'This is a book which, widely read as it will certainly be, may well affect the thought of a generation. Gombrich writes conversationally and intimately. His learning, though very perceptible to any student of the subject, is worn lightly, but he has something new to say on almost every subject. He can illuminate with a few words the whole atmosphere of a period.'

The Times Literary Supplement, reviewing the 1st edition, 27 January 1950

'A pure delight, intellectually and physically.'

Professor H.W. Janson, New York University, 1950

'Almost as well known as the *Mona Lisa*, Sir Ernst Gombrich's *The Story of Art* unites learning and pleasure.'

Pierre Rosenberg, former Président-Directeur, Musée du Louvre, Paris

'Like every art historian of my generation, my way of thinking about pictures has been in large measure shaped by Ernst Gombrich. I was 15 when I read *The Story of Art* and like millions since, I felt I had been given a map of a great country, and with it the confidence to explore further without fear of being overwhelmed.'

Neil MacGregor, Director of the British Museum, London, former Director of the National Gallery, London

'It is hard to overstate my enthusiasm for ... one of the pivotal works in the great cause of bringing people and art together ... A book to read, re-read, and ... to savour lovingly like a classic vintage.'

J. Carter Brown, former Director Emeritus, National Gallery of Art, Washington DC, Chairman, US Commission of Fine Arts

The Story of Art

The Story of Art

E.H. Gombrich

Contents

Preface

This book is intended for all who feel in need of some first
orientation in a strange and fascinating field. It may serve to
show newcomers the lie of the land without confusing them
with details; to enable them to bring some intelligible order
into the wealth of names, periods and styles which crowd the
pages of more ambitious works, and so to equip them for
consulting more specialized books. In writing it I thought first
and foremost of readers in their teens who had just discovered
the world of art for themselves. But I never believed that books
for young people should differ from books for adults except
for the fact that they must reckon with the most exacting class
of critics, critics who are quick to detect and resent any
trace of pretentious jargon or bogus sentiment. I know from
experience that these are the vices which may render people
suspicious of all writing on art for the rest of their lives.
I have striven sincerely to avoid these pitfalls and to use plain
language even at the risk of sounding casual or unprofessional.
Difficulties of thought, on the other hand, I have not avoided,
and so I hope that no readers will attribute my decision
to get along with a minimum of art historian's conventional
terms to any desire on my part to 'talk down' to them. For is
it not rather those who misuse 'scientific' language, not to
enlighten but to impress the reader, who are 'talking down'
to us – from the clouds?

Apart from this decision to restrict the number of
technical terms, I have tried, in writing this book, to follow
a number of more specific self-imposed rules, all of which
have made my own life as its author more difficult, but may
make that of the reader a little easier. The first of these rules
was that I would not write about works I could not show in
the illustrations; I did not want the text to degenerate into lists
of names which could mean little or nothing to those who
do not know the works in question, and would be superfluous

for those who do. This rule at once limited the choice of artists and works I could discuss to the number of illustrations the book would hold. It forced me to be doubly rigorous in my selection of what to mention and what to exclude. This led to my second rule, which was to limit myself to real works of art, and cut out anything which might merely be interesting as a specimen of taste or fashion. This decision entailed a considerable sacrifice of literary effects. Praise is so much duller than criticism, and the inclusion of some amusing monstrosities might have offered some light relief. But the reader would have been justified in asking why something I found objectionable should find a place in a book devoted to art and not to non-art, particularly if this meant leaving out a true masterpiece. Thus, while I do not claim that all the works illustrated represent the highest standard of perfection, I did make an effort not to include anything which I considered to be without a peculiar merit of its own.

The third rule also demanded a little self-denial. I vowed that I would resist any temptation to be original in my selection, lest the well-known masterpieces be crowded out by my own personal favourites. This book, after all, is not intended merely as an anthology of beautiful things; it is meant for those who look for bearings in a new field, and for them the familiar appearance of apparently 'hackneyed' examples may serve as welcome landmarks. Moreover, the most famous works are really often the greatest by many standards, and if this book can help readers to look at them with fresh eyes it may prove more useful than if I had neglected them for the sake of less well-known masterpieces.

Even so, the number of famous works and masters I had to exclude is formidable enough. I may as well confess that I have found no room for Hindu or Etruscan art, or for masters of the rank of Quercia, Signorelli or Carpaccio, of Peter Vischer, Brouwer, Terborch, Canaletto, Corot, and scores of others who happen to interest me deeply. To include them would have doubled or trebled the length of the book and would, I believe, have reduced its value as a first guide to art. One more rule I have followed in this heart-breaking task of elimination. When in doubt I have always preferred to discuss a work which I had seen in the original rather than one I knew only from photographs. I should have liked to make this an absolute rule, but I did not want the reader to be penalized by the accidents of travel restrictions which sometimes dog the life of the art-lover. Moreover, it was my final rule not to have any absolute rules whatever, but to break my own sometimes, leaving to the reader the fun of finding me out.

These, then, were the negative rules I adopted. My positive aims should be apparent from the book itself. In telling the story of art once more in simple language, it should enable readers to see how it hangs together and help them in their appreciation, not so much by rapturous descriptions, as by providing them with some pointers as to the artists' probable intentions. This method should at least help to clear away the most frequent causes of misunderstanding and to forestall a kind of criticism which misses the point of a work of art altogether. Beyond this the book has a slightly more ambitious goal. It sets out to place the works it discusses in their historical setting and thus to lead towards an understanding of the master's artistic aims. Each generation is at some point in revolt against the standards of its fathers; each work of art derives its appeal to contemporaries not only from what it does but also from what it leaves undone. When young Mozart arrived in Paris he noticed – as he wrote to his father – that all the fashionable symphonies there ended with a quick finale;

so he decided to startle his audience with a slow introduction
to his last movement. This is a trivial example, but it shows
the direction in which a historical appreciation of art must
aim. The urge to be different may not be the highest or
profoundest element of the artist's equipment, but it is rarely
lacking altogether. And the appreciation of this intentional
difference often opens up the easiest approach to the art of
the past. I have tried to make this constant change of aims the
key of my narrative, and to show how each work is related by
imitation or contradiction to what has gone before. Even at
the risk of being tedious, I have referred back for the purpose
of comparison to works that show the distance which artists
had placed between themselves and their forerunners. There is
one pitfall in this method of presentation which I hope to
have avoided but which should not go unmentioned. It is the
naïve misinterpretation of the constant change in art as
a continuous progress. It is true that every artist feels that he
has surpassed the generation before him and that from his
point of view he has made progress beyond anything that was
known before. We cannot hope to understand a work of
art without being able to share this sense of liberation and
triumph which the artist felt when he looked at his own
achievement. But we must realize that each gain or progress in
one direction entails a loss in another, and that this subjective
progress, in spite of its importance, does not correspond
to an objective increase in artistic value. All this may sound a
little puzzling when stated in the abstract. I hope the book
will make it clear.

One more word about the space allotted to the various
arts in this book. To some it will seem that painting is unduly
favoured as compared to sculpture and architecture. One reason
for this bias is that less is lost in the illustration of a painting
than in that of a round sculpture, let alone a monumental

building. I had no intention, moreover, of competing with the many excellent histories of architectural styles which exist. On the other hand, the story of art as here conceived could not be told without reference to the architectural background. While I had to confine myself to discussing the style of only one or two buildings in each period, I tried to restore the balance in favour of architecture by giving these examples pride of place in each chapter. This may help readers to co-ordinate their knowledge of each period and see it as a whole.

As a tailpiece to each chapter I have chosen a characteristic representation of the artist's life and world from the period concerned. These pictures form an independent little series illustrating the changing social position of the artist and his public. Even where their artistic merit is not very high these pictorial documents may help us to build up, in our minds, a concrete picture of the surroundings in which the art of the past sprang to life.

This book would never have been written without the warm-hearted encouragement it received from Elizabeth Senior, whose untimely death in an air raid on London was such a loss to all who knew her. I am also indebted to Dr Leopold Ettlinger, Dr Edith Hoffmann, Dr Otto Kurz, Mrs Olive Renier, Mrs Edna Sweetmann, to my wife and my son Richard for much valuable advice and assistance, and to Phaidon Press for their share in shaping this book.

Preface to the twelfth edition

This book was planned from the outset to tell the story of art in both words and pictures by enabling readers as far as possible to have the illustration discussed in the text in front of them, without having to turn the page. I still treasure the memory of the unconventional and resourceful way in which

Dr Bela Horovitz and Mr Ludwig Goldscheider, the founders
of Phaidon Press, achieved this aim in 1949 by making
me write another paragraph here or suggesting an extra
illustration there. The result of these weeks of intense
collaboration certainly justified the procedure, but the balance
arrived at was so delicate that no major alterations could be
contemplated while the original layout was retained. Only the
last few chapters were slightly modified for the eleventh
edition (1966) when a Postscript was added, but the main
body of the book was left as it was. The decision of the
publishers to present the book in a new form more in keeping
with modern production methods thus offered fresh
opportunities but also posed new problems. The pages of
The Story of Art, in its long career, have become familiar to a far
greater number of people than I had ever thought possible.
Even the majority of the twelve editions in other languages
have been modelled on the original layout. It seemed to
me wrong in the circumstances to omit passages and pictures
which readers might want to look for. Nothing is more
irritating than to discover that something one expects to find
in a book has been left out of the edition one takes from the
shelf. Thus, while I welcomed the chance of showing in larger
illustrations some of the works discussed and of adding some
colour plates, I have eliminated nothing and only exchanged
a very few examples for technical or other compelling reasons.
The possibility, on the other hand, of adding to the number
of works to be discussed and illustrated presented both
an opportunity to be seized and a temptation to be resisted.
Clearly to turn this volume into a heavy tome would have
destroyed its character and defeated its purpose. In the end
I decided to add fourteen examples which seemed to me
not only interesting in themselves – which work of art is
not? – but to make a number of fresh points that enrich the

texture of the argument. It is the argument, after all, that makes this book a story rather than an anthology. If it can again be read, and, I hope, enjoyed, without a distracting hunt for the pictures that go with the text, this is due to the help given in various ways by Mr Elwyn Blacker, Dr I. Grafe and Mr Keith Roberts.

E.H.G., November 1971

Preface to the thirteenth edition

There are many more illustrations in colour in this than in the twelfth edition, but the text (except for the Bibliography) remains unchanged. The other new feature is the Chronological Charts on pages 655-63. Seeing the positions of a few landmarks in the vast panorama of history should help the reader to counteract the perspective illusion which gives such prominence to recent developments at the expense of the more distant past. In thus stimulating reflections on the time scales of the story of art, the charts should serve the same purpose for which I wrote this book some thirty years ago. Here I can still refer the reader to the opening words of the original Preface on page 9.

E.H.G., July 1977

Preface to the fourteenth edition

'Books have a life of their own.' The Roman poet who made this remark could not have imagined that his lines would be copied out by hand for many centuries and would be available on the shelves of our libraries some two thousand years later. By these standards this book is a youngster. Even so, in writing it, I could not have dreamt of its future life, which, as far as the English language editions are concerned, is now chronicled on the imprint page. Some of the changes the book has undergone are mentioned in the Prefaces to the twelfth and thirteenth editions.

These changes have been retained, but the section on art books has again been brought up to date. To keep in step with technical developments and the altered expectations of the public many of the illustrations previously printed in black and white now appear in colour. In addition I have added a Supplement on 'New discoveries', with a brief retrospect on archaeological finds to remind the reader of the extent to which the story of the past has always been subject to revision and unexpected enrichment.

E.H.G., March 1984

Preface to the fifteenth edition

Pessimists sometimes tell us that in this age of television and videos people have lost the habit of reading and that students, in particular, tend to lack the patience to derive pleasure from reading any book from cover to cover. Like all authors I can only hope that the pessimists are wrong. Happy as I am to see this fifteenth edition enriched by new illustrations in colour, a revised and reorganized Bibliography and Index, improved Chronological Charts and even two Geographical Maps, I feel the need to emphasize once more that this book is intended to be enjoyed as a story. To be sure, the story now continues beyond the point at which I left it in the first edition, but even these added episodes can only be fully understood in the light of what has gone before. I still hope for readers who would like to be told from the very beginning how it all happened.

E.H.G., March 1989

Preface to the sixteenth edition

As I sit down to add the preface to this latest edition I am filled with amazement and gratitude. Amazement, because I so well remember my very modest expectations when writing this book, and gratitude to generations of readers – dare I say all over the world? – who must have found it so useful as an introduction to our artistic heritage that they have recommended it to others in ever-increasing numbers. Gratitude, of course, also to my publishers who have responded to this demand by keeping step with the passage of time and bestowed much care on every new and revised edition.

This latest transformation is due to the present owner of Phaidon Press, Richard Schlagman, who wished to return to the original principle of keeping the illustrations before the reader's eye while studying the text, to improve the quality and scale of the illustrations, and, if possible, to increase their numbers.

There was, of course, a strict limit to the realization of this last-mentioned aim, since this book would defeat its purpose if it became too lengthy to serve as an introduction.

Even so, it is hoped that readers will welcome these additions, most of all the fold-outs, one of which, figures 155-6, enabled me to show and discuss the whole of the Ghent altarpiece. Some other additions will be found to make good omissions in earlier editions, notably some images referred to in the text but not illustrated, such as the rendering of Egyptian divinities as shown in The Book of the Dead, figure 38, the family portrait of king Akhnaten, figure 40, the medal showing the original project for St Peter's in Rome, figure 186, Correggio's fresco in the dome of Parma Cathedral, figure 217, and one of the militia portraits of Frans Hals, figure 269.

A few other illustrations were added to clarify the setting or context of works discussed: the whole figure of the

Delphi charioteer, figure 53, Durham cathedral, figure 114,
the north porch of Chartres Cathedral, figure 126, and
the south transept of Strasburg Cathedral, figure 128. I need
not here explain the replacement of some illustrations for
purely technical reasons, nor the purpose of enlarged details
of works, but I must say a word about the eight artists
I decided to include despite my determination not to allow
their number to get out of control: in the Preface to the
first edition I had mentioned Corot as one of the painters I
much admired but could not accommodate. The omission
has haunted me ever since and I have repented at last, hoping
that this change of mind has also profited the discussion
of certain artistic issues.

Otherwise I have restricted the addition of artists
to chapters on the twentieth century, taking over from the
German version of this book two masters of German
Expressionism, Käthe Kollwitz, who exerted such a great
influence on the 'socialist realists' of Eastern Europe, and Emil
Nolde for his powerful use of a new graphic idiom, figures
368-9; Brancusi and Nicholson, figures 380, 382, were to
strengthen the discussion of abstraction, and de Chirico and
Magritte that of Surrealism, figures 388-9. Morandi, finally,
served me as an example of a twentieth-century artist who is
all the more lovable for resisting stylistic labels, figure 399.

I have made these additions in the hope of making the
developments seem less abrupt than they may have looked
in the earlier editions, and therefore more intelligible. For that,
of course, is still the overriding aim of this book. If it has
found friends among art-lovers and students, the reason can
only be that it has made them see how the story of art hangs
together. To memorize a list of names and dates is hard and
irksome; remembering a story needs little effort, once we have
understood the role the various members of the cast play in it

and how the dates point to the passage of time between the
generations and the episodes of the narration.

I mention more than once in the body of this book
that in art any gain in one respect may also lead to a loss
elsewhere. No doubt this also applies to this new edition, but
I sincerely hope that the gains far outweigh any loss.

There remains only to thank my eagle-eyed editor
Bernard Dod for the devotion with which he watched over the
new edition.

E.H.G., December 1994

Preface to the pocket edition

This pocket edition of The Story of Art is the first new edition
to be published since the death of its author in 2001.

As the reader may know, The Story of Art is the most
famous and bestselling introduction to art ever written.
Translated into some 35 languages, and despite numerous
efforts to dislodge it, it remains the finest introduction to art
and the first port of call for so many students, art lovers and
art professionals all over the world.

As the publisher of the sixteenth edition I recall with
great fondness the many sessions (some lasting the entire day)
that I spent with Sir Ernst Gombrich in the preparation
of that edition, and I am reminded not only of the enormous
care that he exercised over each aspect of its design and layout
but also of the genuine fun that transpired from practically
every encounter with him. We have missed him greatly this
time around.

The rationale behind the pocket edition was a simple
one and its portability and convenience should be self-evident.
It is our intention that the sixteenth edition will remain
in print and continue to be available, and will be the obvious

choice for enjoying at home and for retaining in one's library. The pocket edition can be carried around with greater ease. In order to achieve the desired portability, lightweight papers were chosen which necessitated the separation of text from images. However, the provision of ribbon markers should make it easy to allow the pictures to accompany one's reading of the text. The text itself remains identical to that of the sixteenth edition and all of the images illustrated there are included here. Only the very astute reader may notice that the small illustration 'sign-offs' that the author used previously at the end of each chapter, but did not refer to in his story, are missing from this edition as in this layout they would have served no purpose.

If you are reading this preface I would assume that you have read the author's own prefaces written to accompany the various previous editions. If not, I urge you to do so as the background to the writing of this book and the author's clearly stated intentions are of great value.

Sir Ernst Gombrich was a truly remarkable man in many ways, some well known, others less so. Though tempted to do so here, I shall endeavour to write something more about that in a small photographic memoir that we intend to publish in the near future.

Richard Schlagman, July 2006

Introduction

On art and artists

There really is no such thing as Art. There are only artists. Once these were men who took coloured earth and roughed out the forms of a bison on the wall of a cave; today some buy their paints, and design posters for hoardings; they did and do many other things. There is no harm in calling all these activities art as long as we keep in mind that such a word may mean very different things in different times and places, and as long as we realize that Art with a capital A has no existence. For Art with a capital A has come to be something of a bogey and a fetish. You may crush an artist by telling him that what he has just done may be quite good in its own way, only it is not 'Art'. And you may confound anyone enjoying a picture by declaring that what he liked in it was not the Art but something different.

Actually I do not think that there are any wrong reasons for liking a statue or a picture. Someone may like a landscape painting because it reminds him of home, or a portrait because it reminds him of a friend. There is nothing wrong with that. All of us, when we see a painting, are bound to be reminded of a hundred-and-one things which influence our likes and dislikes. As long as these memories help us to enjoy what we see, we need not worry. It is only when some irrelevant memory makes us prejudiced, when we instinctively turn away from a magnificent picture of an alpine scene because we dislike climbing, that we should search our mind for the reason for the aversion which spoils a pleasure we might otherwise have had. There *are* wrong reasons for disliking a work of art.

Most people like to see in pictures what they would also like to see in reality. This is quite a natural preference. We all like beauty in nature, and are grateful to the artists who have preserved it in their works. Nor would these artists themselves have rebuffed us for our taste. When the great Flemish painter Rubens made a drawing of his little boy, figure 1, he was surely proud of his good looks. He wanted us, too, to admire the child. But this bias for the pretty and engaging subject is apt to become a stumbling-block if it leads us to reject works which represent a less appealing subject. The great German painter Albrecht Dürer certainly drew his mother, figure 2, with as much devotion and love as Rubens felt for his chubby child. His truthful study of careworn old age may give us a shock which makes us turn away from it – and yet, if we fight against our first repugnance we may be richly rewarded, for Dürer's drawing in its tremendous sincerity is a great work. In fact, we shall soon discover that the beauty of a picture does not really lie in the beauty of its subject-matter. I do not know whether the little ragamuffins whom the Spanish painter Murillo liked to paint, figure 3, were strictly beautiful or not, but, as he painted them, they certainly have great charm. On the other hand, most people would call the child in Pieter de Hooch's wonderful Dutch interior, figure 4, plain, but it is an attractive picture all the same.

The trouble about beauty is that tastes and standards of what is beautiful vary so much. Figures 5 and 6 were both painted in the fifteenth century, and both represent angels playing the lute. Many will prefer the Italian work by Melozzo da Forlì, figure 5, with its appealing grace and charm, to that of his northern contemporary Hans Memling, figure 6. I myself like both. It may take a little longer to discover the intrinsic beauty of Memling's angel, but once we are no longer disturbed by his faint awkwardness we may find him infinitely lovable.

What is true of beauty is also true of expression. In fact, it is often the expression of a figure in the painting which makes us like or loathe the work. Some people like an expression which they can easily understand, and which therefore moves them profoundly. When the seventeenth-century Italian painter Guido Reni painted the head of Christ on the cross, figure 7, he intended, no doubt, that the beholder should find in this face all the agony and all the glory of the Passion. Many people throughout subsequent centuries have drawn strength and comfort from such a representation of the Saviour. The feeling it expresses is so strong and so clear that copies of this work can be found in simple wayside shrines and remote farmhouses where people know nothing about 'Art'. But even if this intense expression of feeling appeals to us we should not, for that reason, turn away from works whose expression is perhaps less easy to understand. The Italian painter of the Middle Ages who painted the crucifix, figure 8, surely felt as sincerely about the Passion as did Reni, but we must first learn to know his methods of drawing to understand his feelings. When we have come to understand these different languages, we may even prefer works of art whose expression is less obvious than Reni's. Just as some prefer people who use few words and gestures and leave something to be guessed, so some people are fond of paintings or sculptures which leave them something to guess and ponder about. In the more 'primitive' periods, when artists were not as skilled in representing human faces and human gestures as they are now, it is often all the more moving to see how they tried nevertheless to bring out the feeling they wanted to convey.

But here newcomers to art are often brought up against another difficulty. They want to admire the artist's skill in representing the things they see. What they like best are paintings which 'look real'. I do not deny for a moment that this is an important consideration. The patience and skill which go into the faithful rendering of the visible world are indeed to be admired. Great artists of the past have devoted much labour to works in which every tiny detail is carefully recorded. Dürer's watercolour study of a hare, figure 9, is one of the most famous examples of this loving patience. But who would say that Rembrandt's drawing of an elephant, figure 10, is necessarily less good because it shows fewer details? Indeed Rembrandt was such a wizard that he gave us the feel of the elephant's wrinkly skin with a few lines of his chalk.

But it is not sketchiness that mainly offends people who like their pictures to look 'real'. They are even more repelled by works which they consider to be incorrectly drawn, particularly when they belong to a more modern period when the artist 'ought to have known better'. As a matter of fact, there is no mystery about these distortions of nature about which we still hear complaints in discussions on modern art. Everyone who has ever seen a Disney film or a comic strip knows all about it. He knows that it is sometimes right to draw things otherwise than they look, to change and distort them in one way or another. Mickey Mouse does not look very much like a real mouse, yet people do not write indignant letters to the papers about the length of his tail. Those who enter Disney's enchanted world are not worried about Art with a capital A. They do not watch his films armed with the same prejudices they like to take with them when going to an exhibition of modern painting. But if a modern artist draws something in his own way, he is apt to be thought a bungler who can do no better. Now, whatever we may think of modern artists, we may safely credit them with enough knowledge to draw 'correctly'. If they do not do so their reasons may be very similar to those of Walt Disney. Figure 11 shows a plate from an illustrated Natural History by the famous pioneer of the modern movement, Picasso. Surely no one could find fault with his charming representation of a mother hen and her fluffy chicks. But in drawing a cockerel, figure 12, Picasso was not content with giving a mere rendering of the bird's appearance. He wanted to bring out its aggressiveness, its cheek and its stupidity. In other words he resorted to caricature. But what a convincing caricature it is!

There are two things, therefore, which we should always ask ourselves if we find fault with the accuracy of a picture. One is whether the artist may not have had his reasons for changing the appearance of what he saw. We shall hear more about such reasons as the story of art unfolds. The other is that we should never condemn a work for being incorrectly drawn unless we have made quite sure that we are right and the painter is wrong. We are all inclined to be quick with the verdict that 'things do not look like that'. We have a curious habit of thinking that nature must always look like the pictures we are accustomed to. It is easy to illustrate this by an astonishing discovery which was made not very long ago. Generations have watched horses gallop, have attended horse-races and hunts, have enjoyed paintings and sporting prints showing horses charging into battle or running after hounds. Not one of these people seems to have noticed what it 'really looks like' when a horse runs. Pictures and sporting prints usually showed them with outstretched legs in full flight through the air – as the great nineteenth-century French painter Théodore Géricault painted them in a famous representation of the races at Epsom, figure 13. About fifty years later, when the photographic camera had been sufficiently perfected for snapshots of horses in rapid motion to be taken, these snapshots proved that both the painters and their public had been wrong all the while. No galloping horse ever moved in the way which seems so 'natural' to us. As the legs come off the ground they are moved in turn for the next kick-off, figure 14. If we reflect for a moment we shall realize that it could hardly get along otherwise. And yet, when painters began to apply this new discovery, and painted horses moving as they actually do, everyone complained that their pictures looked wrong.

This, no doubt, is an extreme example, but similar errors are by no means as rare as one might think. We are all inclined to accept conventional forms or colours as the only correct ones. Children sometimes think that stars must be star-shaped, though naturally they are not. The people who insist that in a picture the sky must be blue, and the grass green, are not very different from these children. They get indignant if they see other colours in a picture, but if we try to forget all we have heard about green grass and blue skies, and look at the world as if we had just arrived from another planet on a voyage of discovery and were seeing it for the first time, we may find that things are apt to have the most surprising colours. Now painters sometimes feel as if they were on such a voyage of discovery. They want to see the world afresh, and to discard all the accepted notions and prejudices about flesh being pink and apples yellow or red. It is not easy to get rid of these preconceived ideas, but the artists who succeed best in doing so often produce the most exciting works. It is they who teach us to see in nature new beauties of whose existence we have never dreamt. If we follow them and learn from them, even a glance out of our own window may become a thrilling adventure.

There is no greater obstacle to the enjoyment of great works of art than our unwillingness to discard habits and prejudices. A painting which represents a familiar subject in an unexpected way is often condemned for no better reason than that it does not seem right. The more often we have seen a story represented in art, the more firmly do we become convinced that it must always be represented on similar lines. About biblical subjects, in particular, feelings are apt to run high. Though we all know that the Scriptures tell us nothing about the appearance of Jesus, and that God Himself cannot be visualized in human form, and though we know that it was the artists of the past who first created the images we have become used to, some are still inclined to think that to depart from these traditional forms amounts to blasphemy.

As a matter of fact, it was usually those artists who read the Scriptures with the greatest devotion and attention who tried to build up in their minds an entirely fresh picture of the incidents of the sacred story. They tried to forget all the paintings they had seen, and to imagine what it must have been like when the Christ Child lay in the manger and the shepherds came to adore Him, or when a fisherman began to preach the gospel. It has happened time and again that such efforts of a great artist to read the old text with entirely fresh eyes have shocked and outraged thoughtless people. A typical 'scandal' of this kind flared up round Caravaggio, a very bold and revolutionary Italian painter, who worked round about 1600. He was given the task of painting a picture of St Matthew for the altar of a church in Rome. The saint was to be represented writing the gospel, and, to show that the gospels were the word of God, an angel was to be represented inspiring his writings. Caravaggio, who was a highly imaginative and uncompromising young artist, thought hard about what it must have been like when an elderly, poor, working man, a simple publican, suddenly had to sit down to write a book. And so he painted a picture of St Matthew, figure 15, with a bald head and bare, dusty feet, awkwardly gripping the huge volume, anxiously wrinkling his brow under the unaccustomed strain of writing. By his side he painted a youthful angel, who seems just to have arrived from on high, and who gently guides the labourer's hand as a teacher may do to a child. When Caravaggio delivered this picture to the church where it was to be placed on the altar, people were

scandalized at what they took to be a lack of respect for the
saint. The painting was not accepted, and Caravaggio had
to try again. This time he took no chances. He kept strictly to
the conventional ideas of what an angel and a saint should
look like, figure 16. The outcome is still quite a good picture,
for Caravaggio tried hard to make it look lively and
interesting, but we feel that it is less honest and sincere than
the first had been.

This story illustrates the harm that may be done by
those who dislike and criticize works of art for wrong reasons.
What is more important, it brings home to us that what we
call 'works of art' are not the results of some mysterious
activity, but objects made by human beings for human beings.
A picture looks so remote when it hangs glazed and framed
on the wall. And in our museums it is – very properly –
forbidden to touch the objects on view. But originally they
were made to be touched and handled, they were bargained
about, quarrelled about, worried about. Let us also remember
that every one of their features is the result of a decision by
the artist: that he may have pondered over them and changed
them many times, that he may have wondered whether to
leave that tree in the background or to paint it over again, that
he may have been pleased by a lucky stroke of his brush
which gave a sudden unexpected brilliance to a sunlit cloud,
and that he put in these figures reluctantly at the insistence of
a buyer. For most of the paintings and statues which are
now lined up along the walls of our museums and galleries
were not meant to be displayed as Art. They were made for
a definite occasion and a definite purpose which were in the
artist's mind when he set to work.

Those ideas, on the other hand, that we outsiders
usually worry about, ideas about beauty and expression, are
rarely mentioned by artists. It was not always like that, but it

was so for many centuries in the past, and it is so again now. The reason is partly that artists are often shy people who would think it embarrassing to use big words like 'Beauty'. They would feel rather priggish if they were to speak about 'expressing their emotions' and to use similar catchwords. Such things they take for granted and find it useless to discuss. That is one reason, and, it seems, a good one. But there is another. In the actual everyday worries of the artist these ideas play a much smaller part than outsiders would, I think, suspect. What an artist worries about as he plans his pictures, makes his sketches, or wonders whether he has completed his canvas, is something much more difficult to put into words. Perhaps he would say he worries about whether he has got it 'right'. Now it is only when we understand what he means by that modest little word 'right' that we begin to understand what artists are really after.

I think we can only hope to understand this if we draw on our own experience. Of course we are no artists, we may never have tried to paint a picture and may have no intention of ever doing so. But this need not mean that we are never confronted with problems similar to those which make up the artist's life. In fact, I am anxious to prove that there is hardly any person who has not got at least an inkling of this type of problem, be it in ever so modest a way. Anybody who has ever tried to arrange a bunch of flowers, to shuffle and shift the colours, to add a little here and take away there, has experienced this strange sensation of balancing forms and colours without being able to tell exactly what kind of harmony it is he is trying to achieve. We just feel a patch of red here may make all the difference, or this blue is all right by itself but it does not 'go' with the others, and suddenly a little stem of green leaves may seem to make it come 'right'. 'Don't touch it any more,' we exclaim, 'now it is perfect.' Not everybody, I admit, is quite so careful over the arrangement of flowers, but nearly everybody has something he wants to get 'right'. It may just be a matter of finding the right belt to match a certain dress, or nothing more impressive than the worry over the right proportion of, say, pudding and cream on one's plate. In every such case, however trivial, we may feel that a shade too much or too little upsets the balance and that there is only one relationship which is as it should be.

People who worry like this over flowers, dresses or food, we may call fussy, because we may feel these things do not warrant so much attention. But what may sometimes be a bad habit in daily life and is often, therefore, suppressed or concealed, comes into its own in the realm of art. When it is a matter of matching forms or arranging colours an artist must always be 'fussy' or rather fastidious to the extreme. He may see differences in shades and texture which we should hardly notice. Moreover, his task is infinitely more complex than any of those we may experience in ordinary life. He has not only to balance two or three colours, shapes or tastes, but to juggle with any number. He has, on his canvas, perhaps hundreds of shades and forms which he must balance till they look 'right'. A patch of green may suddenly look too yellow because it was brought into too close proximity with a strong blue – he may feel that all is spoiled, that there is a jarring note in the picture and that he must begin it all over again. He may suffer agonies over this problem. He may ponder about it in sleepless nights; he may stand in front of his picture all day trying to add a touch of colour here or there and rubbing it out again, though you and I might not have noticed the difference either way. But once he has succeeded we all feel that he has achieved something to which nothing could be added, something which is right – an example of perfection in our very imperfect world.

Take one of Raphael's famous Madonnas: the 'Virgin in the meadow', for instance, figure 17. It is beautiful, no doubt, and engaging; the figures are admirably drawn, and the expression of the Holy Virgin as she looks down on the two children is quite unforgettable. But if we look at Raphael's sketches for the picture, figure 18, we begin to realize that these were not the things he took most trouble about. These he took for granted. What he tried again and again to get was the right balance between the figures, the right relationship which would make the most harmonious whole. In the rapid sketch in the left-hand corner, he thought of letting the Christ Child walk away looking back and up at His mother. And he tried different positions of the mother's head to answer the movement of the Child. Then he decided to turn the Child round and to let Him look up at her. He tried another way, this time introducing the little St John – but, instead of letting the Christ Child look at him, made him turn out of the picture. Then he made another attempt, and apparently became impatient, trying the head of the Child in many different positions. There were several leaves of this kind in this sketch-book, in which he searched again and again to find how best to balance these three figures. But if we now look back at the final picture we see that he did get it right in the end. Everything in the picture seems in its proper place, and the pose and harmony Raphael has achieved by his hard work seem so natural and effortless that we hardly notice them. Yet it is just this harmony which makes the beauty of the Madonna more beautiful and the sweetness of the children more sweet.

It is fascinating to watch an artist thus striving to achieve the right balance, but if we were to ask him why he did this or changed that, he might not be able to tell us. He does not follow any fixed rules. He just feels his way. It is true

that some artists or critics in certain periods have tried to
formulate laws of their art; but it always turned out that poor
artists did not achieve anything when trying to apply these
laws, while great masters could break them and yet achieve a
new kind of harmony no one had thought of before. When
the great English painter Sir Joshua Reynolds explained to
his students in the Royal Academy that blue should not be put
into the foreground of paintings but should be reserved for
the distant backgrounds, for the fading hills on the horizon,
his rival Gainsborough – so the story goes – wanted to prove
that such academic rules are usually nonsense. He painted the
famous 'Blue boy', whose blue costume, in the central
foreground of the picture, stands out triumphantly against the
warm brown of the background.

The truth is that it is impossible to lay down rules of
this kind because one can never know in advance what effect
the artist may wish to achieve. He may even want a shrill,
jarring note if he happens to feel that that would be right. As
there are no rules to tell us when a picture or statue is right it
is usually impossible to explain in words exactly why we feel
that it is a great work of art. But that does not mean that one
work is just as good as any other, or that one cannot discuss
matters of taste. If they do nothing else, such discussions make
us look at pictures, and the more we look at them the more
we notice points which have escaped us before. We begin to
develop a feeling for the kind of harmony each generation
of artists has tried to achieve. The greater our feeling for these
harmonies the more we shall enjoy them, and that, after all,
is what matters. The old proverb that you cannot argue about
matters of taste may well be true, but that should not conceal
the fact that taste can be developed. This is again a matter
of common experience which everybody can test in a modest
field. To people who are not used to drinking tea one blend

may taste exactly like another. But if they have the leisure, will and opportunity to search out such refinements as there may be, they may develop into true 'connoisseurs' who can distinguish exactly what type and mixture they prefer, and their greater knowledge is bound to add to their enjoyment of the choicest blends.

Admittedly, taste in art is something infinitely more complex than taste in food and drink. It is not only a matter of discovering various subtle flavours; it is something more serious and more important. After all, the great masters have given their all in these works, they have suffered for them, sweated blood over them, and the least they have a right to ask of us is that we try to understand what they wanted to do.

One never finishes learning about art. There are always new things to discover. Great works of art seem to look different every time one stands before them. They seem to be as inexhaustible and unpredictable as real human beings. It is an exciting world of its own with its own strange laws and its own adventures. Nobody should think he knows all about it, for nobody does. Nothing, perhaps, is more important than just this: that to enjoy these works we must have a fresh mind, one which is ready to catch every hint and to respond to every hidden harmony: a mind, most of all, not cluttered up with long high-sounding words and ready-made phrases. It is infinitely better not to know anything about art than to have the kind of half-knowledge which makes for snobbishness. The danger is very real. There are people, for instance, who have picked up the simple points I have tried to make in this chapter, and who understand that there are great works of art which have none of the obvious qualities of beauty of expression or correct draughtsmanship, but who become so proud of their knowledge that they pretend to like only those works which are neither beautiful nor correctly drawn. They are always haunted by the fear that they might be considered uneducated if they confessed to liking a work which seems too obviously pleasant or moving. They end by being snobs who lose their true enjoyment of art and who call everything 'very interesting' which they really find somewhat repulsive. I should hate to be responsible for any similar misunderstanding. I would rather not be believed at all than be believed in such an uncritical way.

In the chapters which follow I shall discuss the history of art, that is the history of buildings, of picture-making and of statue-making. I think that knowing something of this history helps us to understand why artists worked in a particular way, or why they aimed at certain effects. Most of all it is a good way of sharpening our eyes for the particular characteristics of works of art, and of thereby increasing our sensitivity to the finer shades of difference. Perhaps it is the only way of learning to enjoy them in their own right. But no way is without its dangers. One sometimes sees people walking through a gallery, catalogue in hand. Every time they stop in front of a picture they eagerly search for its number. We can watch them thumbing through their books, and as soon as they have found the title or the name they walk on. They might just as well have stayed at home, for they have hardly looked at the painting. They have only checked the catalogue. It is a kind of mental short circuit which has nothing to do with enjoying a picture.

People who have acquired some knowledge of art history are sometimes in danger of falling into a similar trap. When they see a work of art they do not stay to look at it, but rather search their memory for the appropriate label. They may have heard that Rembrandt was famous for his *chiaroscuro* – which is the Italian technical term for light and shade – so they nod wisely when they see a Rembrandt, mumble 'wonderful *chiaroscuro*', and wander on to the next picture. I want to be quite frank about this danger of half-knowledge and snobbery, for we are all apt to succumb to such temptations, and a book like this could increase them. I should like to help to open eyes, not to loosen tongues. To talk cleverly about art is not very difficult, because the words critics use have been employed in so many different contexts that they have lost all precision. But to look at a picture with fresh eyes and to venture on a voyage of discovery into it is a far more difficult but also a much more rewarding task. There is no telling what one might bring home from such a journey.

1

Strange Beginnings

Prehistoric and primitive peoples; Ancient America

We do not know how art began any more than we know how language started. If we take art to mean such activities as building temples and houses, making pictures and sculptures, or weaving patterns, there is no people in all the world without art. If, on the other hand, we mean by art some kind of beautiful luxury, something to enjoy in museums and exhibitions or something special to use as a precious decoration in the best parlour, we must realize that this use of the word is a very recent development and that many of the greatest builders, painters or sculptors of the past never dreamed of it. We can best understand this difference if we think of architecture. We all know that there are beautiful buildings and that some of them are true works of art. But there is scarcely any building in the world which was not erected for a particular purpose. Those who use these buildings as places of worship or entertainment, or as dwellings, judge them first and foremost by standards of utility. But apart from this, they may like or dislike the design or the proportions of the structure, and appreciate the efforts of the good architect to make it not only practical but 'right'. In the past the attitude to paintings and statues was often similar. They were not thought of as mere works of art but as objects which had a definite function. He would be a poor judge of houses who did not know the requirements for which they were built. Similarly, we are not likely to understand the art of the past if we are quite ignorant of the aims it had to serve. The further we go back in history, the more definite but also the more strange are the aims which art was supposed to serve. The same applies if we leave towns and cities and go to the peasants or, better still, if we leave our civilized countries and travel to the peoples whose ways of life still resemble the conditions in which our remote ancestors lived. We call these people 'primitive' not because they are simpler than we are – their processes of thought are often more complicated than ours – but because they are closer to the state from which all mankind once emerged. Among these primitives, there is no difference between building and image-making as far as usefulness is concerned. Their huts are there to shelter them from rain, wind and sunshine and the spirits which produce them; images are made to protect them against other powers which are, to them, as real as the forces of nature. Pictures and statues, in other words, are used to work magic.

We cannot hope to understand these strange beginnings of art unless we try to enter into the mind of the primitive peoples and find out what kind of experience it is which makes them think of pictures, not as something nice to look at, but as something powerful to use. I do not think it is really so difficult to recapture this feeling. All that is needed is the will to be absolutely honest with ourselves and see whether we, too, do not retain something of the 'primitive' in us. Instead of beginning with the Ice Age, let us begin with ourselves. Suppose we take a picture of our favourite champion from today's paper – would we enjoy taking a needle and poking out the eyes? Would we feel as indifferent about it as if we poked a hole anywhere else in the paper? I do not think so. However well I know with my waking thoughts that what I do to his picture makes no difference to my friend or hero, I still feel a vague reluctance to harm it. Somewhere there remains the absurd feeling that what one does to the picture is done to the person it represents. Now, if I am right there, if this queer and unreasonable idea really survives, even among us, into the age of atomic power, it is perhaps less surprising that such ideas existed almost everywhere among the so-called primitive peoples. In all parts of the world medicine men or witches have tried to work magic in some such way – they have made

little images of an enemy and have then pierced the heart of
the wretched doll, or burnt it, and hoped that their enemy
would suffer. Even the guy we burn in Britain on Guy Fawkes
Day is a remnant of such a superstition. The primitives are
sometimes even more vague about what is real and what is a
picture. On one occasion, when a European artist made
drawings of cattle in an African village, the inhabitants were
distressed: 'If you take them away with you, what are we to
live on?'

All these strange ideas are important because they may
help us to understand the oldest paintings which have come
down to us. These paintings are as old as any trace of human
skill. And yet, when they were first discovered on the walls
of caves and rocks in Spain, figure 19, and in southern France,
figure 20, in the nineteenth century, archaeologists refused
at first to believe that such vivid and lifelike representations
of animals could have been made by men in the Ice Age.
Gradually the rude implements of stone and of bone found in
these regions made it increasingly certain that these pictures
of bison, mammoth or reindeer were indeed scratched or
painted by men who hunted this game and therefore knew it
so very well. It is a strange experience to go down into these
caves, sometimes through low and narrow corridors, far into
the darkness of the mountain and suddenly to see the guide's
electric torch light up the picture of a bull. One thing is clear,
no one would have crawled so far into the eerie depth of the
earth simply to decorate such an inaccessible place. Moreover,
few of these pictures are clearly distributed on the roofs or
walls of the cave except some paintings in the cave of Lascaux,
figure 21. On the contrary, they are sometimes painted or
scratched on top of each other without any apparent order.
The most likely explanation of these finds is still that they are
the oldest relics of that universal belief in the power of

picture-making; in other words, that these primitive hunters thought that if they only made a picture of their prey – and perhaps belaboured it with their spears or stone axes – the real animals would also succumb to their power.

Of course, this is guesswork – but guesswork pretty well supported by the use of art among those primitive peoples of our own day who have still preserved their ancient customs. True, we do not find any now, as far as I know, who try to work exactly this kind of magic; but most art for them is also closely bound up with similar ideas about the power of images. There are still primitive peoples who use nothing but stone implements and who scratch pictures of animals on rocks for magic purposes. There are other tribes who have regular festivals when they dress up as animals and move like animals in solemn dances. They, too, believe that somehow this will give them power over their prey. Sometimes they even believe that certain animals are related to them in some fairy-tale manner, and that the whole tribe is a wolf tribe, a raven tribe or a frog tribe. It sounds strange enough, but we must not forget that even these ideas are not as far removed from our own times as one might think. The Romans believed that Romulus and Remus had been suckled by a she-wolf, and they had an image in bronze of the she-wolf on the sacred Capitol in Rome. Until recently they kept a living she-wolf in a cage near the steps to the Capitol. No living lions are kept in Trafalgar Square – but the British Lion has led a vigorous life in political cartoons. Of course, there remains a vast difference between this kind of heraldic or cartoon symbolism and the deep seriousness with which tribesmen look on their relationship with the totem, as they call their animal relatives. For it seems that they sometimes live in a kind of dream-world in which they can be man and animal at the same time. Many tribes have special ceremonies in which they wear masks with the features of these animals, and when they put them on they seem to feel that they are transformed, that they have become ravens, or bears. It is very much as if children played at pirates or detectives till they no longer knew where play-acting ended and reality began. But with children there is always the grown-up world about them, the people who tell them 'Don't be so noisy', or 'It is nearly bed-time'. For the primitive there is no such other world to spoil the illusion, because all the members of the tribe take part in the ceremonial dances and rites with their fantastic games of pretence. They have all learned their significance from former generations and are so absorbed in them that they have little chance of stepping outside them and seeing their behaviour critically. We all have beliefs which we take as much for granted as the 'primitives' take theirs – usually so much so that we are not even aware of them unless we meet people who question them.

All this may seem to have little to do with art, but in fact these conditions influence art in many ways. Many of the artists' works are meant to play a part in these strange rituals, and what matters then is not whether the sculpture or painting is beautiful by our standards, but whether it 'works', that is to say, whether it can perform the required magic. Moreover, the artists work for people of their own tribe who know exactly what each form or each colour is meant to signify. They are not expected to change these things, but only to apply all their skill and knowledge to the execution of their work.

Again we do not have to go far to think of parallels. The point of a national flag is not to be a beautifully coloured piece of cloth which any maker can change according to his fancy – the point of a wedding ring is not to be an ornament which can be worn or changed as we think fit. Yet even within the prescribed rites and customs of our lives, there remains a certain element of choice and scope for taste and skill. Let us think of the Christmas tree. Its principal features are laid down by custom. Each family, in fact, has its own traditions and its own predilections without which the tree does not look right. Nevertheless, when the great moment comes to decorate the tree there remains much to be decided. Should this branch get a candle? Is there enough tinsel on top? Does not this star look too heavy or this side too overloaded? Perhaps to an outsider the whole performance would look rather strange. He might think that trees are much nicer without tinsel. But to us, who know the significance, it becomes a matter of great importance to decorate the tree according to our idea.

Primitive art works on just such pre-established lines, and yet leaves the artist scope to show his mettle. The technical mastery of some tribal craftsmen is indeed astonishing. We should never forget, when talking of primitive art, that the word does not imply that the artists have only a primitive knowledge of their craft. On the contrary, many remote tribes have developed a truly amazing skill in carving, in basket work, in the preparation of leather, or even in the working of metals. If we realize with what simple tools these works are made we can only marvel at the patience and sureness of touch which these primitive craftsmen have acquired through centuries of specialization. The Maoris of New Zealand, for instance, have learned to work veritable wonders in their woodcarvings, figure 22. Of course, the fact that a thing was difficult to make does not necessarily prove that it is a work of art. If it were so, the men who make models of sailing ships in glass bottles would rank among the greatest artists. But this proof of tribal skill should warn us against the belief that their work looks odd because they cannot do any better. It is not their standard of craftsmanship which is different from ours, but their ideas. It is important to realize this from the outset, because the whole story of art is not a story of progress in technical proficiency, but a story of changing ideas and requirements. There is increasing evidence that under certain conditions tribal artists can produce work which is just as correct in the rendering of nature as the most skilful work by a Western master. A number of bronze heads were discovered a few decades ago in Nigeria which are the most convincing likenesses that can be imagined, figure 23. They seem to be many centuries old, and there is no evidence to show that the native artists learned their skill from anyone outside.

What, then, can be the reason for so much of tribal art looking utterly remote? Once more we should return to ourselves and the experiments we can all perform. Let us take a piece of paper and scrawl on it any doodle of a face. Just a circle for the head, a stroke for the nose, another for the mouth. Then look at the eyeless doodle. Does it look unbearably sad? The poor creature cannot see. We feel we must 'give it eyes' – and what a relief it is when we make the two dots and at last it can look at us! To us all this is a joke, but to the native it is not. A wooden pole to which he has given a simple face looks to him totally transformed. He takes the impression it makes as a token of its magic power. There is no need to make it any more lifelike provided it has eyes to see. Figure 24 shows the figure of a Polynesian 'God of War' called Oro. The Polynesians are excellent carvers, but they obviously did not find it essential to make this a correct representation of a man. All we see is a piece of wood covered with woven fibre. Only its eyes and arms are roughly shown by this fibre braid, but once we notice them, this is enough to give the pole a look of uncanny power. We are still not quite in the realm of art, but our doodle experiment may teach us something more. Let us vary the shape of our scribbled face in all possible ways. Let us change the shape of the eyes from dots to crosses or any other form which has not the remotest resemblance to real eyes. Let us make the nose a circle and the mouth a scroll. It will hardly matter, as long as their relative position remains roughly the same. Now to the native artist this discovery probably meant much. For it taught him to build up his figures or faces out of those forms which he liked best and which were most suited to his particular craft. The result might not be very lifelike, but it would retain a certain unity and harmony of pattern which is just what our first doodle probably lacked. Figure 25 shows a mask from New Guinea. It may not be a thing of beauty, but it is not meant to be – it is intended for a ceremony in which the young men of the village dress up as ghosts and frighten the women and children. But, however fantastic or repulsive this 'ghost' may look to us, there is something satisfying in the way the artist has built up his face out of geometrical shapes.

In some parts of the world primitive artists have developed elaborate systems to represent the various figures and totems of their myths in such ornamental fashion. Among the native North Americans, for instance, artists combine a very acute observation of natural forms with this disregard for what we call the real appearance of things. As hunters, they know the true shape of the eagle's beak, or the beaver's ears, much better than any of us. But they regard one such feature as quite sufficient. A mask with an eagle's beak just is an eagle. Figure 26 is a model of a chieftain's house of the Haida tribe of the north-west with three so-called totem poles in front of it. We may see only a jumble of ugly masks, but to the native this pole illustrates an old legend of his tribe. The legend itself may strike us as nearly as odd and incoherent as its representation, but we ought no longer to feel surprised that native ideas differ from ours.

> Once there was a young man in the town of Gwais Kun who used
> to laze about on his bed the whole day till his mother-in-law
> remarked on it; he felt ashamed, went away and decided to slay a
> monster which lived in a lake and fed on humans and whales.
> With the help of a fairy bird he made a trap of a tree trunk and
> dangled two children over it as bait. The monster was caught, the
> young man dressed in its skin and caught fishes, which he
> regularly left on his critical mother-in-law's doorstep. She was so
> flattered at these unexpected offerings that she thought of herself
> as a powerful witch. When the young man undeceived her at last,
> she felt so ashamed that she died.

All the participants in this story are represented on the central
pole. The mask below the entrance is one of the whales the
monster used to eat. The big mask above the entrance is the
monster; on top of it the human form of the unfortunate
mother-in-law. The mask with the beak over her is the bird
who helped the hero, and he himself is seen further up dressed
in the monster's skin, with fishes he has caught. The human
figures at the end are the children the hero used as bait.

It is tempting to regard such a work as the product of
an odd whim, but to those who made such things this was a
solemn undertaking. It took years to cut these huge poles with
the primitive tools at the disposal of the natives, and sometimes
the whole male population of the village helped in the task.
It was to mark and honour the house of a powerful chieftain.

Without explanation we could never understand the
meaning of such carvings, on which so much love and labour
were spent. It is frequently so with works of primitive art.
A mask such as figure 28 may strike us as witty, but its meaning
is anything but funny. It represents a man-eating mountain
demon with a blood-stained face. But though we may fail to
understand it, we can appreciate the thoroughness with which

the shapes of nature are transformed into a consistent pattern. There are many great works of this kind dating from the strange beginnings of art whose exact explanation is probably lost for ever but which we can still admire. All that remains to us of the great civilizations of ancient America is their 'art'. I have put the word in quotation marks not because these mysterious buildings and images lack beauty – some of them are quite fascinating – but because we should not approach them with the idea that they were made for the sake of pleasure or 'decoration'. The terrifying carving of a death head from an altar of the ruins of Copan in present-day Honduras, figure 27, reminds us of the gruesome human sacrifices which were demanded by the religions of these peoples. However little may be known about the exact meaning of such carvings, the thrilling efforts of the scholars who have discovered these works and have tried to get at their secrets have taught us enough to compare them with other works of primitive cultures. Of course, these people were not primitive in the usual sense of the word. When the Spanish and Portuguese conquerors of the sixteenth century arrived, the Aztecs in Mexico and the Incas in Peru ruled over mighty empires. We also know that in earlier centuries the Mayas of Central America had built big cities and developed a system of writing and of calculating calendars which is anything but primitive. Like the Negroes of Nigeria, the pre-Columbian Americans were perfectly capable of representing the human face in a lifelike manner. The ancient Peruvians liked to shape certain vessels in the form of human heads which are strikingly true to nature, figure 29. If most works of these civilizations look remote and unnatural to us, the reason lies in the ideas they are meant to convey.

Figure 30 represents a statue from Mexico which is believed to date from the Aztec period, the last before the conquest. Scholars think that it represents the rain-god, whose name was Tlaloc. In these tropical zones rain is often a question of life or death for the people; for without rain their crops may fail and they may have to starve. No wonder that the god of rains and thunderstorms assumed in their minds the shape of a terrifyingly powerful demon. The lightning in the sky appeared to their imagination like a big serpent, and many American peoples therefore considered the rattlesnake to be a sacred and mighty being. If we look more closely at the figure of Tlaloc we see, in fact, that his mouth is formed of two heads of rattlesnakes facing each other, with their big, poisonous fangs protruding from their jaws, and that his nose, too, seems to be formed out of the twisted bodies of the snakes. Perhaps even his eyes might be seen as coiled serpents. We see how far the idea of 'building up' a face out of given forms can lead away from our ideas of lifelike sculpture. We also get an inkling of the reasons which may sometimes have led to this method. It was certainly fitting to form the image of the rain-god out of the body of the sacred snakes which embodied the power of lightning. If we try to enter into the mentality which created these uncanny idols we may begin to understand how image-making in these early civilizations was not only connected with magic and religion but was also the first form of writing. The sacred serpent in ancient Mexican art was not only the picture of a rattlesnake but could also develop into a sign for lightning, and so into a character by which a thunderstorm could be commemorated or, perhaps, conjured up. We know very little about these mysterious origins, but if we want to understand the story of art we do well to remember, once in a while, that pictures and letters are really blood-relations.

Art for Eternity

Egypt, Mesopotamia, Crete

Some form of art exists everywhere on the globe, but the story of art as a continuous effort does not begin in the caves of southern France or among the North American Indians. There is no direct tradition which links these strange beginnings with our own days, but there is a direct tradition, handed down from master to pupil, and from pupil to admirer or copyist, which links the art of our own days, any house or any poster, with the art of the Nile Valley of some five thousand years ago. For we shall see that the Greek masters went to school with the Egyptians, and we are all the pupils of the Greeks. Thus the art of Egypt has a tremendous importance for us.

Everyone knows that Egypt is the land of the pyramids, figure 31, those mountains of stone which stand like weathered landmarks on the distant horizon of history. However remote and mysterious they seem, they tell us much of their own story. They tell us of a land which was so thoroughly organized that it was possible to pile up these gigantic mounds in the lifetime of a single king, and they tell us of kings who were so rich and powerful that they could force thousands and thousands of workers or slaves to toil for them year in, year out, to quarry the stones, to drag them to the building site, and to shift them with the most primitive means till the tomb was ready to receive the king. No king and no people would have gone to such expense, and taken so much trouble, for the creation of a mere monument. In fact, we know that the pyramids had their practical importance in the eyes of the kings and their subjects. The king was considered a divine being who held sway over them, and on his departure from this earth he would again ascend to the gods whence he had come. The pyramids soaring up to the sky would probably help him to make his ascent. In any case they would preserve his sacred body from decay. For the

Egyptians believed that the body must be preserved if the soul is to live on in the beyond. That is why they prevented the corpse from decaying by an elaborate method of embalming it, and binding it up in strips of cloth. It was for the mummy of the king that the pyramid had been piled up, and his body was laid right in the centre of the huge mountain of stone in a stone coffin. Everywhere round the burial chamber, spells and incantations were written to help him on his journey to the other world.

But it is not only these oldest relics of human architecture which tell of the role played by age-old beliefs in the story of art. The Egyptians held the belief that the preservation of the body was not enough. If the likeness of the king was also preserved, it was doubly sure that he would continue to exist for ever. So they ordered sculptors to chisel the king's head out of hard, imperishable granite, and put it in the tomb where no one saw it, there to work its spell and to help his soul to keep alive in and through the image. One Egyptian word for sculptor was actually 'He-who-keeps-alive'.

At first these rites were reserved for kings, but soon the nobles of the royal household had their minor tombs grouped in neat rows round the king's mound; and gradually every self-respecting person had to make provision for his after-life by ordering a costly grave which would house his mummy and his likeness, and where his soul could dwell and receive the offerings of food and drink which were given to the dead. Some of these early portraits from the pyramid age, the fourth 'dynasty' of the 'Old Kingdom', are among the most beautiful works of Egyptian art, figure 32. There is a solemnity and simplicity about them which one does not easily forget. One sees that the sculptor was not trying to flatter his sitter, or to preserve a fleeting expression. He was concerned only with essentials. Every lesser detail he left out. Perhaps it is just because of this strict concentration on the basic forms of the human head that these portraits remain so impressive. For, despite their almost geometrical rigidity, they are not primitive as are the native masks discussed in Chapter 1, figures 25, 28. Nor are they as lifelike as the naturalistic portraits of the artists of Nigeria, figure 23. The observation of nature, and the regularity of the whole, are so evenly balanced that they impress us as being lifelike and yet remote and enduring.

This combination of geometric regularity and keen observation of nature is characteristic of all Egyptian art. We can study it best in the reliefs and paintings that adorned the walls of the tombs. The word 'adorned', it is true, may hardly fit an art which was meant to be seen by no one but the dead man's soul. In fact, these works were not intended to be enjoyed. They, too, were meant to 'keep alive'. Once, in a grim distant past, it had been the custom when a powerful man died to let his servants and slaves accompany him into the grave. They were sacrificed so that he should arrive in the beyond with a suitable train. Later, these horrors were considered either too cruel or too costly, and art came to the rescue. Instead of real servants, the great ones of this earth were given images as substitutes. The pictures and models found in Egyptian tombs were connected with the idea of providing the soul with helpmates in the other world, a belief that is found in many early cultures.

To us these reliefs and wall-paintings provide an extraordinarily vivid picture of life as it was lived in Egypt thousands of years ago. And yet, looking at them for the first time, one may find them rather bewildering. The reason is that the Egyptian painters had a very different way from ours of representing real life. Perhaps this is connected with the different purpose their paintings had to serve. What mattered most was not prettiness but completeness. It was the artists' task to preserve everything as clearly and permanently as possible. So they did not set out to sketch nature as it appeared to them from any fortuitous angle. They drew from memory, according to strict rules which ensured that everything that had to go into the picture would stand out in perfect clarity. Their method, in fact, resembled that of the map-maker rather than that of the painter. Figure 33 shows it in a simple example, representing a garden with a pond. If we had to draw such a motif we might wonder from which angle to approach it. The shape and character of the trees could be seen clearly only from the sides, the shape of the pond would be visible only if seen from above. The Egyptians had no compunction about this problem. They would simply draw the pond as if it were seen from above, and the trees from the side. The fishes and birds in the pond, on the other hand, would hardly look recognizable as seen from above, so they were drawn in profile.

In such a simple picture, we can easily understand the artist's procedure. A similar method is often used by children. But the Egyptians were much more consistent in their application of these methods than children ever are. Everything had to be represented from its most characteristic angle. Figure 34 shows the effect which this idea had on the representation of the human body. The head was most easily seen in profile so they drew it sideways. But if we think of the human eye we think of it as seen from the front. Accordingly, a full-face eye was planted into the side view of the face. The top half of the body, the shoulders and chest, are best seen from the front, for then we see how the arms are hinged to the body. But arms and legs in movement are much more clearly seen sideways. That is the reason why Egyptians in these pictures look so strangely flat and contorted. Moreover, the Egyptian artists found it hard to visualize either foot seen

from the outside. They preferred the clear outline from the
big toe upwards. So both feet are seen from the inside, and
the man on the relief looks as if he had two left feet. It must
not be supposed that Egyptian artists thought that human
beings looked like that. They merely followed a rule which
allowed them to include everything in the human form
that they considered important. Perhaps this strict adherence
to the rule had something to do with their magic purpose.
For how could a man with his arm 'foreshortened' or 'cut off'
bring or receive the required offerings to the dead?

Here as always, Egyptian art is not based on what the
artist could see at a given moment, but rather on what he
knew belonged to a person or a scene. It was out of these
forms which he had learned, and which he knew, that he built
his representations, much as the tribal artist builds his figures
out of the forms he can master. It is not only his knowledge
of forms and shapes that the artist embodies in his picture, but
also his knowledge of their significance. We sometimes call a
man a 'big boss'. The Egyptian drew the boss bigger than his
servants or even his wife.

Once we have grasped these rules and conventions, we
understand the language of the pictures in which the life of
the Egyptians is chronicled. Figure 35 gives a good idea of the
general arrangement of a wall in the tomb of a high Egyptian
dignitary of the so-called 'Middle Kingdom', some nineteen
hundred years before our era. The inscriptions in hieroglyphs
tell us exactly who he was, and what titles and honours he had
collected in his lifetime. His name, we read, was Khnumhotep,
the Administrator of the Eastern Desert, Prince of Menat
Khufu, Confidential Friend of the King, Royal Acquaintance,
Superintendent of the Priests, Priest of Horus, Priest of Anubis,
Chief of all the Divine Secrets, and – most impressive of all –
Master of all the Tunics. On the left side we see him hunting

wildfowl with a kind of boomerang, accompanied by his wife Kheti, his concubine Jat, and one of his sons who, despite his tiny size in the picture, held the title of Superintendent of the Frontiers. Below, in the frieze, we see fishermen under their superintendent Mentuhotep hauling in a big catch. On top of the door Khnumhotep is seen again, this time trapping waterfowl in a net. Understanding the methods of the Egyptian artist, we can easily see how this device worked. The trapper sat hidden behind a screen of reeds, holding a cord, which was linked with the open net (seen from above). When the birds had settled on the bait, he pulled the rope and the net closed over them. Behind Khnumhotep is his eldest son Nacht, and his Superintendent of the Treasures, who was also responsible for the ordering of the tomb. On the right side, Khnumhotep, who is called 'great in fish, rich in wildfowl, loving the goddess of the chase', is seen spearing fish, figure 36. Once more we can observe the conventions of the Egyptian artist who lets the water rise among the reeds to show us the clearing with the fish. The inscription reads: 'Canoeing in the papyrus beds, the pools of wildfowl, the marshes and the streams, spearing with the two-pronged spear, he transfixes thirty fish; how delightful is the day of hunting the hippopotamus.' Below is an amusing episode with one of the men who had fallen into the water being fished out by his mates. The inscription round the door records the days on which offerings are to be given to the dead, and includes prayers to the gods.

When we have become accustomed to looking at these Egyptian pictures we are as little troubled by their unrealities as we are by the absence of colour in a photograph. We even begin to realize the great advantages of the Egyptian method. Nothing in these pictures gives the impression of being haphazard, nothing looks as if it could

just as well be somewhere else. It is worth while taking a pencil
and trying to copy one of these 'primitive' Egyptian drawings.
Our attempts always look clumsy, lopsided and crooked. At least
my own do. For the Egyptian sense of order in every detail is
so strong that any little variation seems to upset it entirely.
The Egyptian artist began his work by drawing a network of
straight lines on the wall, and he distributed his figures with
great care along these lines. And yet all this geometrical sense
of order did not prevent him from observing the details of
nature with amazing accuracy. Every bird or fish is drawn with
such truthfulness that zoologists can still recognize the species.
Figure 37 shows such a detail of figure 35 – the birds in the tree
by Khnumhotep's fowling net. It was not only his great
knowledge which guided the artist, but also an eye for pattern.

It is one of the greatest things in Egyptian art that all
the statues, paintings and architectural forms seem to fall into
place as if they obeyed one law. We call such a law, which all
creations of a people seem to obey, a 'style'. It is very difficult
to explain in words what makes a style, but it is far less
difficult to see. The rules which govern all Egyptian art give
every individual work the effect of poise and austere harmony.

The Egyptian style comprised a set of very strict laws,
which every artist had to learn from his earliest youth. Seated
statues had to have their hands on their knees; men had to be
painted with darker skin than women; the appearance of every
Egyptian god was strictly laid down: Horus, the sky-god, had
to be shown as a falcon or with a falcon's head; Anubis, the
god of funeral rites, as a jackal or with a jackal's head, figure 38.
Every artist also had to learn the art of beautiful script. He had
to cut the images and symbols of the hieroglyphs clearly and
accurately in stone. But once he had mastered all these rules he
had finished his apprenticeship. No one wanted anything
different, no one asked him to be 'original'. On the contrary,

he was probably considered the best artist who could make his statues most like the admired monuments of the past. So it happened that in the course of three thousand years or more Egyptian art changed very little. Everything that was considered good and beautiful in the age of the pyramids was held to be just as excellent a thousand years later. True, new fashions appeared, and new subjects were demanded of the artists, but their mode of representing man and nature remained essentially the same.

Only one man ever shook the iron bars of the Egyptian style. He was a king of the Eighteenth Dynasty, in the period known as the 'New Kingdom', which was founded after a catastrophic invasion of Egypt. This king, Amenophis IV, was a heretic. He broke with many of the customs hallowed by age-old tradition. He did not wish to pay homage to the many strangely shaped gods of his people. For him only one god was supreme, Aten, whom he worshipped and whom he had represented in the shape of the sun-disk sending down its rays, each one endowed with a hand. He called himself Akhnaten, after his god, and he moved his court out of reach of the priests of the other gods, to a place which is now called Tell-el-Amarna.

The pictures which he commissioned must have shocked the Egyptians of his day by their novelty. In them none of the solemn and rigid dignity of the earlier Pharaohs was to be found. Instead, he had himself represented with his wife Nefertiti, figure 40, fondling their children beneath the blessing sun. Some of his portraits show him as an ugly man, figure 39 – perhaps he wanted the artists to portray him in all his human frailty or, perhaps, he was so convinced of his unique importance as a prophet that he insisted on a true likeness. Akhnaten's successor was Tutankhamun, whose tomb with its treasures was discovered in 1922. Some of these works

are still in the modern style of the Aten religion – particularly
the back of the king's throne, figure 42, which shows the king
and queen in a homely idyll. He is sitting on his chair in an
attitude which might have scandalized the strict Egyptian
conservative – almost lolling, by Egyptian standards. His wife
is no smaller than he is, and gently puts her hand on his
shoulder while the Sun-god again is stretching his hands in
blessing down to them.

It is not impossible that this reform of art in the
Eighteenth Dynasty was made easier for the king because he
could point to foreign works that were much less strict and
rigid than the Egyptian products. On an island overseas, in
Crete, there dwelt a gifted people whose artists delighted in
the representation of swift movement. When the palace
of their king at Knossos was excavated at the end of the nineteenth century, people could hardly believe that such a free
and graceful style could have been developed in the second
millennium before our era. Works in this style were also found
on the Greek mainland; a dagger from Mycenae with a lion
hunt, figure 41, shows a sense of movement and flowing lines
which must have impressed any Egyptian craftsman who had
been permitted to stray from the hallowed rules of his style.

But this opening of Egyptian art did not last long.
Already during the reign of Tutankhamun the old beliefs were
restored, and the window to the outside world was shut again.
The Egyptian style, as it had existed for more than a thousand
years before his time, continued to exist for another
thousand years or more, and the Egyptians doubtless believed
it would continue for all eternity. Many Egyptian works in
our museums date from this later period, and so do nearly all
Egyptian buildings such as temples and palaces. New themes
were introduced, new tasks performed, but nothing essentially
new was added to the achievement of art.

Egypt, of course, was only one of the great and
powerful empires which existed in the Near East for several
thousand years. We all know from the Bible that little Palestine
lay between the Egyptian kingdom of the Nile and the
Babylonian and Assyrian empires, which had developed in the
valley of the two rivers Euphrates and Tigris. The art of
Mesopotamia, as the valley of the two rivers was called in
Greek, is less well known to us than the art of Egypt. This is at
least partly due to accident. There were no stone quarries in
these valleys, and most buildings were made of baked brick
which, in course of time, weathered away and fell to dust.
Even sculpture in stone was comparatively rare. But this is not
the only explanation of the fact that relatively few early works
of that art have come down to us. The main reason is probably
that these people did not share the religious belief of
the Egyptians that the human body and its likeness must be
preserved if the soul is to continue. In the very early times,
when a people called the Sumerians ruled in the city of Ur,
kings were still buried with their whole household, slaves and
all, so that they should not lack a following in the world
beyond. Graves of this period have been discovered, and we
can admire some of the household goods of these ancient,
barbarous kings in the British Museum. We see how much
refinement and artistic skill can go together with primitive
superstition and cruelty. There was, for instance, a harp in one
of the tombs, decorated with fabulous animals, figure 43. They
look rather like our heraldic beasts, not only in their general
appearance but also in their arrangement, for the Sumerians had
a taste for symmetry and precision. We do not know exactly
what these fabulous animals were meant to signify, but it
is almost certain that they were figures from the mythology of
these early days, and that the scenes which look to us like pages
from a children's book had a very solemn and serious meaning.

Though artists in Mesopotamia were not called upon to decorate the walls of tombs, they too had to ensure, in a different way, that the image helped to keep the mighty alive. From early times onwards it was the custom of Mesopotamian kings to commission monuments to their victories in war, which told of the tribes that had been defeated, and the booty that had been taken. Figure 44 shows such a relief representing the king who tramples on the body of his slain foe, while others of his enemies beg for mercy. Perhaps the idea behind these monuments was not only to keep the memory of these victories alive. In early times, at least, the ancient beliefs in the power of the image may still have influenced those who ordered them. Perhaps they thought that, as long as the picture of their king with his foot on the neck of the prostrate enemy stood there, the defeated tribe would not be able to rise again.

In later times such monuments developed into complete picture-chronicles of the king's campaign. The best-preserved of these chronicles date from a relatively late period, the reign of King Asurnasirpal II of Assyria, who lived in the ninth century BC, a little later than the biblical King Solomon. In them we see all the episodes of a well-organized campaign; figure 45 shows the details of an attack on a fortress, with the siege machines in action, the defenders tumbling down, and on the top of a tower a woman wailing in vain. The way in which these scenes are represented is rather similar to Egyptian methods, but perhaps a little less tidy and rigid. As one looks at them, one feels as if one were watching the news of two thousand years ago. It all looks so real and convincing. But as we look more carefully we discover a curious fact: there are plenty of dead and wounded in these gruesome wars – but not one of them is an Assyrian. The art of boasting and propaganda was well advanced in these early days. But perhaps we can take a slightly more charitable view of these Assyrians.

Perhaps even they were still ruled by the old superstition which has come into this story so often: the superstition that there is more in a picture than a mere picture. Perhaps they did not want to represent wounded Assyrians for some such reason. In any case, the tradition which then began had a very long life. On all the monuments which glorify the warlords of the past, war is no trouble at all. You just appear, and the enemy is scattered like chaff in the wind.

The Great Awakening

Greece, seventh to fifth century BC

It was in the great oasis lands, where the sun burns mercilessly, and where only the land watered by the rivers provides food, that the earliest styles of art had been created under Oriental despots, and these styles remained almost unchanged for thousands of years. Conditions were very different in the milder climes of the sea which bordered these empires, on the many islands, large and small, of the eastern Mediterranean and the many-creeked coasts of the peninsulas of Greece and Asia Minor. These regions were not subject to one ruler. They were the hiding-places of adventurous seamen, or pirate-kings who travelled far and wide and piled up great wealth in their castles and harbour-towns by means of trade and sea-raiding. The main centre of these areas was originally the island of Crete, whose kings were at times sufficiently rich and powerful to send embassies to Egypt, and whose art created an impression even there, *page 57*.

No one knows exactly who the people were who ruled in Crete, and whose art was copied on the Greek mainland, particularly in Mycenae. Recent discoveries make it likely that they spoke an early form of Greek. Later, about 1000 BC, a fresh wave of warlike tribes from Europe penetrated to the rugged peninsula of Greece and to the shores of Asia Minor, and fought and defeated the former inhabitants. Only in the songs which tell of these battles does something survive of the splendour and beauty of the art which was destroyed in these protracted wars, for these songs are the Homeric poems, and among the new arrivals were the Greek tribes we know from history.

In the first few centuries of their domination of Greece the art of these tribes looked harsh and primitive enough. There is nothing of the gay movement of the Cretan style in these works; rather they seemed to outdo the Egyptians in rigidity. Their pottery was decorated with simple geometric patterns, and where a scene was to be represented it formed part of this strict design. Figure 46, for instance, represents the mourning for a dead man. He is lying on his bier, while wailing women right and left raise their hands to their heads in the ritual lament which is the custom in nearly all primitive societies.

Something of this simplicity and clear arrangement seems to have gone into the style of building which the Greeks introduced in these early days, and which, strange to say, still lives on in our own towns and villages. Figure 50 shows a Greek temple of the old style which is called after the Doric tribe. This was the tribe to which the Spartans belonged, who were noted for their austerity. There is, indeed, nothing unnecessary in these buildings, nothing, at least, of which we do not see, or believe we see, the purpose. Probably the earliest of such temples were built of timber, and consisted of little else than a small walled cubicle to hold the image of the god, and around it, strong props to carry the weight of the roof. About the year 600 BC the Greeks began to imitate these simple structures in stone. The wooden props were turned into columns which supported strong crossbeams of stone. These crossbeams are called architraves, and the whole unit resting on the columns goes under the name of entablature. We can see traces of the timber structure in the upper part, which looks as if the ends of beams were showing. These ends were usually marked with three slits, and are therefore called by the Greek word triglyphs, which means 'three slits'. The space between these beams is called the metope. The astonishing thing in these early temples, which so clearly imitate wooden structures, is the simplicity and harmony of the whole. If the builders had used simple square pillars, or cylindrical columns, the temples might have looked heavy and clumsy. Instead, they took care to shape the columns so that there was a slight swelling towards the middle and a tapering off towards the top. The result is that they look almost as though they were elastic, and as though the weight of the roof was just slightly compressing them, without, however, squeezing them out of shape. It almost seems as if they were living beings who carried their loads with ease. Though some of these temples are large and imposing, they are not colossal like Egyptian buildings. One feels that they were built by human beings, and for human beings. In fact, there was no divine ruler over the Greeks who could or would have forced a whole people to slave for him. The Greek tribes had settled down in various small cities and harbour-towns. There was much rivalry and friction between these small communities, but none of them succeeded in lording it over all the others.

Of these Greek city-states, Athens in Attica became by far the most famous and the most important in the history of art. It was here, above all, that the greatest and most astonishing revolution in the whole history of art bore fruit. It is hard to tell when and where this revolution began – perhaps roughly at the time when the first temples of stone were being built in Greece, in the sixth century BC. We know that before that time the artists of the old Oriental empires had striven for a peculiar kind of perfection. They had tried to emulate the art of their forefathers as faithfully as possible, and to adhere strictly to the sacred rules they had learned. When Greek artists began to make statues of stone, they started where the Egyptians and Assyrians had left off. Figure 47 shows that they studied and imitated Egyptian models, and that they learned from them how to make the figure of a standing young man, how to mark the divisions of the body and the muscles which hold it together. But it also shows that the artist who made these statues was not content to follow any formula, however good, and that he began experimenting for himself. He was obviously interested in finding out what knees really looked like. Perhaps he did not quite succeed; perhaps the knees of his statues are even less convincing than those of Egyptian examples; but the point was that he had decided to have a look for himself instead of following the old prescription. It was no longer a question of learning a ready-made formula for representing the human body. Every Greek sculptor wanted to know how *he* was to represent a particular body. The Egyptians had based their art on knowledge. The Greeks began to use their eyes. Once this revolution had begun, there was no stopping it. The sculptors in their workshops tried out new ideas and new ways of representing the human figure, and each innovation was eagerly taken up by others who added their own discoveries. One discovered how to chisel the trunk, another found out that a statue may look much more alive if the feet are not both placed firmly on the ground. Yet another would discover that he could make a face come alive by simply bending the mouth upwards so that it appeared to smile. Of course, the Egyptian method was in many ways safer. The experiments of the Greek artists sometimes misfired. The smile might look like an embarrassed grin, or the less rigid stance might give the impression of affectation. But the Greek artists were not easily frightened by these difficulties. They had set out on a road on which there was no turning back.

The painters followed suit. We know little of their work except what the Greek writers tell us, but it is important to realize that many Greek painters were even more famous in their time than the Greek sculptors. The only way in which we can form a vague idea of what early Greek painting was like is by looking at the pictures on pottery. These painted vessels are generally called vases, although they were intended more often to hold wine or oil than flowers. The painting of these vases developed into an important industry in Athens, and the humble craftsmen employed in these workshops were just as eager as the other artists to introduce the latest discoveries into their products. In the early vases, painted in the sixth century BC, we still see traces of the Egyptian methods, figure 48. We see the two heroes from Homer, Achilles and Ajax, playing draughts in their tent. Both figures are still shown strictly in profile. Their eyes still look as seen from the front. But their bodies are no longer drawn in the Egyptian fashion, nor are their arms and hands set out so clearly and so rigidly. The painter had obviously tried to imagine what it would really look like if two people were facing each other in that way. He was no longer afraid of showing only a small part of Achilles' left hand, the rest being hidden behind the shoulder. He no longer thought that everything he knew to be there must also be shown. Once this ancient rule was broken, once the artist began to rely on what he saw, a veritable landslide started. Painters made the greatest discovery of all, the discovery of foreshortening. It was a tremendous moment in the history of art when, perhaps a little before 500 BC, artists dared for the first time in all history to paint a foot as seen from in front. In all the thousands of Egyptian and Assyrian works which have come down to us, nothing of that kind had ever happened. A Greek vase, figure 49, shows with what pride this discovery was taken up. We see a young warrior putting on his armour for battle. His parents on either side, who assist him and probably give him good advice, are still represented in rigid profile. The head of the youth in the middle is also shown in profile, and we can see that the painter did not find it too easy to fit his head on to the body, which we see from the front. The right foot, too, is still drawn in the 'safe' way, but the left foot is foreshortened – we see the five toes like a row of five little circles. It may seem exaggerated to dwell for long on such a small detail, but it really meant that the old art was dead and buried. It meant that the artist no longer aimed at including everything in the picture in its most clearly visible form, but took account of the angle from which he saw an object. And immediately beside the foot he showed what he meant. He drew the youth's shield, not in the shape in which we might see it in our imagination as a round, but seen from the side, leaning against a wall.

But as we look at this picture and the previous one, we also realize that the lessons of Egyptian art had not simply been discarded and thrown overboard. Greek artists still tried to make their figures as clear in outline as possible, and to include as much of their knowledge of the human body as would go into the picture without doing violence to its appearance. They still loved firm outlines and balanced design. They were far from trying to copy any casual glimpse of nature as they saw it. The old formula, the type of human form as it had developed in all these centuries, was still their starting-point. Only they no longer considered it sacred in every detail.

The great revolution of Greek art, the discovery of natural forms and of foreshortening, happened at the time which is altogether the most amazing period of human history. It is the time when people in the Greek cities began to question the old traditions and legends about the gods, and inquired without prejudice into the nature of things. It is the time when science, as we understand the term today, and philosophy first awoke among men, and when the theatre first developed out of the ceremonies in honour of Dionysus. We must not imagine, however, that the artists in those days were among the intellectual classes of the city. The rich Greeks who managed the affairs of their city, and who spent their time in the market-place in endless arguments, perhaps even

the poets and philosophers, mostly looked down on the
sculptors and painters as inferior persons. Artists worked with
their hands, and they worked for a living. They sat in their
foundries, covered with sweat and grime, they toiled like
ordinary navvies, and so they were not considered members
of polite society. Nevertheless, their share in the life of the
city was infinitely greater than that of an Egyptian or an
Assyrian craftsman, because most Greek cities, Athens in
particular, were democracies in which these humble workers
who were despised by the well-to-do snobs were yet allowed
to share to some extent in the business of government.

It was at the time when Athenian democracy had
reached its highest level that Greek art came to the summit of
its development. After Athens had defeated the Persian
invasion, the people, under the leadership of Pericles, began
to build again what the Persians had destroyed. In 480 BC the
temples on the sacred rock of Athens, the Acropolis, had
been burned down and sacked by the Persians. Now they
were to be built in marble and with a splendour and nobility
never known before, figure 50. Pericles was no snob. The
ancient writers imply that he treated the artists of his time as
his equals. The man he entrusted with the planning of the
temples was the architect Iktinos, and the sculptor who was
to fashion the figures of the gods and to supervise the
decoration of the temples was Pheidias.

The fame of Pheidias is founded on works which no
longer exist. But it is important to try to imagine what they
were like, because we forget too easily what purpose Greek
art still served at that time. We read in the Bible how the
prophets inveighed against the worship of idols, but we do
not usually connect any very concrete ideas with these words.
There are many passages like the following from Jeremiah
(x. 3-5):

For the customs of the people are vain: for one cutteth a tree out
of the forest, the work of the hands of the workman, with the
axe. They deck it with silver and with gold; they fasten it with
nails and with hammers, that it move not. They are upright as the
palm tree, but speak not: they must needs be borne, because they
cannot go. Be not afraid of them; for they cannot do evil, neither
also is it in them to do good.

What Jeremiah had in mind were the idols of Mesopotamia,
made of wood and precious metals. But his words would
apply almost exactly to the works of Pheidias, made only a
few centuries after the prophet's lifetime. As we walk along
the rows of white marble statues from classical antiquity
in the great museums, we too often forget that among them
are these idols of which the Bible speaks; that people prayed
before them, that sacrifices were brought to them amidst
strange incantations, and that thousands and tens of thousands
of worshippers may have approached them with hope and
fear in their hearts – wondering, as the prophet says, whether
these statues and graven images were not really at the same
time gods themselves. In fact, the very reason why nearly all
the famous statues of the ancient world perished was that
after the victory of Christianity it was considered a pious duty
to smash any statue of the heathen gods. The sculptures in
our museums are, for the most part, only secondhand copies
made in Roman times for travellers and collectors as
souvenirs, and as decorations for gardens or public baths. We
must be very grateful for these copies, because they give us at
least a faint idea of the famous masterpieces of Greek art; but
unless we use our imagination these weak imitations can also
do much harm. They are largely responsible for the
widespread idea that Greek art was lifeless, cold and insipid,
and that Greek statues had that chalky appearance and vacant

look which reminds one of old-fashioned drawing classes.
The Roman copy of the great idol of Pallas Athene, for instance,
which Pheidias made for her shrine in the Parthenon, figure 51,
hardly looks very impressive. We must turn to old descriptions
and try to picture what it was like: a gigantic wooden image,
some 36 feet (11 metres) high, as high as a tree, covered
all over with precious material – the armour and garments of
gold, the skin of ivory. There was also plenty of strong,
shining colour on the shield and other parts of the armour,
not forgetting the eyes, which were made of coloured stones.
There were griffons on the golden helmet of the goddess,
and the eyes of a huge snake which was coiled inside the
shield were, no doubt, also marked by shining stones. It must
have been an awe-inspiring and uncanny sight when one
entered the temple and suddenly stood face to face with this
gigantic statue. There was no doubt something almost
primitive and savage in some of its features, something which
still linked an idol of this kind with the ancient superstitions
against which the prophet Jeremiah had preached. But already
these primitive ideas about the gods as formidable demons
who dwelt in the statues had ceased to be the main
thing. Pallas Athene, as Pheidias saw her and as he fashioned
her statue, was more than the mere idol of a demon. From
all accounts we know that his statue had a dignity which
gave the people quite a different idea of the character and
meaning of their gods. The Athene of Pheidias was like
a great human being. Her power lay less in any magic spells
than in her beauty. People realized at the time that the art
of Pheidias had given the people of Greece a new conception
of the divine.

The two great works of Pheidias, his Athene and his
famous statue of Zeus in Olympia, have been irretrievably lost,
but the temples in which they were placed still exist, and with

them some of the decorations that were made at the time of
Pheidias. The temple in Olympia is the older one; it was
perhaps begun round about 470 BC and finished before 457 BC.
In the squares (metopes) over the architrave the deeds of
Hercules were represented. Figure 52 shows the episode when
he was sent to fetch the apples of the Hesperides. That was a
task which even Hercules could not, or would not, perform.
He entreated Atlas, who bore the heavens on his shoulders, to
do it for him and Atlas agreed on condition that Hercules
would carry his burden in the meantime. On this relief Atlas is
shown returning with the golden apples to Hercules, who
stands taut beneath his huge load. Athene, his cunning helper
in all his deeds, has put a cushion on his shoulder to make it
easier for him. In her right hand she once held a metal spear.
The whole story is told with a wonderful simplicity and
clarity. We feel that the artist still preferred to show a figure in
a straightforward attitude, from the front or side. Athene is
shown squarely facing us, and only her head is turned sideways
towards Hercules. It is not difficult to sense in the figures the
lingering influence of the rules which governed Egyptian art.
But we feel that the greatness, the majestic calm and strength
which belong to Greek sculpture, are also due to this
observance of ancient rules. For these rules had ceased to be
a hindrance, cramping the artist's freedom. The old idea that it
was important to show the structure of the body – its main
hinges, as it were, which help us to realize how it all hangs
together – spurred the artist on to explore the anatomy of the
bones and muscles, and to build up a convincing picture of
the human figure which remains visible even under the flow
of the drapery. The way, in fact, in which Greek artists used the
drapery to mark these main divisions of the body still shows
what importance they attached to the knowledge of form. It is
this balance between an adherence to rules and a freedom

within the rules which has made Greek art so much admired
in later centuries. It is for this that artists have returned again
and again to the masterpieces of Greek art for guidance and
for inspiration.

The type of work which Greek artists were frequently
asked to do may have helped them to perfect their knowledge
of the human body in action. A temple like that of Olympia
was surrounded by statues of victorious athletes dedicated to
the gods. To us this may seem a strange custom for, however
popular our champions may be, we do not expect them to have
their portraits made and presented to a church in thanksgiving
for a victory achieved in the latest match. But the great sports
rallies of the Greeks, of which the Olympic Games were, of
course, the most famous, were something very different from
our modern contests. They were much more closely connected
with the religious beliefs and rites of the people. Those who
took part in them were not sportsmen – whether amateur or
professional – but members of the leading families of Greece,
and the victor in these games was looked upon with awe as a
man whom the gods had favoured with the spell of
invincibility. It was to find out on whom this blessing of
victoriousness rested that the games were originally held, and
it was to commemorate and perhaps to perpetuate these signs
of divine grace that the winners commissioned their statues
from the most renowned artists of their time.

Diggings in Olympia have unearthed a good many of
the pedestals on which these famous statues rested, but the
statues themselves have disappeared. They were mostly made
of bronze and were probably melted down when metal
became scarce in the Middle Ages. Only in Delphi has one of
these statues been found, the figure of a charioteer, figure 53.
His head, shown in figure 54, is amazingly different from the
general idea one may easily form of Greek art when one only

looks at copies. The eyes, which often look so blank and
expressionless in marble statues or are empty in bronze
heads, are marked in coloured stones – as they always were at
that time. The hair, eyes and lips were slightly gilt, which gave
an effect of richness and warmth to the whole face. And
yet such a head never looked gaudy or vulgar. We can see that
the artist was not out to imitate a real face with all its
imperfections but that he shaped it out of his knowledge of
the human form. We do not know whether the charioteer is
a good likeness – probably it is no 'likeness' at all in the sense
in which we understand the word. But it is a convincing
image of a human being, of wonderful simplicity and beauty.

Works like this which are not even mentioned by the
classical Greek writers remind us what we must have lost in
the most famous of these statues of athletes such as the
'Discobolos' (Discus thrower) by the Athenian sculptor Myron,
who probably belonged to the same generation as Pheidias.
Various copies of this work have been found which allow us at
least to form a general idea of what it looked like, figure 55.
The young athlete was represented at the moment when he is
just about to hurl the heavy discus. He has bent down and
swung his arm backwards so as to be able to throw with
greater force. At the next moment he will spin round and let
fly, supporting the throw with a turn of his body. The attitude
looks so convincing that modern athletes have taken it for
a model and have tried to learn from it the exact Greek style
of throwing the discus. But this has proved less easy than they
had hoped. They had forgotten that Myron's statue is not
a 'still' from a sports film but a Greek work of art. In fact if we
look at it more carefully we shall find that Myron has achieved
his astonishing effect of movement mainly through a new
adaptation of very ancient artistic methods. Standing in front
of the statue and thinking only of its outlines, we become

suddenly aware of its relation to the tradition of Egyptian art.
Like the Egyptian painters, Myron has given us the trunk in
front view, the legs and arms in side view; like them he has
composed his picture of a man's body out of the most
characteristic views of its parts. But under his hands this old
and outworn formula has become something entirely
different. Instead of fitting these views together into an
unconvincing likeness of a rigid pose, he asked a real model
to take up a similar attitude and so adapted it that it seems like
a convincing representation of a body in motion. Whether or
not this corresponds to the exact movement most suitable for
throwing the discus is hardly relevant. What matters is that
Myron conquered movement just as the painters of his time
conquered space.

Of all Greek originals which have come down to us
the sculptures from the Parthenon perhaps reflect this new
freedom in the most wonderful way. The Parthenon, figure 50,
was completed some twenty years after the temple of
Olympia, and in that brief span of time artists had acquired
an ever greater ease and facility in solving the problems of
convincing representation. We do not know who the sculptors
were who made these decorations of the temple, but as
Pheidias made the statue of Athene in the shrine it seems likely
that his workshop also provided the other sculptures.

Figures 56 and 57 show fragments of the long band or
frieze that ran high up round the inside of the building and
represented the annual procession on the solemn festival
of the goddess. There were always games and sports displays
during these festivities, one of which consisted in the
dangerous feat of driving a chariot and jumping on and off
while the four horses galloped along. It is such a display that
is shown in figure 56. At first it may be difficult to find one's
way about on this fragment because the relief is very badly

damaged. Not only is part of the surface broken off, but the
whole of the colour has gone, which probably made
the figures stand out brightly against an intensely coloured
background. To us the colour and texture of fine marble is
something so wonderful that we would never want to cover
it with paint, but the Greeks even painted their temples
with strong contrasting colours such as red and blue. But,
however little may be left of the original work, it is always
worth while with Greek sculptures to try to forget what
is not there for the sheer joy of discovering what is left. The
first we see in our fragment is the horses, four of them, one
behind the other. Their heads and their legs are sufficiently
well preserved to give us an idea of the mastery with which
the artist contrived to show the structure of the bones and
muscles without the whole looking stiff or dry. Soon we see
that the same must also have been true of the human figures.
We can imagine, from the traces that are left, how freely they
moved and how clearly the muscles of their bodies stood out.
Foreshortening no longer presented a great problem to the
artist. The arm with the shield is drawn with perfect ease, and
so is the fluttering crest of the helmet and the bulging cloak
which is blown by the wind. But all these new discoveries do
not 'run away' with the artist. However much he may have
enjoyed this conquest of space and movement, we do not feel
that he is eager to show off what he can do. Lively and
spirited as the groups have become, they still fit well into the
arrangement of the solemn procession which moves along
the wall of the building. The artist has retained something
of the wisdom of arrangement which Greek art derived from
the Egyptians and from the training in geometrical patterns
which had preceded the Great Awakening. It is this sureness
of hand which makes every detail of the Parthenon frieze
so lucid and 'right'.

Every Greek work from that great period shows this wisdom and skill in the distribution of figures, but what the Greeks of the time valued even more was something else: the new-found freedom to represent the human body in any position or movement could be used to reflect the inner life of the figures represented. We hear from one of his disciples that this is what the great philosopher Socrates, who had himself been trained as a sculptor, urged artists to do. They should represent the 'workings of the soul' by accurately observing the way 'feelings affect the body in action'.

Once more the craftsmen who painted vases tried to keep step with these discoveries of the great masters whose works are lost. Figure 58 represents the moving episode from the story of Ulysses when the hero has come home after nineteen years of absence, disguised as a beggar with crutch, bundle and bowl, and is recognized by his old nurse, who notices the familiar scar on his leg while washing his feet. The artist must have illustrated a slightly different version from the one we read in Homer (where the nurse has a different name from the one inscribed on the vase and where Eumaios the swineherd is not present); perhaps he had seen a play in which this scene was enacted, for we remember that it was in this century also that the Greek playwrights created the art of the drama. But we do not need the exact text to sense that something dramatic and moving is happening, for the glance exchanged between the nurse and the hero tells us almost more than words could. Greek artists had indeed mastered the means of conveying something of the unspoken feelings set up between people.

It is this capacity to make us see the 'workings of the soul' in the poise of the body that turns a simple tombstone like figure 59 into a great work of art. The relief shows Hegeso, who is buried under the stone, as she was in life. A servant girl stands in front of her and offers her a casket, from which she seems to select a piece of jewellery. It is a quiet scene which we might compare to the Egyptian representation of Tutankhamun on his throne, with his wife adjusting his collar, figure 42. The Egyptian work, too, is wonderfully clear in its outline, but despite the fact that it dates from an exceptional period of Egyptian art it is rather stiff and unnatural. The Greek relief has shed all these awkward limitations, but it has retained the lucidity and beauty of the arrangement, which is no longer geometrical and angular but free and relaxed. The way the upper half is framed by the curve of the two women's arms, the way these lines are answered in the curves of the stool, the simple method by which Hegeso's beautiful hand becomes the centre of attention, the flow of the drapery round the forms of the body so expressive of calm – all combine to produce that simple harmony which only came into the world with Greek art of the fifth century.

4

The Realm of Beauty

Greece and the Greek world,
fourth century BC to first century AD

The great awakening of art to freedom had taken place in the hundred years between, roughly, 520 and 420 BC. Towards the end of the fifth century, artists had become fully conscious of their power and mastery, and so had the public. Though artists were still looked upon as craftsmen and, perhaps, despised by the snobs, an increasing number of people began to be interested in their work for its own sake, and not only for the sake of its religious or political functions. People compared the merits of the various 'schools' of art; that is to say, of the various methods, styles and traditions which distinguished the masters in different cities. There is no doubt that the comparison and competition between these schools stimulated the artist to ever greater efforts, and helped to create that variety which we admire in Greek art. In architecture, various styles began to be used side by side. The Parthenon had been built in the Doric style, figure 50, but in the later buildings on the Acropolis the forms of the so-called Ionic style were introduced. The principle of these temples is the same as that of the Doric ones, but the whole appearance and character are different. The building which shows it at its most perfect is the temple called the Erechtheion, figure 60. The columns of the Ionic temple are much less robust and strong. They are like slender shafts, and the capital or headpiece is no longer a simple unadorned cushion, but is richly decorated with volutes on the sides; these again seem to express the function of the part carrying the beam on which the roof rests. The whole impression of these buildings with their finely wrought details is one of infinite grace and ease.

The same character of grace and ease also marks the sculpture and painting of this period, which begins with the generation after Pheidias. Athens at this time was involved in a fearful war with Sparta, which ended her prosperity and that of Greece. In 408 BC, during a brief spell of peace, a carved balustrade was added to the small temple of the goddess of victory on the Acropolis, and its sculptures and ornaments show the change of taste towards delicacy and refinement which is also reflected in the Ionic style. The figures have been sadly mutilated, but I should like nevertheless to illustrate one of them, figure 61, to show how beautiful this broken figure still is, even without head or hands. It is the figure of a girl, one of the goddesses of victory, stooping to fasten a loosened sandal as she walks. With what charm this sudden halt is portrayed, and how softly and richly the thin drapery falls over the beautiful body! We can see in these works that the artist could do whatever he wanted. He was no longer struggling with any difficulty in representing movement or foreshortening. This very ease and virtuosity made him perhaps a little self-conscious. The artist of the Parthenon frieze, figures 56-7, did not seem to think overmuch about his art or what he was doing. He knew that his task was to represent a procession, and he took pains to represent it as clearly and well as he could. He was hardly conscious of the fact that he was a great master of whom old and young alike would still be talking thousands of years later. The frieze of the Victory temple shows, perhaps, the beginning of a change of attitude. This artist was proud of his immense power, as well he might be. And so, gradually, during the fourth century, the approach to art changed. Pheidias' statues of gods had been famous all over Greece as representations of gods. The great temple statues of the fourth century earned their reputation more by virtue of their beauty as works of art. The educated Greeks now discussed paintings and statues as they discussed poems and plays; they praised their beauty or criticized their form and conception.

   The greatest artist of that century, Praxiteles, was above all famed for the charm of his work and for the sweet and

insinuating character of his creations. His most celebrated
work, whose praise was sung in many poems, represented the
goddess of Love, the youthful Aphrodite, stepping into her
bath. But this work has disappeared. One work which was
found in Olympia in the nineteenth century is thought by
many to be an original by his hands, figures 62-3. But we
cannot be sure. It may only be an accurate marble copy after
a bronze statue. It represents the god Hermes holding the
young Dionysus on his arm and playing with him. If we look
back at figure 47, we see what an enormous distance Greek art
had travelled in two hundred years. In the work of Praxiteles
all traces of rigidity have gone. The god stands before us
in a relaxed pose which does not impair his dignity. But if
we think about the way in which Praxiteles has achieved his
effect, we begin to realize that even then the lesson of
ancient art had not been forgotten. Praxiteles, too, takes care
to show us the hinges of the body, to make us understand its
working as clearly as possible. But he can now do all that
without keeping his statue stiff and lifeless. He can show the
muscles and bones swelling and moving under the soft skin,
and can give the impression of a living body in all its
grace and beauty. Nevertheless, it is necessary to understand
that Praxiteles and the other Greek artists achieved this
beauty through knowledge. There is no living body quite
as symmetrical, well-built and beautiful as those of the Greek
statues. People often think that what the artists did was to
look at many models and to leave out any feature they did
not like; that they started by carefully copying the appearance
of a real man, and then beautified it by omitting any
irregularities or traits which did not conform to their idea of
a perfect body. They say that Greek artists 'idealized' nature,
and they think of it in terms of a photographer who touches
up a portrait by deleting small blemishes. But a touched-up

photograph and an idealized statue usually lack character and vigour. So much has been left out and deleted that little remains but a pale and insipid ghost of the model. The Greek approach was really exactly the opposite. Through all these centuries, the artists we have been discussing were concerned with infusing more and more life into the ancient husks. In the time of Praxiteles their method bore its ripest fruits. The old types had begun to move and breathe under the hands of the skilful sculptor, and they stand before us like real human beings, and yet as beings from a different, better world. They are, in fact, beings from a different world, not because the Greeks were healthier or more beautiful than other men – there is no reason to think they were – but because art at that moment had reached a point at which the typical and the individual were poised in a new and delicate balance.

Many of the most famous works of classical art which were admired in later times as representing the most perfect types of human beings are copies or variants of statues which were created in this period, the middle of the fourth century BC. The Apollo Belvedere, figure 64, shows the ideal model of a man's body. As he stands before us in his impressive pose, holding up the bow in the extended arm and with his head turned sideways as if he were following the arrow with his eyes, we have no difficulty in recognizing the faint echo of the ancient scheme in which each part of the body was given its most characteristic view. Among the famous classical statues of Venus, the Venus of Milo (so called because it was found on the island of Melos) is perhaps the best known, figure 65. Probably it belonged to a group of Venus and Cupid which was made in a somewhat later period, but which used the achievements and the methods of Praxiteles. It was designed to be seen from the side (Venus was extending her arms towards Cupid), and again we can admire the clarity and simplicity with which the artist modelled the beautiful body, the way he marked its main divisions without ever becoming harsh or vague.

Of course, this method of creating beauty by making a general and schematic figure more and more lifelike until the marble's surface seems to live and breathe has one drawback. It was possible to create convincing human types by this means, but would this method ever lead to the representation of real individual human beings? Strange as it may sound to us, the idea of a portrait, in the sense in which we use the word, did not occur to the Greeks until rather late in the fourth century. True, we hear of portraits made in earlier times, *page 73, figure 54*, but these statues were probably not very good likenesses. A portrait of a general was little more than a picture of any good-looking soldier with a helmet and a staff. The artist never reproduced the shape of his nose, the furrows of his brow or his individual expression. It is a strange fact, which we have not yet discussed, that Greek artists in the works we have seen have avoided giving the heads a particular expression. This is really more astonishing than it seems at first sight, because we can hardly scribble any simple face on a scrap of paper without giving it some marked (usually a funny) expression. The heads of Greek statues or paintings of the fifth century, of course, are not expressionless in the sense of looking dull or blank, but their features never seem to express any strong emotion. It was the body and its movements which were used by these masters to express what Socrates had called 'the workings of the soul', *page 77, figure 58*, because they sensed that the play of features would distort and destroy the simple regularity of the head.

In the generation after Praxiteles, towards the end of the fourth century, this restraint was gradually lifted and artists discovered means of animating the features without destroying their beauty. More than that: they learned how to seize the workings of the individual soul, the particular character of a physiognomy, and to make portraits in our sense of the word. It was in the time of Alexander that people started to discuss this new art of portraiture. A writer of that period, satirizing the irritating habits of flatterers and toadies, mentions that they always burst out in loud praise of the striking likeness of their patron's portrait. Alexander himself preferred to be portrayed by his court sculptor Lysippus, the most celebrated artist of the day, whose faithfulness to nature astonished his contemporaries. His portrait of Alexander is thought to be reflected in a free copy, figure 66, which shows how much art had changed since the time of the Delphic charioteer, or even since the time of Praxiteles, who was only a generation older than Lysippus. Of course, the trouble with all ancient portraits is that we really cannot pronounce on their likeness – much less, in fact, than the flatterer in the story. Perhaps if we could see a snapshot of Alexander we should find it quite unlike the bust. Possibly the statues of Lysippus resembled a god much more than they did the real conqueror of Asia. But so much we can say: a man such as Alexander, a restless spirit, immensely gifted but rather spoilt by success, might have looked like this bust with its upraised eyebrows and its lively expression.

The foundation of an empire by Alexander was an enormously important event for Greek art, for thereby it developed from being the concern of a few small cities into the pictorial language of almost half the world. This change was bound to affect its character. We usually refer to this art of the later period not as Greek art, but as Hellenistic art, because that is the name commonly given to the empires founded by Alexander's successors on eastern soil. The rich capital cities of these empires, Alexandria in Egypt, Antioch in Syria and Pergamon in Asia Minor, made different demands on the

artists from those to which they had been accustomed in
Greece. Even in architecture the strong and simple forms of
the Doric style and the easy grace of the Ionic style were
not enough. A new form of column was preferred, which had
been invented early in the fourth century and which was
called after the wealthy merchant city of Corinth, figure 67.
In the Corinthian style, foliage was added to the Ionic spiral
volutes to decorate the capital, and there are generally more
and richer ornaments all over the building. The luxurious
mode suited the sumptuous buildings which were laid out on
a vast scale in the newly founded cities of the East. Few of
them have been preserved, but what remains from later
periods gives us an impression of great magnificence and
splendour. The styles and inventions of Greek art were applied
on the scale, and to the traditions, of the Oriental kingdoms.

   I have said that the whole of Greek art was bound to
undergo a change in the Hellenistic period. This change can be
noticed in some of the most famous sculptures of that age.
One of them is an altar from the city of Pergamon which was
erected around 160 BC, figure 68. The group on it represents the
struggle between the gods and the Giants. It is a magnificent
work, but we look in vain for the harmony and refinement of
early Greek sculpture. The artist was obviously aiming at
strong dramatic effects. The battle rages with terrible violence.
The clumsy Giants are overwhelmed by the triumphant gods,
and they look up in agony and frenzy. Everything is full of
wild movement and fluttering drapery. To make the effect still
more striking, the relief is no longer set flat on the wall but is
composed of almost free-standing figures which, in their
struggle, seem to overflow on to the steps of the altar as if
they hardly troubled about where they belonged. Hellenistic
art loved such wild and vehement works; it wished to be
impressive, and impressive it certainly is.

Some of the works of classical sculpture which have enjoyed the greatest fame in later times were created in the Hellenistic period. When the group of the Laocoön, *figure 69*, came to light in 1506, artists and art-lovers were quite overwhelmed by the effect of this tragic group. It represents the terrible scene which is also described in Virgil's *Aeneid*: the Trojan priest Laocoön has warned his compatriots against accepting the wooden horse in which Greek soldiers were hiding. The gods who see their plans of destroying Troy thwarted send two gigantic snakes from the sea which catch the priest and his two unfortunate sons in their coils and suffocate them. It is one of the stories of senseless cruelty perpetrated by the Olympians against poor mortals which are quite frequent in Greek and Latin mythologies. One would like to know how the story struck the Greek artist who conceived this impressive group. Did he want us to feel the horror of a scene in which an innocent victim is made to suffer for having spoken the truth? Or did he mainly want to show off his own power of representing a terrifying and somewhat sensational fight between man and beast? He had every reason to be proud of his skill. The way in which the muscles of the trunk and the arms convey the effort and the suffering of the hopeless struggle, the expression of pain in the face of the priest, the helpless wriggling of the two boys and the way all this turmoil and movement are frozen into a permanent group have excited admiration ever since. But I cannot help suspecting sometimes that this was an art which was meant to appeal to a public which also enjoyed the horrible sights of the gladiatorial fights. Perhaps it is wrong to blame the artist for that. The fact is probably that by this time, the period of Hellenism, art had largely lost its old connection with magic and religion. Artists became interested in the problems of their craft for its own sake, and the problem of how to represent such a dramatic contest with all its movement, its expression and its tension, was just the type of task which would test an artist's skill. The rights or wrongs of Laocoön's fate may not have occurred to the sculptor at all.

It was in this time, and in this atmosphere, that rich people began to collect works of art, to have famous ones copied if they could not get hold of originals, and to pay fabulous prices for those which they could obtain. Writers began to be interested in art and wrote about the artists' lives, collected anecdotes about their oddities and composed guide-books for tourists. Many of the masters most famous among the ancients were painters rather than sculptors, and we know nothing about their works except what we find in those extracts from classical art books which have come down to us. We know that these painters, too, were interested in the special problems of their craft rather than in their art serving a religious purpose. We hear of masters who specialized in subjects from everyday life, who painted barbers' shops or scenes from the theatre, but all these paintings are lost to us. The only way in which we can form some idea of the character of ancient painting is by looking at the decorative wall-paintings and mosaics which have come to light in Pompeii and elsewhere. Pompeii was a well-to-do country town, and was buried beneath the ashes of Mount Vesuvius when it erupted in 79 AD. Almost every house and villa in that town had paintings on its walls, painted columns and vistas, imitations of framed pictures and of the stage. These paintings are, of course, not all masterpieces, though it is astonishing to see how much good work there was in such a small and rather unimportant town. We should hardly cut so good a figure if one of our seaside resorts were to be excavated by posterity. The interior decorators of Pompeii and neighbouring cities such as Herculaneum and Stabiae obviously drew freely on the stock of inventions made by the great Hellenistic artists. Among much that is humdrum we sometimes discover a figure of such exquisite beauty and grace as figure 70, which represents one of the Hours, picking a blossom as if in a dance. Or we find such details as the head of a faun, figure 71, from another painting, which gives us an idea of the mastery and freedom which these artists had acquired in the handling of expression.

Nearly every kind of thing that would go into a picture is to be found in these decorative wall-paintings: pretty still lifes, for instance, such as two lemons with a glass of water, and pictures of animals. Even landscape paintings existed there. This was perhaps the greatest innovation of the Hellenistic period. Ancient Oriental art had no use for landscapes except as settings for their scenes of human life or of military campaigns. For Greek art at the time of Pheidias or Praxiteles, man remained the main subject of the artist's interest. In the Hellenistic period, the time when poets like Theocritus discovered the charm of simple life among shepherds, artists also tried to conjure up the pleasures of the countryside for sophisticated town-dwellers. These paintings are not actual views of particular country houses or beauty-spots. They are rather collections of everything which makes up an idyllic scene: shepherds and cattle, simple shrines and distant villas and mountains, figure 72. Everything was charmingly arranged in these pictures, and all the set-pieces were looking their best. We really feel that we are looking at a peaceful scene. Nevertheless, even these works are much less realistic than we might think at first glance. If we were to start asking awkward questions, or try to draw a map of the locality, we should soon find out that it could not be done. We do not know how great the distance between the shrine and the villa is supposed to be, nor how near or how far the bridge from the shrine. The fact is that even Hellenistic artists did not know what we call the laws of perspective. The famous avenue of poplars, which recedes to a vanishing point and which so many of us drew at school, was not then a standard task. Artists drew distant things small, and near or important things large, but the law of regular diminution of objects as they become more distant, the fixed framework in which we can represent a view, was not adopted by classical antiquity. Indeed, it took more than another thousand years before it was applied. Thus even the latest, freest and most confident works of ancient art still preserve at least a remnant of the principle which we discussed in our description of Egyptian painting. Even here, knowledge of the characteristic outline of individual objects counts for as much as the actual impression received through the eye. We have long recognized that this quality is not a fault in works of art, to be regretted and looked down upon, but that it is possible to achieve artistic perfection within any style. The Greeks broke through the rigid taboos of early Oriental art, and went out on a voyage of discovery to add more and more features from observation to the traditional images of the world. But their works never look like mirrors in which any odd corner of nature is reflected. They always bear the stamp of the intellect which made them.

World Conquerors

Romans, Buddhists, Jews and Christians,
first to fourth century AD

We have seen that Pompeii, which was a Roman town, contained many reflections of Hellenistic art. For art remained more or less unchanged while the Romans conquered the world and founded their own empire on the ruins of the Hellenistic kingdoms. Most artists who worked in Rome were Greeks, and most Roman collectors bought works of the great Greek masters, or copies of them. Nevertheless art did change, to some extent, when Rome became mistress of the world. The artists were given new tasks and had to adapt their methods accordingly. The most outstanding achievement of the Romans was probably in civil engineering. We all know about their roads, their aqueducts, their public baths. Even the ruins of these buildings still look extremely impressive. One feels like an ant when walking in Rome between their enormous pillars. It was, in fact, these ruins which made it impossible for later centuries to forget 'the grandeur that was Rome'.

The most famous of these Roman buildings is, perhaps, the huge arena known as the Colosseum, figure 73. It is a characteristic Roman building, which excited much admiration in later days. On the whole it is a utilitarian structure, with three storeys of arches, one above the other, to support the seats of the vast amphitheatre inside. But in front of these arches the Roman architect has put a kind of screen of Greek forms. Indeed, he has applied all the three styles of building used for Greek temples. The ground floor is a variation on the Doric style – even the metopes and triglyphs are preserved; the second storey has Ionic, and the third and fourth Corinthian half-columns. This combination of Roman structures with Greek forms or 'orders' had an enormous influence on later architects. If we look round in our own towns we may easily see examples of this influence.

Perhaps none of their architectural creations made a more lasting impression than the triumphal arches the

Romans set up all over their Empire in Italy, France, figure 74, North Africa and Asia. Greek architecture had generally been composed in identical units and the same is even true of the Colosseum; but the triumphal arches use the orders to frame and accent the large central gateway and to flank it by narrower openings. It was an arrangement that could be used for architectural composition much as a chord is used in music.

The most important feature in Roman architecture, however, is the use of arches. This invention had played little or no part in Greek buildings though it may have been known to Greek architects. To construct an arch out of separate wedge-formed stones is quite a difficult feat of engineering. Once this art is mastered the builder can use it for increasingly bold designs. He can span the pillars of a bridge or of an aqueduct, or he can even make use of this device for constructing a vaulted roof. The Romans became great experts in the art of vaulting by various technical devices. The most wonderful of these buildings is the Pantheon or temple of all the gods. It is the only temple of classical antiquity which always remained a place of worship – it was converted into a church in the early Christian era and was therefore never allowed to fall into ruin. Its interior, figure 75, is a huge round hall with a vaulted roof and a circular opening at the top through which one sees the open sky. There is no other window, but the whole room receives ample and even light from above. I know few buildings which convey a similar impression of serene harmony. There is no feeling of heaviness. The enormous dome seems to hover freely over you like a second dome of heaven.

It was typical of the Romans to take from Greek architecture what they liked, and to apply it to their own needs. They did the same in all fields. One of their principal needs was for good, lifelike portraits. Such portraits had played a part in the early religion of the Romans. It had been customary to carry wax images of ancestors in funeral processions. There is little doubt that this usage had been connected with the belief that the likeness preserves the soul, which we know from ancient Egypt. Later, when Rome became an empire, the bust of the emperor was still looked upon with religious awe. We know that every Roman had to burn incense in front of this bust in token of his loyalty and allegiance, and we know that the persecution of Christians began because of their refusal to comply with this demand. The strange thing is that, despite this solemn significance of portraits, the Romans allowed their artists to make them more lifelike and uncomplimentary than anything the Greeks had attempted. Perhaps they sometimes used death-masks and thus acquired their astounding knowledge of the structure and features of the human head. At any rate, we know Pompey, Augustus, Titus, or Nero, almost as if we had seen their faces on the screen. There is no flattery in the bust of Vespasian, figure 76 – nothing to mark him out as a god. He might be any wealthy banker or owner of a shipping line. Nevertheless, there is nothing petty in these Roman portraits. Somehow the artists succeeded in being lifelike without being trivial.

Another new task which the Romans set the artist revived a custom which we know from the ancient Orient, page 59, figure 45. They, too, wanted to proclaim their victories and to tell the story of their campaigns. Trajan, for instance, erected a huge column to show a whole picture chronicle of his wars and victories in Dacia (the modern Romania). There we see the Roman legionaries foraging, fighting and conquering, figure 78. All the skill and achievements of centuries of Greek art were used in these feats of war reporting. But the importance which the Romans attached to an accurate rendering of all details, and to a clear narrative which would impress the feats of the campaign on the stay-at-homes, rather changed the character of art. The main aim was no longer that of harmony, beauty or dramatic expression. The Romans were a matter-of-fact people, and cared less for fancy goods. Yet their pictorial methods of telling the deeds of a hero proved of great value to the religions which came into contact with their far-flung empire.

During the centuries after Christ, Hellenistic and Roman art completely displaced the arts of the Oriental kingdoms, even in their own former strongholds. Egyptians still buried their dead as mummies, but instead of adding their likenesses in the Egyptian style, they had them painted by artists who knew all the tricks of Greek portraiture, figure 79. These portraits, which were certainly made by humble craftsmen at a low price, still astonish us by their vigour and realism. There are few works of ancient art which look so fresh and 'modern' as these.

The Egyptians were not the only ones to adapt the new methods of art to their religious needs. Even in far-distant India, the Roman way of telling a story, and of glorifying a hero, was adopted by artists who set themselves the task of illustrating the story of a peaceful conquest, the story of the Buddha.

The art of sculpture had flourished in India long before this Hellenistic influence reached the country; but it was in the frontier region of Gandhara that the figure of Buddha was first shown in the reliefs which became the model for later Buddhist art. Figure 80 represents the episode from the Buddha legend of The Great Renunciation. The young Prince Gautama is leaving the palace of his parents to become a hermit in the wilderness. He thus addresses his favourite charger Kanthaka: 'My dear Kanthaka, please carry me once more for this one night. When I shall have become Buddha with your help, I shall bring salvation to the world of gods and men.' If Kanthaka had only so much as neighed or made a sound with his hoofs the

city would have been roused and the prince's departure
discovered. So the gods muffled his voice and placed their
hands under his hooves wherever he stepped.

Greek and Roman art, which had taught men to visualize
gods and heroes in beautiful form, also helped the Indians to
create an image of their saviour. The beautiful head of the
Buddha, with its expression of deep repose, was also made in
this frontier region of Gandhara, figure 81.

Yet another Oriental religion that learned to represent
its sacred stories for the instruction of believers was that
of the Jews. Jewish Law actually forbade the making of images
for fear of idolatry. Nevertheless, the Jewish colonies in eastern
towns took to decorating the walls of their synagogues
with stories from the Old Testament. One of these paintings
was discovered in recent times in a small Roman garrison
in Mesopotamia called Dura-Europos. It is not a great work of
art by any means, but it is an interesting document from the
third century AD. The very fact that the style seems clumsy and
that the scene looks rather flat and primitive is not without
interest, figure 82. It represents Moses striking water from the
rock. But it is not so much an illustration of the biblical account
as an explanation, in pictures, of its significance to the Jewish
people. That may be the reason why Moses is represented as a
tall figure standing in front of the Holy Tabernacle in which
we can still discern the seven-branched candlestick. In order to
signify that each tribe of Israel received its share of the
miraculous water the artist has shown twelve rivulets, each
flowing to a small figure standing before a tent. The artist was
doubtless not very skilful, and that accounts for his simple
methods. But perhaps he was not really much concerned with
drawing lifelike figures. The more lifelike they were, the more
they sinned against the Commandment forbidding images. His
main intention was to remind the beholder of the occasions

when God had manifested His power. The humble wall-painting from the Jewish synagogue is of interest to us, because similar considerations began to influence art when the Christian religion spread from the East and also took art into its service.

When Christian artists were first called upon to represent the Saviour and His apostles it was again the tradition of Greek art which came to their aid. Figure 83 shows one of the earliest representations of Christ, from the fourth century AD. Instead of the bearded figure to which we have become accustomed through later illustrations, we see Christ in youthful beauty, enthroned between St Peter and St Paul, who look like dignified Greek philosophers. There is one detail, in particular, which reminds us how closely such a representation is still linked with the methods of pagan Hellenistic art: to indicate that Christ is enthroned above the heavens the sculptor has made His feet rest on the canopy of the firmament, held aloft by the ancient god of the sky.

The origins of Christian art go even farther back than this example, but the earliest monuments never show Christ Himself. The Jews of Dura had painted scenes from the Old Testament in their synagogue, not so much to adorn it but rather to tell the sacred tale in visible form. The artists who were first called upon to paint images for Christian places of burial – the Roman catacombs – acted very much in the same spirit. Paintings such as that of the 'Three men in the fiery furnace', figure 84, probably from the third century AD, show that these artists were familiar with the methods of Hellenistic painting used in Pompeii. They were quite capable of conjuring up the idea of a human figure with a few rough strokes of the brush. But we also feel that these effects and tricks did not interest them very much. The picture no longer existed as a beautiful thing in its own right. Its main purpose was to remind the faithful of one of the examples of God's mercy and power. We read in the Bible (Daniel III) of three high Jewish officials under King Nebuchadnezzar who refused to fall down and worship on a given signal when a gigantic golden image of the King was set up in the plain of Dura in the province of Babylon. Like so many Christians of the period when these paintings were made, they had to pay the penalty for their refusal. They were thrown into a fiery furnace 'in their coats, their hosen, and their hats'. But, lo, the fire had no power upon their bodies 'nor was an hair of their heads singed, neither were their coats changed'. The Lord 'sent His angel and delivered His servants'.

We need only imagine what the master of the Laocoön, figure 69, would have made of such a subject to realize the different direction art was taking. The painter in the catacombs did not want to represent a dramatic scene for its own sake. To present the consoling and inspiring example of fortitude and salvation it was quite sufficient if the three men in their Persian dress, the flames and the dove – a symbol of Divine help – were recognizable. Everything which was not strictly relevant was better left out. Once more ideas of clarity and simplicity began to outweigh ideals of faithful imitation. Yet there is something touching in the very effort which the artist made to tell his story as clearly and simply as possible. These three men seen from the front, looking at the beholder, their hands raised in prayer, seem to show that mankind had begun to concern itself with other things besides earthly beauty.

It is not only in religious works of the period of the decline and fall of the Roman Empire that we can detect something of that shifting of interest. Few artists seemed to care much for what had been the glory of Greek art, its refinement and harmony. Sculptors no longer had the patience to work marble with a chisel, and to treat it with that delicacy

and taste which had been the pride of the Greek craftsmen.
Like the painter of the catacomb picture, they used more
rough-and-ready methods, such as, for instance, a mechanical
drill with which to mark the principal features of a face or
a body. It has often been said that ancient art declined in these
years, and it is certainly true that many secrets of the best
period were lost in the general turmoil of wars, revolts and
invasions. But we have seen that this loss in skill is not the
whole story. The point is that artists at this time seemed no
longer satisfied with the mere virtuosity of the Hellenistic
period, and tried to achieve new effects. Some of the portraits
of this period, the fourth and fifth centuries AD in particular,
show perhaps most clearly what it was these artists aimed at,
figure 85. To a Greek of the time of Praxiteles these works
would have looked crude and barbaric. Indeed, the heads are
not beautiful by any common standards. A Roman, used to the
striking likenesses of portraits such as that of Vespasian,
figure 76, might have dismissed them as of poor workmanship.
And yet, to us, these figures seem to have a life of their own,
and a very intense expression which is due to the firm
marking of the features and the care bestowed on such traits
as the part around the eyes and the furrows of the brow. They
portray the people who witnessed, and finally accepted, the
rise of Christianity, which meant the end of the ancient world.

6

A Parting of Ways

Rome and Byzantium, fifth to thirteenth century

When, in the year 311 AD, the Emperor Constantine established
the Christian Church as a power in the State, the problems
with which it saw itself confronted were enormous. During
the periods of persecution there had been no need, and
indeed no possibility, of building public places of worship.
The churches and assembly halls that did exist were small and
inconspicuous. But once the Church had become the greatest
power in the realm, its whole relationship to art had to be
reconsidered. The places of worship could not be modelled on
the ancient temples, for their function was entirely different.
The interior of the temple was usually only a small shrine for
the statue of the god. Processions and sacrifices took place
outside. The church, on the other hand, had to find room for
the whole congregation that assembled for service when
the priest read Mass at the high altar, or delivered his sermon.
Thus it came about that churches were not modelled on pagan
temples, but on the type of large assembly halls which had
been known in classical times under the name of 'basilicas',
which means roughly 'royal halls'. These buildings were
used as covered market-halls and public law-courts, and mainly
consisted of large, oblong halls with narrower, lower
compartments on the longer sides, divided from the main hall
by rows of columns. At the far end there was often room for
a semicircular dais (or apse), where the chairman of the
meeting, or the judge, could take his seat. The mother of the
Emperor Constantine erected such a basilica to serve as a
church, and so the term established itself for churches of this
type. The semicircular niche or apse would be used for the
high altar, towards which the eyes of the worshippers were
directed. This part of the building, where the altar stood, came
to be known as the choir. The main central hall, where the
congregation assembled, was known later as the nave, which
really means 'ship', while the lower compartments at the side

were called side-aisles, which means 'wings'. In most of the basilicas, the lofty nave was simply roofed with timber, and the beams of the loft were visible. The side-aisles were often flat-roofed. The columns which separated the nave from the aisles were often sumptuously decorated. None of the earliest basilicas has remained quite unchanged, but despite the alterations and renovations made in the course of the one-and-a-half thousand years since that time, we can still form an idea of what these buildings generally looked like, *figure 86*.

The question of how to decorate these basilicas was a much more difficult and serious one, because here the whole issue of the image and its use in religion came up again and caused very violent disputes. On one thing nearly all early Christians were agreed: there must be no statues in the House of God. Statues were too much like those graven images and heathen idols that were condemned in the Bible. To place a figure of God, or of one of His saints, on the altar seemed altogether out of the question. For how would the poor pagans who had just been converted to the new faith grasp the difference between their old beliefs and the new message, if they saw such statues in churches? They might too easily have thought that such a statue really 'represented' God, just as a statue by Pheidias was thought to represent Zeus. Thus they might have found it even more difficult to grasp the message of the one Almighty and Invisible God, in whose semblance we are made. But, although all devout Christians objected to large lifelike statues, their ideas about paintings differed a good deal. Some thought them useful because they helped to remind the congregation of the teachings they had received, and kept the memory of these sacred episodes alive. This view was mainly taken in the Latin, Western part of the Roman Empire. Pope Gregory the Great, who lived at the end of the sixth century AD, took this line. He reminded the people who

were against all paintings that many members of the Church
could neither read nor write, and that, for the purpose of
teaching them, these images were as useful as the pictures in
a picture-book are for children. 'Painting can do for the
illiterate what writing does for those who can read,' he said.

It was of immense importance for the history of art
that such a great authority had come out in favour of painting.
His saying was to be quoted again and again whenever people
attacked the use of images in churches. But it is clear that the
type of art which was thus admitted was of a rather restricted
kind. If Gregory's purpose was to be served, the story had
to be told as clearly and simply as possible, and anything that
might divert attention from this main and sacred aim should
be omitted. At first, artists still used the methods of story-
telling that had been developed by Roman art, but gradually
they came to concentrate more and more on what was strictly
essential. Figure 87 shows a work in which these principles
have been applied with the greatest consistency. It comes from
a basilica in Ravenna, which was then, round about 500 AD,
a great seaport and the capital city on Italy's east coast. It
illustrates the story from the Gospels in which Christ fed five
thousand people on five loaves and two fishes. A Hellenistic
artist might have seized the opportunity to portray a large
crowd of people in a gay and dramatic scene. But this master
chose a very different method. His work is not a painting done
with deft strokes of the brush – it is a mosaic, laboriously put
together, of stone or glass cubes which yield deep, full colours
and give to the church interior, covered with such mosaics,
an appearance of solemn splendour. The way in which the
story is told shows the spectator that something miraculous
and sacred is happening. The background is laid out with
fragments of golden glass and on this gold background no
natural or realistic scene is enacted. The still and calm figure

of Christ occupies the centre of the picture. It is not the
bearded Christ known to us, but the long-haired young man
as He lived in the imagination of the early Christians.
He wears a purple robe, and stretches out His arms in blessing
on both sides, where stand two apostles offering Him the
bread and fishes in order that the miracle may be accomplished. They carry the food with covered hands, as subjects
bringing tribute for their rulers used to do at that time.
Indeed, the scene looks like a solemn ceremony. We see that
the artist attached a deep significance to what he represented.
To him it was not only a strange miracle which had happened
a few hundred years before in Palestine. It was the symbol
and token of Christ's abiding power which was embodied in
the Church. That explains, or helps to explain, the way in
which Christ looks steadfastly at the beholder: it is he whom
Christ will feed.

At first glance, such a picture looks rather stiff and
rigid. There is nothing of the mastery of movement and
expression which was the pride of Greek art, and which
persisted until Roman times. The way in which the figures
are planted in strict frontal view may almost remind us of
certain children's drawings. And yet the artist must have been
very well acquainted with Greek art. He knew exactly how
to drape a cloak round a body so that the main joints should
remain visible through the folds. He knew how to mix
stones of differing shades in his mosaic to convey the colours
of flesh or of the rocks. He marked the shadows on the
ground, and had no difficulty in representing foreshortening.
If the picture looks rather primitive to us, it must be because
the artist wanted it to be simple. The Egyptian ideas about
the importance of clarity in the representation of all objects
had returned with great force because of the stress which the
Church laid on clarity. But the forms which the artists used in

this new attempt were not the simple forms of primitive art, but the developed forms of Greek painting. Thus Christian art of the Middle Ages became a curious mixture of primitive and sophisticated methods. The power of observation of nature, which we saw awakening in Greece about 500 BC, was put to sleep again about 500 AD. Artists no longer checked their formulae against reality. They no longer set out to make discoveries about how to represent a body, or how to create the illusion of depth. But the discoveries which had been made were never lost. Greek and Roman art provided an immense stock of figures standing, sitting, bending down or falling. All these types could prove useful in the telling of a story, and so they were assiduously copied and adapted to ever-new contexts. But the purpose for which they were used was now so radically different that we cannot be surprised that, superficially, the pictures betray little of their classical origin.

This question of the proper purpose of art in churches proved of immense importance for the whole history of Europe. For it was one of the principal issues on which the Eastern, Greek-speaking parts of the Roman Empire, whose capital was Byzantium or Constantinople, refused to accept the lead of the Latin Pope. One party was against all images of a religious nature. They were called iconoclasts or image-smashers. In 754 AD they gained the upper hand and all religious art was forbidden in the Eastern Church. But their opponents were even less in agreement with Pope Gregory's ideas. To them images were not just useful, they were holy. The arguments with which they tried to justify this point of view were as subtle as those used by the other party: 'If God in His mercy could decide to reveal Himself to mortal eyes in the human nature of Christ,' they argued, 'why should He not also be willing to manifest Himself in visible images? We do not worship these images themselves as the pagans did.

We worship God and the Saints through or across their images.'
Whatever we may think of the logic of this plea, its importance
for the history of art was tremendous. For when this party
had returned to power after a century of repression, the
paintings in a church could no longer be regarded as mere
illustrations for the use of those who could not read. They
were looked upon as mysterious reflections of the supernatural
world. The Eastern Church, therefore, could no longer allow
the artist to follow his fancy in these works. Surely it was not
any beautiful painting of a mother with her child that could
be accepted as the true sacred image or 'icon' of the Mother of
God, but only types hallowed by an age-old tradition.

Thus, the Byzantines came to insist almost as strictly as
the Egyptians on the observance of traditions. But there were
two sides to this question. By asking the artist who painted
sacred images to keep strictly to the ancient models, the
Byzantine Church helped to preserve the ideas and achievement of Greek art in the types used for drapery, faces or
gestures. If we look at a Byzantine altar-painting of the Holy
Virgin like figure 88, it may seem very remote from the achievements of Greek art. And yet, the way the folds are draped
round the body and radiate round the elbows and knees, the
method of modelling the face and hands by marking the
shadows, and even the sweep of the Virgin's throne, would have
been impossible without the conquests of Greek and
Hellenistic painting. Despite a certain rigidity, Byzantine art
therefore remained closer to nature than the art of the West in
subsequent periods. On the other hand, the stress on tradition,
and the necessity of keeping to certain permitted ways of
representing Christ or the Holy Virgin, made it difficult for
Byzantine artists to develop their personal gifts. But this
conservatism developed only gradually, and it is wrong to
imagine that the artists of the period had no scope whatever.

It was they, in fact, who transformed the simple illustrations
of early Christian art into the great cycles of large and solemn
images that dominate the interior of Byzantine churches.
As we look at the mosaics done by these Greek artists in the
Balkans and in Italy in the Middle Ages, we see that this
Oriental empire had in fact succeeded in reviving something
of the grandeur and majesty of ancient Oriental art, and in
using it for the glorification of Christ and His power. Figure 89
gives an idea of how impressive this art could be. It shows the
apse of the cathedral of Monreale, in Sicily, which was
decorated by Byzantine craftsmen shortly before 1190. Sicily
itself belonged to the Western or Latin Church, which
accounts for the fact that among the saints arrayed on each
side of the window we find the earliest representation of
St Thomas Becket, the news of whose murder some twenty
years earlier had resounded throughout Europe. But apart
from this choice of saints the artists have kept close to their
native Byzantine tradition. The faithful assembled in the
cathedral would find themselves face to face with the majestic
figure of Christ, represented as the Ruler of the Universe,
His right hand raised in blessing. Below is the Holy Virgin,
enthroned like an Empress, flanked by two archangels and the
solemn row of saints.

Images such as these, looking down on us from the
golden, glimmering walls, seemed to be such perfect symbols
of the Holy Truth that there appeared to be no need ever to
depart from them. Thus they continued to hold their sway in
all countries ruled by the Eastern Church. The holy images
or 'icons' of the Russians still reflect these great creations of
Byzantine artists.

Looking Eastwards

Islam, China, second to thirteenth century

Before we return to the Western world and take up the story
of art in Europe, we must at least cast a glance at what
happened in other parts of the world during these centuries
of turmoil. It is interesting to see how two other great religions
reacted to the question of images, which so engaged the
mind of the Western world. The religion of the Middle East,
which swept everything before it in the seventh and eighth
centuries AD, the religion of the Muslim conquerors of
Persia, Mesopotamia, Egypt, North Africa and Spain, was
even more rigorous in this matter than Christianity had been.
The making of images was forbidden. But art as such cannot
so easily be suppressed, and the craftsmen of the East,
who were not permitted to represent human beings, let their
imagination play with patterns and forms. They created the
most subtle lacework ornamentation known as arabesques.
It is an unforgettable experience to walk through the court-
yards and halls of the Alhambra, figure 90, and to admire
the inexhaustible variety of these decorative patterns. Even
outside the Islamic dominions the world became familiar
with these inventions through Oriental rugs, figure 91. Ultimately
we may owe their subtle designs and rich colour schemes
to Muhammad, who directed the mind of the artist away
from the objects of the real world to this dream-world of lines
and colours. Later sects among the Muslims were less strict in
their interpretation of the ban on images. They did allow the
painting of figures and illustrations as long as they had no
connection with religion. The illustrating of romances, histories
and fables done in Persia from the fourteenth century
onwards, and later also in India under Muslim (Mogul) rulers,
shows how much the artists of these lands had learned from
the discipline which had confined them to the designing of
patterns. The moonlight scene in a garden, figure 92, from a
Persian romance of the fifteenth century is a perfect example

of this wonderful skill. It looks like a carpet which has somehow come to life in a fairy-tale world. There is as little illusion of reality in it as in Byzantine art. Perhaps even less. There is no foreshortening, and no attempt to show light and shade or the structure of the body. The figures and plants look a little as if they had been cut out of coloured paper and distributed over the page to make a perfect pattern. But, because of that, the illustration fits even better into the book than it might have done if the artist had wanted to create the illusion of a real scene. We can read such a page almost as we read a text. We can look from the hero, as he stands with his arms crossed in the right-hand corner, to the heroine, who approaches him, and we can let our imagination wander through the moonlit fairy garden without ever getting too much of it.

The impact of religion on art was even stronger in China. We know little about the beginnings of Chinese art, except the fact that the Chinese had been skilled in the art of casting bronze at a very early date, and that some of the bronze vessels used in the ancient temples go back to the first millennium before Christ – some say even earlier. Our records of Chinese painting and sculpture, however, are not so old. In the centuries immediately before and after Christ, the Chinese adopted burial customs somewhat reminiscent of the Egyptians, and in these burial chambers, as in the Egyptian ones, there are a number of vivid scenes which reflect the life and the habits of those long bygone days, figure 93. At that time, much of what we call typically Chinese in art had already developed. The artists were less fond of rigid angular forms than the Egyptians had been, and preferred swerving curves. When a Chinese artist had to represent a prancing horse, he seemed to fit it together out of a number of rounded shapes. We can see the same in Chinese sculpture, which always seems to twist and turn without, however, losing its solidity and firmness, figure 94.

Some of the great teachers of China appear to have had a similar view of the value of art to that held by Pope Gregory the Great. They thought of art as a means of reminding people of the great examples of virtue in the golden ages of the past. One of the earliest illustrated Chinese book-scrolls to have been preserved is a collection of great examples of virtuous ladies, written in the spirit of Confucius. It is said to go back to the painter Ku K'ai-chi, who lived in the fourth century AD. The illustration, figure 95, shows a husband unjustly accusing his wife, and it has all the dignity and grace we connect with Chinese art. It is as clear in its gestures and arrangement as one might expect from a picture which also aims at driving home a lesson. It shows, moreover, that the Chinese artist had mastered the difficult art of representing movement. There is nothing rigid in this early Chinese work, because the predilection for undulating lines imparts a sense of movement to the whole picture.

However, the most important impulse to Chinese art probably came through yet another religious influence: that of Buddhism. The monks and ascetics of Buddha's circle were often represented in amazingly lifelike statues, figure 96. Once more we see the curved outlines in the shape of the ears, the lips or the cheeks, but they do not distort the real forms; they only weld them together. We feel that such a work is not haphazard, but that everything is in its place and contributes to the effect of the whole. The old principle of the primitive masks, figure 28, serves its turn even in such a convincing representation of a face.

Buddhism influenced Chinese art not only by providing the artists with new tasks. It introduced an entirely new approach to pictures, a reverence for the artist's achievement such as did not exist either in ancient Greece or in Europe up to the time of the Renaissance. The Chinese were the first people who did not think of the making of pictures as a rather menial task, but who placed the painter on the same level as the inspired poet. The religions of the East taught that nothing was more important than the right kind of meditation.

To meditate is to think and ponder about the same holy truth for many hours on end, to fix an idea in one's mind and to look at it from all sides without letting go of it. It is a kind of mental exercise for Orientals, to which they used to attach even greater importance than we attach to physical exercise or sport. Some monks meditated on single words, turning them over in their minds while they sat quite still for whole days and listened to the stillness which preceded and followed the holy syllable. Others meditated on things in nature, on water, for instance, and what we can learn from it, how humble it is, how it yields and yet wears away solid rock, how it is clear and cool and soothing and gives life to the thirsting field; or on mountains, how strong and lordly they are, and yet how good, for they allow the trees to grow on them. That is, perhaps, how religious art in China came to be employed less for telling the legends of the Buddha and the Chinese teachers, less for the teaching of a particular doctrine – as Christian art was to be employed in the Middle Ages – than as an aid to the practice of meditation. Devout artists began to paint water and mountains in a spirit of reverence, not in order to teach any particular lesson, nor merely as decorations, but to provide material for deep thought. Their pictures on silk scrolls were kept in precious containers and only unrolled in quiet moments, to be looked at and pondered over as one might open a book of poetry and read and reread a beautiful verse. That is the purpose behind the greatest of the Chinese landscape paintings of the twelfth and thirteenth centuries.

It is not easy for us to recapture that mood, because we are
fidgety Westerners with little patience and little knowledge of
the technique of meditation – no more, I suppose, than the
old Chinese had of the technique of physical training. But if we
look long and carefully at a picture such as figure 97, we shall
perhaps begin to feel something of the spirit in which it was
painted and of the high purpose it was to serve. We must not,
of course, expect any portraits of real landscapes, or picture-
postcards of beauty spots. Chinese artists did not go out into
the open, to sit down in front of some motif and sketch it.
They even learned their art by a strange method of meditation
and concentration in which they first acquired skill in 'how to
paint pine trees', 'how to paint rocks', 'how to paint clouds',
by studying not nature but the works of renowned masters.
Only when they had thoroughly acquired this skill did they
travel and contemplate the beauty of nature so as to capture
the moods of the landscape. When they came home they would
then try to recapture these moods by putting together their
images of pine trees, rocks and clouds much in the way a poet
might string together a number of images which had come
into his mind during a walk. It was the ambition of these
Chinese masters to acquire such a facility in the handling of
brush and ink that they could write down their vision while
their inspiration was still fresh. Often they would write a few
lines of poetry and paint a picture on the same scroll of silk.
The Chinese, therefore, consider it childish to look for details
in pictures and then to compare them with the real world. They
want, rather, to find in them the visible traces of the artist's
enthusiasm. It may not be easy for us to appreciate the boldest
of these works, such as figure 98, which consists only of some
vague forms of mountain peaks emerging out of clouds. But
once we try to put ourselves in the place of the painter, and to
experience something of the awe he must have felt for these

majestic peaks, we may at least get an inkling of what the Chinese value most highly in art. For us it is easier to admire the same skill and concentration in more familiar subjects. The painting of three fishes in a pond, figure 99, gives an idea of the patient observation that must have gone into the artist's study of his simple subject, and of the ease and mastery with which he handled it when he came to paint this picture. Again we see how fond the Chinese artists were of graceful curves, and how they could exploit their effects to suggest movement. The forms do not seem to make any clear symmetrical pattern. They are not evenly distributed as in the Persian miniature. Nevertheless we feel that the artist has balanced them with immense assurance. One can look at such a picture for a long stretch of time without getting bored. It is an experiment well worth trying.

There is something wonderful in this restraint of Chinese art, in its deliberate limitation to a few simple motifs of nature. But it almost goes without saying that this approach to painting also had its dangers. As time went on, nearly every type of brushstroke with which a stem of bamboo or a rugged rock could be painted was laid down and labelled by tradition, and so great was the general admiration for the works of the past that artists dared less and less to rely on their own inspiration. The standards of painting remained very high throughout the subsequent centuries both in China and in Japan (which adopted the Chinese conceptions) but art became more and more like a graceful and elaborate game which has lost much of its interest as so many of its moves are known. It was only after a new contact with the achievements of Western art in the eighteenth century that Japanese artists dared to apply the Eastern methods to new subjects. We shall see how fruitful these new experiments also became for the West when it first got to know them.

Western Art
in the Melting Pot

Europe, sixth to eleventh century

We have taken the story of Western art up to the period of Constantine, and to the centuries in which it was to adapt itself to the precept of Pope Gregory the Great that images are useful for teaching laymen the sacred word. The period which followed this early Christian era, the period after the collapse of the Roman Empire, is generally known by the uncomplimentary title of the Dark Ages. We call these ages dark, partly to convey that the people who lived during these centuries of migrations, wars and upheavals were themselves plunged in darkness and had little knowledge to guide them, but also to imply that we ourselves know rather little about these confused and confusing centuries which followed upon the decline of the ancient world and preceded the emergence of the European countries in the shape, roughly, in which we know them now. There are, of course, no fixed limits to the period, but for our purpose we may say that it lasted almost five hundred years – approximately from 500 to 1000 AD. Five hundred years is a long time, in which much can change and much, in fact, did change. But what is most interesting to us is that these years did not see the emergence of any one clear and uniform style, but rather the conflict of a great number of different styles, which only began to fuse towards the end of that period. To those who know something of the history of the Dark Ages this is hardly surprising. It was not only a dark, it was a patchy period, with tremendous differences among various peoples and classes. Throughout these five centuries there existed men and women, particularly in the monasteries and convents, who loved learning and art, and who had a great admiration for those works of the ancient world which had been preserved in libraries and treasure-houses. Sometimes these learned and educated monks or clergy held positions of power and influence at the courts of the mighty, and tried to revive the arts which they most admired. But frequently their work came to naught because of new wars and invasions by armed raiders from the north, whose opinions about art were very different indeed. The various Teutonic tribes, the Goths, the Vandals, the Saxons, the Danes and the Vikings, who swept through Europe raiding and pillaging, were considered barbarians by those who valued Greek and Roman achievements in literature and art. In a sense they certainly were barbarians, but this need not mean that they had no feeling for beauty, no art of their own. They had skilled craftsmen experienced in finely wrought metalwork, and excellent woodcarvers, comparable to those of the New Zealand Maoris, figure 22. They loved complicated patterns which included the twisted bodies of dragons or birds mysteriously interlaced. We do not know exactly where these patterns originated in the seventh century or what they signified, but it is not unlikely that the ideas of these Teutonic tribes about art resembled the ideas of primitive tribes elsewhere. There are reasons for believing that they, too, thought of such images as a means of working magic and exorcizing evil spirits. The carved figures of dragons from Viking sledges and ships give a good idea of the character of this art, figure 101. One can well imagine that these threatening heads of monsters were something more than just innocent decorations. In fact, we know that there were laws among the Norwegian Vikings which required the captain of a ship to remove these figures before entering his home port, 'so as not to frighten the spirits of the land'.

The monks and missionaries of Celtic Ireland and Saxon England tried to apply the traditions of these northern craftsmen to the tasks of Christian art. They built churches and steeples in stone imitating the timber structures used by local craftsmen, figure 100, but the most amazing monuments to their success are some of the manuscripts made in England

and Ireland during the seventh and eighth centuries. Figure 103 is a page from the famous Lindisfarne Gospels, made in Northumbria shortly before 700 AD. It shows the Cross composed of an incredibly rich lacework of intertwined dragons and serpents, standing against a background of an even more complicated pattern. It is exciting to try to find one's way through this bewildering maze of twisted shapes, and to follow the coils of these interwoven bodies. It is even more astonishing to see that the result is not confusion, but that the various patterns strictly correspond to each other and form a complex harmony of design and colour. One can hardly imagine how anyone could have thought out such a scheme and had the patience and perseverance to finish it. It proves, if proof were needed, that the artists who took up this native tradition were certainly not lacking either in skill or in technique.

It is all the more surprising to look at the way in which human figures were represented by these artists in the illustrated manuscripts of England and Ireland. They do not look quite like human figures but rather like strange patterns made of human forms, figure 102. One can see that the artist used some example he had found in an old Bible, and transformed it to suit his taste. He changed the folds of the dress to something like interlacing ribbons, the locks of hair and even the ears into scrolls, and turned the whole face into a rigid mask. These figures of evangelists and saints look almost as stiff and quaint as primitive idols. They show that the artists who had grown up in the tradition of their native art found it difficult to adapt themselves to the new requirements of Christian books. Yet it would be wrong to look upon such pictures as being merely crude. The training of hand and eye which the artists had received, and which enabled them to make a beautiful pattern on the page, helped them to bring a new element into Western art. Without this influence, Western

art might have developed on similar lines to those of the art
of Byzantium. Thanks to the clash of the two traditions, the
classical tradition and the taste of the native artists, something
entirely new began to grow up in Western Europe.

For the knowledge of the earlier achievements of
classical art was by no means lost altogether. At the court of
Charlemagne, who regarded himself as the successor of the
Roman Emperors, the tradition of Roman craftsmanship was
eagerly revived. The church that Charlemagne had built about
800 AD at his residence in Aachen, figure 104, is a fairly close
copy of a famous church that had been built in Ravenna some
three hundred years earlier.

We have seen before that our modern notion that
an artist must be 'original' was by no means shared by most
peoples of the past. An Egyptian, a Chinese or a Byzantine
master would have been greatly puzzled by such a demand.
Nor would a medieval artist of Western Europe have understood why he should invent new ways of planning a church,
of designing a chalice or of representing the sacred story
when the old ones served their purpose so well. The pious
donor who wanted to dedicate a new shrine for a holy relic
of his patron saint not only tried to procure the most precious
material he could afford, he would also seek to provide the
master with an old and venerable example of how the legend
of the saint should be correctly represented. Nor would
the artist feel hampered by this type of commission. There
remained enough scope for him to show whether he was a
master or a bungler.

Perhaps we can best understand this attitude if we
think of our own approach to music. If we ask a musician to
perform at a wedding we do not expect him to compose
something new for the occasion, any more than the medieval
patron expected a new invention if he asked for a painting of

the Nativity. We indicate the type of music we want and the size of the orchestra or choir we may be able to afford. It still is up to the musician to produce a wonderful performance of an ancient masterpiece or to make a mess of things. And just as two equally great musicians may interpret the same piece very differently, so two great medieval masters might make very different works of art on the same theme and even on the same ancient model. An example should make this clear: figure 105 shows a page from a gospel book produced at the court of Charlemagne. It represents the figure of St Matthew writing the gospel. It had been customary in Greek and Roman books to have the portrait of the author represented on the opening page and this picture of the writing evangelist must be an extraordinarily faithful copy of this type of portrait. The way the saint is draped in his toga in the best classical fashion, the way his head is modelled in many shades of light and colour, convinces us that the medieval artist had strained every nerve to give an accurate and worthy rendering of a venerated model.

The painter of another manuscript of the ninth century, figure 106, probably had before him the same or a very similar ancient example from early Christian times. We can compare the hands, the left hand holding an inkhorn and resting on the lectern, the right hand holding the pen; we can compare the feet and even the drapery round the knees. But while the artist of figure 105 had done his very best to copy the original as faithfully as possible, the artist of figure 106 must have aimed at a different interpretation. Perhaps he did not want to represent the evangelist like any serene old scholar, sitting quietly in his study. To him St Matthew was an inspired man, writing down the Word of God. It was an immensely important and immensely exciting event in the history of mankind that he wanted to portray, and he succeeded in conveying something of his own sense of awe and excitement in this figure of a writing man. It is not mere clumsiness and ignorance which made him draw the saint with wide open, protruding eyes and enormous hands. He intended to give him that expression of tense concentration. The very brushwork of the drapery and of the background looks as if it had been done in a mood of intense excitement. This impression, I think, is partly due to the evident enjoyment with which the artist seized on every opportunity to draw scrolly lines and zigzagging folds. There may have been something in the original to suggest such a treatment, but it probably appealed to the medieval artist because it reminded him of those interlaced ribbons and lines which had been the greatest achievement of northern art. In pictures like these we see the emergence of a new medieval style which made it possible for art to do something that neither ancient Oriental nor classical art had done: the Egyptians had largely drawn what they knew to exist, the Greeks what they saw; in the Middle Ages the artist also learned to express in his picture what he felt.

One cannot do justice to any medieval work of art without keeping this purpose in mind. For these artists were not out to create a convincing likeness of nature or to make beautiful things – they wanted to convey to their brothers in the faith the content and the message of the sacred story. And in this they were perhaps more successful than most artists of earlier or later times. Figure 107 is from a gospel book which was illustrated (or 'illuminated') in Germany more than a century later, around the year 1000. It represents the incident told in the Gospel of St John (XIII. 8-9) when Christ, after the Last Supper, washed the disciples' feet:

> *Peter saith unto him, 'Thou shalt never wash my feet.'*
> *Jesus answered him, 'If I wash thee not, thou hast no part with*
> *me.' Simon Peter saith unto him, 'Lord, not my feet only but my*
> *hands and my head.'*

This exchange alone is what mattered to the artist. He saw no reason to represent the room in which the scene occurred; it might merely have diverted attention from the inner meaning of the event. He rather placed his principal figures before a flat, luminous golden ground, on which the gestures of the speakers stand out like a solemn inscription: the imploring movement of St Peter, the calm teaching gesture of Christ. A disciple on the right takes off his sandals, another brings a basin, the others crowd behind St Peter. All eyes are rigidly turned towards the centre of the scene and thus give us the feeling that something of infinite significance is happening here. What does it matter if the basin is not evenly rounded, and if the painter has to wrench the leg of St Peter up, the knee somewhat forward, to get his foot clearly into the water? He was concerned with the message of divine humility, and this he conveyed.

It is interesting to glance back for a moment to another scene representing the washing of feet, the Greek vase painted in the fifth century BC, figure 58. It was in Greece that the art of showing the 'workings of the soul' was discovered, and however differently the medieval artist interpreted this aim, the Church could never have used pictures for its own ends without this heritage.

We remember the teaching of Pope Gregory the Great that 'painting can do for the illiterate what writing does for those who can read', page 105. This search for clarity comes out not only in the painted illustrations but also in works of sculpture such as the panel from a bronze door which was commissioned for the church of Hildesheim in Germany shortly after the year 1000, figure 108. It shows the Lord approaching Adam and Eve after the Fall. Again there is nothing in this relief that does not strictly belong to the story. But this concentration on the things which matter makes the figures stand out all the more clearly against the plain background – and we can almost read off what their gestures say: God points to Adam, Adam to Eve, and Eve to the serpent on the ground. The shifting of guilt and the origin of evil are expressed with such forcefulness and clarity that we soon forget that the proportions of the figures are perhaps not strictly correct and the bodies of Adam and Eve not beautiful by our standards.

We need not imagine, though, that all art in this period existed exclusively to serve religious ideas. Not only churches were built in the Middle Ages, but castles as well, and the barons and feudal lords to whom the castles belonged also occasionally employed artists. The reason why we are inclined to forget these works when we speak of the art of the earlier Middle Ages is simple: castles were often destroyed when churches were spared. Religious art was, on the whole, treated with greater respect, and looked after more carefully, than mere decorations of private apartments. When these became old-fashioned they were removed or thrown away – just as happens nowadays. But, fortunately, one great example of this latter type of art has come down to us – and that because it was preserved in a church. It is the famous Bayeux Tapestry, which illustrates the story of the Norman Conquest. We do not know exactly when this tapestry was made, but most scholars agree that it was within living memory of the scenes it illustrates – perhaps round about the year 1080. The tapestry is a picture-chronicle of the kind we know from ancient Oriental and Roman art (Trajan's Column, for example, figure 78) – the story of a campaign and a victory. It tells its story with wonderful liveliness. In *figure 109* we see, as the inscription tells, how Harold swears his oath to William and in *figure 110* how he returns to England. Nothing could be clearer than the way in which the story is told – we see William on his throne watching Harold laying his hand on the sacred relics to swear allegiance – it was this oath which served William as pretext for his claims on England. I particularly like the man on the balcony in the next scene, who holds his hands above his eyes to espy Harold's ship as it arrives from afar. It is true that his arms and fingers look rather quaint and that all the figures in the story are strange little manikins which are not drawn with the assurance of the Assyrian or Roman chroniclers. When the medieval artist of this period had no model to copy, he drew rather like a child. It is easy to smile at him, but by no means so easy to do what he did. He tells the epic with such an economy of means, and with such concentration on what seemed important to him, that the final result remains more memorable than the realistic accounts in our newspapers and on television.

9

The Church Militant

The twelfth century

Dates are indispensable pegs on which to hang the tapestry of history, and since everybody knows the date 1066, that may serve us as a convenient peg. No complete buildings have survived in England from the Saxon period, and there are very few churches of the period before that date still existing anywhere in Europe. But the Normans who landed in England brought with them a developed style of building, which had taken shape within their generation in Normandy and elsewhere. The bishops and nobles who were the new feudal lords of England soon began to assert their power by founding abbeys and minsters. The style in which these buildings were erected is known as the Norman style in England, and as the Romanesque style on the Continent. It flourished for a hundred years and more after the Norman invasion.

Today it is not easy to imagine what a church meant to the people of that period. Only in some old villages in the countryside can we still get a glimpse of its importance. The church was often the only stone building anywhere in the neighbourhood; it was the only considerable structure for miles around, and its steeple was a landmark to all who approached from afar. On Sundays and during services all the inhabitants of the town might meet there, and the contrast between the lofty building and the primitive and humble dwellings in which these people spent their lives must have been overwhelming. Small wonder that the whole community was interested in the building of these churches and took pride in their decoration. Even from the economic point of view the building of a minster, which took years, must have transformed a whole town. The quarrying and transport of stone, the erection of suitable scaffolding, the employment of itinerant craftsmen, who brought tales from distant lands, all this was a real event in those far-off days.

The Dark Ages had by no means blotted out the memory of the first churches, the basilicas, and the forms which the Romans had used in their building. The ground-plan was usually the same – a central nave leading to an apse or choir, and two or four aisles at the side. Sometimes this simple plan was enriched by a number of additions. Some architects liked the idea of building churches in the form of a cross, and they thus added what is called a transept between the choir and the nave. The general impression made by these Norman or Romanesque churches is nevertheless very different from that of the old basilicas. In the earliest basilicas classical columns carrying straight 'entablatures' had been used. In Romanesque and Norman churches we generally find round arches resting on massive piers. The whole impression which these churches make, both inside and outside, is one of massive strength. There are few decorations, even few windows, but firm unbroken walls and towers which remind one of medieval fastnesses, figure 111. These powerful and almost defiant piles of stone erected by the Church in lands of peasants and warriors who had only recently been converted from their heathen way of life seem to express the very idea of the Church Militant – the idea, that is, that here on earth it is the task of the Church to fight the powers of darkness till the hour of triumph dawns on doomsday, figure 112.

There was one problem in connection with the building of churches that engaged the minds of all good architects. It was the task of giving these impressive stone buildings a worthy roof of stone. The timber roofs which had been usual for basilicas lacked dignity, and were dangerous because they easily caught fire. The Roman art of vaulting such large buildings demanded a great amount of technical knowledge and calculation which had largely been lost. Thus the eleventh and twelfth centuries became a period of ceaseless

experiment. It was no small matter to span the whole breadth
of the main nave by a vault. The simplest solution, it would
seem, was to bridge the distance as one throws a bridge across
a river. Tremendous pillars were built up on both sides, which
were to carry the arches of those bridges. But it soon became
clear that a vault of this kind had to be very firmly joined if it
was not to crash, and that the weight of the necessary stones
was very great. To carry this enormous load the walls and pillars
had to be made even stronger. Huge masses of stone were
needed for these early 'tunnel'-vaults.

Norman architects therefore began to try out a different
method. They saw that it was not really necessary to make the
whole roof so heavy. It was sufficient to have a number of firm
arches spanning the distance and to fill in the intervals with
lighter material. It was found that the best method of doing
this was by spanning the arches or 'ribs' crosswise between
the pillars and then filling in the triangular sections between
them. This idea, which was soon to revolutionize building
methods, can be traced as far back as the Norman cathedral
of Durham, figure 114, though the architect who, after the
Conquest, designed the first 'rib-vault' for its mighty interior,
figure 113, was hardly aware of its technical possibilities.

It was in France that Romanesque churches began
to be decorated with sculptures, though here again the word
'decorate' is rather misleading. Everything that belonged to
the church had its definite function and expressed a definite
idea connected with the teaching of the Church. The porch
of the late twelfth-century church of St-Trophime at Arles, in
southern France, is one of the most complete examples of
this style, figure 115. Its shape recalls the principle of the Roman
triumphal arch, figure 74. In the field above the lintel – called
the tympanum, figure 116 – we see Christ in glory, surrounded
by the symbols of the four Evangelists. These symbols, the lion

for St Mark, the angel for St Matthew, the ox for St Luke and
the eagle for St John, were derived from the Bible. In the Old
Testament we read of the vision of Ezekiel (Ezek. I. 4-12),
in which he describes the throne of the Lord, carried by four
creatures with the heads of a lion, a man, an ox and an eagle.

Christian theologians thought the supporters of God's
throne signified the four Evangelists, and such a vision was
a fitting subject for the entrance to the church. On the lintel
below we see twelve seated figures, the twelve apostles,
and we can discern, on Christ's left, a row of naked figures
in chains – they are lost souls being dragged off to hell –
while on Christ's right we see the blessed, their faces turned
towards Him in eternal bliss. Below, we see the rigid figures
of saints, each marked by his emblem, reminding the faithful
of those who can intercede for them when their souls stand
before the ultimate Judge. Thus the teachings of the Church
about the final goal of our life here below were embodied
in these sculptures on the portal of the church. These images
lived on in the minds of the people even more powerfully
than did the words of the preacher's sermon. A late medieval
French poet, François Villon, has described this effect in the
moving verses he wrote for his mother:

> I am a woman, poor and old,
> Quite ignorant, I cannot read.
> They showed me at my village church
> A painted Paradise with harps
> And Hell where the damned souls are boiled,
> One gives me joy, the other frightens me …

We must not expect such sculptures to look as natural,
graceful and light as classical works. They are all the more
impressive because of their massive solemnity. It becomes

much easier to see at a glance what is represented, and they fit in much better with the grandeur of the whole building.

Every detail inside the church was just as carefully thought out to fit its purpose and its message. Figure 117 shows a candlestick made for Gloucester Cathedral about the year 1110. The intertwined monsters and dragons of which it is formed remind us of the work of the Dark Ages, page 120, figures 101, 103. But now a more definite meaning is given to these uncanny shapes. A Latin inscription round its crown says roughly: 'This bearer of light is the work of virtue — with its shine it preaches the doctrine, so that man should not be darkened by vice.' And really, as we penetrate with our eyes into the jungle of strange creatures we not only find once more (round the knob in the middle) the symbols of the Evangelists, who stand for the doctrine, but also naked figures of men. Like Laocoön and his sons, figure 69, they are assailed by snakes and monsters; but theirs is not a hopeless struggle. 'The light that shineth in the darkness' can make them triumph over the power of evil.

The font of a church in Liège (Belgium), made about 1113, provides another example of the part taken by the theologians in advising the artists, figure 118. It is made of brass and shows in the middle a relief of the baptism of Christ — the most appropriate subject for a font. There are Latin inscriptions explaining the meaning of every figure; for instance, we read 'Angelis ministrantes' (ministering angels) over the two figures waiting at the side of the River Jordan to receive Christ. But it is not only these inscriptions that underline the importance attached to the meaning of every detail. Again, the whole font was given such a meaning. Even the figures of oxen on which it stands are not there merely for the sake of ornament or decoration. We read in the Bible (2 Chronicles IV) how King Solomon engaged a cunning workman from Tyre in Phoenicia who was an expert in brass

foundry. Among the things he made for the temple in
Jerusalem the Bible describes:

> A molten sea of ten cubits from brim to brim, round in compass.
> ... It stood upon twelve oxen, three looking towards the north,
> and three looking towards the west, and three looking towards
> the south, and three looking towards the east: and the sea was set
> upon them, and all their hinder parts were inward.

It was this sacred model, then, which the artist of Liège,
another expert in brass foundry, was asked to keep in mind
two thousand years or more after the time of Solomon.

The forms which the artist uses for his images of Christ,
of the angels and of St John, look more natural and at the same
time more calm and majestic than those of the bronze doors of
Hildesheim, figure 108. We remember that the twelfth century is
the century of the Crusades. There was naturally more contact
than formerly with the art of Byzantium, and many artists of the
twelfth century tried to imitate and emulate the majestic sacred
images of the Eastern Church, figures 88, 89.

At no other time, in fact, did European art approach the
ideals of this kind of Eastern art more closely than at the
height of the Romanesque style. We have seen the rigid and
solemn arrangement of the sculptures of Arles, figures 115-16,
and we see the same spirit in many illuminated manuscripts
of the twelfth century. Figure 119, for instance, represents
the Annunciation. It looks almost as stiff and motionless as
an Egyptian relief. The Virgin is seen from in front, her
hands raised as in astonishment, while the dove of the Holy
Spirit descends on her from on high. The Angel is seen half
in profile, his right hand extended in a gesture which in
medieval art signifies the act of speaking. If, looking at such
a page, we expect a vivid illustration of a real scene, we may

well find it disappointing. But if we remember once more that the artist was not concerned with an imitation of natural forms, but rather with the arrangement of traditional sacred symbols, which were all he needed to illustrate the mystery of the Annunciation, we shall no longer feel the lack of what he never intended to give us.

For we must realize how great the possibilities were that opened up before the artists as soon as they finally discarded all ambition to represent things as we see them. Figure 120 shows a page from a calendar for the use of a German monastery. It marks the principal feasts of saints to be commemorated in the month of October, but, unlike our own calendars, it marks them not only in words but also by illustrations. In the middle, under the arches, we see St Willimarus the priest and St Gall with the bishop's crozier and a companion who carries the luggage of the wandering missionary. The curious pictures on top and below illustrate the story of two martyrdoms which are remembered in October. In later times, when art had returned to the detailed representation of nature, such cruel scenes were often painted with a profusion of horrible detail. Our artist was able to avoid all this. To remind us of St Gereon and his companions, whose heads were cut off and thrown into a well, he arranged the beheaded trunks in a neat circle around the image of the well. St Ursula who, according to the legend, had been massacred with her eleven thousand maidens by the heathens, is seen enthroned, literally surrounded by her followers. An ugly savage with bow and arrows and a man brandishing his sword are placed outside the frame and aiming at the saint. We are able to read the story off the page without being forced to visualize it. And as the artist could dispense with any illusion of space or any dramatic action he could arrange his figures and forms on purely ornamental lines. Painting was indeed on the way to becoming a form of writing in pictures; but this return to more simplified methods of representation gave the artist of the Middle Ages a new freedom to experiment with more complex forms of composition (composition = putting together). Without these methods the teachings of the Church could never have been translated into visible shapes.

As with forms so with colours. As the artists no longer felt obliged to study and imitate the real gradations of shades that occur in nature they were free to choose any colour they liked for their illustrations. The bright gold and luminous blues of their goldsmiths' works, the intense colours of their book illuminations, the glowing red and deep greens of their stained-glass windows, figure 121, show that these masters put their independence of nature to good use. It was this freedom from the need to imitate the natural world that was to enable them to convey the idea of the supernatural.

10

The Church Triumphant

The thirteenth century

We have just compared the art of the Romanesque period with the art of Byzantium and even of the ancient Orient. But there is one respect in which Western Europe always differed profoundly from the East. In the East these styles lasted for thousands of years, and there seemed no reason why they should ever change. The West never knew this immobility. It was always restless, groping for new solutions and new ideas. The Romanesque style did not even outlast the twelfth century. Hardly had the artists succeeded in vaulting their churches and arranging their statues in the new and majestic manner, when a fresh idea made all these Norman and Romanesque churches look clumsy and obsolete. The new idea was born in northern France. It was the principle of the Gothic style. At first one might call it mainly a technical invention, but in its effect it became much more. It was the discovery that the method of vaulting a church by means of crosswise arches could be developed much more consistently and to much greater purpose than the Norman architects had dreamt of. If it was true that pillars were sufficient to carry the arches of the vaulting between which the other stones were held as mere filling, then all the massive walls between the pillars were really superfluous. It was possible to erect a kind of scaffolding of stone which held the whole building together. All that was needed were slim pillars and narrow 'ribs'. Anything in between could be left out without danger of the scaffolding collapsing. There was no need for heavy stone walls – instead one could put in large windows. It became the ideal of architects to build churches almost in the manner in which we build greenhouses. Only they had no steel frames or iron girders – they had to make them of stone, and that needed a great amount of careful calculation. Provided, however, that the calculation was correct, it was possible to build a church of an entirely new kind; a building of stone and glass such as the world had never seen before. This is the leading idea of the Gothic cathedrals, which was developed in northern France in the second half of the twelfth century.

Of course, the principle of crosswise 'ribs' alone was not sufficient for this revolutionary style of Gothic building. A number of other technical inventions were necessary to make the miracle possible. The round arches of the Romanesque style, for instance, were unsuited to the aims of the Gothic builders. The reason is this: if I am given the task of bridging the gap between two pillars with a semicircular arch, there is only one way of doing it. The vaulting will always reach one particular height, no more and no less. If I wanted to reach higher I should have to make the arch steeper. The best thing, in this case, is not to have a rounded arch at all, but to fit two segments together. That is the idea of the pointed arch. Its great advantage is that it can be varied at will, made flatter or more pointed according to the requirements of the structure.

There was one more thing to be considered. The heavy stones of the vaulting press not only downwards but also sideways, much like a bow which has been drawn. Here, too, the pointed arch was an improvement over the round one, but even so pillars alone were not sufficient to withstand this outward pressure. Strong frames were needed to keep the whole structure in shape. In the vaulted side-aisles this did not prove very difficult. Buttresses could be built outside. But what could be done with the high nave? This had to be kept in shape from outside, across the roofs of the aisles. To do that, the builders had to introduce their 'flying buttresses', which complete the scaffolding of the Gothic vault, figure 122. A Gothic church seems to be suspended between these slender structures of stone as a bicycle wheel, held in shape by its flimsy spokes, carries its load. In both cases it is the even distribution of weight that makes it possible to reduce the material needed for the construction more and more without endangering the firmness of the whole.

It would be wrong, however, to look at these churches mainly as feats of engineering. The artist saw to it that we feel and enjoy the boldness of their design. Looking at a Doric temple, figure 50, we sense the function of the row of columns which carry the load of the horizontal roof. Standing inside a Gothic interior, figure 123, we are made to understand the complex interplay of thrust and pull that holds the lofty vault in its place. There are no blank walls or massive pillars anywhere. The whole interior seems to be woven out of thin shafts and ribs; their network covers the vault, and runs down along the walls of the nave to be gathered up by the pillars, which are formed by a bundle of stone rods. Even the windows are overspread by these interlacing lines known as tracery, figure 124.

The great cathedrals, the bishops' own churches (cathedra = bishop's throne), of the late twelfth and early thirteenth century were mostly conceived on such a bold and magnificent scale that few, if any, were ever completed exactly as planned. But even so, and after the many alterations which they have undergone in the course of time, it remains an unforgettable experience to enter these vast interiors whose very dimensions seem to dwarf anything that is merely human and petty. We can hardly imagine the impression which these buildings must have made on those who had only known the heavy and grim structures of the Romanesque style. These older churches in their strength and power may have conveyed something of the 'Church Militant' that offered shelter against the onslaught of evil. The new cathedrals gave the faithful a glimpse of a different world. They would have heard in sermons and hymns of the Heavenly Jerusalem with its gates

of pearl, its priceless jewels, its streets of pure gold and transparent glass (Revelation XXI). Now this vision had descended
from heaven to earth. The walls of these buildings were
not cold and forbidding. They were formed of stained glass
that shone like rubies and emeralds. The pillars, ribs and
tracery were glistening with gold. Everything that was heavy,
earthly or humdrum was eliminated. The faithful who sur-
rendered themselves to the contemplation of all this beauty
could feel that they had come nearer to understanding the
mysteries of a realm beyond the reach of matter.

Even as seen from afar these miraculous buildings
seemed to proclaim the glories of heaven. The façade of
Notre-Dame in Paris is perhaps the most perfect of them all,
figure 125. So lucid and effortless is the arrangement of the
porches and windows, so lithe and graceful the tracery of the
gallery, that we forget the weight of this pile of stone and
the whole structure seems to rise up before us like a mirage.

There is a similar feeling of lightness and weightless-
ness in the sculptures that flank the porches like heavenly
hosts. While the Romanesque master of Arles, figure 115, made
his figures of saints look like solid pillars firmly fitted into the
architectural framework, the master who worked on the
northern porch of the Gothic cathedral of Chartres, figures 126,
127, made each of his figures come to life. They seem to move,
and look at each other solemnly, and the flow of their drapery
indicates once more that there is a body underneath. Each
of them is clearly marked, and should have been recognizable
to anyone who knew his Old Testament. We have no difficulty
in recognizing Abraham, the old man with his son Isaac held
before him, ready to be sacrificed. We can also recognize Moses,
because he holds the tablets on which the Ten Commandments
were inscribed, and the column with the brazen serpent by
which he cured the Israelites. The man on the other side of

Abraham is Melchizedek, King of Salem, of whom we read
in the Bible (Genesis XIV. 18) that he was 'a priest of the
most high God' and that he 'brought forth bread and wine'
to welcome Abraham after a successful battle. In medieval
theology he was therefore considered the model of the priest
who administers the sacraments, and that is why he is marked
by the chalice and censer of the priest. In this way nearly
every one of the figures that crowd the porches of the great
Gothic cathedrals is clearly marked by an emblem so that
its meaning and message could be understood and pondered
by the faithful. Taken together they form as complete an
embodiment of the teachings of the Church as the works
discussed in the preceding chapter. And yet we feel that
the Gothic sculptor has approached his task in a new spirit.
To him these statues are not only sacred symbols, solemn
reminders of a moral truth. Each of them must have been for
him a figure in its own right, different from its neighbour
in its attitude and type of beauty and each imbued with an
individual dignity.

The cathedral of Chartres still largely belonged to
the late twelfth century. After the year 1200 many new and
magnificent cathedrals sprang up in France and also in
the neighbouring countries, in England, in Spain and in the
German Rhineland. Many of the masters busy on the new
sites had learned their craft while working on the first buildings
of this kind, but they all tried to add to the achievements
of their elders.

Figure 129, from the early thirteenth-century Gothic
cathedral of Strasbourg, shows the novel approach of these
Gothic sculptors. It represents the Death of the Virgin. The
twelve apostles surround her bed, St Mary Magdalene kneels
before her. Christ, in the middle, is receiving the Virgin's
soul into His arms. We see that the artist was still anxious to

preserve something of the solemn symmetry of the early
period. We can imagine that he sketched out the group
beforehand to arrange the heads of the apostles around the
arch, the two apostles at the bedside corresponding to each
other, and the figure of Christ in the centre. But he was no
longer content with a purely symmetrical arrangement such
as the twelfth-century master of *figure 120*, preferred. He
clearly wanted to breathe life into his figures. We can see the
expression of mourning in the beautiful faces of the apostles,
with their raised eyebrows and their intent look. Three of
them lift their hands to their faces in the traditional gesture
of grief. Even more expressive are the face and figure of
St Mary Magdalene, who cowers at the bedside and wrings her
hands, and it is marvellous how the artist succeeded in
contrasting her features with the serene and blissful look on
the face of the Virgin. The draperies are no longer the empty
husks and purely ornamental scrolls we see on early medieval
work. The Gothic artists wanted to understand the ancient
formula for draped bodies, which had been handed down to
them. Perhaps they turned for enlightenment to the remnants
of pagan stonework, Roman tombstones and triumphal arches,
of which several could be seen in France. Thus they regained
the lost classical art of letting the structure of the body show
under the folds of the drapery. Our artist, in fact, is proud of
his ability to handle this difficult technique. The way in which
the Virgin's feet and hands and Christ's hand appear under
the cloth shows that these Gothic sculptors were no longer
interested only in what they represented, but also in the
problems of how to represent. Once more, as in the time of
the great awakening in Greece, they began to look at nature,
not so much to copy it as to learn from it how to make a
figure look convincing. Yet there is a vast difference between
Greek art and Gothic art, between the art of the temple and

that of the cathedral. The Greek artists of the fifth century were mainly interested in how to build up the image of a beautiful body. To the Gothic artist all these methods and tricks were only a means to an end, which was to tell his sacred story more movingly and more convincingly. He does not tell it for its own sake, but for the sake of its message, and for the solace and edification the faithful could derive from it. The attitude of Christ as He looks at the dying Virgin was clearly more important to the artist than skilful rendering of muscles.

In the course of the thirteenth century, some artists went even further in their attempts to make the stone come to life. The sculptor who was given the task of representing the founders of Naumburg Cathedral in Germany, round about 1260, almost convinces us that he portrayed actual knights of his time, figure 130. It is not very likely that he really did – these founders had been dead for many years, and were nothing but a name to him. But his statues of men and women seem to be ready at any moment to step down from the pedestals and to join the company of those vigorous knights and gracious ladies whose deeds and suffering fill the pages of our history books.

To work for cathedrals was the main task of the northern sculptors of the thirteenth century. The most frequent task of the northern painters of that time was still the illumination of manuscripts, but the spirit of these illustrations was very diffrent from that of the solemn Romanesque book pages. If we compare the Annunciation from the twelfth century, figure 119, with a page from a thirteenth-century Psalter, figure 131, we gain a measure of this change. It shows the entombment of Christ, similar in subject and in spirit to the relief from Strasbourg Cathedral, figure 129. Once more we see how important it has become to the artist to show us the feelings of his figures. The Virgin bends over the dead body of Christ and embraces it, while St John wrings his hands in grief. As in the relief, we see what pains the artist took to fit his scene into a regular pattern: the angels in the top corners coming out of the clouds with censers in their hands, and the servants with their strange pointed hats – such as were worn by the Jews in the Middle Ages – supporting the body of Christ. This expression of intense feeling, and this regular distribution of the figures on the page, were obviously more important to the artist than any attempt to make his figures lifelike, or to represent a real scene. He does not mind that the servants are smaller than the holy personages, and he does not give us any indication of the place or the setting. We understand what is happening without any such external indications. Though it was not the artist's aim to represent things as we see them in reality, his knowledge of the human body, like that of the Strasbourg master, was nevertheless much greater than that of the painter of the twelfth-century miniature.

It was in the thirteenth century that artists occasionally abandoned their pattern books, in order to represent something because it interested them. We can hardly imagine today what this meant. We think of an artist as a person with a sketchbook who sits down and makes a drawing from life whenever he feels inclined. But we know that the whole training and upbringing of the medieval artist was very different. He started by being apprenticed to a master, whom he assisted at first by carrying out his instructions and filling in relatively unimportant parts of a picture. Gradually he would learn how to represent an apostle, and how to draw the Holy Virgin. He would learn to copy and rearrange scenes from old books, and fit them into different frames, and he would finally acquire enough facility in all this to be able even to illustrate a scene for which he knew no pattern. But never in his career would he be faced with the necessity of taking a sketchbook and drawing something from life. Even when he was asked to represent a particular person, the ruling king or a bishop, he would not make what we should call a likeness. There were no portraits as we understand them in the Middle Ages. All the artists did was to draw a conventional figure and to give it the insignia of office – a crown and sceptre for the king, a mitre and crozier for the bishop – and perhaps write the name underneath so that there would be no mistake. It may seem strange to us that artists who were able to make such lifelike figures as the Naumburg founders, *figure 130*, should have found it difficult to make a likeness of a particular person. But the whole idea of sitting down in front of a person or an object and copying it was alien to them. It is all the more remarkable that, on certain occasions, artists in the thirteenth century did in fact draw something from life. They did it when they had no conventional pattern on which they could rely. *Figure 132* shows such an exception. It is the picture of an elephant drawn by the English historian Matthew Paris (died 1259) in the middle of the thirteenth century. This elephant had been sent by St Louis, King of France, to Henry III in 1255. It was the first that had been seen in England. The figure of the servant by its side is not a very convincing likeness, though we are given his name, Henricus de Flor. But what is interesting is that in this case the artist was very anxious to get the right proportions. Between the legs of the elephant there is a Latin inscription saying: 'By the size of the man portrayed here you may imagine the size of the beast represented here.' To us this elephant may look a little odd, but it does show, I think, that medieval artists, at least in the thirteenth century, were very well aware of such things as proportions, and that, if they ignored them so often, they did so not out of ignorance but simply because they did not think they mattered.

In the thirteenth century, the time of the great cathedrals, France was the richest and most important country in
Europe. The University of Paris was the intellectual centre of
the Western World. In Italy, which was a land of warring cities,
the ideas and methods of the great French cathedral builders,
which had been so eagerly imitated in Germany and England,
did not at first meet with much response.

It was only in the second half of the thirteenth century
that an Italian sculptor began to emulate the example of the
French masters and to study the methods of classical sculpture
in order to represent nature more convincingly. This artist was
Nicola Pisano, who worked in the great seaport and trading
centre of Pisa. Figure 133 shows one of the reliefs on a pulpit he
completed in 1260. At first it is not too easy to see what
subject is represented because Pisano followed the medieval
practice of combining various stories within one frame.
Thus the left corner of the relief is taken up with the group
of the Annunciation and the middle with the Birth of Christ.
The Virgin is lying on a bedstead, St Joseph is crouching
in a corner, and two servants are engaged in bathing the Child.
They seem to be jostled about by a herd of sheep, but these
really belong to a third scene – the story of the Annunciation
to the Shepherds, which is represented in the top right-hand
corner, where the Christ Child appears once more in the
manger. But if the scene appears a little crowded and confusing
the sculptor has nevertheless contrived to give each episode
its proper place and its vivid details. One can see how he
enjoyed such touches of observation as the goat in the lower
right-hand corner scratching its head with its hoof, and one
realizes how much he owed to the study of classical and early
Christian sculpture, figure 83, when one looks at his treatment of
heads and garments. Like the master of Strasbourg who worked
a generation before him, or like the master of Naumburg who

may have been about his age, Nicola Pisano had learned the methods of the ancients to show the forms of the body under the drapery and to make his figures look both dignified and convincing.

Italian painters were even slower than Italian sculptors in responding to the new spirit of the Gothic masters. Italian cities such as Venice were in close contact with the Byzantine Empire and Italian craftsmen looked to Constantinople rather than to Paris for inspiration and guidance (see figure 8). In the thirteenth century Italian churches were still decorated with solemn mosaics in the 'Greek manner'.

It might have seemed as if this adherence to the conservative style of the East would prevent all change, and indeed the change was long delayed. But when it came towards the end of the thirteenth century, it was this firm grounding in the Byzantine tradition which enabled Italian art not only to catch up with the achievements of the northern cathedral sculptors but to revolutionize the whole art of painting.

We must not forget that the sculptor who aims at reproducing nature has an easier task than the painter who sets himself a similar aim. The sculptor need not worry about creating an illusion of depth through foreshortening or through modelling in light and shade. His statue stands in real space and in real light. Thus the sculptors of Strasbourg or Naumburg could reach a degree of lifelikeness which no thirteenth-century painting could match. For we remember that northern painting had given up all pretence of creating an illusion of reality. Its principles of arrangement and of story-telling were governed by quite different aims.

It was Byzantine art which ultimately allowed the Italians to leap the barrier that separates sculpture from painting. For all its rigidity, Byzantine art had preserved more of the discoveries of the Hellenistic painters than had survived the picture-writing of the Dark Ages in the West. We remember how many of these achievements still lay hidden, as it were, under the frozen solemnity of a Byzantine painting like figure 88; how the face is modelled in light and shade and how the throne and the footstool show a correct understanding of the principles of foreshortening. With methods of this kind a genius who broke the spell of Byzantine conservatism could venture out into a new world and translate the lifelike figures of Gothic sculpture into painting. This genius Italian art found in the Florentine painter Giotto di Bondone (c. 1267-1337).

It is usual to start a new chapter with Giotto; the Italians were convinced that an entirely new epoch of art had begun with the appearance of that great painter. We shall see that they were right. But for all that, it may be useful to remember that in real history there are no new chapters and no new beginnings, and that it detracts nothing from Giotto's greatness if we realize that his methods owe much to the Byzantine masters, and his aims and outlook to the great sculptors of the northern cathedrals.

Giotto's most famous works are wall-paintings or frescoes (so called because they must be painted on the wall while the plaster is still fresh, that is, wet). Between 1302 and 1305 he covered the wall of a small church in Padua in northern Italy with stories from the life of the Virgin and of Christ. Underneath he painted personifications of virtues and vices such as had sometimes been placed on the porches of northern cathedrals.

Figure 134 shows Giotto's figure of Faith, a matron with a cross in one hand, a scroll in the other. It is easy to see the similarity of this noble figure to the works of the Gothic sculptors. But this is no statue. It is a painting which gives the illusion of a statue in the round. We see the foreshortening of the arms, the modelling of the face and neck, the deep shadows in the flowing folds of the drapery. Nothing like this had been done for a thousand years. Giotto had rediscovered the art of creating the illusion of depth on a flat surface.

For Giotto this discovery was not only a trick to be displayed for its own sake. It enabled him to change the whole conception of painting. Instead of using the methods of picture-writing he could create the illusion that the sacred story was happening before our very eyes. For this it was no longer sufficient to look at older representations of the same scene and adapt these time-honoured models to a new use. He rather followed the advice of the preaching friars who exhorted the people to visualize in their mind, when reading the Bible and the legends of the saints, what it must have looked like when a carpenter's family fled to Egypt or when the Lord was nailed to the cross. He did not rest till he had thought it all out afresh: how would a man stand, how would he act, how would he move, if he took part in such an event? Moreover, how would such a gesture or movement present itself to our eyes?

We can best gauge the extent of this revolution if we compare one of Giotto's frescoes from Padua, figures 135-6, with a similar theme in the thirteenth-century miniature in figure 131. The subject is the mourning over the dead body of Christ, with the Virgin embracing her Son for the last time. In the miniature the artist was not interested in representing the scene as it might have happened. He varied the size of the figures so as to fit them well into the page, and if we try to imagine the space between the figures in the foreground and St John in the background – with Christ and the Virgin in between – we realize how everything is squeezed together, and how little the artist cared about space. It is the same indifference to the real place where the scene is happening which led Nicola Pisano to represent different episodes within one frame. Giotto's method is completely different. Painting, for him, is more than a substitute for the written word. We seem to witness the real event as if it were enacted on a stage. Compare the conventional gesture of the mourning St John in the miniature with the passionate movement of St John in Giotto's painting as he bends forward, his arms extended sideways. If we try here to imagine the distance between the cowering figures in the foreground and St John, we immediately feel that there is air and space between them, and that they can all move. These figures in the foreground show how entirely new Giotto's art was in every respect. We remember that early Christian art had reverted to the old Oriental idea that to tell a story clearly every figure had to be shown completely, almost as was done in Egyptian art. Giotto abandoned these ideas. He did not need such simple devices. He shows us so convincingly how each figure reflects the grief of the tragic scene that we sense the same grief in the cowering figures whose faces are hidden from us.

Giotto's fame spread far and wide. The people of Florence were proud of him. They were interested in his life, and told anecdotes about his wit and dexterity. This, too, was rather a new thing. Nothing quite like it had happened before. Of course, there had been masters who had enjoyed general esteem, and been recommended from monastery to monastery, or from bishop to bishop. But, on the whole, people did not think it necessary to preserve the names of these masters for posterity. They thought of them as we think of a good cabinet-maker or tailor. Even the artists themselves were not much interested in acquiring fame or notoriety. Very often they did not even sign their work. We do not know the names of the masters who made the sculptures of Chartres, Strasbourg or Naumburg. No doubt they were appreciated in their time, but they gave the honour to the cathedral for which they worked.

In this respect too, the Florentine painter Giotto begins an entirely new chapter in the history of art. From his day onwards the history of art, first in Italy and then in other countries also, is the history of the great artists.

11

Courtiers and Burghers

The fourteenth century

The thirteenth century had been the century of the great
cathedrals, in which nearly all branches of art had their share.
Work on these immense enterprises continued into the fourteenth century and even beyond, but they were no longer
the main focus of art. We must remember that the world had
changed a great deal during that period. In the middle of the
twelfth century, when the Gothic style was first developed,
Europe was still a thinly populated continent of peasants with
monasteries and barons' castles as the main centres of power
and learning. The ambition of the great bishops' sees to have
mighty cathedrals of their own was the first indication of an
awakening civic pride in the towns. But a hundred and fifty
years later these towns had grown into teeming centres of trade
whose burghers felt increasingly independent of the power
of the Church and the feudal lords. Even the nobles no longer
lived a life of grim seclusion in their fortified manors, but
moved to the cities with their comfort and fashionable luxury,
there to display their wealth at the courts of the mighty. We
can get a very vivid idea of what life in the fourteenth century
was like if we turn to the works of Chaucer, with his knights
and squires, friars and artisans. This was no longer the world
of the Crusades, and of those paragons of chivalry, which
we remember when looking at the founders of Naumburg,
figure 130. It is never safe to generalize too much about periods
and styles. There are always exceptions and examples which
would not fit any such generalization. But, with that reservation,
we may say that the taste of the fourteenth century was rather
for the refined than for the grand.

This is exemplified in the architecture of the period. In
England we distinguish between the pure Gothic style of the
early cathedrals, which is known as Early English, and the later
development of these forms, known as the Decorated style. The
name indicates the change of taste. The Gothic builders of the

fourteenth century were no longer content with the clear majestic outline of the earlier cathedrals. They liked to show their skill in decoration and complicated tracery. The west window of Exeter Cathedral is a typical example of this style, figure 137.

Churches were no longer the main tasks of the architects. In the growing and prosperous cities many secular buildings had to be designed – town halls, guild halls, colleges, palaces, bridges and city gates. One of the most celebrated and characteristic buildings of this kind is the Doges' Palace in Venice, figure 138, which was begun in the fourteenth century, when the power and prosperity of that city were at their height. It shows that this later development of the Gothic style, for all its delight in ornament and tracery, could yet achieve its own effect of grandeur.

The most characteristic works of sculpture in the fourteenth century are perhaps not those of stone, which were still made in great numbers for the churches of the period, but rather the smaller works of precious metal or ivory, in which the craftsmen of the period excelled. Figure 139 shows a little silver-gilt statue of the Virgin and Child made by a French goldsmith. Works of this kind were not intended for public worship. Rather, they were to be placed in a palace chapel for private prayer. They are not meant to proclaim a truth in solemn aloofness, like the statues of the great cathedrals, but to excite love and tenderness. The Paris goldsmith was thinking of the Virgin as a real mother, and of Christ as a real child, thrusting His hand at His mother's face. He took care to avoid any impression of rigidity. That is why he gave the figure a slight bend – she rests her arm on her hip to support the child, while her head is bent towards Him. Thus the whole body seems to sway slightly in a gentle curve, very much like an S, and Gothic artists of the period were very fond of this motif.

In fact the artist who made this statue probably did not invent either the peculiar posture of Our Lady, or the motif of the Child playing with her. In such things he was following the general trend of fashion. His own contribution lay in the exquisite finish of every detail, the beauty of the hands, the little creases in the baby's arms, the wonderful surface of gilded silver and enamel, and, last but not least, the exact proportion of the statue, with its small and graceful head on a long and slender body. There is nothing haphazard in these works by the great Gothic craftsmen. Such details as the drapery falling over the right arm show the infinite care the artist has taken to compose it into graceful and melodious lines. We can never do these works justice if we just pass them by in our museums, and devote no more than a quick glance to them. They were made to be appreciated by real connoisseurs, and treasured as pieces worthy of devotion.

The love of fourteenth-century painters for graceful and delicate details is seen in such famous illustrated manuscripts as the English Psalter known as 'Queen Mary's Psalter'. Figure 140 shows Christ in the Temple, conversing with the learned scribes. They have put Him on a high chair, and He is seen explaining some point of doctrine with the characteristic gesture used by medieval artists when they wanted to draw a teacher. The Jewish scribes raise their hands in attitudes of awe and astonishment, and so do Christ's parents, who are just coming on to the scene, looking at each other wonderingly. The method of telling the story is still rather unreal. The artist has evidently not yet heard of Giotto's discovery of the way in which to stage a scene so as to give it life. Christ, who was twelve at the time, as the Bible tells us, is minute in comparison with the grown-ups, and there is no attempt on the part of the artist to give us any idea of the space between the figures. Moreover, we can see that all the faces are more or less drawn according to one simple formula, with the curved eyebrows, the mouth drawn downwards and the curly hair and beard. It is all the more surprising to look down the same page and to see that another scene has been added, which has nothing to do with the sacred text. It is a theme from the daily life of the time, the hunting of ducks with a hawk. Much to the delight of the man and women on horseback, and of the boy in front of them, the hawk has just got hold of a duck, while two others are flying away. The artist may not have looked at real twelve-year-old boys when he painted the scene above, but he had undoubtedly looked at real hawks and ducks when he painted the scene below. Perhaps he had too much reverence for the biblical narrative to bring his observation of actual life into it. He preferred to keep the two things apart: the clear symbolic way of telling a story with easily readable gestures and no distracting details, and, on the margin of the page, the slice of real life, which reminds us once more that this is Chaucer's century. It was only in the course of the fourteenth century that the two elements of this art, the graceful narrative and the faithful observation, were gradually fused. Perhaps this would not have happened so soon without the influence of Italian art.

In Italy, particularly in Florence, the art of Giotto had changed the whole idea of painting. The old Byzantine manner suddenly seemed stiff and outmoded. Nevertheless it would be wrong to imagine that Italian art was suddenly set apart from the remainder of Europe. On the contrary, Giotto's ideas gained influence in the countries north of the Alps, while the ideals of the Gothic painters of the north also began to have their effect on the southern masters. It was particularly in Siena, another Tuscan town and a great rival of Florence, that the taste and fashion of these northern artists made a very deep impression. The painters of Siena had not broken with

the earlier Byzantine tradition in such an abrupt and revolutionary manner as Giotto in Florence. Their greatest master
of Giotto's generation, Duccio (c. 1255/60 - c. 1315/18), had
tried – and tried successfully – to breathe new life into the
old Byzantine forms instead of discarding them altogether.
The altar panel of figure 141 was made by two younger
masters of his school, Simone Martini (1285?-1344) and Lippo
Memmi (died 1347?). It shows to what an extent the ideals
and the general atmosphere of the fourteenth century
had been absorbed by Sienese art. The painting represents the
Annunciation – the moment when the Archangel Gabriel
arrives from Heaven to greet the Virgin, and we can read his
words coming out of his mouth: '*Ave gratia plena*'. In his left
hand he holds an olive branch, symbol of peace; his right
hand is lifted as if he were about to speak. The Virgin has been
reading. The appearance of the angel has taken her by surprise.
She shrinks away in a movement of awe and humility, while
looking back at the messenger from Heaven. Between the
two there stands a vase with white lilies, symbols of virginity,
and high up in the central pointed arch we see the dove,
symbol of the Holy Ghost, surrounded by four-winged
cherubim. These masters shared the predilection of the French
and English artists of figure 139 and 140 for delicate forms and
a lyrical mood. They enjoyed the gentle curves of the flowing
drapery and the subtle grace of slender bodies. The whole
painting, in fact, looks like some precious goldsmith's work,
with its figures standing out from a golden background,
so skilfully arranged that they form an admirable pattern. One
can never cease to wonder at the way in which these figures
are fitted into the complicated shape of the panel; the way in
which the angel's wings are framed by the pointed arch to
the left, and the Virgin's figure shrinks back into the shelter of
the pointed arch to the right, while the empty space between

them is filled by the vase and the dove over it. The painters
had learned this art of fitting the figures into a pattern from
the medieval tradition. We had occasion, earlier, to admire the
way in which medieval artists arranged the symbols of the
sacred stories so as to form a satisfying arrangement. But we
know that they did so by ignoring the real shape and
proportion of things, and by forgetting about space altogether.
That was no longer the way of the Sienese artists. Perhaps we
may find their figures a little strange, with their slanting eyes
and curved mouths. But we need only look at some details to
see that the achievements of Giotto had by no means been lost
on them. The vase is a real vase standing on a real stone floor,
and we can tell exactly where it stands in relation to the angel
and the Virgin. The bench on which the Virgin sits is a real
bench, receding into the background, and the book she holds
is not just the symbol of a book, but a real prayer book with
light falling on it and with shade between the pages, which
the artist must have studied from a prayer book in his studio.

Giotto was a contemporary of the great Florentine poet
Dante, who mentions him in his *Divine Comedy*. Simone Martini,
the master of figure 141, was a friend of Petrarch, the greatest
Italian poet of the next generation. Petrarch's fame today rests
mainly on the many love-sonnets he wrote for Laura. We know
from them that Simone Martini painted a portrait of Laura
which Petrarch treasured. We remember that portraits in our
sense had not existed during the Middle Ages and that artists
were content to use any conventional figure of a man or
woman, and to write on it the name of the person it was
intended to represent. Unfortunately, Simone Martini's portrait
of Laura is lost, and we do not know how far it was a real likeness. We do know, however, that this artist and other masters
in the fourteenth century painted likenesses from nature, and
the art of portraiture developed during that period. Perhaps the

way in which Simone Martini looked at nature and observed details had something to do with this, for the artists of Europe had ample opportunity of learning from his achievements. Like Petrarch himself, Simone Martini spent many years at the court of the Pope, which was at that time not in Rome but at Avignon in southern France. France was still the centre of Europe, and French ideas and styles had a great influence everywhere. Germany was ruled by a family from Luxemburg who had their residence in Prague. There is a wonderful series of busts dating from this period (between 1379 and 1386) in the cathedral of Prague. They represent benefactors of the church and thus serve the same purpose as the figures of the Naumburg Founders, figure 130. But here we need no longer be in doubt. These are real portraits. For the series includes busts of contemporaries including one of the artist in charge, Peter Parler the Younger (1330-99), which is in all probability the first real self-portrait of an artist known to us, figure 142.

Bohemia became one of the centres through which this influence from Italy and France spread more widely. Its contacts reached as far as England, where Richard II married Anne of Bohemia. England traded with Burgundy. Europe, or at least the Europe of the Latin Church, was still one large unit. Artists and ideas travelled from one centre to another, and no one thought of rejecting an achievement because it was 'foreign'. The style which arose out of this mutual give-and-take towards the end of the fourteenth century is known among historians as the 'International style'. A wonderful example of it in England, possibly painted by a French master for an English king, is the so-called Wilton Diptych, figure 143. It is interesting to us for many reasons, including the fact that it, too, records the features of a real historical personage, and that of no other than Anne of Bohemia's unlucky husband – King Richard II. He is seen kneeling in prayer while St John

the Baptist and two patron saints of the royal family commend
him to the Holy Virgin, who seems to stand on the flowery
meadow of Paradise, surrounded by angels of radiant beauty, all
of whom wear the badge of the king, the white hart with
golden antlers. The lively Christ Child is bending forward as if
to bless or welcome the king and assure him that his prayers
have been answered. Perhaps something of the ancient magical
attitude towards the image still survives in the custom of
'donors' portraits' to remind us of the tenacity of these beliefs
which we have found in the very cradle of art. Who can tell
whether the donor did not feel somehow reassured in the
rough and tumble of life, in which his own part was perhaps
not always very saintly, to know that in some quiet church or
chapel there was something of himself – a likeness fixed there
through the artist's skill, which always kept company with the
saints and angels and never ceased praying?

It is easy to see how the art of the Wilton Diptych is
linked with the works we have discussed before, how it shares
with them the taste for beautiful flowing lines and for dainty
and delicate motifs. The way in which the Virgin touches the
foot of the Christ Child and the gestures of the angels, with
their long and slender hands, remind us of figures we have
seen before. Once more we see how the artist showed his
skill in foreshortening, for instance in the posture of the angel
kneeling on the left side of the panel, and how he enjoyed
making use of studies from nature in the many flowers which
adorn the paradise of his imagination.

The artists of the International style applied the same
power of observation, and the same delight in delicate and
beautiful things, to their portrayal of the world around them.
It had been customary in the Middle Ages to illustrate calendars
with pictures of the changing occupations of the months,
of sowing, hunting, harvesting. A calendar attached to a prayer

book which a rich Burgundian duke had ordered from the
workshop of the Limbourg brothers, figure 144, shows how
these pictures from real life had gained in liveliness and
observation, even since the time of Queen Mary's Psalter of
figure 140. The miniature represents the annual spring festival
of the courtiers. They are riding through a wood in gay
attire, wreathed with branches and flowers. We can see how
the painter enjoyed the spectacle of the pretty girls in their
fashionable dresses, and how he took pleasure in bringing
the whole colourful pageantry on to his page. Once more we
may think of Chaucer and his pilgrims; for our artist, too,
took pains to distinguish the different types, so skilfully that
we almost seem to hear them talking. Such a picture was
probably painted with a magnifying glass, and it should be
studied with the same loving attention. All the choice details
which the artist has crowded on to his page combine to
build up a picture which looks nearly like a scene from real
life. Nearly, but not quite; for when we notice that the artist
has closed the background with a kind of curtain of trees,
beyond which we see the roof-tops of a vast castle, we realize
that what he gives us is not an actual scene from nature.
His art seems so far removed from the symbolic way of telling
a story which earlier painters had used, that it needs an effort
to realize that even he cannot represent the space in which
his figures move, and that he achieves the illusion of reality
mainly through his close attention to detail. His trees are not
real trees painted from nature, but rather a row of symbolic
trees, one beside the other, and even his human faces are
still developed more or less out of one charming formula.
Nevertheless, his interest in all the splendour and gaiety
of the real life around him shows that his ideas about the
aims of painting were very different from those of the artists
of the early Middle Ages. The interest had gradually shifted,

from the best way of telling a sacred story as clearly and impressively as possible, to the methods of representing a piece of nature in the most faithful way. We have seen that the two ideals do not necessarily clash. It was certainly possible to place this newly acquired knowledge of nature at the service of religious art, as the masters of the fourteenth century had done, and as other masters were to do after them; but, for the artist, the task had nevertheless changed. Formerly it was sufficient training to learn the ancient formulas for representing the main figures of the sacred story and to apply this knowledge in ever-new combinations. Now the artist's job included a different skill. He had to be able to make studies from nature and to transfer them to his pictures. He began to use a sketchbook, and to lay up a store of sketches of rare and beautiful plants and animals. What had been an exception in the case of Matthew Paris, *page 147, figure 132*, was soon to be the rule. A drawing such as *figure 145*, made by the north Italian artist Antonio Pisanello (1397-1455?) only some twenty years after the Limbourg miniature, shows how this habit led artists to study a live animal with loving interest. The public which looked at the artist's works began to judge them by the skill with which nature was portrayed, and by the wealth of attractive details which the artist managed to bring into his pictures. The artists, however, wanted to go one better. They were no longer content with the newly acquired mastery of painting such details as flowers or animals from nature; they wanted to explore the laws of vision, and to acquire sufficient knowledge of the human body to build it up in their statues and pictures as the Greeks and Romans had done. Once their interest took this turn, medieval art was really at an end. We come to the period usually known as the Renaissance.

12

The Conquest of Reality

The early fifteenth century

The word renaissance means rebirth or revival, and the idea of such a rebirth had gained ground in Italy ever since the time of Giotto. When people of the period wanted to praise a poet or an artist, they said that his work was as good as that of the ancients. Giotto had been exalted in this way as a master who had led to a true revival of art; by this, people meant that his art was as good as that of the famous masters whose work they found praised in the ancient writers of Greece and Rome. It is not surprising that this idea became popular in Italy. The Italians were very much aware of the fact that in the distant past Italy, with Rome her capital, had been the centre of the civilized world, and that her power and glory had waned since the Germanic tribes, Goths and Vandals, had invaded the country and broken up the Roman Empire. The idea of a revival was closely connected in the minds of the Italians with the idea of a rebirth of 'the grandeur that was Rome'. The period between the classical age, to which they looked back with pride, and the new era of rebirth for which they hoped was merely a sad interlude, 'the time between'. Thus the idea of a rebirth or renaissance was responsible for the idea that the intervening period was a Middle Age – and we still use this terminology. Since the Italians blamed the Goths for the downfall of the Roman Empire, they began to speak of the art of this interven-ing period as Gothic, by which they meant barbaric – much as we speak of vandalism when we refer to the useless destruction of beautiful things.

We now know that these ideas of the Italians had little basis in fact. They were, at best, a crude and much simplified picture of the actual course of events. We have seen that some seven hundred years separated the Goths from the rise of the art that we now call Gothic. We also know that the revival of art, after the shock and turmoil of the Dark Ages, came gradually and that the Gothic period itself saw this revival

getting into its full stride. Possibly we can understand the
reason why the Italians were less aware of this gradual growth
and unfolding of art than the people living farther north. We
have seen that they lagged behind during part of the Middle
Ages, so that the new achievements of Giotto came to them as
a tremendous innovation, a rebirth of all that was noble and
great in art. The Italians of the fourteenth century believed that
art, science and scholarship had flourished in the classical
period, that all these things had been almost destroyed by the
northern barbarians and that it was for them to help to revive
the glorious past and thus bring about a new era.

In no city was this feeling of confidence and hope more
intense than in the wealthy merchant city of Florence, the city
of Dante and of Giotto. It was there, in the first decades of the
fifteenth century, that a group of artists deliberately set out to
create a new art and to break with the ideas of the past.

The leader of this group of young Florentine artists was
an architect, Filippo Brunelleschi (1377-1446). Brunelleschi
was employed on the completion of the cathedral of Florence.
It was a Gothic cathedral, and Brunelleschi had fully mastered
the technical inventions which formed part of the Gothic
tradition. His fame, in fact, rests partly on an achievement in
construction and design which would not have been possible
without his knowledge of the Gothic methods of vaulting.
The Florentines wished to have their cathedral crowned by a
mighty dome, but no artist was able to span the immense
space between the pillars on which the dome was to rest, till
Brunelleschi devised a method of accomplishing this, figure 146.
When Brunelleschi was called upon to design new churches
or other buildings, he decided to discard the traditional style
altogether, and to adopt the programme of those who longed
for a revival of Roman grandeur. It is said that he travelled to
Rome and measured the ruins of temples and palaces, and

made sketches of their forms and ornaments. It was never his intention to copy these ancient buildings outright. They could hardly have been adapted to the needs of fifteenth-century Florence. What he aimed at was the creation of a new way of building, in which the forms of classical architecture were freely used to create new modes of harmony and beauty.

What remains most astonishing in Brunelleschi's achievement is the fact that he actually succeeded in making his programme come true. For nearly five hundred years the architects of Europe and America followed in his footsteps. Wherever we go in our cities and villages we find buildings in which classical forms, such as columns or pediments, are used. It was only in the present century that architects began to question Brunelleschi's programme and to revolt against the Renaissance tradition in building, just as he had revolted against the Gothic tradition. But many houses which are being built now, even those that have no columns or similar trimmings, still somewhere preserve remnants of classical form in the shape of mouldings on doors and window-frames, or in the measurements and proportions of the building. If Brunelleschi wanted to create the architecture of a new era, he certainly succeeded.

Figure 147 shows the façade of a little church which Brunelleschi built for the powerful family of the Pazzi in Florence. We see at once that it has little in common with any classical temple, but even less with the forms used by Gothic builders. Brunelleschi has combined columns, pilasters and arches in his own way to achieve an effect of lightness and grace which is different from anything that had gone before. Details such as the framing of the door, with its classical gable or pediment, show how carefully Brunelleschi had studied the ancient ruins, and buildings such as the Pantheon, figure 75. Compare how the arch is formed and how it cuts into the

upper storey with its pilasters (flat half-columns). We see
his study of Roman forms even more clearly as we enter the
church, figure 148. Nothing in this bright and well-propor-
tioned interior has any of the features which Gothic architects
valued so highly. There are no high windows, no slim pillars.
Instead, the blank white wall is subdivided by grey pilasters,
which convey the idea of a classical 'order', although they
serve no real function in the construction of the building.
Brunelleschi only put them there to emphasize the shape and
proportion of the interior.

Brunelleschi was not only the initiator of Renaissance
architecture. To him, it seems, is due another momentous
discovery in the field of art, which also dominated the art of
subsequent centuries – that of perspective. We have seen that
even the Greeks, who understood foreshortening, and the
Hellenistic painters, who were skilled in creating the illusion
of depth, *page 91*, *figure 72*, did not know the mathematical laws
by which objects appear to diminish in size as they recede
from us. We remember that no classical artist could have drawn
the famous avenue of trees leading back into the picture until
it vanishes on the horizon. It was Brunelleschi who gave artists
the mathematical means of solving this problem; and the
excitement which this caused among his painter-friends must
have been immense. Figure 149 shows one of the first paintings
which were made according to these mathematical rules. It is
a wall-painting in a Florentine Church, and represents the Holy
Trinity with the Virgin and St John under the cross, and the
donors – an elderly merchant and his wife – kneeling outside.
The artist who painted this was called Masaccio (1401-28),
which means 'clumsy Thomas'. He must have been an
extraordinary genius, for we know that he died when hardly
twenty-eight years of age, and that by then he had already
brought about a complete revolution in painting. This revolution

did not consist only in the technical trick of perspective painting, though that in itself must have been startling enough
when it was new. We can imagine how amazed the Florentines
must have been when this wall-painting was unveiled and
seemed to have made a hole in the wall through which they
could look into a new burial chapel in Brunelleschi's modern
style. But perhaps they were even more amazed at the simplicity
and grandeur of the figures which were framed by this new
architecture. If the Florentines had expected something in
the vein of the International style, which was as fashionable in
Florence as elsewhere in Europe, they must have been disappointed. Instead of delicate grace, they saw massive heavy figures;
instead of easy-flowing curves, solid angular forms; and, instead
of dainty details such as flowers and precious stones, a stark
tomb with a skeleton placed on it. But if Masaccio's art was less
pleasing to the eye than the paintings they had been accustomed
to, it was all the more sincere and moving. We can see that
Masaccio admired the dramatic grandeur of Giotto, though he
did not imitate him. The simple gesture with which the Holy
Virgin points to her crucified Son is so eloquent and impressive
because it is the only movement in the whole solemn painting.
Its figures, in fact, look like statues. It is this effect, more than
anything else, that Masaccio has heightened by the perspective
frame in which he placed his figures. We feel we can almost
touch them, and this feeling brings them and their message
nearer to us. To the great masters of the Renaissance, the new
devices and discoveries of art were never an end in themselves.
They always used them to bring the meaning of their subject
still nearer to our minds.

 The greatest sculptor of Brunelleschi's circle was the
Florentine master Donatello (1386?-1466). He was older than
Masaccio by fifteen years, but he lived much longer. *Figure 151*
shows one of his earlier works. It was commissioned by the

guild of the armourers, whose patron saint, St George, it represents, and was destined for a niche on the outside of a Florentine church (Or San Michele). If we think back to the Gothic statues outside the great cathedrals, figure 127, we realize how completely Donatello broke with the past. These Gothic statues hovered at the side of the porches in calm and solemn rows, looking like beings from a different world. Donatello's St George stands firmly on the ground, his feet planted resolutely on the earth as if he were determined not to yield an inch. His face has none of the vague and serene beauty of medieval saints – it is all energy and concentration, figure 150. He seems to watch the approach of the enemy and to take its measure, his hands resting on his shield, his whole attitude tense with defiant determination. The statue has remained famous as an unrivalled picture of youthful dash and courage. But it is not only Donatello's imagination which we must admire, his faculty of visualizing the knightly saint in such a fresh and convincing manner; his whole approach to the art of sculpture shows a completely new conception. Despite the impression of life and movement which the statue conveys it remains clear in outline and solid as a rock. Like Masaccio's paintings, it shows us that Donatello wanted to re-place the gentle refinement of his predecessors by a new and vigorous observation of nature. Such details as the hands or the brow of the saint show a complete independence from the traditional models. They prove a fresh and determined study of the real features of the human body. For these Florentine masters of the beginning of the fifteenth century were no longer content to repeat the old formulas handed down by medieval artists. Like the Greeks and Romans, whom they admired, they began to study the human body in their studios and workshops by asking models or fellow artists to pose for them in the required attitudes. It is this new method and this new interest which makes Donatello's work look so strikingly convincing.

Donatello acquired great fame in his lifetime. Like Giotto a century earlier, he was frequently called to other Italian cities to add to their beauty and glory. Figure 152 shows a bronze relief he made for a font at Siena some ten years after the 'St George'. Like the medieval font of figure 118, it illustrates a scene from the life of St John the Baptist. It shows the gruesome moment when the princess Salome had asked King Herod for the head of St John as a reward for her dancing, and got it. We look into the royal banqueting hall, and beyond it to the musicians' gallery and a sequence of rooms and stairs behind. The executioner has just entered and knelt down before the king carrying the head of the saint on a charger. The king shrinks back and raises his hands in horror, children cry and run away; Salome's mother, who instigated the crime, is seen talking to the king, trying to explain the deed. There is a great void around her as the guests recoil. One of them covers his eyes with his hand, others crowd round Salome, who seems just to have stopped in her dance. One need not explain at length what features were new in such a work of Donatello's. They all were. To people accustomed to the clear and graceful narratives of Gothic art, Donatello's way of telling a story must have come as a shock. Here there was no desire to form a neat and pleasing pattern, but rather to produce the effect of sudden chaos. Like Masaccio's figures, Donatello's are harsh and angular in their movements. Their gestures are violent, and there is no attempt to mitigate the horror of the story. To his contemporaries, the scene must have looked almost uncannily alive.

The new art of perspective further increases the illusion of reality. Donatello must have begun by asking himself: 'What must it have been like when the head of the saint was brought into the hall?' He did his best to represent a classical palace, such as the one in which the event might have taken place, and he chose Roman types for the figures in the background, figure 153. We can see clearly, in fact, that by this time Donatello, like his friend Brunelleschi, had begun a systematic study of Roman remains to help him bring about the rebirth of art. It is quite wrong, however, to imagine that this study of Greek and Roman art *caused* the rebirth or 'Renaissance'. Almost the opposite is true. The artists round Brunelleschi longed so passionately for a revival of art that they turned to nature, to science and to the remains of antiquity to realize their new aims.

The mastery of science and the knowledge of classical art remained for some time the exclusive possession of the Italian artists of the Renaissance. But the passionate will to create a new art, which should be more faithful to nature than anything that had ever been seen before, also inspired the artists of the same generation in the North.

Just as Donatello's generation in Florence became tired of the subtleties and refinements of the International Gothic style and longed to create more vigorous, austere figures, so a sculptor beyond the Alps strove for an art more lifelike and more forthright than the delicate works of his predecessors. This sculptor was Claus Sluter, who worked from about 1380 to 1405 at Dijon, at that time the capital of the rich and prosperous Duchy of Burgundy. His most famous work is a group of prophets which once formed the base of a large crucifix marking the fountain of a popular place of pilgrimage, figure 154. They are the men whose words were interpreted as the prediction of the Passion. Each of them holds in his hand a large book or scroll, on which these words were inscribed, and seems to be meditating on this coming tragedy. These are no longer the solemn and rigid figures that flanked the porches of Gothic cathedrals, figure 127. They differ from these earlier works just as much as does Donatello's 'St George'. The man with the turban is Daniel, the bare-headed old prophet, Isaiah.

As they stand before us, larger than life, still enlivened by gold
and colour, they look less like statues than like impressive
characters from one of the medieval mystery plays, just about
to recite their parts. But with all this striking illusion of lifelikeness we should not forget the artistic sense with which
Sluter has created these massive figures with the sweep of their
drapery and the dignity of their bearing.

Yet it was not a sculptor who carried out the final conquest of reality in the North. For the artist whose revolutionary
discoveries were felt from the beginning to represent something
entirely new was the painter Jan van Eyck (1390?-1441).
Like Sluter, he was connected with the court of the Dukes of
Burgundy, but he mostly worked in the part of the Netherlands
that is now Belgium. His most famous work is a huge altarpiece
with many scenes in the city of Ghent, figures 155-6. It is said
to have been begun by Jan's elder brother Hubert, of whom
little is known, and was completed by Jan in 1432. Thus it was
painted during the very years that saw the completion of the
great works of Masaccio and Donatello already described.

For all their obvious differences there are a number of
similarities between Masaccio's fresco in Florence, figure 149,
and this altarpiece painted for a church in distant Flanders.
Both show the pious donor and his wife in prayer at the sides,
figure 155, and both centre on a large symbolic image – that
of the Holy Trinity in the fresco, and on the altar the mystic
vision of the Adoration of the Lamb, the lamb, of course
symbolizing Christ, figure 156. The composition is mainly based
on a passage in the Revelations of St John (VII. 9), 'And I
beheld ... a great multitude, which no man could number, of
all nations and kindred and people and tongues [which] stood
before the throne and before the lamb ...', a text that is related
by the Church to the Feast of All Saints, to which there are
further allusions in the painting. Above, we see God the Father,

as majestic as Masaccio's but enthroned in splendour like a
Pope, between the Holy Virgin and St John the Baptist, who first
called Jesus the Lamb of God.

The altar, figure 156, with its many images, could be
shown open, which happened on feast days, when its glowing
colours would be revealed, or shut (on weekdays) when it
presented a more sober appearance, figure 155. Here the artist
represented St John the Baptist and St John the Evangelist as
statues, much as Giotto had represented the figures of
Virtues and Vices in the Arena Chapel, figure 134. Above, we are
shown the familiar scene of the Annunciation, and we need
only look back again at the wonderful panel by Simone
Martini, painted a hundred years earlier, figure 141, to gain a
first impression of van Eyck's wholly novel 'down to earth'
approach to the sacred story.

His most striking demonstration of his new conception
of art, however, he reserved for the inner wings: the figures
of Adam and Eve after the Fall. The Bible tells us that it was
only after having eaten from the Tree of Knowledge that they
'knew they were naked'. Stark naked indeed they look, despite
the fig leaves they hold in their hands. Here there is really
no parallel with the masters of the early Renaissance in Italy
who never quite abandoned the traditions of Greek and Roman
art. We remember that the ancients had 'idealized' the human
figure in such works as the Venus of Milo or the Apollo
Belvedere, figures 64-5. Jan van Eyck would have had none of
this. He must have placed naked models in front of him and
painted them so faithfully that later generations were somewhat shocked by so much honesty. Not that the artist had no
eye for beauty. He clearly also enjoyed evoking the splendours
of Heaven no less than the master of the Wilton Diptych,
figure 143, had done a generation earlier. But look again at the
difference, at the patience and mastery with which he studied

and painted the sheen of the precious brocades worn by the music-making angels and the sparkle of jewellery everywhere. In this respect the Van Eycks did not break as radically with the traditions of the International Style as Masaccio had done. They rather pursued the methods of such artists as the Limbourg brothers and brought them to such a pitch of perfection that they left the ideas of medieval art behind. They, like other Gothic masters of their period, had enjoyed crowding their pictures with charming and delicate details taken from observation. They were proud to show their skill in painting flowers and animals, buildings, gorgeous costumes and jewellery, and to present a delightful feast to the eye. We have seen that they did not concern themselves overmuch with the real appearance of the figures and landscapes, and that their drawing and perspective were therefore not very convincing. One cannot say the same thing of Van Eyck's pictures. His observation of nature is even more patient, his knowledge of details even more exact. The trees and the building in the background show this difference clearly. The trees of the Limbourg brothers, as we remember, were rather schematic and conventional, figure 144. Their landscape looked like a back-cloth or a tapestry rather than actual scenery. All this is quite different in Van Eyck's picture. In the details shown in figure 157, we have real trees and a real landscape leading back to the city and castle on the horizon. The infinite patience with which the grass on the rocks and the flowers growing in the crags are painted bears no comparison with the ornamental undergrowth in the Limbourg miniature. What is true of the landscape is true of the figures. Van Eyck seems to have been so intent on reproducing every minute detail on his picture that we almost seem able to count the hairs of the horses' manes, or on the fur trimmings of the riders' costumes. The white horse in the Limbourg miniature looks a little like a rocking-horse.

Van Eyck's horse is very similar in shape and posture, but it is alive. We can see the light in its eye, and the creases in its skin, and, while the earlier horse looks almost flat, Van Eyck's horse has rounded limbs which are modelled in light and shade.

It may seem petty to look out for all these small details and to praise a great artist for the patience with which he observed and copied nature. It would certainly be wrong to think less highly of the work of the Limbourg brothers or, for that matter, of any other painting, because it lacked this faithful imitation of nature. But if we want to understand the way in which northern art developed we must appreciate this infinite care and patience of Jan van Eyck. The southern artists of his generation, the Florentine masters of Brunelleschi's circle, had developed a method by which nature could be represented in a picture with almost scientific accuracy. They began with the framework of perspective lines, and they built up the human body through their knowledge of anatomy and of the laws of foreshortening. Van Eyck took the opposite way. He achieved the illusion of nature by patiently adding detail upon detail till his whole picture became like a mirror of the visible world. This difference between northern and Italian art remained important for many years. It is a fair guess to say that any work which excels in the representation of the beautiful surface of things, of flowers, jewels or fabric, will be by a northern artist, most probably by an artist from the Netherlands; while a painting with bold outlines, clear perspective and a sure mastery of the beautiful human body, will be Italian.

To carry out his intention of holding up a mirror to reality in all its details, Van Eyck had to improve the technique of painting. He was the inventor of oil-painting. There has been much discussion about the exact meaning and truth of this assertion, but the details matter comparatively little. His was not a discovery like that of perspective, which constituted something entirely new. What he achieved was a new prescription for the preparation of paints before they were put on the panel. Painters at that time did not buy ready-made colours in tubes or boxes. They had to prepare their own pigments, mostly from coloured plants and minerals. These they ground to powder between two stones – or let their apprentice grind them – and, before use, they added some liquid to bind the powder into a kind of paste. There were various methods of doing this, but all through the Middle Ages the main ingredient of the liquid had been made of an egg, which was quite suitable except that it dried rather quickly. The method of painting with this type of colour-preparation was called tempera. It seems that Jan van Eyck was dissatisfied with this formula, because it did not allow him to achieve smooth transitions by letting the colours shade off into each other. If he used oil instead of egg, he could work much more slowly and accurately. He could make glossy colours which could be applied in transparent layers or 'glazes', he could put on the glittering highlights with a pointed brush, and achieve those miracles of accuracy which astonished his contemporaries and soon led to a general acceptance of oil-painting as the most suitable medium.

Van Eyck's art reached perhaps its greatest triumph in the painting of portraits. One of his most famous portraits is figure 158, which represents an Italian merchant, Giovanni Arnolfini, who had come to the Netherlands on business, with his bride Jeanne de Chenany. In its own way it was as new and as revolutionary as Donatello's or Masaccio's work in Italy. A simple corner of the real world had suddenly been fixed on to a panel as if by magic. Here it all was – the carpet and the slippers, the rosary on the wall, the little brush beside the bed, and the fruit on the window-sill. It is as if we could pay a visit to the Arnolfini in their house. The picture probably represents a solemn moment in their lives – their betrothal. The young

woman has just put her right hand into Arnolfini's left and he
is about to put his own right hand into hers as a solemn
token of their union. Probably the painter was asked to record
this important moment as a witness, just as a notary might be
asked to declare that he has been present at a similar solemn
act. This would explain why the master has put his name in a
prominent position on the picture with the Latin words
'Johannes de eyck fuit hic' (Jan van Eyck was here). In the mirror
at the back of the room we see the whole scene reflected from
behind, and there, so it seems, we also see the image of the
painter and witness, figure 159. We do not know whether it was
the Italian merchant or the northern artist who conceived the
idea of making this use of the new kind of painting, which
may be compared to the legal use of a photograph, properly
endorsed by a witness. But whoever it was that originated this
idea, he had certainly been quick to understand the tremendous possibilities which lay in Van Eyck's new way of painting.
For the first time in history the artist became the perfect eye-
witness in the truest sense of the term.

In this attempt to render reality as it appeared to the eye,
Van Eyck, like Masaccio, had to give up the pleasing patterns
and flowing curves of the International Gothic style. To some,
his figures may even look stiff and clumsy compared with the
exquisite grace of such paintings as the Wilton Diptych, figure 143.
But everywhere in Europe artists of that generation, in their
passionate search for truth, defied the older ideas of beauty
and probably shocked many elderly people. One of the most
radical of these innovators was a Swiss painter called Konrad
Witz (1400?-1446?). Figure 161 is from an altarpiece he painted
for Geneva in 1444. It is dedicated to St Peter and represents
the saint's encounter with Christ after the Resurrection as it is
told in the Gospel of St John (Chapter XXI). Some apostles
and their companions had gone to fish in the sea of Tiberias,

but had caught nothing. When the morning came Jesus stood on the shore, but they did not recognize Him. He told them to cast the net on the right side of the ship and it was so full of fish that they were unable to pull it in. At that moment one of them said, 'It is the Lord', and when St Peter heard this, 'he girt his fisher's coat unto him (for he was naked) and did cast himself into the sea. And the other disciples came in a little ship', after which they partook of a meal with Jesus. A medieval painter who was asked to illustrate this miraculous event would probably have been satisfied with a conventional row of wavy lines to mark the sea of Tiberias. But Witz desired to bring home to the burghers of Geneva what it must have looked like when Christ stood by the waters. Thus he painted not just any lake but a lake they all knew, the lake of Geneva with the broad ridge of Mont Salève in the background. It is a real landscape which everyone could see, which exists today, and still looks very much as it does in the painting. It is perhaps the first exact representation, the first 'portrait' of a real view ever attempted. On this real lake, Witz painted real fishermen: not the dignified apostles of older pictures, but uncouth men of the people, busy with their fishing tackle and struggling rather clumsily to keep the boat steady. St Peter looks somewhat helpless in the water, and so, surely, he ought. Only Christ Himself is standing quietly and firmly. His solid figure recalls those in Masaccio's great fresco, *figure 149*. It must have been a moving experience for the worshippers in Geneva when they looked at their new altar for the first time and saw the apostles as men like themselves, fishing on their own lake, with the risen Christ miraculously appearing to them on its familiar shore to give them help and comfort.

13

Tradition
and Innovation: I

The later fifteenth century in Italy

The new discoveries which had been made by the artists of Italy and Flanders at the beginning of the fifteenth century created a stir all over Europe. Painters and patrons alike were fascinated by the idea that art could not only be used to tell the sacred story in a moving way, but might serve to mirror a fragment of the real world. Perhaps the most immediate result of this great revolution in art was that artists everywhere began to experiment and to search for new and startling effects. This spirit of adventure which took hold of art in the fifteenth century marks the real break with the Middle Ages.

There is one effect of this break which we must consider first. Until about 1400, art in different parts of Europe had developed on similar lines. We remember that the style of the Gothic painters and sculptors of that period is known as the International style, *page 161*, because the aims of the leading masters in France and Italy, in Germany and Burgundy, were all very similar. Of course, national differences had existed all through the Middle Ages – we remember the differences between France and Italy during the thirteenth century – but on the whole these were not very important. This applies not to the field of art alone, but also to the world of learning and even to politics. The learned men of the Middle Ages all spoke and wrote Latin and did not much mind whether they taught at the University of Paris, Padua or Oxford.

The noblemen of the period shared the ideas of chivalry; their loyalty to their king or their feudal overlord did not imply that they considered themselves the champions of any partic- ular people or nation. All this had gradually changed towards the end of the Middle Ages, when the cities with their burghers and merchants became increasingly more important than the castles of the barons. The merchants spoke their native tongue and stood together against any foreign competitor or intruder. Each city was proud and jealous of its own position and privileges in trade and industry. In the Middle Ages a good master might travel from building site to building site, he might be recommended from one monastery to another, and few would trouble to ask what his nationality was. But as soon as the cities gained in importance, artists, like all artisans and craftsmen, were organized into guilds. These guilds were in many respects similar to our trade unions. It was their task to watch over the rights and privileges of their members and to ensure a safe market for their produce. To be admitted into the guild the artist had to show that he was able to reach certain standards, that he was, in fact, a master of his craft. He was then allowed to open a workshop, to employ apprentices, and to accept commissions for altar-paintings, portraits, painted chests, banners and coats of arms, or any other work of the kind.

The guilds and corporations were usually wealthy companies who had a say in the government of the city and who not only helped to make it prosperous, but also did their best to make it beautiful. In Florence and elsewhere the guilds, the goldsmiths, the wool-workers, the armourers and others, devoted part of their funds to the foundation of churches, the building of guild halls and the dedication of altars and chapels. In this respect they did much for art. On the other hand they watched anxiously over the interests of their own members, and therefore made it difficult for any foreign artist to get employment or to settle among them. Only the most famous of artists sometimes managed to break down this resistance and to travel as freely as had been possible at the period when the great cathedrals were being built.

All this has a bearing on the history of art, because, thanks to the growth of the cities, the International style was perhaps the last international style Europe has seen – at least until the twentieth century. In the fifteenth century art broke up into a number of different 'schools' – nearly every city or small town in Italy, Flanders and Germany had its own 'school of painting'. 'School' is rather a misleading word. In those days there were no art schools where young students attended classes. If a boy decided that he would like to become a painter, his father apprenticed him at an early age to one of the leading masters of the town. He usually lived in, ran errands for the master's family, and had to make himself useful in every possible way. One of his first tasks might be to grind the colours, or to assist in the preparation of the wooden panels or the canvas which the master wanted to use. Gradually he might be given some minor piece of work like the painting of a flagstaff. Then, one day when the master was busy, he might ask the apprentice to help with the completion of some unimportant or inconspicuous part of a major work – to paint the background which the master had traced out on the canvas, to finish the costumes of the bystanders in a scene. If he showed talent and knew how to imitate his master's manner to perfection, the youth would gradually be given more important things to do – perhaps paint a whole picture from the master's sketch and under his supervision. These, then, were the 'schools of painting' of the fifteenth century. They were indeed excellent schools and there are many painters nowadays who wish they had received so thorough a training. The manner in which the masters of a town handed down their skill and experience to the young generation also explains why the 'school of painting' in these towns developed such a clear individuality of its own. One can recognize whether a fifteenth-century picture comes from Florence or Siena, Dijon or Bruges, Cologne or Vienna.

To gain a vantage point from which we can survey this immense variety of masters, 'schools' and experiments, we had best return to Florence, where the great revolution in art had begun. It is fascinating to watch how the generation which

followed Brunelleschi, Donatello and Masaccio tried to make
use of their discoveries and apply them to all the tasks with
which they were confronted. That was not always easy.
The main tasks which the patrons commissioned had, after all,
remained fundamentally unchanged since the earlier period.
The new and revolutionary methods sometimes seemed to
clash with the traditional commissions. Take the case of architecture: Brunelleschi's idea had been to introduce the forms of
classical buildings, the columns, pediments and cornices
which he had copied from Roman ruins. He had used these
forms in his churches. His successors were eager to emulate
him in this. Figure 162 shows a church planned by the
Florentine architect Leon Battista Alberti (1404-72), who
conceived its façade as a gigantic triumphal arch in the
Roman manner, figure 74. But how was this new programme
to be applied to an ordinary dwelling-house in a city street?
Traditional houses and palaces could not be built in
the manner of temples. No private houses had survived from
Roman times, and even if they had, needs and customs had
changed so much that they might have offered little guidance.
The problem, then, was to find a compromise between the
traditional house, with walls and windows, and the classical
forms which Brunelleschi had taught the architects to use.
It was again Alberti who found the solution that remained
influential up to our own days. When he built a palace for
the rich Florentine merchant family of Rucellai, figure 163, he
designed an ordinary three-storeyed building. There is little
similarity between this façade and any classical ruin. And yet
Alberti stuck to Brunelleschi's programme and used classical
forms for the decoration of the façade. Instead of building
columns or half-columns, he covered the house with a network
of flat pilasters and entablatures which suggested a classical
order without changing the structure of the building. It is easy

to see where Alberti had learned this principle. We remember
the Roman Colosseum, figure 73, in which various Greek
'orders' were applied to the various storeys. Here, too, the
lowest storey is an adaptation of the Doric order, and here,
too, there are arches between the pilasters. But though Alberti
had thus given the old city palace a modern look by reverting
to Roman forms he did not quite break with Gothic traditions.
We need only compare the palace windows with those on
the façade of Notre-Dame in Paris, figure 125, to discover an
unexpected similarity. Alberti has merely 'translated' a Gothic
design into classical forms by smoothing out the 'barbaric'
pointed arch and using the elements of the classical order in
a traditional context.

This achievement of Alberti is typical. Painters and sculptors in fifteenth-century Florence also often found themselves
in a situation in which they had to adapt the new programme
to an old tradition. The mixture between new and old, between
Gothic traditions and modern forms, is characteristic of many
masters in the middle of the century.

The greatest of these Florentine masters who succeeded
in reconciling the new achievements with the old tradition
was a sculptor of Donatello's generation, Lorenzo Ghiberti
(1378-1455). Figure 164 shows one of his reliefs for the same
font in Siena for which Donatello made the 'Dance of Salome',
figure 152. Of Donatello's work we could say that everything
was new; Ghiberti's looks much less startling at first sight.
We notice that the arrangement of the scene is not so very
different from the one used by the famous brassfounder of
Liège in the twelfth century, figure 118: Christ in the centre,
flanked by St John the Baptist and the ministering angels with
God the Father and the Dove appearing up in Heaven. Even in
the treatment of details Ghiberti's work recalls that of his
medieval forerunners – the loving care with which he arranges

the folds of the drapery may remind us of such fourteenth-century goldsmith's work as the Holy Virgin on figure 139. And yet Ghiberti's relief is in its own way as vigorous and as convincing as Donatello's companion piece. He, too, has learned to characterize each figure and to make us understand the part each plays: the beauty and humility of Christ, the Lamb of God; the solemn and energetic gesture of St John, the emaciated prophet from the wilderness; and the heavenly host of angels who silently look at each other in joy and wonder. And while Donatello's new dramatic way of representing the sacred scene somewhat upset the clear arrangement which had been the pride of earlier days, Ghiberti took care to remain lucid and restrained. He does not give us the idea of real space at which Donatello was aiming. He prefers to give us only a hint of depth and to let his principal figures stand out clearly against a neutral background.

Just as Ghiberti remained faithful to some of the ideas of Gothic art, without refusing to make use of the new discoveries of his century, the great painter Fra Angelico (brother Angelico) of Fiesole near Florence (1387-1455) applied the new methods of Masaccio mainly in order to express the traditional ideas of religious art. Fra Angelico was a friar of the Dominican order, and the frescoes he painted in his Florentine monastery of San Marco round about 1440 are among his most beautiful works. He painted a sacred scene in each monk's cell and at the end of every corridor, and as one walks from one to the other in the stillness of the old building one feels something of the spirit in which these works were conceived. Figure 165 shows a picture of the Annunciation which he painted in one of the cells. We see at once that the art of perspective presented no difficulty to him. The cloister where the Virgin kneels is represented as convincingly as the vault in Masaccio's famous fresco, figure 149. Yet it was clearly not Fra Angelico's main intention to 'break a hole into the wall'. Like Simone Martini in the fourteenth century, figure 141, he only wanted to represent the sacred story in all its beauty and simplicity. There is hardly any movement in Fra Angelico's painting and hardly any suggestion of real solid bodies. But I think it is all the more moving because of its humility, which is that of a great artist who deliberately renounced any display of modernity despite his profound understanding of the problems which Brunelleschi and Masaccio had introduced into art.

We can study the fascination of these problems and also their difficulty in the work of another Florentine, the painter Paolo Uccello (1397 - 1475), among whose best-preserved works is the battle scene in the National Gallery, figure 166. The picture was probably intended to be placed above the wainscoting (panelling covering the lower part of the wall) of a room in the Palazzo Medici, the city palace of the most powerful and wealthy of the Florentine merchant families. It represents an episode from Florentine history, still topical when the picture was painted, the rout of San Romano in 1432, when Florentine troops defeated their enemies in one of the many battles between the Italian factions. Superficially the picture may look medieval enough. These knights in armour with their long and heavy lances, riding as if to a tournament, may remind us of a medieval romance of chivalry; nor does the way in which the scene is represented strike us at first as very modern. Both horses and men look a little wooden, almost like toys, and the whole gay picture seems very remote from the reality of war. But if we ask ourselves why it is that these horses look somewhat like rocking-horses and the whole scene reminds us a little of a puppet-show, we shall make a curious discovery. It is precisely because the painter was so fascinated by the new possibilities of his art that he did everything to make his figures stand out in space as if they were carved and not painted.

It was said of Uccello that the discovery of perspective had so impressed him that he spent nights and days drawing objects in foreshortening, and setting himself ever new problems. His fellow artists used to tell that he was so engrossed in these studies that he would hardly look up when his wife called him to go to bed, and would exclaim: 'What a sweet thing perspective is!' We can see something of this fascination in the painting. Uccello obviously took great pains to represent the various pieces of armour which litter the ground in correct foreshortening. His greatest pride was probably the figure of the fallen warrior lying on the ground, the foreshortened representation of which must have been most difficult, figure 167. No such figure had been painted before and, though it looks rather too small in relation to the other figures, we can imagine what a stir it must have caused. We find traces all over the picture of the interest which Uccello took in perspective and of the spell it exerted over his mind. Even the broken lances lying on the ground are so arranged that they point towards their common 'vanishing point'. It is this neat mathematical arrangement which is partly responsible for the artificial appearance of the stage on which the battle seems to take place. If we turn back from this pageant of chivalry to Van Eyck's picture of knights, figure 157, and the Limbourg miniature, figure 144, with which we compared it, we may see more clearly what Uccello owed to the Gothic tradition, and how he transformed it. Van Eyck, in the north, had changed the forms of the International style by adding more and more details from observation and trying to copy the surfaces of things down to the minutest shade. Uccello rather chose the opposite approach. By means of his beloved art of perspective, he tried to construct a convincing stage on which his figures would appear solid and real. Solid they undoubtedly look, but the effect is a little reminiscent of the stereoscopic pictures which one looks at through a pair of lenses. Uccello had not yet learned how to use the effects of light and shade and air to mellow the harsh outlines of a strictly perspective rendering. But if we stand in front of the actual painting in the National Gallery, we do not feel that anything is amiss, for, despite his preoccupation with applied geometry, Uccello was a real artist.

While painters such as Fra Angelico could make use of the new without changing the spirit of the old, while Uccello in his turn was completely captivated by the problems of the new, less devout and less ambitious artists applied the new methods gaily without worrying overmuch about their difficulty. The public probably liked these masters who gave them the best of both worlds. Thus the commission for painting the walls of the private chapel in the city palace of the Medici went to Benozzo Gozzoli (c.1421-97), a pupil of Fra Angelico, but apparently a man of very different outlook. He covered the walls of the chapel with a picture of the cavalcade of the three Magi and made them travel in truly royal state through a smiling landscape, figure 168. The biblical episode gives him the opportunity of displaying beautiful finery and gorgeous costumes, a fairy world of charm and gaiety. We have seen how this taste for representing the pageantry of noble pastimes developed in Burgundy, figure 144, with which the Medici entertained close trade relations. Gozzoli seems intent upon showing that the new achievements can be used to make these gay pictures of contemporary life even more vivid and enjoyable. We have no reason to quarrel with him for that. The life of the period was indeed so picturesque and colourful that we must be grateful to those minor masters who preserved a record of these delights in their works, and no one who goes to Florence should miss the joy of a visit to this small chapel, in which something of the zest and savour of a festive life seems still to linger.

Meanwhile, other painters in the cities north and south of Florence had absorbed the message of the new art of Donatello and Masaccio, and were perhaps even more eager to profit by it than the Florentines themselves. There was Andrea Mantegna (1431-1506), who worked first in the famous university town of Padua, and then at the court of the lords of Mantua, both in northern Italy. In a Paduan church, quite near the chapel where Giotto had painted his famous frescoes, Mantegna painted a series of wall-paintings illustrating the legend of St James. The church was heavily damaged by bombing during World War II, and most of these wonderful paintings by Mantegna were destroyed. It is a sad loss, because they were surely among the greatest works of art of all time. One of them, figure 169, showed St James being escorted to his place of execution. Like Giotto or Donatello, Mantegna tried to imagine quite clearly what the scene must have looked like in reality, but the standards of what he called reality had become much more exacting since Giotto's day. What had mattered to Giotto was the inner meaning of the story – how men and women would move and behave in a given situation. Mantegna was also interested in the outward circumstances. He knew that St James had lived in the period of the Roman Emperors, and he was anxious to reconstruct the scene just as it might have actually happened. He had made a special study of classical monuments for this purpose. The city gate through which St James has just been led is a Roman triumphal arch, and the soldiers of the escort all wear the dress and armour of Roman legionaries as we see them represented on authentic classical monuments. It is not only in these details of costume and ornament that the painting reminds us of ancient sculpture. The whole scene breathes the

spirit of Roman art in its harsh simplicity and austere grandeur.
The differences, indeed, between the Florentine frescoes of
Benozzo Gozzoli and Mantegna's works which were painted
approximately during the same years could hardly be more
pronounced. In Gozzoli's gay pageantry we recognized a
return to the taste of the International Gothic style. Mantegna,
on the other hand, carries on where Masaccio had left off. His
figures are as statuesque and impressive as Masaccio's. Like
Masaccio, he uses the new art of perspective with eagerness,
but he does not exploit it as Uccello did to show off the new
effect which could be achieved by means of this magic.
Mantegna rather uses perspective to create the stage on which
his figures seem to stand and move like solid, tangible beings.
He distributes them as a skilled theatrical producer might
have done, so as to convey the significance of the moment
and the course of the episode. We can see what is happening:
the procession escorting St James has halted for a moment
because one of the persecutors has repented and has thrown
himself at the feet of the saint, to receive his blessing. The
saint has turned round calmly to bless the man, while the
Roman soldiers stand by and watch, one of them impassively,
the other lifting his hand in an expressive gesture which
seems to convey that he, too, is moved. The round of the arch
frames this scene and separates it from the turmoil of the
watching crowds pushed back by the guards.

While Mantegna was thus applying the new methods of
art in northern Italy, another great painter, Piero della Francesca
(1416?-92), did the same in the region south of Florence, in
the towns of Arezzo and Urbino. Like Gozzoli's and Mantegna's
frescoes, Piero della Francesca's were painted shortly after the
middle of the fifteenth century, that is about a generation after
Masaccio. The episode in figure 170 shows the famous legend
of the dream which made the Emperor Constantine accept the

Christian faith. Before a crucial battle with his rival, he dreamt
that an angel showed him the Cross and said: 'Under this
sign you will be victorious.' Piero's fresco represents the scene
at night in the Emperor's camp before the battle. We look into
the open tent, where the Emperor lies asleep on his camp bed.
His bodyguard sits by his side, while two soldiers are also
keeping guard. This quiet night scene is suddenly illuminated
by a flash of light as an angel rushes down from Heaven
holding the symbol of the Cross in his outstretched hand. As
with Mantegna, we are somewhat reminded of a scene in a
play. There is a stage quite clearly marked, and there is nothing
to divert our attention from the essential action. Like Mantegna,
Piero has taken pains over the dress of his Roman legionaries
and, like him, he has avoided the gay and colourful details
which Gozzoli crowded into his scenes. Piero, too, had mastered
the art of perspective completely, and the way in which he
shows the figure of the angel in foreshortening is so bold as
to be almost confusing, especially in a small reproduction. But
to these geometrical devices suggesting the space of the stage
he has added a new one of equal importance: the treatment
of light. Medieval artists had taken hardly any notice of light.
Their flat figures cast no shadows. Masaccio had also been a
pioneer in this respect – the round and solid figures of his
paintings were forcefully modelled in light and shade, figure 149.
But no one had seen the immense new possibilities of this
means as clearly as Piero della Francesca. In this picture, light
not only helps to model the forms of the figures, but is equal
in importance to perspective in creating the illusion of depth.
The soldier in front stands like a dark silhouette before the
brightly lit opening of the tent. We thus feel the distance which
separates the soldiers from the steps on which the bodyguard
is sitting, whose figure, in turn, stands out in the flash of light
that emanates from the angel. We are made to feel the round-

ness of the tent, and the hollow it encloses, just as much by means of this light as by foreshortening and perspective. But Piero lets light and shade perform an even greater miracle. They help him to create the mysterious atmosphere of the scene in the depth of night when the Emperor had a vision which was to change the course of history. This impressive simplicity and calm make Piero perhaps the greatest heir to Masaccio.

While these and other artists were applying the inventions of the great generation of Florentine masters, artists in Florence became increasingly aware of the new problems that these inventions had created. In the first flush of triumph, they may have thought that the discovery of perspective and the study of nature could solve all their difficulties. But we must not forget that art is altogether different from science. The artist's means, his technical devices, can be developed, but art itself can hardly be said to progress in the way in which science progresses. Each discovery in one direction creates a new difficulty somewhere else. We remember that medieval painters were unaware of the rules of correct draughtsmanship, but that this very shortcoming enabled them to distribute their figures over the picture in any way they liked in order to create the perfect pattern. The twelfth-century illustrated calendar, figure 120, or the thirteenth-century relief of the 'Death of the Virgin', figure 129, are examples of this skill. Even fourteenth-century painters like Simone Martini, figure 141, were still able to arrange their figures so that they formed a lucid design on the ground of gold. As soon as the new concept of making the picture a mirror of reality was adopted, this question of how to arrange the figures was no longer so easy to solve. In reality figures do not group themselves harmoniously, nor do they stand out clearly against a neutral background. In other words, there was a danger that the new power of the artist would ruin his most precious gift of creating a pleasing and satisfying whole. The problem was particularly serious where big altar-paintings and similar tasks confronted the artist. These paintings had to be seen from afar and had to fit into the architectural framework of the whole church. Moreover, they had to present the sacred story to the worshippers in a clear and impressive outline. Figure 171 shows the way in which a Florentine artist of the second half of the fifteenth century, Antonio Pollaiuolo (1432?-98), tried to solve this new problem of making a picture both accurate in draughtsmanship and harmonious in composition. It is one of the first attempts of its kind to solve this question, not by tact and instinct alone, but by the application of definite rules. It may not be an altogether successful attempt, nor is it a very attractive picture, but it clearly shows how deliberately the Florentine artists set about it. The picture represents the martyrdom of St Sebastian, who is tied to a stake while six executioners are grouped around him. This group forms a very regular pattern in the form of a steep triangle. Each executioner on one side is matched by a similar figure on the other side.

The arrangement, in fact, is so clear and symmetrical as to be almost too rigid. The painter was obviously aware of this drawback and tried to introduce some variety. One of the executioners bending down to adjust his crossbow is seen from the front, the corresponding figure from behind, and the same with the shooting figures. In this simple way, the painter has endeavoured to relieve the rigid symmetry of the composition and to introduce a sense of movement and counter-movement very much as in a piece of music. In Pollaiuolo's picture this device is still used rather self-consciously and his composition looks somewhat like an exercise. We can imagine that he used the same model, seen from different sides, for the corresponding figures, and we feel that his pride in his mastery of muscles and movements has almost made him forget the true subject of his picture. Moreover, Pollaiuolo was not wholly successful in what he set out to do. It is true that he applied the new art of perspective to a wonderful vista of the Tuscan landscape in the background, but the main theme and the background do not really blend. There is no path from the hill in the foreground on which the martyrdom is enacted to the scenery behind. One almost wonders whether Pollaiuolo would not have done better to place his composition against something like a neutral or golden background, but one soon realizes that this expedient was barred to him. Such vigorous and lifelike figures would look out of place on a golden background. Once art had chosen the path of vying with nature, there was no turning back. Pollaiuolo's picture shows the kind of problem that artists of the fifteenth century must have discussed in their studios. It was by finding a solution to this problem that Italian art reached its greatest heights a generation later.

Among the Florentine artists of the second half of the fifteenth century who strove for a solution to this question was the painter Sandro Botticelli (1446-1510). One of his most famous pictures represents not a Christian legend but a classical myth – the birth of Venus, figure 172. The classical poets had been known all through the Middle Ages, but only at the time of the Renaissance, when the Italians tried so passionately to recapture the former glory of Rome, did the classical myths become popular among educated laymen. To these men, the mythology of the admired Greeks and Romans represented something more than gay and pretty fairy-tales. They were so convinced of the superior wisdom of the ancients that they believed these classical legends must contain some profound and mysterious truth. The patron who commissioned the Botticelli painting for his country villa was a member of the rich and powerful family of the Medici. Either he himself, or

one of his learned friends, probably explained to the painter
what was known of the way the ancients had represented
Venus rising from the sea. To these scholars the story of her
birth was the symbol of mystery through which the divine
message of beauty came into the world. One can imagine that
the painter set to work reverently to represent this myth in a
worthy manner. The action of the picture is quickly understood.
Venus has emerged from the sea on a shell which is driven to
the shore by flying wind-gods amidst a shower of roses. As she
is about to step on to the land, one of the Hours or Nymphs
receives her with a purple cloak. Botticelli has succeeded where
Pollaiuolo failed. His picture forms, in fact, a perfectly
harmonious pattern. But Pollaiuolo might have said that
Botticelli had done so by sacrificing some of the achievements
he had tried so hard to preserve. Botticelli's figures look less
solid. They are not so correctly drawn as Pollaiuolo's or
Masaccio's. The graceful movements and melodious lines of
his composition recall the Gothic tradition of Ghiberti and
Fra Angelico, perhaps even the art of the fourteenth century –
works such as Simone Martini's 'Annunciation' figure 141, or
the French goldsmith's work, figure 139, in which we
remarked on the gentle sway of the body and the exquisite fall
of the drapery. Botticelli's Venus is so beautiful that we do
not notice the unnatural length of her neck, the steep fall of
her shoulders and the queer way her left arm is hinged to
the body. Or, rather, we should say that these liberties which
Botticelli took with nature in order to achieve a graceful
outline add to the beauty and harmony of the design because
they enhance the impression of an infinitely tender and
delicate being, wafted to our shores as a gift from Heaven.

The rich merchant who commissioned this picture
from Botticelli, Lorenzo di Pierfrancesco de' Medici, was also
the employer of a Florentine who was destined to give his

name to a continent. It was in the service of his firm that
Amerigo Vespucci sailed to the New World. We have reached
the period which later historians selected as the 'official' end
of the Middle Ages. We remember that in Italian art there
were various turning-points that might be described as the
beginning of a new age – the discoveries of Giotto round
about 1300, those of Brunelleschi round about 1400. But even
more important, perhaps, than these revolutions in method
was a gradual change that had come over art in the course of
these two centuries. It is a change that is more easily sensed
than described. A comparison of the medieval book illuminations discussed in the preceding chapters, figure 131 and figure
140, with a Florentine specimen of that art made about 1475,
figure 173, might give an idea of the different spirit in which
the same art can be employed. It is not that the Florentine
master lacked reverence or devotion. But the very powers his
art had gained made it impossible for him to think of it only
as a means of conveying the meaning of the sacred story.
Rather did he want to use this power to turn the page into a
gay display of wealth and luxury. This function of art, to add to
the beauty and graces of life, had never been entirely forgotten.
In the period we call the Italian Renaissance it came
increasingly to the fore.

14

Tradition
and Innovation: II

The fifteenth century in the North

We have seen that the fifteenth century brought a decisive change in the history of art because the discoveries and innovations of Brunelleschi's generation in Florence had lifted Italian art on to a new plane, and had separated it from the development of art in the rest of Europe. The aims of the northern artists of the fifteenth century did not, perhaps, differ so much from those of their Italian fellow artists as did their means and methods. The difference between the North and Italy is most clearly marked in architecture. Brunelleschi had put an end to the Gothic style in Florence by introducing the Renaissance method of using classical motifs for his buildings. It was nearly a century before the artists outside Italy followed his example. All through the fifteenth century they continued developing the Gothic style of the preceding century. But though the forms of these buildings still contained such typical elements of Gothic architecture as the pointed arch or the flying buttress, the taste of the times had greatly changed. We remember that in the fourteenth century architects liked to use graceful lacework and rich ornamentation. We remember the Decorated style, in which the window of Exeter Cathedral was designed, figure 137. In the fifteenth century this taste for complicated tracery and fantastic ornament went even further.

Figure 174, the Palace of Justice in Rouen, is an example of this last phase of French Gothic, sometimes referred to as the Flamboyant style. We see how the designers covered the whole building with an infinite variety of decorations, not, apparently, considering whether they performed any function in the structure. Some of these buildings have a fairy-tale quality of overwhelming wealth and invention; but one feels that in them the designers had exhausted the last possibility of Gothic building, and that a reaction was bound to set in sooner or later. There are, in fact, indications that even without the direct influence of Italy the architects of the North would have evolved a new style of greater simplicity.

It is particularly in England that we can see these tendencies at work in the last phase of the Gothic style which is known as the Perpendicular. This name was invented to convey the character of later fourteenth- and fifteenth-century buildings in England because in their decorations straight lines are more frequent than the curves and arches of earlier 'decorated' tracery. The most famous example of this style is the wonderful chapel of King's College in Cambridge, *figure 175*, which was begun in 1446. The shape of this church is much more simple than those of earlier Gothic interiors – there are no side-aisles, and therefore no pillars and no steep arches. The whole makes the impression of a lofty hall rather than of a medieval church. But while the general structure is thus sober and perhaps more worldly than that of the great cathedrals, the imagination of the Gothic craftsmen is given free rein in the details, particularly in the form of the vault ('fan-vault'), with its fantastic lace-work of curves and lines recalling the miracles of Celtic and Northumbrian manuscripts, *figure 103*.

The development of painting and sculpture in the countries outside Italy runs to a certain extent parallel with this development of architecture. In other words, while the Renaissance had been victorious in Italy along the whole front, the North in the fifteenth century remained still faithful to the Gothic tradition. Despite the great innovations of the Van Eyck brothers, the practice of art continued to be a matter of custom and usage rather than of science. The mathematical rules of perspective, the secrets of scientific anatomy, the study of Roman monuments did not yet trouble the peace of mind of the northern masters. For this reason we may say that they were still 'medieval artists', while their colleagues across the Alps already belonged to the 'modern era'. But the problems facing the artists on both sides of the Alps were nevertheless strikingly similar. Jan van Eyck had taught them how to make the picture a mirror of nature by carefully adding detail upon detail until the whole frame was filled with painstaking observation, figures 157-8. But just as Fra Angelico and Benozzo Gozzoli in the south, figures 165, 168, had used Masaccio's innovations in the spirit of the fourteenth century, so there were artists in the North who applied Van Eyck's discoveries to more traditional themes. The German painter Stefan Lochner (1410?-51), for instance, who worked in Cologne in the middle of the fifteenth century, was somewhat like a northern Fra Angelico. His charming picture of the Virgin in a rose-bower, figure 176, surrounded by little angels who make music, scatter flowers, or offer fruit to the Christ Child, shows that the master was aware of the new methods of Van Eyck, just as Fra Angelico was aware of the discoveries of Masaccio. And yet his picture is nearer in spirit to the Gothic Wilton Diptych, figure 143, than it is to Van Eyck. It may be interesting to look back at the earlier example and compare the two works. We see at once that the later master had learned one thing which had presented difficulties to the earlier painter. Lochner could suggest the space in which the Virgin is enthroned on the grass bank. Compared with his figures, those of the Wilton Diptych look a little flat. Lochner's Holy Virgin still sits enthroned before a background of gold, but in front of it there is a real stage. He has even added two charming angels holding back the curtain, which seems to hang from the frame. It was paintings like those by Lochner and Fra Angelico which first captured the imagination of the romantic critics of the nineteenth century, men such as Ruskin and the painters of the Pre-Raphaelite Brotherhood. They saw in them all the charm of simple devotion and a childlike heart. In a way they were right. These works are perhaps so fascinating because for us, used to real space in pictures, and more or less correct drawing, they are easier to understand than the works of the earlier medieval masters, whose spirit they nevertheless preserved.

Other painters in the North correspond rather to Benozzo Gozzoli, whose frescoes in the Palazzo Medici in Florence reflect the gay pageantry of the elegant world, in the traditional spirit of the International style. This applies particularly to the painters who designed tapestries, and to those who decorated the pages of precious manuscripts. The page illustrated in figure 177 was painted about the middle of the fifteenth century, as were Gozzoli's frescoes. In the background is the traditional scene showing the author handing the finished book to his noble patron who had ordered it. But the painter found this theme rather dull by itself. He therefore gave it the setting of an entrance hall, and showed us the happenings all around. Behind the city gate there is a party apparently making ready for the chase – at least there is one rather dandyish figure carrying a falcon on his fist, while others stand around like pompous burghers. We see the stalls and booths inside and in front of the city gate, with the merchants displaying their goods and the buyers inspecting them. It is a lifelike picture of a medieval city of the time. Nothing like it could have been done a hundred years earlier, or, indeed, at any earlier time. We have to go back to ancient Egyptian art to find pictures which portray the daily life of the people as faithfully as this; and even the Egyptians did not look at their own world with so much accuracy and humour. It is the spirit of the drollery of which we saw an example in 'Queen Mary's Psalter', figure 140, that came to fruition in these charming portrayals of daily life. Northern art, which was less preoccupied with attaining ideal harmony and beauty than

Italian art, was to favour this type of representation to an increasing extent.

Nothing, however, would be more wrong than to imagine that these two 'schools' developed in watertight compartments. Of the leading French artist of the period, Jean Fouquet (1420?-80?), we know, in fact, that he visited Italy in his youth. He went to Rome, where he painted the Pope in 1447. Figure 178 shows a donor's portrait which he probably made a few years after his return. As in the Wilton Diptych, figure 143, the saint protects the kneeling and praying figure of the donor. As the donor's name was Estienne (which is old French for Stephen), the saint by his side is his patron, St Stephen, who, as the first deacon of the Church, wears a deacon's robe. He carries a book and on it is a large sharp stone, for, according to the Bible, St Stephen was stoned. If we look back to the Wilton Diptych, we see once more what strides had been made by art in the representation of nature in half a century. The saints and donor of the Wilton Diptych look as though they were cut out of paper and placed upon the picture; those of Jean Fouquet look as if they had been modelled. In the earlier picture there is no trace of light and shade; Fouquet uses light almost as Piero della Francesca did, figure 170. The way in which these calm and statuesque figures stand as in real space shows that Fouquet had been deeply impressed by what he had seen in Italy. And yet, his manner of painting is different from that of the Italians. The interest he takes in the texture and surface of things – the fur, the stone, the cloth and the marble – shows that his art remains indebted to the northern tradition of Jan van Eyck.

Another great northern artist who went to Rome (for a pilgrimage in 1450) was Rogier van der Weyden (1400?-64). Very little is known about this master except that he enjoyed great fame and lived in the southern Netherlands, where

Jan van Eyck had also worked. *Figure 179* shows a large altar-painting which represents the Descent from the Cross.
We see that Rogier, like Van Eyck, could faithfully reproduce every detail, every hair and every stitch. Nevertheless, his picture does not represent a real scene. He has placed his figures on a kind of shallow stage against a neutral background. Remembering Pollaiuolo's problems, *pages 196-7, figure 171*, we can appreciate the wisdom of Rogier's decision. He, too, had to make a large altar-painting to be seen from afar, and had to display the sacred theme to the faithful in the church. It had to be clear in outline, and satisfying as a pattern. Rogier's picture fulfils these requirements without looking forced and self-conscious as does Pollaiuolo's. The body of Christ, which is turned full face towards the beholder, forms the centre of the composition. The weeping women frame it on both sides. St John, bending forward, like St Mary Magdalene on the other side, tries in vain to support the fainting Virgin, whose movement corresponds to that of Christ's descending body. The calm bearing of the old men forms an effective foil to the expressive gestures of the principal actors. For they really seem like actors in a mystery play or in a *tableau vivant* grouped or posed by an inspired producer who had studied the great works of the medieval past and wanted to imitate them in his own medium. In this way, by translating the main ideas of Gothic art into the new, lifelike style, Rogier did a great service to northern art. He saved much of the tradition of lucid design that might otherwise have been lost under the impact of Jan van Eyck's discoveries. Henceforward northern artists tried, each in his own way, to reconcile the new demands on art with its old religious purpose.

We can study these efforts in a work of one of the greatest Flemish painters of the second half of the fifteenth century, Hugo van der Goes (died 1482). He is one of the few northern masters of this early period of whom we know some personal details. We hear that he spent the last years of his life in voluntary retirement in a monastery and that he was haunted by feelings of guilt and attacks of melancholy. There is indeed something tense and serious in his art that makes it very different from the placid moods of Jan van Eyck. Figure 180 shows his painting of the 'Death of the Virgin'. What strikes us first is the admirable way in which the artist has represented the varying reactions of the twelve apostles to the event they are witnessing – the range of expression from quiet brooding to passionate sympathy and almost indiscreet gaping. We can best gain a measure of Van der Goes's achievement if we turn back to the illustration of the same scene over the porch of Strasbourg Cathedral, figure 129. Compared to the painter's many types, the apostles of the sculpture look very much alike. And how easy it was for the earlier artist to arrange his figures in a clear design! He did not have to wrestle with foreshortening and the illusion of space as was expected of Van der Goes. We can feel the efforts of the painter to conjure up a real scene before our eyes and yet to leave no part of the panel's surface empty and meaningless. The two apostles in the foreground and the apparition over the bed show most clearly how he strove to spread his figures out and display them before us. But this visible strain which makes the movements look somewhat contorted also adds to the feeling of tense excitement that surrounds the calm figure of the dying Virgin who, alone in the crowded room, is granted the vision of her Son, who is opening His arms to receive her.

For the sculptors and woodcarvers the survival of Gothic tradition in the new form which Rogier had given to it proved of particular importance. Figure 182 shows a carved altar which was commissioned for the Polish city of Cracow in 1477

(two years after Pollaiuolo's altar-painting, figure 171). Its
master was Veit Stoss, who lived for the greater part of his life
in Nuremberg in Germany and died there at a very advanced
age in 1533. Even on the small illustration we can see the value
of a lucid design. For like the members of the congregation
who stood far away we are able to read off the meaning of the
main scenes without difficulty. The shrine in the centre shows
again the death of the Virgin Mary, surrounded by the twelve
apostles, though this time she is not represented lying on
a bed but kneeling in prayer. Farther up we see her soul being
received into a radiant Heaven by Christ, and at the top we
watch her being crowned by God the Father and His Son. Both
wings of the altar represent important moments in the life of
the Virgin, which (together with her crowning) are known as
the Seven Joys of Mary. The cycle begins in the left top square
with the Annunciation; it continues farther down with the
Nativity and the Adoration of the Magi. In the right-hand wing
we find the remaining three joyous moments after so much
sorrow – the Resurrection of Christ, His Ascension and the
Outpouring of the Holy Ghost at Whitsun. All these stories
the faithful could contemplate when they were assembled in
church on a feast day of the Virgin (the other sides of the
wings were adapted to other feast days). But only if they could
approach close to the shrine could they admire the truthfulness
and expressiveness of Veit Stoss's art in the wonderful heads
and hands of his apostles, figure 183.

In the middle of the fifteenth century a decisive technical
invention had been made in Germany, which had a tremendous effect on the future development of art, and not of art
alone – the invention of printing. The printing of pictures had
preceded the printing of books by several decades. Small leaflets,
with images of saints and the text of prayers, had been printed
for distribution among pilgrims and for private devotion.

The method of printing these images was simple enough. It was the same as was later developed for the printing of letters. You took a wood-block and cut away with a knife everything that should *not* appear on the print. In other words, everything that was to look white in the final product was to be cut hollow and everything that was to look black was left standing in narrow ridges. The result looked like any rubber stamp we use today, and the principle of printing it on to paper was practically the same: you covered the surface with printer's ink made of oil and soot and pressed it on to the leaflet. You could make a good many impressions from one block before it wore out. This simple technique of printing pictures is called woodcut. It was a very cheap method and soon became popular. Several wood-blocks together could be used for a little series of pictures printed together as a book; these books printed from whole blocks are called block-books. Woodcuts and block-books were soon on sale at popular fairs; playing-cards were made in this way; there were humorous pictures and prints for devotional use. Figure 184 shows a page from one of these early block-books, which was used by the Church as a picture-sermon. Its purpose was to remind the faithful of the hour of death and to teach them – as the title says – 'The art of dying well'. The woodcut shows the pious man on his death-bed with the monk by his side putting a lighted candle into his hand. An angel is receiving his soul, which has come out of his mouth in the shape of a little praying figure. In the background we see Christ and His saints, towards whom the dying man should turn his mind. In the foreground we see a host of devils in the most ugly and fantastic shapes, and the inscriptions which come out of their mouths tell us what they say: 'I am raging', 'We are disgraced', 'I am dumbfounded', 'This is no comfort', 'We have lost his soul'. Their grotesque antics are in vain. The man who possesses the art of dying well need not fear the powers of Hell.

When Gutenberg made his great invention of using
movable letters held together by a frame, instead of whole
wood-blocks, such block-books became obsolete. But methods
were soon found of combining a printed text with a wood-
block for illustration, and many books of the latter half of the
fifteenth century were illustrated with woodcuts.

For all its usefulness, however, the woodcut was a rather
crude way of printing pictures. It is true that this crudeness
itself is sometimes effective. The quality of these popular prints
of the late Middle Ages reminds one sometimes of our best
posters – they are simple in outline and economical in their
means. But the great artists of the period had rather different
ambitions. They wanted to show their mastery of detail
and their powers of observation, and for this the woodcut was
not suitable. These masters, therefore, chose another medium,
which gave more subtle effects. Instead of wood, they used
copper. The principle of the copper-plate engraving is a little
different from that of the woodcut. In the woodcut you
cut away everything except the lines you want to show. In the
engraving you take a special tool, called a burin, and press
it into the copper plate. The line which you thus engrave into
the surface of the metal will hold any colour or printer's
ink you spread over the surface. What you do, therefore, is to
cover your engraved copper plate with printer's ink and then
wipe the blank metal clean. If then you press the plate very
hard against a piece of paper, the ink which has remained
in the lines cut by the burin is squeezed on to the paper, and
the print is ready. In other words, the copper-engraving is
really a negative of the woodcut. The woodcut is made by
leaving the lines standing, the engraving by cutting them into
the plate. Now, however hard it may be to handle the burin
firmly and to control the depth and strength of your lines, it is
clear that, once you have mastered this craft, you can obtain

much more detail and much more subtle effects from a copper-engraving than you can from a woodcut.

One of the greatest and most famous masters of engraving in the fifteenth century was Martin Schongauer (1453?-91), who lived on the upper Rhine at Colmar, in present-day Alsace. *Figure 185* shows Schongauer's engraving of the Holy Night. The scene is interpreted in the spirit of the great masters of the Netherlands. Like them, Schongauer was anxious to convey every little homely detail of the scene, and to make us feel the very texture and surfaces of the objects he represents. That he should have succeeded in doing so without the help of brush and colour, and without the medium of oil, borders on the miraculous. One can look at his engravings through a magnifying glass and study the way he characterizes the broken stones and bricks, the flowers in the crags, the ivy creeping along the vault, the fur of the animals and the hair and beards of the shepherds. But it is not only his patience and craftsmanship we must admire. We can enjoy his tale of Christmas without any knowledge of the difficulties of working with the burin. There is the Virgin kneeling in the ruined chapel which is used as a stable. She kneels in adoration of the Child, whom she has carefully placed on the corner of her cloak, and St Joseph, lantern in hand, looks at her with a worried and fatherly expression. The ox and the ass are worshipping with her. The humble shepherds are just about to cross the threshold; one of them, in the background, receives the message from the angel. Up in the right-hand corner we have a glimpse of the heavenly chorus singing 'Peace on Earth'. In themselves, these motifs are all deeply rooted in the tradition of Christian art, but the way in which they are combined and distributed over the page was Schongauer's own. The problems of composition for the printed page and for the altar-picture are in some respects similar. In both cases, the suggestion of space and the faithful imitation of reality must not be allowed to destroy the balance of the composition. It is only if we think of this problem that we can fully appreciate Schongauer's achievement. We now understand why he has chosen a ruin as setting – it allowed him to frame the scene solidly with the pieces of broken masonry that form the opening through which we look. It enabled him to place a black foil behind the principal figures and to leave no part of the engraving empty or without interest. We can see how carefully he planned his composition if we lay two diagonals across the page: they meet at the head of the Virgin, which is the true centre of the print.

The art of the woodcut and of engraving soon spread all over Europe. There are engravings in the manner of Mantegna and Botticelli in Italy, and others from the Netherlands and France. These prints became yet another means through which the artists of Europe learned of each other's ideas. At that time it was not yet considered dishonourable to take over an idea or a composition from another artist, and many of the humbler masters made use of engravings as pattern books from which they borrowed. Just as the invention of printing hastened the exchange of ideas without which the Reformation might never have come about, so the printing of images ensured the triumph of the art of the Italian Renaissance in the rest of Europe. It was one of the forces which put an end to the medieval art of the North, and brought about a crisis in the art of these countries which only the greatest masters could overcome.

15

Harmony Attained

Tuscany and Rome, early sixteenth century

We left Italian art at the time of Botticelli, that is, at the end of the fifteenth century, which the Italians by an awkward trick of language called the *Quattrocento*, that is to say, the 'four hundreds'. The beginning of the sixteenth century, the *Cinquecento*, is the most famous period of Italian art, one of the greatest periods of all time. This was the time of Leonardo da Vinci and Michelangelo, of Raphael and Titian, of Correggio and Giorgione, of Dürer and Holbein in the North, and of many other famous masters. One may well ask why it was that all these great masters were born in the same period, but such questions are more easily asked than answered. One cannot explain the existence of genius. It is better to enjoy it. What we have to say, therefore, can never be a full explanation of the great period which is called the High Renaissance, but we can try to see what the conditions were which made this sudden efflorescence of genius possible.

We have seen the beginning of these conditions far back in the period of Giotto. His fame was so great that the Commune of Florence was proud of him and anxious to have the bell-tower of their cathedral designed by that widely renowned master. This pride of the cities, which vied with each other in securing the services of the greatest artists to beautify their buildings and to create works of lasting fame, was a great incentive to the masters to outdo each other – an incentive which did not exist to the same extent in the feudal countries of the North, where cities had much less independence and local pride. Then came the period of the great discoveries, when Italian artists turned to mathematics to study the laws of perspective, and to anatomy to study the build of the human body. Through these discoveries, the artist's horizon widened. He was no longer a craftsman among craftsmen, ready to carry out commissions for shoes, or cupboards, or paintings, as the case might be. He was a master in his own right, who could not achieve fame and glory without exploring the mysteries of nature and probing into the secret laws of the universe. It was natural that the leading artists who had these ambitions felt aggrieved by their social status. This was still the same as it had been at the time of ancient Greece, when snobs might have accepted a poet who worked with his brain, but never an artist who worked with his hands. Here was another challenge for the artists to meet, another spur which urged them on towards yet greater achievements that would compel the surrounding world to accept them, not only as respectable heads of prosperous workshops, but as men of unique and precious gifts. It was a difficult struggle, which was not immediately successful. Social snobbery and prejudice are strong forces, and there were many who would gladly have invited to their tables a scholar who spoke Latin, and knew the right turn of phrase for every occasion, but would have hesitated to extend a similar privilege to a painter or a sculptor. It was again the love of fame on the part of the patrons which helped the artists to break down such prejudices. There were many small courts in Italy which were badly in need of honour and prestige. To erect magnificent buildings, to commission splendid tombs, to order great cycles of frescoes, or to dedicate a painting for the high altar of a famous church, was considered a sure way of perpetuating one's name and securing a worthy monument to one's earthly existence. As there were many centres competing for the services of the most renowned masters, the masters in turn could dictate their terms. In earlier times it was the prince who bestowed his favours on the artist. Now it almost came to pass that the roles were reversed, and that the artist granted a favour to a rich prince or potentate by accepting a commission from him. Thus it came about that the artists could frequently choose the kind of commission which they liked, and that they no longer needed to accommodate their

works to the whims and fancies of their employers. Whether
or not this new power was an unmixed blessing for art in the
long run is difficult to decide. But at first, at any rate, it had
the effect of a liberation which released a tremendous amount
of pent-up energy. At last, the artist was free.

In no sphere was the effect of this change so marked
as in architecture. Since the time of Brunelleschi, *page 168*, the
architect had to have some of the knowledge of a classical
scholar. He had to know the rules of the ancient 'orders', of
the right proportions and measurements of the Doric, Ionic
and Corinthian columns and entablatures. He had to measure
ancient ruins, and pore over the manuscripts of classical
writers like Vitruvius, who had codified the conventions of
the Greek and Roman architects, and whose works contained
many difficult and obscure passages, which challenged the
ingenuity of Renaissance scholars. In no other field was the
conflict between the requirements of the patrons and the
ideals of the artists more apparent than in this field of architecture. What these learned masters really longed to do was to
build temples and triumphal arches – what they were asked
to do was to build city palaces and churches. We have seen
how a compromise was reached in this fundamental conflict
by masters such as Alberti, *page 187, figure 163*, who wedded
the ancient 'orders' to the modern city palace. But the true
aspiration of the Renaissance architect was still to design a
building irrespective of its use; simply for the beauty of its
proportions, the spaciousness of its interior and the imposing
grandeur of its ensemble. They craved for a perfect symmetry
and regularity such as they could not achieve while concentrating on the practical requirements of an ordinary building.
It was a memorable moment when one of them found a
mighty patron willing to sacrifice tradition and expediency for
the sake of the fame he would acquire by erecting a stately

structure that would outshine the seven wonders of the world. Only in this way can we understand the decision of Pope Julius II in 1506 to pull down the venerable Basilica of St Peter, which stood at the place where, according to tradition, St Peter lay buried, and to have it built anew in a manner which defied the age-old traditions of church-building and the usages of divine service. The man to whom he entrusted this task was Donato Bramante (1444-1514), an ardent champion of the new style. One of the few of his buildings which have survived intact shows how far Bramante had gone in absorbing the ideas and standards of classical architecture without becoming a slavish imitator, figure 187. It is a chapel, or 'Tempietto' (little temple) as he called it, which should have been surrounded by a cloister in the same style. It takes the form of a small pavilion, a round building on steps, crowned by a cupola and encircled by a colonnade of the Doric order. The balustrade on top of the cornice adds a light and graceful touch to the whole building, and the small structure of the actual chapel and the decorative colonnade are held in a harmony as perfect as that in any temple of classical antiquity.

To this master, then, the Pope had given the task of designing the new church of St Peter, and it was understood that this should become a true marvel of Christendom. Bramante was determined to disregard the Western tradition of a thousand years, according to which a church of this kind should be an oblong hall with the worshippers looking eastwards towards the main altar, where Mass is read.

In his craving for that regularity and harmony that alone could be worthy of the place, he designed a square church with chapels symmetrically arranged round a gigantic cross-shaped hall. This hall was to be crowned by a huge dome resting on colossal arches, which we know from the foundation medal, figure 186. Bramante hoped, it was said, to combine the effect of the largest ancient building, the Colosseum, figure 73, whose towering ruins still impressed the visitor to Rome, with that of the Pantheon, figure 75. For one brief moment, admiration for the art of the ancients and ambition to create something unheard of overruled considerations of expediency and time-honoured traditions. But Bramante's plan for St Peter's was not destined to be carried out. The enormous building swallowed up so much money that, in trying to raise sufficient funds, the Pope precipitated the crisis which led to the Reformation. It was the practice of selling indulgences against contributions for the building of the new church that led Luther in Germany to his first public protest. Even within the Catholic Church, opposition to Bramante's plan increased, and over the years the idea of an all-round symmetrical church was abandoned. St Peter's, as we know it today, has little in common with the original plan, except its gigantic dimensions.

The spirit of bold enterprise which made Bramante's plan for St Peter's possible is characteristic of the period of the High Renaissance, the period around 1500 which produced so many of the world's greatest artists. To these men nothing seemed impossible, and that may be the reason why they did sometimes achieve the apparently impossible. Once more, it was Florence which gave birth to some of the leading minds of that great epoch. Since the days of Giotto round about 1300, and of Masaccio in the early 1400s, Florentine artists had cultivated their tradition with special pride, and their excellence was recognized by all people of taste. We shall see that nearly all the greatest artists grew out of such a firmly established tradition, and that is why we should not forget the humbler masters in whose workshops they learned the elements of their craft.

Leonardo da Vinci (1452-1519), the oldest of these famous masters, was born in a Tuscan village. He was apprenticed to a leading Florentine workshop, that of the painter and sculptor Andrea del Verrocchio (1435-88). Verrocchio's fame was very great, so great indeed that the city of Venice commissioned from him the monument to Bartolommeo Colleoni, one of their generals, to whom they owed gratitude for a number of charities he had founded rather than for any particular deed of military prowess. The equestrian statue which Verrocchio made, figures 188-9, shows that he was a worthy heir to the tradition of Donatello. He minutely studied the anatomy of the horse, and we see how clearly he observed the muscles of Colleoni's face and neck. But most admirable of all is the posture of the horseman, who seems to be riding ahead of his troops with an expression of bold defiance. Later times have made us so familiar with these riders of bronze that have come to people our towns and cities, representing more or less worthy emperors, kings, princes and generals, that it may take us some time to realize the greatness and simplicity of Verrocchio's work – in the clear outline which his group presents from nearly all aspects, and the concentrated energy which seems to animate the man in armour and his mount.

In a workshop capable of producing such masterpieces, the young Leonardo could certainly learn many things. He would be introduced into the technical secrets of foundry-work and other metalwork, he would learn to prepare pictures and statues carefully by making studies from the nude and from draped models. He would learn to study plants and curious animals for inclusion in his pictures, and he would receive a thorough grounding in the optics of perspective and in the use of colours. In the case of any other gifted boy, this training would have been sufficient to make a respectable artist, and many good painters and sculptors did in fact emerge from Verrocchio's prosperous workshop. But Leonardo was more than a gifted boy. He was a genius whose powerful mind will always remain an object of wonder and admiration to ordinary mortals. We know something of the range and productivity of Leonardo's mind because his pupils and admirers carefully preserved for us his sketches and notebooks, thousands of pages covered with writings and drawings, with excerpts from books Leonardo read, and drafts for books he intended to write. The more one reads of these papers, the less can one understand how one human being could have excelled in all these different fields of research and made important contributions to nearly all of them. Perhaps one of the reasons is that Leonardo was a Florentine artist and not a trained scholar. He thought that the artist's business was to explore the visible world just as his predecessors had done, only more thoroughly and with greater intensity and accuracy. He was not interested in the bookish knowledge of the scholars. Like Shakespeare, he probably had 'little Latin and less Greek'. At a time when the learned men at the universities relied on the authority of the admired ancient writers, Leonardo, the painter, would never accept what he read without checking it with his own eyes. Whenever he came across a problem, he did not rely on authorities but tried an experiment to solve it. There was nothing in nature which did not arouse his curiosity and challenge his ingenuity. He explored the secrets of the human body by dissecting more than thirty corpses, figure 190. He was one of the first to probe into the mysteries of the growth of the child in the womb; he investigated the laws of waves and currents; he spent years in observing and analysing the flight of insects and birds, which was to help him to devise a flying machine which he was sure would one day become a reality. The forms of rocks and clouds, the effect of the atmosphere on the colour of distant objects, the laws governing the growth of trees and plants, the harmony of sounds, all these were the objects of his ceaseless research, which was to be the foundation of his art.

His contemporaries looked upon Leonardo as a strange and rather uncanny being. Princes and generals wanted to use this astonishing wizard as a military engineer for the building of fortifications and canals, of novel weapons and devices. In time of peace, he would entertain them with mechanical toys of his own invention, and with the designing of new effects for stage performances and pageantries. He was admired as a great artist, and sought after as a splendid musician, but, for all that, few people can have had an inkling of the importance of his ideas or the extent of his knowledge. The reason is that Leonardo never published his writings, and that very few can even have known of their existence. He was left-handed, and had taken to writing from right to left so that his notes can only be read in a mirror. It is possible that he was afraid of divulging his discoveries for fear that his opinions would be found heretical. Thus we find in his writings the five words 'The sun does not move', which shows that Leonardo anticipated the theories of Copernicus which were later to bring Galileo into trouble. But it is also possible that he undertook his researches and experiments simply because of his insatiable curiosity, and that, once he had solved a problem for himself, he was apt to lose interest because there were so many other mysteries still to be explored.

Most of all, it is likely that Leonardo himself had no ambition to be considered a scientist. All this exploration of nature was to him first and foremost a means of gaining knowledge of the visible world, such as he would need for his art. He thought that by placing it on scientific foundations he could transform his beloved art of painting from a humble craft into an honoured and gentlemanly pursuit. To us, this preoccupation with the social rank of artists may be difficult to understand, but we have seen what importance it had for the men of the period. Perhaps if we remember Shakespeare's *A Midsummer Night's Dream* and the roles he assigns to Snug the joiner, Bottom the weaver and Snout the tinker, we can understand the background of this struggle. Aristotle had codified the snobbishness of classical antiquity in distinguishing between certain arts that were compatible with a 'liberal education' (the so-called Liberal Arts such as grammar, logic, rhetoric, or geometry) and pursuits that involved working with the hands, which were 'manual' and therefore 'menial', and thus below the dignity of a gentleman. It was the ambition of such men as Leonardo to show that painting was a Liberal Art, and that the manual labour involved in it was no more essential than was the labour of writing in poetry. It is possible that this view often affected Leonardo's relationships with his patrons. Perhaps he did not want to be considered the owner of a shop where anyone could commission a picture. At any rate, we know that Leonardo often failed to carry out his commissions. He would start on a painting and leave it unfinished, despite the urgent requests of the patron. Moreover, he obviously insisted that it was he himself who had to decide when a work of his was considered finished, and he refused to let it go out of his hands unless he was satisfied with it. It is not surprising, therefore, that few of Leonardo's works were ever completed, and that his contemporaries regretted the way in which this outstanding genius seemed to fritter away his time, moving restlessly from Florence to Milan, from Milan to Florence, and to the service of the notorious adventurer Cesare Borgia, then to Rome, and finally to the court of King Francis I in France, where he died in the year 1519, more admired than understood.

By a singular misfortune, the few works which Leonardo did complete in his mature years have come down to us in a very bad state of preservation. Thus when we look at what remains of Leonardo's famous wall-painting of 'The Last Supper', figures 191-2, we must try to imagine how it may have appeared to the monks for whom it was painted. The painting covers one wall of an oblong hall that was used as a refectory by the monks of the monastery of Santa Maria delle Grazie in Milan. One must visualize what it was like when the painting was uncovered, and when, side by side with the long tables of the monks, there appeared the table of Christ and his apostles. Never before had the sacred episode appeared so close and so lifelike. It was as if another hall had been added to theirs, in which the Last Supper had assumed tangible form. How clear the light fell on to the table, and how it added roundness and solidity to the figures. Perhaps the monks were first struck by the truth to nature with which all details were portrayed, the dishes on the tablecloth, and the folds of the draperies. Then, as now, works of art were often judged by laymen according to their degree of lifelikeness. But that can only have been the first reaction. Once they had sufficiently admired this extraordinary illusion of reality, the monks would turn to the way in which Leonardo had presented the biblical story. There was nothing in this work that resembled older representations of the same theme. In these traditional versions, the apostles were seen sitting quietly at the table in a row – only Judas being segregated from the rest – while Christ was calmly dispensing the Sacrament. The new picture was very different from any of these paintings. There was drama in it, and excitement. Leonardo, like Giotto before him, had gone back to the text of the Scriptures, and had striven to visualize what it must have been like when Christ said, '"Verily I say unto you, that one of you shall betray me"', and they were

exceeding sorrowful and began every one of them to say
unto him "Lord, is it I?"' (Matthew XXVI. 21-2). The Gospel of
St John adds that 'Now there was leaning on Jesus' bosom one
of his disciples, whom Jesus loved. Simon Peter therefore
beckoned to him, that he should ask who it should be of
whom he spake' (John XIII. 23-4). It is this questioning and
beckoning that bring movement into the scene. Christ has
just spoken the tragic words, and those on His side shrink back
in terror as they hear the revelation. Some seem to protest their
love and innocence, others gravely to dispute whom the Lord
may have meant, others again seem to look to Him for an
explanation of what He has said. St Peter, most impetuous of
all, rushes towards St John, who sits to the right of Jesus. As he
whispers something into St John's ear, he inadvertently pushes
Judas forward. Judas is not segregated from the rest, and yet
he seems isolated. He alone does not gesticulate and question.
He bends forward and looks up in suspicion or anger, a
dramatic contrast to the figure of Christ sitting calm and
resigned amidst this surging turmoil. One wonders how long
it took the first spectators to realize the consummate art by
which all this dramatic movement was controlled. Despite the
excitement which Christ's words have caused, there is nothing
chaotic in the picture. The twelve apostles seem to fall quite
naturally into four groups of three, linked to each other
by gestures and movements. There is so much order in this
variety, and so much variety in this order, that one can never
quite exhaust the harmonious interplay of movement and
answering movement. Perhaps we can only fully appreciate
Leonardo's achievement in this composition if we think back
to the problem we discussed in the description of Pollaiuolo's
'St Sebastian', pages 196-7, figure 171. We remember how the
artists of that generation had struggled to combine the demands
of realism with those of design. We remember how rigid and

artificial Pollaiuolo's solution of this problem looked to us.
Leonardo, who was only a little younger than Pollaiuolo,
had solved it with apparent ease. If one forgets for a moment
what the scene represents, one can still enjoy the beautiful
pattern formed by the figures. The composition seems to have
the effortless balance and harmony which it had in Gothic
paintings, and which artists like Rogier van der Weyden and
Botticelli, each in his own way, had tried to recapture for art.
But Leonardo did not find it necessary to sacrifice correctness
of drawing, or accuracy of observation, to the demands of
a satisfying outline. If one forgets the beauty of the
composition, one suddenly feels confronted with a piece of
reality as convincing and striking as any we saw in the works
of Masaccio or Donatello. And even this achievement hardly
touches upon the true greatness of the work. For, beyond such
technical matters as composition and draughtsmanship, we
must admire Leonardo's deep insight into the behaviour and
reactions of men, and the power of imagination which
enabled him to put the scene before our eyes. An eye-witness
tells us that he often saw Leonardo at work on 'The Last
Supper'. He would get on to the scaffolding and stand there
for whole days with folded arms just looking critically at what
he had done before painting another stroke. It is the result
of this thought that he has bequeathed to us, and, even in its
ruined state, 'The Last Supper' remains one of the great
miracles wrought by human genius.

There is another work of Leonardo's which is perhaps
even more famous than 'The Last Supper'. It is the portrait of
a Florentine lady whose name was Lisa, 'Mona Lisa', figure 193.
A fame as great as that of Leonardo's 'Mona Lisa' is not an
unmixed blessing for a work of art. We become so used to
seeing it on picture postcards, and even advertisements, that
we find it difficult to see it with fresh eyes as the painting

by a real man portraying a real woman of flesh and blood. But
it is worth while to forget what we know, or believe we know,
about the picture, and to look at it as if we were the first people
ever to set eyes on it. What strikes us first is the amazing
degree to which Lisa looks alive. She really seems to look at us
and to have a mind of her own. Like a living being, she seems
to change before our eyes and to look a little different every
time we come back to her. Even in photographs of the picture
we experience this strange effect, but in front of the original
in the Louvre it is almost uncanny. Sometimes she seems to
mock at us, and then again we seem to catch something like
sadness in her smile. All this sounds rather mysterious, and so
it is; that is so often the effect of a great work of art.
Nevertheless, Leonardo certainly knew how he achieved this
effect, and by what means. That great observer of nature knew
more about the way we use our eyes than anybody who
had ever lived before him. He had clearly seen a problem
which the conquest of nature had posed to artists – a problem
no less intricate than the one of combining correct drawing
with a harmonious composition. The great works of the
Italian *Quattrocento* masters who followed the lead given by
Masaccio have one thing in common: their figures look
somewhat hard and harsh, almost wooden. The strange thing
is that it clearly is not lack of patience or lack of knowledge
that is responsible for this effect. No one could be more
patient in his imitation of nature than Van Eyck, figure 158; no
one could know more about correct drawing and perspective
than Mantegna, figure 169. And yet, for all the grandeur and
impressiveness of their representations of nature, their figures
look more like statues than living beings. The reason may be
that the more conscientiously we copy a figure line by line
and detail by detail, the less we can imagine that it ever really
moved and breathed. It looks as if the painter had suddenly

cast a spell over it, and forced it to stand stock-still for
evermore, like the people in 'The Sleeping Beauty'. Artists had
tried various ways out of this difficulty. Botticelli, for instance,
figure 172, had tried to emphasize in his pictures the waving
hair and the fluttering garments of his figures, to make them
look less rigid in outline. But only Leonardo found the true
solution to the problem. The painter must leave the beholder
something to guess. If the outlines are not quite so firmly
drawn, if the form is left a little vague, as though
disappearing into a shadow, this impression of dryness and
stiffness will be avoided. This is Leonardo's famous invention
which the Italians call 'sfumato' – the blurred outline and
mellowed colours that allow one form to merge with another
and always leave something to our imagination.

If we now return to the 'Mona Lisa', figure 194, we may
understand something of its mysterious effect. We see that
Leonardo has used the means of his 'sfumato' with the utmost
deliberation. Everyone who has ever tried to draw or scribble
a face knows that what we call its expression rests mainly
in two features: the corners of the mouth, and the corners of
the eyes. Now it is precisely these parts which Leonardo has
left deliberately indistinct, by letting them merge into a soft
shadow. That is why we are never quite certain in what mood
Mona Lisa is really looking at us. Her expression always seems
just to elude us. It is not only vagueness, of course, which
produces this effect. There is much more behind it. Leonardo
has done a very daring thing, which perhaps only a painter
of his consummate mastery could risk. If we look carefully at
the picture, we see that the two sides do not quite match.
This is most obvious in the fantastic dream landscape in the
background. The horizon on the left side seems to lie much
lower than the one on the right. Consequently, when we focus
on the left side of the picture, the woman looks somehow

taller or more erect than if we focus on the right side. And
her face, too, seems to change with this change of position,
because, even here, the two sides do not quite match. But with
all these sophisticated tricks, Leonardo might have produced
a clever piece of jugglery rather than a great work of art, had
he not known exactly how far he could go, and had he not
counterbalanced his daring deviation from nature by an almost
miraculous rendering of the living flesh. Look at the way in
which he modelled the hand, or the sleeves with their minute
folds. Leonardo could be as painstaking as any of his
forerunners in the patient observation of nature. Only he was
no longer merely the faithful servant of nature. Long ago, in
the distant past, people had looked at portraits with awe,
because they had thought that in preserving the likeness the
artist could somehow preserve the soul of the person he
portrayed. Now the great scientist, Leonardo, had made some
of the dreams and fears of these first image-makers come true.
He knew the spell which would infuse life into the colours
spread by his magic brush.

The second great Florentine whose work makes Italian
art of the Cinquecento so famous was Michelangelo Buonarroti
(1475-1564). Michelangelo was twenty-three years younger
than Leonardo and survived him by forty-five years. In his
long lifetime he witnessed a complete change in the position
of the artist. To some degree it was he himself who brought
about this change. In his youth Michelangelo was trained
like any other craftsman. As a boy of thirteen he was apprenticed
for three years to the busy workshop of one of the leading
masters of late Quattrocento Florence, the painter Domenico
Ghirlandaio (1449-94). Ghirlandaio was one of those masters
whose works we enjoy rather for the way in which they
mirror the colourful life of the period than for the greatness
of their genius. He knew how to tell the sacred story

pleasantly, as if it had just happened among the rich Florentine citizens of the Medici circle who were his patrons. Figure 195 represents the birth of the Virgin Mary, and we see the relatives of her mother, St Anne, coming to visit and congratulate her. We look into a fashionable apartment of the late fifteenth century, and witness the formal visit of well-to-do ladies of society. Ghirlandaio proved that he knew how to arrange his groups effectively and how to give pleasure to the eye. He showed that he shared the taste of his contemporaries for the themes of ancient art, for he took care to depict a relief of dancing children, in the classical manner, in the background of the room.

In his workshop the young Michelangelo could certainly learn all the technical tricks of the trade, a solid technique in painting frescoes, and a thorough grounding in draughtsman-ship. But, as far as we know, Michelangelo did not enjoy his days in this successful painter's firm. His ideas about art were different. Instead of acquiring the facile manner of Ghirlandaio, he went out to study the work of the great masters of the past, of Giotto, Masaccio, Donatello, and of the Greek and Roman sculptors whose works he could see in the Medici collection. He tried to penetrate into the secrets of the ancient sculptors, who knew how to represent the beautiful human body in motion, with all its muscles and sinews. Like Leonardo, he was not content with learning the laws of anatomy secondhand, as it were, from antique sculpture. He made his own research into human anatomy, dissected bodies, and drew from models, till the human figure did not seem to hold any secrets for him. But, unlike Leonardo, for whom man was only one of the many fascinating riddles of nature, Michelangelo strove with an incredible singleness of purpose to master this one problem, but to master it fully. His power of concentration and his retentive memory must have been so outstanding that soon there was no posture and no movement which he found difficult to draw. In fact, difficulties only seemed to attract him. Attitudes and angles which many a great *Quattrocento* artist might have hesitated to introduce into his pictures, for fear of failing to represent them convincingly, only stimulated his artistic ambition, and soon it was rumoured that this young artist not only equalled the renowned masters of classical antiquity but actually surpassed them. The time was to come when young artists spent several years at art schools studying anatomy, the nude, perspective, and all the tricks of draughtsmanship. And today many an unambitious commercial artist may have acquired facility in drawing human figures from all angles. Thus it may not be easy for us to grasp the tremendous admiration which Michelangelo's sheer skill and knowledge aroused in his day. By the time he was thirty, he was generally acknowledged to be one of the outstanding masters of the age, equal in his way to the genius of Leonardo. The city of Florence honoured him by commissioning him and Leonardo each to paint an episode from Florentine history on a wall of their council chamber. It was a dramatic moment in the history of art when these two giants competed for the palm, and all Florence watched with excitement the progress of their preparations. Unfortunately, the works were never completed. In 1506 Leonardo returned to Milan and Michelangelo received a call which kindled his enthusiasm even more. Pope Julius II wanted his presence in Rome to erect a tomb for him that should be worthy of the overlord of Christendom. We have heard of the ambitious plans of this great-minded but ruthless ruler of the Church, and it is not difficult to imagine how fascinated Michelangelo must have been to work for a man who possessed the means and the will to carry out the boldest plans. With the Pope's permission, he immediately travelled to the famous marble quarries at Carrara, there to select the blocks from which to carve a gigantic mausoleum. The young artist was overwhelmed by the sight of all these marble rocks, which seemed to be waiting for his chisel to turn them into statues such as the world had never seen. He stayed more than six months at the quarries, buying, selecting and rejecting, his mind seething with images. He wanted to release the figures from the stones in which they were slumbering. But when he returned and started to work he soon discovered that the Pope's enthusiasm for the great enterprise had markedly cooled. We know, today, that one of the main reasons for the Pope's embarrassment was that his plan for a tomb had come into conflict with that plan of his which was even dearer to his heart: the plan for a new St Peter's. For the tomb had originally been destined to stand in the old building, and if that was to be pulled down, where was the mausoleum to be housed? Michelangelo, in his boundless disappointment, suspected different reasons. He smelt intrigue, and even feared that his rivals, above all Bramante, the architect of the new St Peter's, wanted to poison him. In a fit of fear and fury he left Rome for Florence, and wrote a rude letter to the Pope saying that if he wanted him, he could come and look for him.

What was so remarkable in this incident was that the Pope did not lose his temper, but started formal negotiations with the head of the city of Florence to persuade the young sculptor to return. All concerned seemed to agree that the movements and plans of this young artist were as important as any delicate matter of State. The Florentines even feared that the Pope might turn against them if they continued to give him shelter. The head of the city of Florence therefore persuaded Michelangelo to return to the service of Julius II, and gave him a letter of recommendation in which he said that his art was unequalled throughout Italy, perhaps even throughout the world, and that if only he met with kindness 'he would achieve things which would amaze the whole world'. For once a diplomatic note had uttered the truth. When Michelangelo returned to Rome, the Pope made him accept another commission. There was a chapel in the Vatican which had been built by Pope Sixtus IV, and was therefore called the Sistine Chapel, figure 196. The walls of this chapel had been decorated by the most famous painters of the former generation, by Botticelli, Ghirlandaio and others. But the vault was still blank. The Pope suggested that Michelangelo should paint it. Michelangelo did all he could to evade this commission. He said that he was not really a painter, but a sculptor. He was convinced that this thankless commission had been palmed off on him through the intrigues of his enemies. When the Pope remained firm, he started to work out a modest scheme of twelve apostles in niches, and to engage assistants from Florence to help him with the painting. But suddenly he shut himself up in the chapel, let no one come near him, and started to work alone on a plan which has indeed continued to 'amaze the whole world' from the moment it was revealed.

It is very difficult for any ordinary mortal to imagine how it could be possible for one human being to achieve what Michelangelo achieved in four years of lonely work on the scaffolding of the papal chapel, figure 198. The mere physical exertion of painting this huge fresco on the ceiling of the chapel, of preparing and sketching the scenes in detail and transferring them to the wall, is fantastic enough. Michelangelo had to lie on his back and paint looking upwards. In fact, he became so used to this cramped position that even when he received a letter during this period he had to hold it over his head and bend backwards to read it. But the physical performance of one man covering this vast space unaided is as nothing compared to the intellectual and artistic achievement.

The wealth of ever-new inventions, the unfailing mastery of execution in every detail, and, above all, the grandeur of the visions which Michelangelo revealed to those who came after him, have given mankind a quite new idea of the power of genius.

One often sees illustrations of details of this gigantic work, and one can never look at them enough. But the impression given by the whole, when one steps into the chapel, is still very different from the sum of all the photographs one may ever see. The chapel resembles a very large and high assembly hall, with a shallow vault. High up on the walls, we see a row of paintings of the stories of Moses and of Christ in the traditional manner of Michelangelo's forerunners. But, as we look upwards, we seem to look into a different world. It is a world of more than human dimensions. In the vaultings that rise between the five windows on either side of the chapel, Michelangelo placed gigantic images of the Old Testament prophets who spoke to the Jews of the coming Messiah, alternating with images of Sibyls, who, according to an old tradition, predicted the coming of Christ to the pagans. He painted them as mighty men and women, sitting deep in thought, reading, writing, arguing, or as though they were listening to an inner voice. Between these rows of over life-size figures, on the ceiling proper, he painted the story of the Creation and of Noah. But, as though this immense task had not satisfied his urge for creating ever-new images, he filled the framework between these pictures with an overwhelming host of figures, some of them like statues, others like living youths of supernatural beauty, holding festoons and medallions with yet more stories. And even this is only the centrepiece. Beyond that, in the vaultings and directly below them, he painted an endless succession of men and women in infinite variation – the ancestors of Christ as they are enumerated in the Bible.

When we see all this wealth of figures in a photographic reproduction, we may suspect that the whole ceiling may look crowded and unbalanced. It is one of the great surprises, when one comes into the Sistine Chapel, to find how simple and harmonious the ceiling looks if we regard it merely as a piece of superb decoration, and how clear the whole arrangement. Since it was cleaned of its many layers of candle-soot and dust in the 1980s the colours have been revealed as strong and luminous, a necessity if the ceiling was to be visible in a chapel with so few and narrow windows. (This is a point rarely considered by those who have admired these paintings in the strong electric light that is now thrown on to the ceiling.)

Figure 197 shows one sector of the work, vaulting across the ceiling, that exemplifies the way in which Michelangelo distributed the figures flanking the scenes of the Creation. On the one side there is the prophet Daniel holding a huge volume which he supports on his knees with the help of a little boy, and turning aside to take a note of what he has read. Next to him is the Cumaean Sibyl peering into her book. On the opposite side there is the Persian Sibyl, an old woman in Oriental costume, holding a book close to her eyes – equally engrossed in her researches into the sacred texts – and the Old Testament prophet Ezekiel, turning violently as if in argument. The marble seats on which they sit are adorned with statues of playing children, and above them, one on each side, are two of the nudes gaily about to tie the medallion to the ceiling. In the triangular spandrels he represented ancestors of Christ as they are mentioned in the Bible, surmounted by more contorted bodies. The astonishing nude figures display all Michelangelo's mastery in drawing the human body in any position and from any angle. They are young athletes with wonderful muscles, twisting and turning in every conceivable direction, but always contriving to remain graceful. There are no fewer than twenty of them on the ceiling, each one more masterly than the last, and there is little doubt that many of the ideas which were to have come to life out of the marbles of Carrara now crowded upon Michelangelo's mind when he painted the Sistine ceiling. One can feel how he enjoyed his stupendous mastery and how his disappointment and his wrath at being prevented from continuing to work in the material he preferred spurred him on even more to show his enemies, real or suspected, that, if they forced him to paint – well, he would show them!

We know how minutely Michelangelo studied every detail, and how carefully he prepared each figure in his drawings. Figure 199 shows a leaf from his sketch-book on which he studied the forms of a model for one of the Sibyls. We see the interplay of muscles as no one had observed and portrayed it since the Greek masters. But, if he proved himself an unsurpassed virtuoso in these famous 'nudes', he proved to be infinitely more than that in the illustrations of biblical themes which form the centre of the composition. There we see the Lord calling forth, with powerful gestures, the plants, the heavenly bodies, animal life, and man. It is hardly an exaggeration to say that the picture of God the Father – as it has lived in the minds of generation after generation, not only of artists but of humble people, who perhaps have never heard the name of Michelangelo – was shaped and moulded through the direct and indirect influence of these great visions in which Michelangelo illustrated the act of creation. Perhaps the most famous and most striking of them is the creation of Adam on one of the large fields, figure 200. Artists before Michelangelo had already painted Adam lying on the ground and being called to life by a mere touch of the hand of God, but none of them had even come near to expressing the greatness of the mystery of creation with such simplicity and force. There is nothing in the picture to divert attention from the main subject. Adam is lying on the ground in all the vigour and beauty that befit the first man; from the other side God the Father is approaching, carried and supported by His angels, wrapped in a wide and majestic mantle blown out by the wind like a sail, and suggesting the ease and speed with which He floats through the void. As He stretches out His hand, not even touching Adam's finger, we almost see the first man waking, as from a profound sleep, and gazing into the fatherly face of his Maker. It is one of the greatest miracles in art how Michelangelo has contrived thus to make the touch of the Divine hand the centre and focus of the picture, and how he has made us see the idea of omnipotence by the ease and power of this gesture of creation.

Michelangelo had hardly finished his great work on the Sistine ceiling, in 1512, when he eagerly returned to his marble blocks to go on with the tomb of Julius II. He had intended to adorn it with a number of statues of prisoners, such as he had seen on Roman monuments – although it is likely he planned to give to these figures a symbolic meaning. One of these is the 'Dying slave', figure 201.

If anyone had thought that after the tremendous exertion in the chapel Michelangelo's imagination had run dry, he was soon proved wrong. For when he returned to his beloved material, his powers seemed greater than ever. While in the 'Adam' Michelangelo had depicted the moment when life entered the beautiful body of a vigorous youth, he now, in the 'Dying slave', chose the moment when life was just fading, and the body was giving way to the laws of dead matter. There is unspeakable beauty in this last moment of final relaxation and release from the struggle of life – this gesture of lassitude and resignation. It is difficult to think of this work as being a statue of cold and lifeless stone, as we stand before it in the

Louvre. It seems to move before our eyes, and yet to remain at rest. This is probably the effect Michelangelo aimed at. It is one of the secrets of his art that has been admired ever since, that, however much he lets the bodies of his figures twist and turn in violent movement, their outline always remains firm, simple and restful. The reason for this is that, from the very beginning, Michelangelo always tried to conceive his figures as lying hidden in the block of marble on which he was working; the task he set himself as a sculptor was merely to remove the stone which covered them. Thus the simple shape of a block was always reflected in the outline of the statues, and held it together in one lucid design, however much movement there was in the figure.

If Michelangelo had been famous when Julius II called him to Rome, his fame after the completion of these works was something no artist had ever enjoyed before. But this tremendous fame began to be something like a curse to him: for he was never allowed to complete the dream of his youth – the tomb of Julius II. When Julius died, another pope required the services of the most famous artist of his time, and each successive pope seemed more eager than his predecessor to have his name linked with that of Michelangelo. Yet, while princes and popes were outbidding each other to secure the services of the ageing master, he seemed to retire more and more into himself and to become more exacting in his standards. The poems he wrote show that he was troubled by doubts as to whether his art had been sinful, while his letters make it clear that the higher he rose in the esteem of the world, the more bitter and difficult he became. He was not only admired, but feared for his temper, and he spared neither high nor low. There is no doubt he was very conscious of his social position, which was so different from anything he remembered from the days of his youth.

Indeed, when he was seventy-seven, he once rebuffed a compatriot for having addressed a letter to 'the Sculptor Michelangelo'. 'Tell him', he wrote, 'not to address his letters to the sculptor Michelangelo, for here I am known only as Michelangelo Buonarroti ... I have never been a painter or sculptor, in the sense of having kept a shop ... although I have served the popes; but this I did under compulsion.'

How sincere he was in this feeling of proud independence is best shown by the fact that he refused payment for his last great work, which occupied him in his old age: the completion of the work of his one-time enemy Bramante – the crowning cupola of St Peter's. This work on the principal church of Christendom the aged master regarded as a service to the greater glory of God, which should not be sullied by worldly profit. As it rises over the city of Rome, supported, it seems, by a ring of twin columns and soaring up with its clean majestic outline, it serves as a fitting monument to the spirit of this singular artist whom his contemporaries called 'divine'.

At the time when Michelangelo and Leonardo were competing with each other in Florence in 1504, a young painter arrived there from the small city of Urbino, in the province of Umbria. He was Raffaello Santi, whom we know as Raphael (1483-1520), who had shown great promise in the workshop of the leader of the 'Umbrian' school, Perugino (1446-1523). Like Michelangelo's master, Ghirlandaio, and Leonardo's master, Verrocchio, Raphael's teacher, Perugino, belonged to the generation of highly successful artists who needed a large staff of skilled apprentices to help them carry out the many commissions they received. Perugino was one of those masters whose sweet and devout manner in painting altarpieces commanded general respect. The problems with which earlier *Quattrocento* artists had wrestled with such zeal no longer presented much difficulty to him. Some of his most successful works, at any rate, show that he knew how to achieve a sense of depth without upsetting the balance of the design, and he had learned to handle Leonardo's 'sfumato' so as to avoid giving his figures a harsh and rigid appearance. Figure 202 is an altar-painting dedicated to St Bernard. The saint looks up from his book to see the Holy Virgin standing in front of him. The arrangement could hardly be simpler – and yet there is nothing stiff or forced in this almost symmetrical layout. The figures are distributed to form a harmonious composition, and each of them moves with calm and ease. It is quite true that Perugino achieved this beautiful harmony at the expense of something else. He sacrificed the faithful portrayal of nature which the great masters of the *Quattrocento* had striven for with such passionate devotion. If we look at Perugino's angels, we see that they all follow, more or less, the same type. It is a type of beauty which Perugino invented and applied in his pictures in ever-new variations. When we see too much of his work, we may tire of his devices, but then his paintings were not meant to be seen, side by side, in picture galleries. Taken singly, some of his best works give us a glimpse into a world more serene and more harmonious than our own.

It was in this atmosphere that the young Raphael grew up, and he had soon mastered and absorbed the manner of his teacher. When he arrived in Florence he was confronted with a stirring challenge. Leonardo and Michelangelo, the one his senior by thirty-one years, the other by eight years, were setting up new standards in art of which nobody had ever dreamed. Other young artists might have become discouraged by the reputations of these giants. Not so Raphael. He was determined to learn. He must have known that he was at a disadvantage in some respects. He had neither the immense range of knowledge of Leonardo, nor the power of Michelangelo. But while these two geniuses were difficult to get on with, unpredictable and elusive to ordinary mortals, Raphael was of a sweetness of temper which would commend him to influential patrons. Moreover he could work, and work he would until he had caught up with the older masters.

Raphael's greatest paintings seem so effortless that one does not usually connect them with the idea of hard and relentless work. To many he is simply the painter of sweet Madonnas which have become so well known as hardly to be appreciated as paintings any more. For Raphael's vision of the Holy Virgin has been adopted by subsequent generations in the same way as Michelangelo's conception of God the Father. We see cheap reproductions of these works in humble dwellings, and we are apt to conclude that paintings with such a general appeal must surely be a little 'obvious'. In fact, their apparent simplicity is the fruit of deep thought, careful planning and immense artistic wisdom, *page 31, figures 17-18*. A painting like Raphael's 'Madonna del Granduca', *figure 203*, is truly 'classical' in the sense that it has served countless generations as a standard of perfection in the same way as the works of Pheidias and Praxiteles. It needs no explanation. In this respect it is indeed 'obvious'. But, if we compare it with the countless representations of the same theme which preceded it, we feel that they have all been groping for the very simplicity that Raphael has attained. We can see what Raphael did owe to the calm beauty of Perugino's types, but what a difference there is between the rather empty regularity of the master and the fullness of life in the pupil! The way the Virgin's face is modelled and recedes into the shade, the way Raphael makes us feel the volume of the body wrapped in the freely flowing mantle, the firm and tender way in which she holds and supports the Christ Child – all this contributes to the effect of perfect poise. We feel that to change the group ever so slightly would upset the whole harmony. Yet there is nothing strained or sophisticated in the composition. It looks as if it could not be otherwise, and as if it had so existed from the beginning of time.

After some years in Florence, Raphael went to Rome. He arrived there probably in 1508, at the time when Michelangelo was just starting work on the Sistine ceiling. Julius II soon found work for this young and amiable artist also. He asked him to decorate the walls of various rooms in the Vatican which have come to be known by the name of the 'Stanze' (rooms). Raphael proved his mastery of perfect design and balanced composition in a series of frescoes on the walls and ceilings of these rooms. To appreciate the full beauty of these works, one must spend some time in the rooms and feel the harmony and diversity of the whole scheme in which movement answers to movement, and form to form. Removed from their setting and reduced in size they tend to look frigid, for the individual figures, which stand before us life-size when we face the frescoes, are too readily absorbed by the groups. Conversely, when taken out of their context as illustrations of 'detail', these figures lose one of their principal functions – that of forming part of the graceful melody of the whole design.

This applies less to a smaller fresco, figure 204, which Raphael painted in the villa (now called the Farnesina) of a rich banker, Agostino Chigi. As subject he chose a verse from a poem by the Florentine Angelo Poliziano which had also helped to inspire Botticelli's 'Birth of Venus'. These lines describe how the clumsy giant Polyphemus sings a love song to the fair sea-nymph Galatea and how she rides across the waves in a chariot drawn by two dolphins, laughing at his uncouth song, while the gay company of other sea-gods and nymphs is milling round her. Raphael's fresco shows Galatea with her gay companions; the picture of the giant was to appear elsewhere in the hall. However long one looks at this lovely and cheerful picture, one will always discover new beauties in its rich and intricate composition. Every figure seems to correspond to some other figure, every movement to answer a counter-movement. We have observed this method in Pollaiuolo's showpiece, figure 171. But how rigid and dull his solution looks in comparison with Raphael's! To start with the small boys with Cupid's bows and arrows who aim at the heart of the nymph: not only do those to right and left echo each other's movements, but the boy swimming beside the chariot corresponds to the one flying at the top of the picture. It is the same with the group of sea-gods which seems to be 'wheeling' round the nymph. There are two on the margins, who blow on their sea-shells, and two pairs in front and behind, who are making love to each other. But what is more admirable is that all these diverse movements are somehow reflected and taken up in the figure of Galatea herself, figure 205. Her chariot had been driving from left to right with her veil blowing backwards, but, hearing the strange love song, she turns round and smiles, and all the lines in the picture, from the love-gods' arrows to the reins she holds, converge on her beautiful face in the very centre of the picture. By these artistic means Raphael has achieved constant movement throughout the picture, without letting it become restless or unbalanced. It is for this supreme mastery of arranging his figures, this consummate skill in composition, that artists have admired Raphael ever since. Just as Michelangelo was found to have reached the highest peak in the mastery of the human body, Raphael was seen to have accomplished what the older generation had striven so hard to achieve: the perfect and harmonious composition of freely moving figures.

There was another quality in Raphael's work that was admired by his contemporaries and by subsequent generations – the sheer beauty of his figures. When he had finished the 'Galatea', Raphael was asked by a courtier where in all the world he had found a model of such beauty. He replied that he did not copy any specific model but rather followed 'a certain idea' he had formed in his mind. To some extent, then, Raphael, like his teacher Perugino, had abandoned the faithful portrayal of nature which had been the ambition of so many *Quattrocento* artists. He deliberately used an imagined type of regular beauty. If we look back to the time of Praxiteles, *figure* 62, we remember how what we call an 'ideal' beauty grew out of a slow approximation of schematic forms to nature. Now the process was reversed. Artists tried to modify nature according to the idea of beauty they had formed when looking at classical statues – they 'idealized' the model. It was a tendency not without its dangers, for, if the artist deliberately 'improves on' nature, his work may easily look mannered or insipid. But if we look once more at Raphael's work, we see that he, at any rate, could idealize without any loss of vitality and sincerity in the result. There is nothing schematic or calculated in Galatea's loveliness. She is an inmate of a brighter world of love and beauty – the world of the classics as it appeared to its admirers in sixteenth-century Italy.

It was for this achievement that Raphael has remained famous throughout the centuries. Perhaps those who connect his name only with beautiful Madonnas and idealized figures from the classical world may even be surprised to see Raphael's portrait of his great patron Pope Leo X of the Medici family, in the company of two cardinals, *figure* 206. There is nothing idealized in the slightly puffed head of the near-sighted Pope, who has just examined an old manuscript (somewhat similar in style and period to the 'Queen Mary's Psalter', *figure* 140). The velvets and damasks in their various rich tones add to the atmosphere of pomp and power, but one can well imagine that these men are not at ease. These were troubled times, for we remember that at the very period when this portrait was painted Luther had attacked the Pope for the way he raised money for the new St Peter's. It so happens that it was Raphael himself whom Leo X had put in charge of this building enterprise after Bramante had died in 1514, and thus he had also become an architect, designing churches, villas and palaces and studying the ruins of ancient Rome. Unlike his great rival Michelangelo, though, he got on well with people and could keep a busy workshop going. Thanks to his sociable qualities, the scholars and dignitaries of the papal court made him their companion. There was even talk of his being made a cardinal when he died on his thirty-seventh birthday, almost as young as Mozart, having crammed into his brief life an astonishing diversity of artistic achievements. One of the most famous scholars of his age, Cardinal Bembo, wrote the epitaph for his tomb in the Pantheon of Rome:

> *This is Raphael's tomb, while he lived he made Mother Nature Fear to be vanquished by him and, as he died, to die too.*

Light and Colour

Venice and northern Italy, early sixteenth century

We must now turn to another great centre of Italian art, second in importance only to Florence itself – the proud and prosperous city of Venice. Venice, whose trade linked it closely with the East, had been slower than other Italian cities in accepting the style of the Renaissance, Brunelleschi's application of classical form to buildings. But when it did, the style there acquired a new gaiety, splendour and warmth which evoke, perhaps more closely than any other buildings in modern times, the grandeur of the great merchant cities of the Hellenistic period, of Alexandria or Antioch. One of the most characteristic buildings of this style is the Library of San Marco, figure 207. Its architect was a Florentine, Jacopo Sansovino (1486-1570), but he had completely adapted his style and manner to the genius of the place, the brilliant light of Venice, which is reflected by the lagoons, and dazzles the eye by its splendour. It may seem a little pedantic to anatomize such a festive and simple building, but to look at it carefully may help us to see how skilled these masters were in weaving a few simple elements into ever-new patterns. The lower storey, then, with its vigorous Doric order of columns, is in the most orthodox classical manner. Sansovino has closely followed the rules of building which the Colosseum, figure 73, exemplified. He adhered to the same tradition when he arranged the upper storey in the Ionic order, carrying a so-called 'attic' crowned with a balustrade and topped by a row of statues. But instead of letting the arched openings between the orders rest on pillars, as had been the case with the Colosseum, Sansovino supported them by another set of small Ionic columns, and thus achieved a rich effect of interlocked orders. With his balustrades, garlands and sculptures he gave the building something of the appearance of tracery such as had been used on the Gothic façades of Venice, figure 138.

This building is characteristic of the taste for which Venetian art in the Cinquecento became famous. The atmosphere of the lagoons, which seems to blur the sharp outlines of objects and to blend their colours in a radiant light, may have taught the painters of this city to use colour in a more deliberate and observant way than other painters in Italy had done so far. Maybe, also, the links with Constantinople and its craftsmen in mosaic had something to do with this bias. It is difficult to talk or write about colours, and no illustration, much reduced in scale, gives an adequate idea of the real appearance of a masterpiece of colour. But so much seems to be clear: the painters of the Middle Ages were no more concerned about the 'real' colours of things than they were about their real shapes. In their miniatures, enamel work and panel paintings, they loved to spread out the purest and most precious colours they could get – with shining gold and flawless ultramarine blue as a favourite combination. The great reformers of Florence were less interested in colour than in drawing. That does not mean, of course, that their pictures were not exquisite in colour – the contrary is true – but few of them regarded colour as one of the principal means of welding the various figures and forms of a picture into one unified pattern. They preferred to do this by means of perspective and composition before they even dipped their brushes into paint. The Venetian painters, it seems, did not think of colour as an additional adornment for the picture after it had been drawn on the panel. When one enters the little church of San Zaccaria in Venice and stands before the picture, figure 208, which the great Venetian painter Giovanni Bellini (1431?-1516) painted over the altar there in 1505 – in his old age – one immediately notices that his approach to colour was very different. Not that the picture is particularly bright or shining. It is rather the mellowness and richness of the colours that impress one before one even begins to look at what the picture represents. I think that even the photograph conveys something of the warm and gilded atmosphere which fills the niche in which the Virgin sits enthroned, with the infant Jesus lifting His little hands to bless the worshippers before the altar. An angel at the foot of the altar softly plays the violin, while the saints stand quietly at either side of the throne: St Peter with his key and book, St Catherine with the palm of martyrdom and the broken wheel, St Lucy and St Jerome, the scholar who translated the Bible into Latin, and whom Bellini therefore represented as reading a book. Many Madonnas with saints have been painted before and after, in Italy and elsewhere, but few were ever conceived with such dignity and repose. In the Byzantine tradition, the picture of the Virgin used to be rigidly flanked by images of the saints, figure 89. Bellini knew how to bring life into this simple symmetrical arrangement without upsetting its order. He also knew how to turn the traditional figures of the Virgin and saints into real and living beings without divesting them of their holy character and dignity. He did not even sacrifice the variety and individuality of real life – as Perugino had done to some extent, figure 202. St Catherine with her dreamy smile, and St Jerome, the old scholar engrossed in his book, are real enough in their own ways, although they, too, no less than Perugino's figures, seem to belong to another more serene and beautiful world, a world transfused with that warm and supernatural light that fills the picture.

Giovanni Bellini belonged to the same generation as Verrocchio, Ghirlandaio and Perugino – the generation whose pupils and followers were the famous *Cinquecento* masters. He, too, was the head of an exceedingly busy workshop out of whose orbit there emerged the famous painters of the Venetian *Cinquecento*, Giorgione and Titian. If the classical painters of central Italy had achieved the new complete harmony within their pictures by means of perfect design and balanced arrangement, it was only natural that the painters of Venice should follow the lead of Giovanni Bellini, who had made such happy use of colour and light to unify his pictures. It was in this sphere that the painter Giorgione (1478?-1510) achieved the most revolutionary results. Very little is known of this artist; scarcely five paintings can be ascribed with absolute certainty to his hand. Yet these suffice to secure him a fame nearly as great as that of the great leaders of the new movement. Strangely enough, even these pictures contain something of a puzzle. We are not quite sure what the most accomplished one, 'The tempest', figure 209, represents; it may be a scene from some classical writer or an imitator of the classics. For Venetian artists of the period had awakened to the charm of the Greek poets and what they stood for. They liked to illustrate the idyllic stories of pastoral love and to portray the beauty of Venus and the nymphs. One day the episode here illustrated may be identified – the story, perhaps, of a mother of some future hero, who was cast out of the city into the wilderness with her child and was there discovered by a friendly young shepherd. For this, it seems, is what Giorgione wanted to represent. But it is not due to its content that the picture is one of the most wonderful things in art. That this is so may be difficult to see in a small-scale illustration, but even such an illustration conveys a shadow, at least, of his revolutionary achievement. Though the figures are not particularly carefully drawn, and though the composition is somewhat artless, the picture is clearly blended into a whole simply by the light and air that permeate it all. It is the weird light of a thunderstorm, and for the first time, it seems, the landscape before which the actors of the picture move is not just a background. It is there, by its own right, as the real subject of the painting. We look from the figures to the scenery which fills the major part of the small panel, and then back again, and we feel somehow that, unlike his predecessors and contemporaries, Giorgione has not drawn things and persons to arrange them afterwards in space, but that he really thought of nature, the earth, the trees, the light, air and clouds and the human beings with their cities and bridges as one. In a way, this was almost as big a step forward into a new realm as the invention of perspective had been. From now on, painting was more than drawing plus colouring. It was an art with its own secret laws and devices.

Giorgione died too young to gather all the fruits of this great discovery. This was done by the most famous of all Venetian painters, Titian (c. 1485-1576). Titian was born in Cadore, in the southern Alps, and was rumoured to be ninety-nine when he died of the plague. During his long life he rose to a fame which nearly matched that of Michelangelo. His early biographers tell us with awe that even the great Emperor Charles V had done him honour by picking up a brush he had dropped. We may not find this very remarkable, but if we consider the strict rules of the court of those times, we realize that the greatest embodiment of worldly power was believed to have humbled himself symbolically before the majesty of genius. Seen in this light, the little anecdote, whether true or not, represented to later ages a triumph for art. All the more so since Titian was neither such a universal scholar as Leonardo, nor such an outstanding personality as Michelangelo, nor such a versatile and attractive man as Raphael. He was principally a painter, but a painter whose handling of paint equalled Michelangelo's mastery of draughtsmanship. This supreme skill enabled him to disregard all the time-honoured rules of composition, and to rely on colour to restore the unity which he apparently broke up. We need but look at figure 210 (which

was begun only some fifteen years after Giovanni Bellini's
'Madonna with saints') to realize the effect which his art must
have had on contemporaries. It was almost unheard of to move
the Holy Virgin out of the centre of the picture, and to place the
two administering saints – St Francis, who is recognizable
by the stigmata (the wounds of the Cross), and St Peter, who has
deposited the key (emblem of his dignity) on the steps of the
Virgin's throne – not symmetrically on each side, as Giovanni
Bellini had done, but as active participants of a scene. In this
altar-painting, Titian had to revive the tradition of donors'
portraits, figure 143, but did it in an entirely novel way. The picture
was intended as a token of thanksgiving for a victory over the
Turks by the Venetian nobleman Jacopo Pesaro, and Titian
portrayed him kneeling before the Virgin while an armoured
standard-bearer drags a Turkish prisoner behind him. St Peter and
the Virgin look down on him benignly while St Francis, on the
other side, draws the attention of the Christ Child to the other
members of the Pesaro family, who are kneeling in the corner of
the picture, figure 211. The whole scene seems to take place in
an open courtyard, with two giant columns which rise into the
clouds where two little angels are playfully engaged in raising
the Cross. Titian's contemporaries may well have been amazed
at the audacity with which he had dared to upset the old-
established rules of composition. They must have expected, at
first, to find such a picture lopsided and unbalanced. Actually
it is the opposite. The unexpected composition only serves to
make it gay and lively without upsetting the harmony of it all.
The main reason is the way in which Titian contrived to
let light, air and colours unify the scene. The idea of making
a mere flag counterbalance the figure of the Holy Virgin would
probably have shocked an earlier generation, but this flag, in
its rich, warm colour, is such a stupendous piece of painting
that the venture was a complete success.

Titian's greatest fame with his contemporaries rested on portraits. We need only look at a head like figure 212, usually called a 'Young Englishman', to understand this fascination. We might try in vain to analyse wherein it consists. Compared with earlier portraits it all looks so simple and effortless. There is nothing of the minute modelling of Leonardo's 'Mona Lisa' in it – and yet this unknown young man seems as mysteriously alive as she does. He seems to gaze at us with such an intense and soulful look that it is almost impossible to believe that these dreamy eyes are only a bit of coloured earth spread on a rough piece of canvas, figure 213.

No wonder that the mighty of this world competed with each other for the honour of being painted by this master. Not that Titian was inclined to produce a specially flattering likeness, but he gave them the conviction that through his art they would go on living. They did, or so we feel when we stand in front of his portrait of Pope Paul III in Naples, figure 214. It shows the aged ruler of the Church turning towards a young relative, Alessandro Farnese, who is about to pay homage while his brother, Ottavio, calmly looks at us. Clearly Titian knew and admired Raphael's portrait of Pope Leo X with his cardinals painted some twenty-eight years earlier, figure 206, but he must also have aimed at surpassing it in lively characterization. The encounter of these personalities is so convincing and so dramatic that we cannot help speculating about their thoughts and emotions. Are the cardinals plotting? Does the Pope see through their schemes? These are probably idle questions, but they may also have obtruded themselves on contemporaries. The painting remained unfinished when the master left Rome to obey a summons to Germany to paint the Emperor Charles V.

It was not only in the great centres like Venice that artists advanced to the discovery of new possibilities and new

methods. The painter who was looked upon by later
generations as the most 'progressive' and most daring innovator
of the whole period led a lonely life in the small northern
Italian town of Parma. He was Antonio Allegri, called Correggio
(1489?-1534). Leonardo and Raphael had died and Titian had
already risen to fame when Correggio painted his more
important works, but we do not know how much he knew of
the art of his time. He probably had an opportunity in the
neighbouring cities of northern Italy to study the works of
some of Leonardo's pupils and to learn about his treatment of
light and shade. It was in this field that he worked out entirely
new effects which greatly influenced later schools of painters.

Figure 215 shows one of his most famous paintings –
'The Holy Night'. The tall shepherd has just had the vision of
the open heavens in which the angels sing their 'Glory to God
on High'; we see them whirling gaily about in the cloud and
looking down on the scene to which the shepherd has rushed
with his long staff. In the dark ruins of the stable he sees
the miracle – the new-born Child that radiates light all round,
lighting up the beautiful face of the happy mother. The
shepherd arrests his movement and fumbles for his cap, ready
to kneel down and worship. There are two servant girls – one
is dazzled by the light from the manger, one looks happily at
the shepherd. St Joseph in the murky dark outside busies
himself with the ass.

At first sight the arrangement looks quite artless and
casual. The crowded scene on the left does not seem to be
balanced by any corresponding group on the right. It is only
balanced through the emphasis which the light gives to the
group of the Virgin and the Child. Correggio even more than
Titian exploited the discovery that colour and light can be
used to balance forms and to direct our eyes along certain
lines. It is we who rush to the scene with the shepherd and

who are made to see what he sees – the miracle of the Light that shone in darkness of which the Gospel of St John speaks.

There is one feature of Correggio's works which was imitated throughout the subsequent centuries; it is the way in which he painted the ceilings and cupolas of churches. He tried to give the worshippers in the nave below the illusion that the ceiling had opened and that they were looking straight into the glory of Heaven. His mastery of light effects enabled him to fill the ceiling with sunlit clouds between which the heavenly hosts seem to hover with their legs dangling downwards. This may not sound very dignified and actually there were people at the time who objected, but when you stand in the dark and gloomy medieval cathedral of Parma and look up towards its dome the impression is nevertheless very great, figure 217. Unfortunately this type of effect cannot easily be reproduced in an illustration. It is fortunate, therefore, that we still have some of his drawings which he made in preparation. Figure 216 shows his first idea for the figure of the Virgin ascending on a cloud and gazing towards the radiance of heaven that awaits her. The drawing is certainly easier to make out than the figure in the fresco, which is even more contorted. Moreover, we are able to see with what simple means Correggio could suggest such a flood of light with a few strokes of his chalk.

7

e New Learning
eads

and the Netherlands, early sixteenth century

The great achievements and inventions of the Italian masters of the Renaissance made a deep impression on the peoples north of the Alps. Everyone who was interested in the revival of learning had become accustomed to looking towards Italy, where the wisdom and the treasures of classical antiquity were being discovered. We know very well that in art we cannot speak of progress in the sense in which we speak of progress in learning. A Gothic work of art may be just as great as a work of the Renaissance. Nevertheless, it is perhaps natural that to the people at that time, who came into contact with the masterpieces from the south, their own art seemed suddenly to be old-fashioned and uncouth. There were three tangible achievements of the Italian masters to which they could point. One was the discovery of scientific perspective, the second the knowledge of anatomy – and with it the perfect rendering of the beautiful human body – and thirdly the knowledge of the classical forms of building, which seemed to the period to stand for everything that was dignified and beautiful.

It is a fascinating spectacle to watch the reactions of various artists and traditions to the impact of this new knowledge, and to see how they asserted themselves – or as sometimes happened, how they succumbed – according to the strength of their character and the breadth of their vision. Architects were perhaps in the most difficult position. Both the Gothic system, to which they were accustomed, and the new revival of ancient buildings are, at least in theory, utterly logical and consistent, but as different from each other in aim and spirit as two styles could possibly be. It took a long time, therefore, before the new fashion in building was adopted north of the Alps. When this did come about, it was frequently on the insistence of princes and noblemen who had visited Italy and wanted to be up to date. Even so, architects often complied only very superficially with the requirements of the new style. They demonstrated their acquaintance with the new ideas by putting a column here and a frieze there – in other words, by adding some of the classical forms to their wealth of decorative motifs. More often than not, the body of the building remained entirely untouched. There are churches in France, England and Germany where the pillars supporting the vault are superficially turned into columns by having capitals affixed to them, or where the Gothic windows are complete with tracery, but the pointed arch has given way to a rounded one, figure 218. There are regular cloisters supported by fantastic bottle-shaped columns, castles bristling with turrets and buttresses, but adorned with classical details, gabled town houses with classical friezes and busts, figure 219. An Italian artist, convinced of the perfection of the classical rules, would probably have turned away from these things in horror, but if we do not measure them by any pedantic academic standard we may often admire the ingenuity and wit with which these incongruous styles were blended.

Things were rather different in the case of painters and sculptors, because for them it was not a matter of taking over certain definite forms such as columns, or arches, piecemeal. Only minor painters could be content with borrowing a figure or a gesture from an Italian engraving which had come their way. Any real artist was bound to feel the urge thoroughly to understand the new principles of art and to make up his mind about their usefulness. We can study this dramatic process in the work of the greatest German artist, Albrecht Dürer (1471-1528), who was throughout his life fully conscious of their vital importance for the future of art.

Albrecht Dürer was the son of a distinguished master-goldsmith who had come from Hungary and settled in the flourishing city of Nuremberg. Even as a boy, the young Dürer showed an astonishing gift for drawing – some of his works of that time have been preserved – and he was apprenticed with the largest workshop for altars and woodcut illustrations. This belonged to the Nuremberg master, Michel Wolgemut. Having completed his apprenticeship, he followed the custom of all young medieval craftsmen and travelled about as a journeyman to broaden his views and to look for a place in which to settle. Dürer's intention had been to visit the workshop of the greatest copper-engraver of this period, Martin Schongauer, *page 213*, but when he arrived at Colmar he found that the master had died some months earlier. However, he stayed with Schongauer's brothers, who had taken charge of the workshop, and then turned to Basle in Switzerland, at that time a centre of learning and of the book trade. Here he made woodcuts for books, and then travelled on, across the Alps into northern Italy, keeping an open eye throughout his journeys and making watercolours of the picturesque places in the Alpine valleys, and studying the works of Mantegna, *pages 192-3*. When he returned to Nuremberg to marry and open his own workshop, he possessed all the technical accomplishments a northern artist could expect to acquire in the South. He soon showed that he had more than mere technical knowledge of his difficult craft, that he possessed that intense feeling and imagination which alone make the great artist. One of his first great works was a series of large woodcuts illustrating the Revelation of St John. It was an immediate success. The terrifying visions of the horrors of doomsday, and of the signs and portents preceding it, had never before been visualized with such force and power. There is little doubt that Dürer's imagination, and the interest of the public, fed on the general discontent with the institutions of the Church which was rife in Germany towards the end of the Middle Ages, and was finally to break out in Luther's Reformation. To Dürer and his

public, the weird visions of the apocalyptic events had
acquired something like topical interest, for there were many
who expected these prophecies to come true within their
lifetime. Figure 220 shows an illustration of Revelation XII.7:

> *And there was war in heaven: Michael and his angels fought against*
> *the dragon; and the dragon fought and his angels, and prevailed not;*
> *neither was their place found any more in heaven.*

To represent this great moment, Dürer discarded all the
traditional poses that had been used time and again to represent,
with a show of elegance and ease, a hero's fight against
a mortal enemy. Dürer's St Michael does not strike any pose.
He is in deadly earnest. He uses both hands in a mighty effort
to thrust his huge spear into the dragon's throat, and this
powerful gesture dominates the whole scene. Round him there
are the hosts of other warring angels fighting as swordsmen
and archers against the fiendish monsters, whose fantastic
appearance defies description. Beneath this celestial battlefield
there lies a landscape untroubled and serene, with Dürer's
famous monogram.

But though Dürer had proved himself a master of the
fantastic and the visionary, a true heir of those Gothic artists
who had created the porches of the great cathedrals, he did
not rest content with this achievement. His studies and sketches
show that it was also his aim to contemplate the beauty of
nature, and to copy it as patiently and as faithfully as any artist
had ever done, since Jan van Eyck had shown the artists of
the North that their task was to mirror nature. Some of these
studies of Dürer have become famous: his hare, figure 9,
for instance, or his watercolour of a piece of turf, figure 221.
It seems that Dürer strove for his perfect mastery in the
imitation of nature, not so much as an aim in itself but as

a better way of presenting a convincing vision of the sacred stories which he was to illustrate in his paintings, engravings, and woodcuts. For the same patience which enabled him to draw these sketches also made him the born engraver, who never tired of adding detail upon detail to build up a true little world within the compass of his copper plate. In his 'Nativity', figure 222, which he made in 1504 (that is, about the time when Michelangelo amazed the Florentines by his display of knowledge of the human body), Dürer took up the theme which Schongauer, figure 185, had represented in his lovely engraving. The older artist had already used the opportunity to depict the rugged walls of dilapidated stables with special love. It would seem, at first glance, that for Dürer this was the main subject. The old farmyard with its cracked mortar and loose tiles, its broken wall from which trees are growing, its ramshackle boards in place of a roof, on which birds are nesting, is thought out and rendered with such quiet and contemplative patience that one feels how much the artist enjoyed the idea of the picturesque old building. Compared with it, the figures seem, indeed, small and almost insignificant: Mary, who has sought shelter in the old shed and is kneeling in front of her Child, and Joseph, who busies himself hauling water from the well and pouring it carefully into a narrow pitcher. One must look carefully to discover one of the adoring shepherds in the background, and one almost needs a magnifying glass to detect the traditional angel in the sky who announces the glad tidings to the world. And yet no one would seriously suggest that Dürer was merely trying to display his skill in rendering old and broken walls. This old, disused farmyard, with its humble visitors, conveys such an atmosphere of idyllic peace that it calls on us to ponder the miracle of the Holy Night in the same mood of devout meditation as went into the making of the engraving.

In engravings like this, Dürer seemed to have summed up and brought to perfection the development of Gothic art, since it had turned towards the imitation of nature. But, at the same time, his mind was busy grappling with the new aims given to art by the Italian artists.

There was one aim which Gothic art had almost excluded and which now stood in the foreground of interest: the representation of the human body in that ideal beauty with which classical art had endowed it.

Here Dürer was soon to find out that any mere imitation of real nature, even when done as diligently and devotedly as Van Eyck's Adam and Eve, figure 156, would never be sufficient to produce the elusive quality of beauty that distinguished southern works of art. Raphael, when confronted with this question, referred to the 'certain idea' of beauty that he found in his mind, pages 243-4, the idea that he had absorbed during years of studying classical sculpture and beautiful models. To Dürer, this was no simple proposition. Not only were his opportunities for study less wide, but he had no firm tradition or sure instinct to guide him in such matters. That is why he went in search of a reliable recipe, as it were, a teachable rule which would explain what makes for beauty in the human form; and he believed that he had found such a rule in the teachings of the classical writers on the proportions of the human body. Their expressions and measurements were rather obscure, but Dürer was not to be deterred by such difficulties. He intended, as he said, to give the vague practice of his forefathers (who had created vigorous works without clear knowledge of the rules of art) a proper teachable foundation. It is thrilling to watch Dürer experimenting with various rules of proportion, to see him deliberately distorting the human frame by drawing overlong, or overbroad, bodies in order to find the right

balance and the right harmony. Among the first results of
these studies, which were to engage him throughout his life,
was the engraving of Adam and Eve, in which he embodied
all his new ideas of beauty and harmony, and which he
proudly signed with his full name in Latin, ALBERTUS DURER
NORICUS FACIEBAT 1504 ('Albrecht Dürer of Nuremberg
made [this engraving] in 1504'), figure 223.

It may not be easy for us to see immediately the
achievement which lay in this engraving. For the artist is
speaking a language which is less familiar to him than that
which he used in our preceding example. The harmonious
forms at which he arrived by diligent measuring and
balancing with compass and ruler are not as convincing and
beautiful as their Italian and classical models. There is some
slight suggestion of artificiality, not only in their form and
posture, but also in the symmetrical composition. But this first
feeling of awkwardness soon disappears when one realizes that
Dürer has not abandoned his real self to worship new idols, as
lesser artists did. As we let him guide us into the Garden of
Eden, where the mouse lies quietly beside the cat, where the
elk, the cow, the rabbit and the parrot do not fear the tread
of human feet, as we look deep into the grove where the tree
of knowledge grows, and watch the serpent giving Eve the
fatal fruit while Adam stretches out his hand to receive it, and
as we notice how Dürer has contrived to let the clear outline
of their white and delicately modelled bodies show up against
the dark shade of the forest with its rugged trees, we come to
admire the first serious attempt to transplant the ideals of the
South into northern soil.

Dürer himself, however, was not easily satisfied. A year
after he had published this engraving, he travelled to Venice to
broaden his horizon and to learn more about the secrets of
southern art. The arrival of so eminent a competitor was not

altogether welcome to the minor Venetian artists, and Dürer
wrote to a friend:

> I have many friends among the Italians who warn me not to eat
> and drink with their painters. Many of them are my enemies;
> they copy my works in the churches and wherever they can find
> them; and then they decry my work and say it was not in the
> manner of the classics and therefore it was no good. But Giovanni
> Bellini has praised me very highly to many noblemen. He wanted
> to have something I have done, and he himself came to me and
> asked me to make something for him – he would pay well.
> Everyone tells me how devout a man he is, which makes me like
> him. He is very old, and still the best in painting.

It is in one of these letters from Venice that Dürer wrote the
touching sentence which shows how keenly he felt the
contrast of his position as an artist in the rigid order of the
Nuremberg guilds compared with the freedom of his Italian
colleagues: 'How I shall shiver for the sun,' he wrote, 'here
I am a lord, at home a parasite.' But Dürer's later life does not
quite bear out these apprehensions. True, at first he had to
bargain and argue with the rich burghers of Nuremberg and
Frankfurt like any artisan. He had to promise them to use
only the best-quality paint for his panels and to apply it in
many layers. But gradually his fame spread, and the Emperor
Maximilian, who believed in the importance of art as an
instrument of glorification, secured Dürer's services for a
number of ambitious schemes. When, at the age of fifty, Dürer
visited the Netherlands, he was, indeed, received like a lord.
He himself, deeply moved, described how the painters of
Antwerp honoured him in their guild hall with a solemn
banquet, 'and when I was led to the table, the people stood,
on both sides, as if they were introducing a great lord, and

among them were many persons of excellence who all bowed their heads in the most humble manner'. Even in the northern countries the great artists had broken down the snobbery which led people to despise men who worked with their hands.

It is a strange and puzzling fact that the only German painter who can be compared with Dürer for greatness and artistic power has been forgotten to such an extent that we are not even quite sure of his name. A writer of the seventeenth century makes rather confused mention of one Matthias Grünewald of Aschaffenburg. He gives a glowing description of some paintings of this 'German Correggio', as he calls him, and thenceforward these paintings and others which must have been painted by the same great artist are usually labelled 'Grünewald'. No record or document of the period, however, mentions any painter of the name of Grünewald, and we must consider it likely that the author had mixed up his facts. Since some of the paintings ascribed to the master bear the initials M.G.N., and since a painter Mathis Gothardt Nithardt is known to have lived and worked near Aschaffenburg in Germany as an approximate contemporary of Albrecht Dürer, it is now believed that this, and not Grünewald, was the true name of the great master. But this theory does not help us much, since we do not know very much about that master Mathis. In short, while Dürer stands before us like a living human being whose habits, beliefs, tastes and mannerisms are intimately known to us, Grünewald is as great a mystery to us as Shakespeare. It is unlikely that this is entirely due to mere coincidence. The reason why we know so much about Dürer is precisely that he saw himself as a reformer and innovator of the art of his country. He reflected on what he was doing and why he did it, he kept records of his journeys and researches, and he wrote books to teach his own generation. There is no indication that

the painter of the 'Grünewald' masterpieces saw himself in a
similar light. On the contrary. The few paintings we have of
his are altar-panels of the traditional type in major and minor
provincial churches, including a large number of painted
'wings' for a great altar at the Alsatian village of Isenheim (the
so-called Isenheim altarpiece). His works afford no indication
that he strove like Dürer to become something different from
a mere craftsman or that he was hampered by the fixed
traditions of religious art as it had developed in the late Gothic
period. Though he was certainly familiar with some of the
great discoveries of Italian art, he made use of them only as far
as they suited his ideas of what art should do. On this score,
he does not seem to have felt any doubts. Art for him did not
consist in the search for the hidden laws of beauty – for him
it could have only one aim, the aim of all religious art in
the Middle Ages – that of providing a sermon in pictures, of
proclaiming the sacred truths as taught by the Church. The
central panel of the Isenheim altarpiece, figure 224, shows that
he sacrificed all other considerations to this one overriding
aim. Of beauty, as the Italian artists saw it, there is none in the
stark and cruel picture of the crucified Saviour. Like a preacher
at Passiontide, Grünewald left nothing undone to bring home
to us the horrors of this scene of suffering: Christ's dying body
is distorted by the torture of the Cross; the thorns of the
scourges stick in the festering wounds which cover the whole
figure. The dark red blood forms a glaring contrast to the sickly
green of the flesh. By His features and the impressive gesture
of His hands, the Man of Sorrows speaks to us of the meaning
of His Calvary. His suffering is reflected in the traditional
group of Mary, in the garb of a widow, fainting in the arms of
St John the Evangelist, to whose care the Lord has commended
her, and in the smaller figure of St Mary Magdalene with
her vessel of ointments, wringing her hands in sorrow. On the

other side of the Cross, there stands the powerful figure of
St John the Baptist with the ancient symbol of the lamb
carrying the cross and pouring out its blood into the chalice
of the Holy Communion. With a stern and commanding
gesture he points towards the Saviour, and over him are written
the words that he speaks (according to the Gospel of St John
III. 30): 'He must increase, but I must decrease.'

There is little doubt that the artist wanted the beholder
of the altar to meditate on these words, which he emphasized
so strongly by the pointing hand of St John the Baptist.
Perhaps he even wanted us to see how Christ must grow and
we diminish. For in this picture, in which reality seems to be
depicted in all its unmitigated horror, there is one unreal and
fantastic trait: the figures differ greatly in size. We need only
compare the hands of St Mary Magdalene under the Cross
with those of Christ to become fully aware of the astonishing
difference in their dimensions. It is clear that in these matters
Grünewald rejected the rules of modern art as it had
developed since the Renaissance, and that he deliberately
returned to the principles of medieval and primitive painters,
who varied the size of their figures according to their
importance in the picture. Just as he had sacrificed the
pleasing kind of beauty for the sake of the spiritual message
of the altar, he also disregarded the new demand for correct
proportions, since this helped him to express the mystic truth
of the words of St John.

Grünewald's work may thus remind us once more that
an artist can be very great indeed without being 'progressive',
because the greatness of art does not lie in new discoveries.
That Grünewald was familiar with these discoveries he showed
plainly enough whenever they helped him to express what he
wanted to convey. And just as he used his brush to depict
the dead and tormented body of Christ, he used it on another

panel to convey its transfiguration at the Resurrection into an unearthly apparition of heavenly light, figure 225. It is difficult to describe this picture because, once more, so much depends on its colours. It seems as if Christ has just soared out of the grave, leaving a trail of radiant light – the shroud in which the body has been swathed reflecting the coloured rays of the halo. There is a poignant contrast between the risen Christ, who is hovering over the scene, and the helpless gestures of the soldiers on the ground, who are dazzled and overwhelmed by this sudden apparition of light. We feel the violence of the shock in the way in which they writhe in their armour. As we cannot assess the distance between foreground and background, the two soldiers behind the grave look like puppets who have tumbled over, and their distorted shapes only serve to throw into relief the serene and majestic calm of the transfigured body of Christ.

A third famous German of Dürer's generation, Lucas Cranach (1472-1553), began as a most promising painter. In his youth he spent several years in southern Germany and Austria. At the time when Giorgione, who came from the southern foothills of the Alps, discovered the beauty of mountain scenery, figure 209, this young painter was fascinated by the northern foothills with their old forests and romantic vistas. In a painting dated 1504 – the year when Dürer published his prints, figures 222-3 – Cranach represented the Holy Family on the Flight into Egypt, figure 226. They are resting near a spring in a wooded mountain region. It is a charming place in the wilderness with shaggy trees and a wide view down a lovely green valley. Crowds of little angels have gathered round the Virgin; one is offering berries to the Christ Child, another is fetching water in a shell while others have settled down to refresh the spirit of the tired refugees with a concert of pipes and flutes. This poetic invention has preserved something of the spirit of Lochner's lyrical art, figure 176.

In his later years Cranach became a rather slick and fashionable court painter in Saxony, who owed his fame mainly to his friendship with Martin Luther. But it seems that his brief stay in the Danube region had been sufficient to open the eyes of the people who lived in the Alpine districts to the beauty of their surroundings. The painter Albrecht Altdorfer, of Regensburg (1480?-1538), went out into the woods and mountains to study the shape of weather-beaten pines and rocks. Many of his watercolours and etchings, and at least one of his oil-paintings, figure 227, tell no story and contain no human being. This is quite a momentous change. Even the Greeks with all their love of nature had painted landscapes only as settings for their pastoral scenes, figure 72. In the Middle Ages a painting which did not clearly illustrate a theme, sacred or profane, was almost inconceivable. Only when the painter's skill as such began to interest people was it possible for him to sell a painting which served no other purpose but that of recording his enjoyment of a beautiful piece of scenery.

The Netherlands, at this great time of the first decades of the sixteenth century, produced not as many outstanding masters as they had done during the fifteenth century, when masters like Jan van Eyck, *page 175*, Rogier van der Weyden, *pages 205-6* and Hugo van der Goes, *pages 206-7*, were famous throughout Europe. Those artists, at least, who strove to absorb the New Learning as Dürer had done in Germany were often torn between their loyalties to old methods and their love for the new. Figure 228 shows a characteristic example by the painter Jan Gossaert, called Mabuse (1478?-1532). According to the legend, St Luke the Evangelist was a painter by profession, and thus he is represented here making a portrait of the Virgin and her Child. The way in which Mabuse painted these figures is quite in accordance with the traditions of Jan van Eyck and his followers, but the setting is quite different. It seems that he wanted to show off his knowledge of the Italian achievements, his skill in scientific perspective, his familiarity with classical architecture, and his mastery of light and shade. The result is a picture which certainly has great charm but which lacks the simple harmony of both its northern and Italian models. One wonders why St Luke found no more suitable place in which to draw the Madonna than this ostentatious but presumably draughty palace courtyard.

Thus it came about that the greatest Netherlandish artist of the period is not found among the adherents of the New Style but among those who, like Grünewald in Germany, refused to be drawn into the modern movement from the South. In the Dutch town of 's Hertogenbosch there lived such a painter, who was called Hieronymus Bosch. Very little is known about him. We do not know how old he was when he died in 1516, but he must have been active for a considerable time since he became an independent master in 1488. Like Grünewald, Bosch showed that the traditions and achievements of painting which had been developed to represent reality most convincingly could be turned round, as it were, to give us an equally plausible picture of things no human eye had seen. He became famous for his terrifying representations of the powers of evil. Perhaps it is no accident that the gloomy King Philip II of Spain, later in the century, had a special predilection for this artist, who was so much concerned with man's wickedness. Figures 229-30 show two wings from one of Bosch's triptychs he bought and which is therefore still in Spain. On the left we watch evil invading the world. The creation of Eve is followed by the temptation of Adam and both are driven out of Paradise, while high above in the sky we see the fall of the rebellious angels, who are hurled from heaven as a swarm of repulsive insects. On the other wing we are shown a vision of hell. There we see horror piled upon horror, fires and torments and all manner of fearful demons, half animal, half human or half machine, who plague and punish the poor sinful souls for all eternity. For the first and perhaps for the only time, an artist had succeeded in giving concrete and tangible shape to the fears that had haunted the minds of man in the Middle Ages. It was an achievement which was perhaps only possible at this very moment, when the old ideas were still vigorous and yet the modern spirit had provided the artist with methods of representing what he saw. Perhaps Hieronymus Bosch could have written on one of his paintings of Hell what Jan van Eyck wrote on his peaceful scene of the Arnolfinis' betrothal: 'I was there'.

8

Crisis of Art

ater sixteenth century

Round about 1520 all lovers of art in the Italian cities seemed
to agree that painting had reached the peak of perfection. Men
such as Michelangelo and Raphael, Titian and Leonardo had
actually done everything that former generations had tried to
do. No problem of draughtsmanship seemed too difficult for
them, no subject-matter too complicated. They had shown
how to combine beauty and harmony with correctness, and
had even surpassed – so it was said – the most renowned
statues of Greek and Roman antiquity. For a boy who wanted
one day to become a great painter himself, this general
opinion was perhaps not altogether pleasant to listen to.
However much he may have admired the works of the great
living masters, he must have wondered whether it was
true that nothing remained to be done because everything art
could possibly do had been achieved. Some appeared to
accept this idea as inevitable, and studied hard to learn what
Michelangelo had learned, and to imitate his manner as
best they could. Michelangelo had loved to draw nudes in
complicated attitudes – well, if that was the right thing to do,
they would copy his nudes, and put them into their pictures
whether they fitted or not. The results were sometimes slightly
ludicrous – the sacred scenes from the Bible were crowded out
by what appeared to be a training team of young athletes.
Later critics, who saw that these young painters had gone
wrong since they merely imitated the manner of Michelangelo
because it was in fashion, have called this the period of
Mannerism. But not all young artists of this period were so
foolish as to believe that all that was asked of art was a
collection of nudes in difficult postures. Many, indeed, doubted
whether art could ever come to a standstill, whether it was not
possible, after all, to surpass the famous masters of the former
generation, if not in their handling of human forms, then,
perhaps, in some other respect. Some wanted to outdo them

in the matter of invention. They wanted to paint pictures full of significance and wisdom – such wisdom, indeed, that it should remain obscure, save to the most learned scholars. Their works almost resemble picture puzzles which cannot be solved save by those who know what the scholars of the time believed to be the true meaning of Egyptian hieroglyphs, and of many half-forgotten ancient writers. Others, again, wanted to attract attention by making their works less natural, less obvious, less simple and harmonious than the works of the great masters. These works, they seem to have argued, are indeed perfect – but perfection is not for ever interesting. Once you are familiar with it, it ceases to excite you. We will aim at the startling, the unexpected, the unheard-of. Of course, there was something slightly unsound in this obsession of the young artists with the task of outdoing the classical masters – it led even the best among them to strange, sophisticated experiments. But in a way, these frantic efforts to go one better were the greatest tribute they could pay to the older artists. Had not Leonardo himself said: 'It is a wretched pupil who does not surpass his master'? To some extent, the great 'classical' artists had themselves begun and encouraged new and unfamiliar experiments; their very fame, and the credit they enjoyed in their later years, had enabled them to try out novel, unorthodox effects in arrangement or colouring, and to explore new possibilities of art. Michelangelo in particular had occasionally shown a bold disregard for all conventions – nowhere more than in architecture, where he sometimes abandoned the sacrosanct rules of classical tradition to follow his own moods and whims. It was he himself who accustomed the public to admire an artist's 'caprices' and 'inventions', and who set the example of a genius not satisfied with the matchless perfection of his own early masterpieces, but constantly and restlessly searching for new methods and modes of expression.

It was only natural that young artists should regard this as a licence to startle the public with their own 'original' inventions. Their efforts resulted in some amusing pieces of design. The window in the form of a face, figure 231, designed by an architect and painter, Federico Zuccaro (1543-1609), gives a good idea of this type of caprice.

Other architects, again, were more intent on displaying their great learning and their knowledge of classical authors in which they did, in fact, surpass the masters of Bramante's generation. The greatest and most learned of these was the architect Andrea Palladio (1508-80). Figure 232 shows his famous Villa Rotonda, or round villa, near Vicenza. In a way, it, too, is a 'caprice', for it has four identical sides, each with a porch in the form of a temple façade, grouped round a central hall which recalls the Roman Pantheon, figure 75. However beautiful the combination may be, it is hardly a building which one would like to live in. The search for novelty and effect has interfered with the ordinary purpose of architecture.

A typical artist of this period was the Florentine sculptor and goldsmith Benvenuto Cellini (1500-71). Cellini has described his own life in a famous book, which gives an immensely colourful and vivid picture of his age. He was boastful, ruthless and vain, but it is hard to be cross with him because he tells the story of his adventures and exploits with such gusto that you think you are reading a novel by Dumas. In his vanity and conceit and in his restlessness, which drove him from town to town and from court to court, picking quarrels and earning laurels, Cellini is a real product of his time. For him, to be an artist was no longer to be a respectable and sedate owner of a workshop: it was to be a 'virtuoso' for whose favour princes and cardinals should compete. One of the few works by his hand which have come down to us is a golden salt-cellar, made for the King of France in 1543,

figure 233. Cellini tells us the story in great detail. We hear
how he snubbed two famous scholars who ventured to suggest
a subject to him, how he made a model in wax of his own
invention representing the Earth and the Sea. To show how
the Earth and the Sea interpenetrate he made the legs of the
two figures interlock: 'The Sea, fashioned as a man, held
a finely wrought ship which could hold enough salt, beneath
I had put four sea-horses and I had given the figure a trident.
The Earth I fashioned as a fair woman, as graceful as I could
do it. Beside her I placed a richly decorated temple to hold
the pepper.' But all this subtle invention makes less interesting
reading than the story of how Cellini carried the gold from
the King's treasurer and was attacked by four bandits, all
of whom he put to flight single-handed. To some of us the
smooth elegance of Cellini's figures may look a little over-
elaborate and affected. Perhaps it is a consolation to know that
their master had enough of that healthy robustness which his
work seems to lack.

Cellini's outlook is typical of the restless and hectic
attempts of the period to create something more interesting
and unusual than former generations had done. We find
the same spirit in the paintings of one of Correggio's
followers, Parmigianino (1503-40). I can well imagine that
some may find his Madonna, figure 234, almost offensive
because of the affectation and sophistication with which a
sacred subject is treated. There is nothing in it of the ease and
simplicity with which Raphael had treated that ancient theme.
The picture is called the 'Madonna with the long neck'
because the painter, in his eagerness to make the Holy Virgin
look graceful and elegant, has given her a neck like that of a
swan. He has stretched and lengthened the proportions of the
human body in a strangely capricious way. The hand of the
Virgin with its long delicate fingers, the long leg of the angel

in the foreground, the lean, haggard prophet with a scroll
of parchment – we see them all as through a distorting mirror.
And yet there can be no doubt that the artist achieved this
effect through neither ignorance nor indifference. He has
taken care to show us that he liked these unnaturally elongated
forms, for, to make doubly sure of his effect, he placed an
oddly shaped high column of equally unusual proportions in
the background of the painting. As for the arrangement of the
picture, he also showed us that he did not believe in
conventional harmonies. Instead of distributing his figures in
equal pairs on both sides of the Madonna, he crammed a
jostling crowd of angels into a narrow corner, and left the
other side wide open to show the tall figure of the prophet, so
reduced in size through the distance that he hardly reaches
the Madonna's knee. There can be no doubt, then, that if this
be madness there is method in it. The painter wanted to be
unorthodox. He wanted to show that the classical solution of
perfect harmony is not the only solution conceivable;
that natural simplicity is one way of achieving beauty, but that
there are less direct ways of getting interesting effects for
sophisticated lovers of art. Whether we like or dislike the road
he took, we must admit that he was consistent. Indeed,
Parmigianino and all the artists of his time who deliberately
sought to create something new and unexpected, even at the
expense of the 'natural' beauty established by the great
masters, were perhaps the first 'modern' artists. We shall see,
indeed, that what is now called 'modern' art may have had its
roots in a similar urge to avoid the obvious and achieve effects
which differ from conventional natural beauty.

Other artists of this strange period, in the shadow of
the giants of art, were less despairing of surpassing them
by ordinary standards of skill and virtuosity. We may not agree
with all they did, but here, too, we are forced to admit that

some of their efforts are startling enough. A typical example is the statue of Mercury, the messenger of the gods, by a Flemish sculptor, Jean de Boulogne (1529-1608), whom the Italians called Giovanni da Bologna or Giambologna, figure 235. He had set himself the task of achieving the impossible – a statue which overcomes the weight of dead matter and which creates the sensation of a rapid flight through the air. And to a certain extent he was successful. Only with a tip of his toe does his famous Mercury touch the ground – rather, not the ground, but a gush of air which comes out of the mouth of a mask representing the South Wind. The whole statue is so carefully balanced that it really seems to hover in the air – almost to speed through it, with swiftness and grace. Perhaps a classical sculptor, or even Michelangelo, might have found such an effect unbecoming to a statue which should remind one of the heavy block of matter out of which it was shaped – but Giambologna, no less than Parmigianino, preferred to defy these well-established rules and to show what surprising effects could be achieved.

Perhaps the greatest of all these masters of the latter part of the sixteenth century lived in Venice. He was called Jacopo Robusti, but nicknamed Tintoretto (1518-94). He too had tired of the simple beauty in forms and colours which Titian had shown to the Venetians – but his discontent must have been more than a mere desire to accomplish the unusual. He seems to have felt that, however incomparable Titian was as a painter of beauty, his pictures tended to be more pleasing than moving; that they were not sufficiently exciting to make the great stories of the Bible and the sacred legends live for us. Whether he was right in this or not, he must, at any rate, have been resolved to tell these stories in a different way, to make the spectator feel the thrill and tense drama of the events he painted. Figure 236 shows that he did indeed succeed in making his pictures unusual and captivating. At first glance this painting looks confused and confusing. Instead of a clear arrangement of the main figures in the plane of the picture, such as Raphael had achieved, we look into the depths of a strange vault. There is a tall man with a halo at the left corner, raising his arm as if to stop something that is happening – and if we follow his gesture we can see that he is concerned with what is going on high under the roof of the vault on the other side of the picture. There are two men about to lower a dead body from a tomb – they have lifted its lid – and a third man in a turban is helping them, while a nobleman in the background with a torch is trying to read the inscription on another tomb. These men are evidently plundering a catacomb. One of the bodies is stretched out on a carpet in strange foreshortening, while a dignified old man in a gorgeous costume kneels beside it and looks at it. In the right corner there is a group of gesticulating men and women, looking with astonishment at the saint – for a saint the figure with the halo must be. If we look more closely we see that he carries a book – he is St Mark the Evangelist, the patron saint of Venice. What is happening? The picture represents the story of how the relics of St Mark were brought from Alexandria (the town of the 'infidel' Muslims) to Venice, where the famous shrine of the church of St Mark was built to house them. The story goes that St Mark had been bishop at Alexandria and had been buried in one of the catacombs there. When the Venetian party had broken into the catacomb on the pious errand of finding the body of the saint, they did not know which of the many tombs contained the treasured relic. But when they came upon the right one, St Mark suddenly appeared and revealed the remains of his earthly existence. That is the moment which Tintoretto selected. The saint commands the men not to continue searching the tombs. His body is found; it lies at his feet,

bathed in light, and already its presence is working miracles.
The writing man on the right is freed from a demon
who had possessed him and who is seen escaping from his
mouth like a wisp of smoke. The nobleman who kneels down
in gratitude and adoration is the donor, a member of the
religious confraternity who had commissioned the painting.
No doubt the whole picture must have struck contemporaries
as eccentric. They may have been rather shocked by the
clashing contrasts of light and shade, of closeness and
distance, by the lack of harmony in gestures and movement.
Yet they must soon have understood that with more ordinary
methods Tintoretto could not have created the impression
of a tremendous mystery unfolding before our eyes. To achieve
this purpose Tintoretto even sacrificed that mellow beauty
of colour that had been the proudest achievement of Venetian
painting, of Giorgione and Titian. His painting of St George's
fight with the dragon, in London, figure 237, shows how the
weird light and the broken tones add to the feeling of tension
and excitement. We feel the drama has just reached its climax.
The princess seems to be rushing right out of the picture
towards us while the hero is removed, against all rules, far into
the background of the scene.

Giorgio Vasari (1511-74), the great Florentine critic
and biographer of the period, wrote of Tintoretto that 'had he
not abandoned the beaten track but rather followed the
beautiful style of his predecessors, he would have become one
of the greatest painters seen in Venice.' As it was, Vasari thought
his work was marred by careless execution and eccentric taste.
He was puzzled by the lack of 'finish' Tintoretto gave his work.
'His sketches', he says, 'are so crude that his pencil strokes
show more force than judgement and seem to have been made
by chance.' It is a reproach which from that time onwards has
often been made against modern artists. Perhaps this is not

altogether surprising, for these great innovators in art have often concentrated on the essential things and refused to worry about technical perfection in the usual sense. In periods like that of Tintoretto, technical excellence had reached such a high standard that anyone with some mechanical aptitude could master some of its tricks. A man like Tintoretto wanted to show things in a new light, he wanted to explore new ways of representing the legends and myths of the past. He considered his painting complete when he had conveyed his vision of the legendary scene. A smooth and careful finish did not interest him, for it did not serve his purpose. On the contrary – it might have distracted our attention from the dramatic happenings of the picture. So he left it at that, and left people wondering.

No one in the sixteenth century took these methods further than a painter from the Greek island of Crete, Domenikos Theotokopoulos (1541?-1614), who was called El Greco ('the Greek') for short. He had come to Venice from an isolated part of the world which had not developed any new kind of art since the Middle Ages. In his homeland, he must have been used to seeing the images of saints in the ancient Byzantine manner – solemn, rigid and remote from any semblance of natural appearance. Not being trained to look at pictures for their correct design, he found nothing shocking in Tintoretto's art, but much that was fascinating. For he too, it seems, was a passionate and devout man, and he felt an urge to tell the sacred stories in a new and stirring manner. After his stay in Venice he settled in a distant part of Europe – in Toledo, Spain, where again he was not likely to be disturbed and harried by critics asking for correct and natural design – for in Spain, too, the medieval ideas on art still lingered on. This may explain why El Greco's art surpasses even Tintoretto's in its bold disregard of natural forms and colours, and in its

stirring and dramatic vision. Figure 238 is one of his most
startling and exciting pictures. It represents a passage from the
Revelation of St John, and it is St John himself whom we see
on one side of the picture in visionary rapture, looking
towards Heaven and raising his arms in a prophetic gesture.

The passage is the one in which the Lamb summons
St John to 'Come and see' the opening of the seven seals. 'And
when he had opened the fifth seal, I saw under the altar the
souls of them that were slain for the word of God, and for the
testimony which they held: And they cried with a loud voice,
saying "How long, O Lord, holy and true, dost thou not judge
and avenge our blood on them that dwell on the earth?"
And white robes were given unto every one of them' (Rev. VI.
9 - 11). The nude figures, with their excited gestures, are
therefore the martyrs who rise to receive the heavenly gift of
white robes. Surely no exact and accurate drawing could ever
have expressed with such an uncanny and convincing force
that terrible vision of doomsday, when the very saints call for
the destruction of this world. It is not difficult to see that
El Greco had learned much from Tintoretto's unorthodox
method of lopsided composition, and that he had also adopted
the mannerism of over-long figures like that of Parmigianino's
sophisticated Madonna, figure 234. But we also realize that
El Greco employed this artistic method with a new purpose.
He lived in Spain, where religion had a mystic fervour
found hardly anywhere else. In this atmosphere, the
sophisticated art of Mannerism lost much of its character of
an art for connoisseurs. Though his work strikes us as
incredibly 'modern', his contemporaries in Spain do not seem
to have raised any objections such as Vasari did to Tintoretto's
works. His greatest portraits, figure 239, can indeed stand beside
those of Titian, figure 212. His studio was always fully
employed. He seems to have engaged a number of assistants to

cope with the many orders he received, and that may explain
why not all the works that bear his name are equally good.
It was only a generation later that people began to criticize his
unnatural forms and colours, and to regard his pictures as
something like a bad joke; and only after the First World War,
when modern artists had taught us not to apply the same
standards of 'correctness' to all works of art, was El Greco's art
rediscovered and understood.

In the northern countries, in Germany, Holland and
England, artists were confronted with a much more real crisis
than their colleagues in Italy and Spain. For these southerners
had only to deal with the problem of how to paint in a new
and startling manner. In the North the question soon faced
them whether painting could and should continue at all. This
great crisis was brought about by the Reformation. Many
Protestants objected to pictures or statues of saints in churches
and regarded them as a sign of Popish idolatry. Thus the
painters in Protestant regions lost their best source of income,
the painting of altar-panels. The stricter among the Calvinists
even objected to other kinds of luxury such as gay decorations
of houses, and even where these were permitted in theory, the
climate and the style of buildings were usually unsuited to
large fresco decorations such as Italian nobles commissioned
for their palaces. All that remained as a regular source of income
for artists was book illustration and portrait painting, and it was
doubtful whether these would suffice to make a living.

We can witness the effect of this crisis in the career of
the greatest German painter of this generation, in the life of
Hans Holbein the Younger (1497-1543). Holbein was twenty-
six years younger than Dürer and only three years older
than Cellini. He was born in Augsburg, a rich merchant city
with close trading relations with Italy; he soon moved to
Basle, a renowned centre of the New Learning.

The knowledge which Dürer strove for so passionately throughout his life thus came more naturally to Holbein. Coming from a painter's family (his father was a respected master) and being exceedingly alert, he soon absorbed the achievements of both the northern and the Italian artists. He was hardly over thirty when he painted the wonderful altar-painting of the Virgin with the family of the burgomaster of Basle as donors, figure 240. The form was traditional in all countries, and we have seen it applied in the Wilton Diptych, figure 143, and Titian's 'Pesaro Madonna', figure 210. But Holbein's painting is still one of the most perfect examples of its kind. The way in which the donors are arranged in seemingly effortless groups on both sides of the Virgin, whose calm and majestic figure is framed by a niche of classical forms, reminds us of the most harmonious compositions of the Italian Renaissance, of Giovanni Bellini, figure 208, and Raphael, figure 203. The careful attention to detail, on the other hand, and a certain indifference to conventional beauty, show that Holbein had learned his trade in the North. He was on his way to becoming the leading master of the German-speaking countries when the turmoil of the Reformation put an end to all such hopes. In 1526 he left Switzerland for England with a letter of recommendation from the great scholar, Erasmus of Rotterdam. 'The arts here are freezing,' Erasmus wrote commending the painter to his friends, among whom was Sir Thomas More. One of Holbein's first jobs in England was to prepare a large portrait of that other great scholar's family, and some detailed studies for this work are still preserved at Windsor Castle, figure 241. If Holbein had hoped to get away from the turmoil of the Reformation he must have been disappointed by later events, but when he finally settled in England for good and was given the official title of Court Painter by Henry VIII he had at least found a sphere of activity which allowed him to live and work. He could no longer paint Madonnas, but the tasks of a Court Painter were exceedingly manifold. He designed jewellery and furniture, costumes for pageantries and decorations for halls, weapons and goblets. His main job, however, was to paint portraits of the royal household, and it is due to Holbein's unfailing eye that we still have such a vivid picture of the men and women of Henry VIII's period. Figure 242 shows his portrait of Sir Richard Southwell, a courtier and official who took part in the dissolution of the monasteries. There is nothing dramatic in these portraits of Holbein, nothing to catch the eye, but the longer we look at them the more they seem to reveal of the sitter's mind and personality. We do not doubt for a moment that they are in fact faithful records of what Holbein saw, drawn without fear or favour. The way in which Holbein has placed the figure in the picture shows the sure touch of the master. Nothing seems left to chance; the whole composition is so perfectly balanced that it may easily seem 'obvious' to us. But this was Holbein's intention. In his earlier portraits he had still sought to display his wonderful skill in the rendering of details, to characterize a sitter through his setting, through the things among which he spent his life, figure 243. The older he grew and the more mature his art became, the less did he seem in need of any such tricks. He did not want to obtrude himself and to divert attention from the sitter. And it is precisely for this masterly restraint that we admire him most.

When Holbein had left the German-speaking countries, painting there began to decline to a frightening extent, and when Holbein died the arts were in a similar plight in England. In fact, the only branch of painting there that survived the Reformation was that of portrait painting, which Holbein had so firmly established. Even in this branch the

fashions of southern Mannerism made themselves increasingly
felt, and ideals of courtly refinement and elegance replaced the
simpler style of Holbein.

The portrait of a young Elizabethan nobleman, figure
244, gives an idea of this new type of portraiture at its best. It
is a 'miniature' by the famous English master Nicholas Hilliard
(1547-1619), a contemporary of Sir Philip Sidney and William
Shakespeare. We may indeed think of Sidney's pastorals or
Shakespeare's comedies when looking at this dainty youth
who leans languidly against a tree, surrounded by thorny wild
roses, his right hand pressed against his heart. Perhaps the
miniature was intended as the young man's gift to the lady he
was wooing, for it bears the Latin inscription 'Dat poenas
laudata fides', which means roughly, 'my praised faith procures
my pain'. We ought not to ask whether these pains were any
more real than the painted thorns on the miniature. A young
gallant in those days was expected to make a show of grief
and unrequited love. These sighs and these sonnets were all
part of a graceful and elaborate game, which nobody took too
seriously but in which everybody wanted to shine by
inventing new variations and new refinements.

If we look at Hilliard's miniature as an object designed
for this game, it may no longer strike us as affected and
artificial. Let us hope that when the maiden received this token
of affection in a precious case and saw the pitiful pose of her
elegant and noble wooer, his 'praised faith' had at last its reward.

There was only one Protestant country in Europe where
art fully survived the crisis of the Reformation – that was the
Netherlands. There, where painting had flourished for so long,
artists found a way out of their predicament: instead of
concentrating on portrait painting alone they specialized in all
those types of subject-matter to which the Protestant Church
could raise no objections. Since the early days of Van Eyck, the

artists of the Netherlands had been recognized as perfect masters in the imitation of nature. While the Italians prided themselves on being unrivalled in the representation of the beautiful human figure in motion, they were ready to recognize that, for sheer patience and accuracy in depicting a flower, a tree, a barn or a flock of sheep, the 'Flemings' were apt to outstrip them. It was therefore quite natural that the northern artists, who were no longer needed for the painting of altar-panels and other devotional pictures, tried to find a market for their recognized specialities and to paint pictures the main object of which was to display their stupendous skill in representing the surface of things. Specialization was not even quite new to the artists of these lands. We remember that Hieronymus Bosch, figures 229-30, had made a speciality of pictures of Hell and of demons even before the crisis of art. Now, when the scope of painting had become more restricted, the painters went further along this road. They tried to develop the traditions of northern art which reach back to the time of the drôleries on the margins of medieval manuscripts, figure 140, and to the scenes of real life represented in fifteenth-century art, figure 177. Pictures in which the painters deliberately cultivated a certain branch or kind of subject, particularly scenes from daily life, later became known as 'genre pictures' (genre being the French word for 'branch' or 'kind').

The greatest of the Flemish sixteenth-century masters of genre was Pieter Bruegel the Elder (1525?-69). We know little of his life except that he had been to Italy, like so many northern artists of his time, and that he lived and worked in Antwerp and Brussels, where he painted most of his pictures in the 1560s, the decade in which the stern Duke of Alva arrived in the Netherlands. The dignity of art and of artists was probably as important to him as it was to Dürer or Cellini, for in one of his splendid drawings he is clearly out to point a contrast between the proud painter and the stupid-looking bespectacled man who fumbles in his purse as he peers over the artist's shoulder, figure 245.

The 'kind' of painting on which Bruegel concentrated was scenes from peasant life. He painted peasants merrymaking, feasting and working, and so people have come to think of him as one of the Flemish peasants. This is a common mistake which we are apt to make about artists. We are often inclined to confuse their work with their person. We think of Dickens as a member of Mr Pickwick's jolly circle, or of Jules Verne as a daring inventor and traveller. If Bruegel had been a peasant himself he could not have painted them as he did. He certainly was a townsman and his attitude towards the rustic life of the village was very likely similar to that of Shakespeare, for whom Quince the Carpenter and Bottom the Weaver were a species of 'clown'. It was the custom at that time to regard the country yokel as a figure of fun. I do not think that either Shakespeare or Bruegel accepted this custom out of snobbery, but in rustic life human nature was less disguised and covered up with a veneer of artificiality and convention than in the life and manners of the gentlemen Hilliard portrayed. Thus, when they wanted to show up the folly of humankind, playwrights and artists often took low life as their subject.

One of the most perfect of Bruegel's human comedies is his famous picture of a country wedding, figure 246. Like most pictures, it loses a great deal in reproduction: all details become much smaller, and we must therefore look at it with double care. The feast takes place in a barn, with straw stacked up high in the background. The bride sits in front of a piece of blue cloth, with a kind of crown suspended over her head. She sits quietly, with folded hands and a grin of utter contentment on her stupid face, figure 247. The old man in the chair and the woman beside her are probably her parents, while the man farther back, who is so busy gobbling his food with his spoon, may be the bridegroom. Most of the people at the table concentrate on eating and drinking, and we notice this is only the beginning. In the left-hand corner a man pours out beer – a good number of empty jugs are still in the basket – while two men with white aprons are carrying ten more platefuls of pie or porridge on an improvised tray. One of the guests passes the plates to the table. But much more is going on. There is the crowd in the background trying to get in; there are the musicians, one of them with a pathetic, forlorn and hungry look in his eyes, as he watches the food being carried past; there are the two outsiders at the corner of the table, the friar and the magistrate, engrossed in their own conversation; and there is the child in the foreground, who has got hold of a plate, and a feathered cap much too large for its little head, and who is completely absorbed in licking the delicious food – a picture of innocent greed. But what is even more admirable than all this wealth of anecdote, wit and observation, is the way in which Bruegel has organized his picture so that it does not look crowded or confusing. Tintoretto himself could not have produced a more convincing picture of a crowded space than did Bruegel with his device of the table receding into the background and the movement of people starting with the crowd at the barn door, leading up to the foreground and the scene of the food carriers, and back again through the gesture of the man serving the table who leads our eyes directly to the small but central figure of the grinning bride.

In these gay, but by no means simple, pictures, Bruegel had discovered a new kingdom for art which the generations of Netherlandish painters after him were to explore to the full.

In France the crisis of art took again a different turn. Situated between Italy and the northern countries, it was influenced by both. The vigorous tradition of French medieval art was at first threatened by the inrush of the Italianate fashion, which French painters found as difficult to adapt as did their colleagues in the Netherlands, figure 228. The form in which Italian art was finally accepted by high society was that of the elegant and refined Italian Mannerists of Cellini's type, figure 233. We can see its influence in the lively reliefs from a fountain by the French sculptor, Jean Goujon (died 1566?), figure 248. There is something both of Parmigianino's fastidious elegance and Giambologna's virtuosity in these exquisitely graceful figures and the way they are fitted into the narrow strips reserved for them.

A generation later an artist arose in France in whose etchings the bizarre inventions of the Italian Mannerists were represented in the spirit of Pieter Bruegel: the Lorrainian, Jacques Callot (1592-1635). Like Tintoretto or even El Greco, he loved to show the most surprising combinations, of tall, gaunt figures and wide unexpected vistas; but, like Bruegel, he used these devices to portray the follies of mankind through scenes from the life of its outcasts, soldiers, cripples, beggars and strolling players, figure 249. But by the time Callot popularized these extravaganzas in his etchings most painters of his day had turned their attention to new problems, which filled the talk of the studios in Rome, Antwerp and Madrid.

19

Vision and Visions

Catholic Europe, first half of the seventeenth century

The history of art is sometimes described as the story of a succession of various styles. We hear how the Romanesque or Norman style of the twelfth century with its round arches was succeeded by the Gothic style with the pointed arch; how the Gothic style was supplanted by the Renaissance, which had its beginnings in Italy in the early fifteenth century and slowly gained ground in all the countries of Europe. The style which followed the Renaissance is usually called Baroque. But, while it is easy to identify the earlier styles by definite marks of recognition, this is not so simple in the case of Baroque. The fact is that from the Renaissance onwards, almost up to our own time, architects have used the same basic forms – columns, pilasters, cornices, entablatures and mouldings, all of which were originally borrowed from classical ruins. In a sense, therefore, it is true to say that the Renaissance style of building has continued from Brunelleschi's days to our own, and many books on architecture speak of this whole period as Renaissance. On the other hand, it is natural that within such a long period tastes and fashions in building should have varied considerably, and it is convenient to have different labels by which to distinguish these changing styles. It is a strange fact that many of these labels which to us are simply names of styles were originally words of abuse or derision. The word 'Gothic' was first used by the Italian art critics of the Renaissance to denote the style which they considered barbarous, and which they thought had been brought into Italy by the Goths who destroyed the Roman Empire and sacked its cities. The word 'Mannerism' still retains for many people its original connotation of affectation and shallow imitation, of which critics of the seventeenth century had accused the artists of the late sixteenth century. The word 'Baroque' was a term employed by critics of a later period who fought against the tendencies of the seventeenth century, and wanted to hold them up to ridicule. Baroque really means absurd or grotesque, and it was used by men who insisted that the forms of classical buildings should never have been used or combined except in the ways adopted by the Greeks and Romans. To disregard the strict rules of ancient architecture seemed to these critics a deplorable lapse of taste – whence they labelled the style Baroque. It is not altogether easy for us to appreciate these distinctions. We have become too accustomed to seeing buildings in our cities which defy the rules of classical architecture or misunderstand them altogether. So we have become insensitive in these matters and the old quarrels seem very remote from the architectural questions which interest us. To us a church façade like that in figure 250 may not seem very exciting, because we have seen so many good and bad imitations of this type of building that we hardly turn our heads to look at them; but when it was first built in Rome, in 1575, it was a most revolutionary building. It was not just one more church in Rome, where there are many churches. It was the church of the newly founded Order of the Jesuits, on which high hopes were set for combating the Reformation all over Europe. Its very shape was to be on a new and unusual plan; the Renaissance idea of round and symmetrical church building had been rejected as unsuited to divine service, and a new, simple and ingenious plan had been worked out which was to be accepted all over Europe. The church was to be in the form of a cross, topped by a high and stately cupola. In the one large, oblong space, known as the nave, the congregation could assemble without hindrance, and look towards the main altar. This stood at the end of the oblong, and behind it was the apse, which was similar in form to that of the early basilicas. To suit the requirements of private devotion and adoration of individual saints, a row of small chapels was distributed on either side of the nave each of which had an

altar of its own, and there were two larger chapels at the
ends of the arms of the cross. It is a simple and ingenious way
of planning a church and has since been widely used. It
combines the main features of medieval churches – their
oblong shape, emphasizing the main altar – with the
achievements of Renaissance planning, in which so much
stress is laid on large and roomy interiors into which the light
would stream through a majestic dome.

Looking closely at the façade of Il Gesù, which was
built by the celebrated architect Giacomo della Porta
(1541?-1602), we soon realize why it must have impressed
contemporaries as being no less new and ingenious than the
interior of the church. We see at once that it is composed
of the elements of classical architecture – we find all the set
pieces together: columns (or rather, half-columns and
pilasters) carrying an 'architrave' crowned by a high 'attic'
which, in turn, carries the upper storey. Even the distribution
of these set pieces employs some features of classical
architecture: the large middle entrance, framed by columns
and flanked by two smaller entrances, recalls the scheme of
triumphal arches, figure 74, which (to repeat) became as firmly
implanted in the architect's mind as the major chord in the
minds of musicians. There is nothing in this simple and
majestic façade to suggest deliberate defiance of the classical
rules for the sake of sophisticated caprice. But the way in
which the classical elements are fused into a pattern shows
that Roman and Greek and even Renaissance rules have been
left behind. The most striking feature in this façade is the
doubling of each column or pilaster, as if to give the whole
structure greater richness, variety and solemnity. The second
trait we notice is the care which the artist has taken to avoid
repetition and monotony and to arrange the parts so as
to form a climax in the centre, where the main entrance is

emphasized by a double frame. If we turn back to earlier buildings composed of similar elements, we immediately see the great change in character. Brunelleschi's Cappella Pazzi, figure 147, looks infinitely light and graceful by comparison, in its wonderful simplicity, and Bramante's Tempietto, figure 187, almost austere in its clear and straightforward arrangement. Even the rich complexities of Sansovino's Library, figure 207, appear simple by comparison, because there the same pattern is repeated again and again. If you have seen a part of it, you have seen it all. In Della Porta's façade of the first Jesuit church everything depends on the effect given by the whole. It is all fused together into one large and complex pattern. Perhaps the most characteristic trait in this respect is the care the architect has taken to connect the upper and lower storeys. He uses a form of volute which has no place at all in classical architecture. We need only imagine a form of this kind somewhere on a Greek temple or a Roman theatre to realize how utterly out of place it would seem. In fact, it is these curves and scrolls that have been responsible for much of the censure showered on Baroque builders by the upholders of pure classical tradition. But if we cover the offending ornaments with a piece of paper and try to visualize the building without them, we must admit that they are not merely ornamental. Without them the building would 'fall apart'. They help to give it that essential coherence and unity which was the aim of the artist. In the course of time, Baroque architects had to use ever more bold and unusual devices to achieve the essential unity of a large pattern. Seen in isolation these devices often look puzzling enough, but in all good buildings they are essential to the architect's purpose.

The development of painting out of the deadlock of Mannerism, into a style far richer in possibilities than that of the earlier great masters, was in some respects similar to that of Baroque architecture. In the great paintings of Tintoretto and of El Greco we have seen the growth of some ideas which gained increasing importance in the art of the seventeenth century: the emphasis on light and colour, the disregard of simple balance, and the preference for more complicated compositions. Nevertheless, seventeenth-century painting is not just a continuation of the Mannerist style. At least people at the time did not feel it to be so. They felt that art had got into a dangerous rut, and must be got out of it. People liked talking about art in those days. In Rome, in particular, there were cultured gentlemen who enjoyed discussions on the various 'movements' among the artists of their time, who liked to compare them with older masters, and to take sides in their quarrels and intrigues. Such discussions were in themselves something new in the world of art. They had begun in the sixteenth century with such questions as whether painting was better than sculpture, or whether design was more important than colour or vice versa (the Florentines backing design, the Venetians colour). Now their topic was different: they talked about two artists who had come to Rome from northern Italy and whose methods seemed to them utterly opposed. One was Annibale Carracci (1560-1609) from Bologna, the other Michelangelo da Caravaggio (1573-1610) from a little place near Milan. Both these artists seemed tired of Mannerism. But the ways in which they overcame its sophistications were very different. Annibale Carracci was a member of a family of painters who had studied the art of Venice and of Correggio. On his arrival in Rome, he fell under the spell of Raphael's works, which he greatly admired. He aimed at recapturing something of their simplicity and beauty instead of deliberately contradicting them, as the Mannerists had done. Later critics have attributed to him the intention of imitating the best in all the great painters of the past. It is unlikely that he ever formulated a programme of this kind (which is called 'eclectic'). That was done later, in the academies or art schools which took his work as a model. Carracci himself was too much of a real artist to adopt such a foolish idea. But the battle-cry of his party among the cliques of Rome was the cultivation of classical beauty. We can see his intention in the altar-picture of the Holy Virgin mourning over the dead body of Christ, figure 251. We need only think back to Grünewald's tormented body of Christ, figure 224, to realize how careful Annibale Carracci was not to remind us of the horrors of death and the agonies of pain. The picture itself is as simple and harmonious in arrangement as that of an early Renaissance painter. Nevertheless, we would not easily mistake it for a Renaissance painting. The way in which the light is made to play over the body of the Saviour, the whole appeal to our emotions, is quite different, is Baroque. It is easy to dismiss such a picture as sentimental, but we must not forget the purpose for which it was made. It is an altar-painting, meant to be contemplated in prayer and devotion with candles burning before it.

Whatever we may feel about Carracci's methods, Caravaggio and his partisans certainly did not think highly of them. The two painters, it is true, were on the best of terms – which was no easy matter in the case of Caravaggio, for he was of a wild and irascible temper, quick to take offence, and even to run a dagger through a man. But his work was on different lines from Carracci's. To be afraid of ugliness seemed to Caravaggio a contemptible weakness. What he wanted was truth. Truth as he saw it. He had no liking for classical models, nor any respect for 'ideal beauty'. He wanted to do away with convention and to think about art afresh, page 27, figures 15, 16. Some people thought he was mainly out to shock the public; that he had no respect for any kind of beauty or tradition.

He was one of the first painters at whom these accusations were levelled and the first whose outlook was summed up by his critics in a slogan: he was condemned as a 'naturalist'. In point of fact, Caravaggio was far too great and serious an artist to fritter away his time in trying to cause a sensation. While the critics argued, he was busy at work. And his work has lost nothing of its boldness in the three centuries and more since he did it. Consider his painting of St Thomas, figure 252: the three apostles staring at Jesus, one of them poking his finger into the wound in His side, look unconventional enough. One can imagine that such a painting struck devout people as being irreverent and even outrageous. They were accustomed to seeing the apostles as dignified figures draped in beautiful folds – here they looked like common labourers, with weathered faces and wrinkled brows. But, Caravaggio would have answered, they were old labourers, common people – and as to the unseemly gesture of Doubting Thomas, the Bible is quite explicit about it. Jesus says to him: 'Reach hither thy hand, and thrust it into my side: and be not faithless, but believing' (St John xx. 27).

Caravaggio's 'naturalism', that is, his intention to copy nature faithfully, whether we think it ugly or beautiful, was perhaps more devout than Carracci's emphasis on beauty. Caravaggio must have read the Bible again and again, and pondered its words. He was one of the great artists, like Giotto and Dürer before him, who wanted to see the holy events before his own eyes as if they had been happening in his neighbour's house. And he did everything possible to make the figures of the ancient texts look more real and tangible. Even his way of handling light and shade helps to this end. His light does not make the body look graceful and soft: it is harsh and almost glaring in its contrast to the deep shadows. But it makes the whole strange scene stand out with an uncompromising honesty which few of his contemporaries could appreciate, but which had a decisive effect on later artists.

Annibale Carracci and Caravaggio fell out of fashion in the nineteenth century, but have come into their own again. But the impulse they both gave to the art of painting can hardly be imagined. Both of them worked in Rome, and Rome, at the time, was the centre of the civilized world. Artists from all parts of Europe came there, took part in the discussions on painting, took sides in the quarrels of the cliques, studied the old masters, and returned to their native countries with tales of the latest 'movements' – much as modern artists used to do with regard to Paris. According to their national traditions and temperaments, artists preferred one or other of the rival schools in Rome, and the greatest of them developed their own personal idiom from what they had learned of these foreign movements. Rome still remains the best vantage point from which to glance at the splendid panorama of painting in the countries adhering to Roman Catholicism. Of the many Italian masters who developed their style in Rome, the most famous was probably Guido Reni (1575-1642), a painter from Bologna who after a brief period of hesitation threw in his lot with the school of the Carracci. His fame, like that of his master, once stood immeasurably higher than it happens to stand just now, figure 7. There was a time when his name ranked with that of Raphael, and if we look at figure 253 we may realize why. Reni painted this fresco on the ceiling of a palace in Rome in 1614. It represents Aurora (the Dawn) and the youthful sun-god Apollo in his chariot, round which the fair maidens of the Hours (the Horae) dance their joyful measure preceded by a torch-bearing child, the Morning Star. Such are the grace and beauty of this picture of the radiant rising day that one can understand how it reminded people of Raphael and his frescoes in the Farnesina, figure 204. Indeed Reni wanted them to think of this great painter, whom he had set out to emulate. If modern critics have often thought less highly of Reni's achievement, this may be the reason. They feel, or fear, that this very emulation of another master has made Reni's work too self-conscious, too deliberate in its striving for pure beauty. We need not quarrel over these distinctions. It is no doubt true that Reni differed from Raphael in his whole approach. With Raphael, we feel that the sense of beauty and serenity flowed naturally from his whole nature and art; with Reni we feel that he chose to paint like this as a matter of principle, and that if perchance Caravaggio's disciples had convinced him that he was wrong, he could have adopted a different style. But it was not Reni's fault that these matters of principle had been brought up and had permeated the minds and the conversation of painters. In fact, it was no one's fault. Art had been developed to such a point that artists were inevitably conscious of the choice of methods before them. And once we accept this, we are free to admire the way in which Reni carried out his programme of beauty, how he deliberately discarded anything in nature that he considered low and ugly or unsuitable for his lofty ideas, and how his quest for forms more perfect and more ideal than reality was rewarded with success. It was Annibale Carracci, Reni and their followers who formulated the programme of idealizing, of 'beautifying' nature, according to the standards set by the classical statues. We call it the neo-classical or 'academic' programme as distinct from classical art, which is not bound up with any programme at all. The disputes over it are not likely to cease soon, but no one denies that among its champions have been great masters who gave us a glimpse of a world of purity and beauty without which we would be the poorer.

The greatest of the 'academic' masters was the Frenchman Nicolas Poussin (1594-1665), who made Rome his adopted home town. Poussin studied the classical statues with passionate zeal, because he wanted their beauty to help him convey his vision of bygone lands of innocence and dignity. Figure 254 represents one of the most famous results of these unremitting studies. It shows a calm, sunny southern landscape. Beautiful young men and a fair and dignified young woman have gathered round a large tomb of stone. One of the shepherds – for shepherds they are, as we see by their wreaths and their shepherds' staffs – has knelt down to try to decipher the inscription on the tomb, and a second one points towards it while he looks at the fair shepherdess who, like her companion opposite, stands in silent melancholy. It is inscribed in Latin ET IN ARCADIA EGO (Even in Arcady I am): I, Death, reign even in the idyllic dreamland of the pastorals, in Arcady. Now we understand the wonderful gesture of awe and contemplation with which the framing figures gaze at the tomb, and we admire even more the beauty with which the reading figures answer each other's movements. The arrangement seems simple enough but it is simplicity born of immense artistic knowledge. Only such knowledge could evoke this nostalgic vision of calm repose in which death has lost its terror.

It is for the same mood of nostalgic beauty that the works of another Italianized Frenchman became famous. He was Claude Lorrain (1600-82), some six years younger than Poussin. Claude studied the landscape of the Roman Campagna, the plains and hills round Rome with their lovely southern hues and their majestic reminders of a great past. Like Poussin, he showed in his sketches that he was a perfect master of the realistic representation of nature, and his studies of trees are a joy to look at. But for his finished pictures and etchings he selected only such motifs as he considered worthy of a place in a dreamlike vision of the past, and he dipped it all in a golden light or a silvery air which appear to transfigure the whole scene, figure 255. It was Claude who first opened people's eyes to the sublime beauty of nature, and for nearly a century after his death travellers used to judge a piece of real scenery according to his standards. If it reminded them of his visions, they called it lovely and sat down to picnic there. Rich Englishmen went even further and decided to model the pieces of nature they called their own, the gardens on their estates, on Claude's dreams of beauty. In this way, many a tract of the lovely English countryside should really bear the signature of the French painter who settled in Italy and made the programme of the Carracci his own.

The one northern artist to come most directly into contact with the Roman atmosphere of Carracci's and Caravaggio's days was a generation older than Poussin and Claude, and about as old as Guido Reni. He was the Fleming Peter Paul Rubens (1577-1640), who came to Rome in 1600 when he was twenty-three years old – perhaps the most impressionable age. He must have listened to many heated discussions on art, and studied a great number of new and older works, not only in Rome, but also in Genoa and Mantua (where he stayed for some time). He listened and learned with keen interest, but does not seem to have joined any of the 'movements' or groups. In his heart he remained a Flemish artist – an artist from the country where Van Eyck and Rogier van der Weyden and Bruegel had worked. These painters from the Netherlands had always been most interested in the variegated surfaces of things: they had tried to use all artistic means known to them to express the texture of cloth and living flesh, in short to paint as faithfully as possible everything the eye could see. They had not troubled about the standards of beauty so sacred to their Italian colleagues, and they had not even always shown much concern for dignified subjects. It was in this tradition that Rubens had grown up, and all his admiration for the new art that was developing in Italy does not seem to have shaken his fundamental belief that a painter's business was to paint the world around him; to paint what he liked, to make us feel that he enjoyed the manifold living beauty of things. To such an approach there was nothing contradictory in Caravaggio's and Carracci's art. Rubens admired the way in which Carracci and his school revived the painting of classical stories and myths and arranged impressive altar-panels for the edification of the faithful; but he also admired the uncompromising sincerity with which Caravaggio studied nature.

When Rubens returned to Antwerp in 1608 he was a man of thirty-one, who had learned everything there was to be learned; he had acquired such facility in handling brush and paint, in representing nudes and drapery, armour and jewels, animals and landscapes, that he had no rival north of the Alps. His predecessors in Flanders had mostly painted on a small scale. He had brought from Italy the predilection for huge canvases to decorate churches and palaces, and this suited the taste of the dignitaries and princes. He had learned the art of arranging the figures on a vast scale, and of using light and colours to increase the general effect. Figure 256, a sketch for the painting over the high altar of an Antwerp church, shows how well he had studied his Italian predecessors, and how boldly he developed their ideas. It is again the old, time-honoured theme of the Holy Virgin surrounded by saints, with which artists had grappled at the time of the Wilton Diptych, figure 143, Bellini's 'Madonna', figure 208, or Titian's 'Pesaro Madonna', figure 210, and it may be worth while to turn to these illustrations once more to see the freedom and ease with which Rubens handled the ancient task. One thing is clear at the first glance: there is more movement, more light, more space, and there are more figures in this painting than in any of the earlier ones. The saints are crowding to the lofty throne of the Virgin in a festive throng. In the foreground the Bishop St Augustine, the Martyr St Lawrence with the grill on which he suffered, and the monk St Nicholas of Tolentino lead the spectator on to their object of worship. St George with the Dragon, and St Sebastian with a quiver and arrows, look into each other's eyes in fervent emotion, while a warrior – the palm of martyrdom in his hand – is about to kneel before the throne. A group of women, among them a nun, are looking up enraptured to the main scene, in which a young girl, assisted by a little angel, is falling on her knees to receive a ring from the little Christ Child, who is bending towards her from His mother's lap. It is the legend of the betrothal of St Catherine, who saw such a scene in a vision and considered herself the Bride of Christ. St Joseph watches benevolently from behind the throne, and St Peter and St Paul – one recognizable by the key, the other by the sword – stand in deep contemplation. They make an effective contrast to the imposing figure of St John on the other side, standing alone, bathed in light, throwing up his arms in ecstatic admiration while two charming little angels drag his reluctant lamb up the steps of the throne. From the sky another pair of little angels come rushing down to hold a wreath of laurels over the Virgin's head.

Having looked at the details, we must once more consider the whole, and admire the grand sweep with which Rubens has contrived to hold all the figures together, and to impart to it all an atmosphere of joyful and festive solemnity. Small wonder that a master who could plan such vast pictures with such sureness of hand and eye soon had more orders for paintings than he could cope with alone. But this did not worry him. Rubens was a man of great organizing ability and great personal charm; many gifted painters in Flanders were proud to work under his direction and thereby to learn from him. If an order for a new picture came from one of the churches, or from one of the kings or princes of Europe, he would sometimes paint only a small coloured sketch. (Figure 256 is such a colour sketch for a large composition.) It would be the task of his pupils or assistants to transfer these ideas on to the large canvas, and only when they had finished grounding and painting according to the master's ideas might he take the brush again and touch up a face here and a silken dress there, or smooth out any harsh contrasts. He was confident that his brushwork could quickly impart life to anything, and he was right. For that was the greatest secret of Rubens's art – his magic skill in making anything alive, intensely and joyfully alive. We can best gauge and admire this mastery of his in some of the simple drawings, figure 1, and paintings done for his own pleasure. Figure 257 shows the head of a little girl, probably Rubens's daughter. There are no tricks of composition here, no splendid robes or streams of light, but a simple *en face* portrait of a child. And yet it seems to breathe and palpitate like living flesh. Compared with this, the portraits of earlier centuries seem somehow remote and unreal – however great they may be as works of art. It is vain to try to analyse how Rubens achieved this impression of gay vitality, but it surely had something to do with the bold and delicate touches of light with which he indicated the moisture of the lips and the modelling of the face and hair. To an even greater degree than Titian before him, he used the brush as his main instrument. His paintings are no longer drawings carefully modelled in colour – they are produced by 'painterly' means, and that enhances the impression of life and vigour.

It was a combination of his unrivalled gifts in arranging
large colourful compositions, and in infusing them with
buoyant energy, that secured a fame and success for Rubens
such as no painter had enjoyed before. His art was so
eminently suitable to enhance the pomp and splendour of
palaces, and to glorify the powers of this world, that he
enjoyed something like a monopoly in the sphere in which
he moved. It was the time during which the religious and
social tensions of Europe came to a head in the fearful Thirty
Years' War on the Continent and in the Civil War in England.
On the one side stood the absolute monarchs and their courts,
most of them supported by the Catholic Church – on the
other the rising merchant cities, most of them Protestant. The
Netherlands themselves were divided into Protestant Holland,
which resisted Spanish 'Catholic' domination, and Catholic
Flanders, ruled from Antwerp under Spanish allegiance. It was
as the painter of the Catholic camp that Rubens rose to his
unique position. He accepted commissions from the Jesuits in
Antwerp and from the Catholic rulers of Flanders, from
King Louis XIII of France and his crafty mother Maria de'
Medici, from King Philip III of Spain and King Charles I of
England, who conferred a knighthood on him. When
travelling from court to court as an honoured guest, he was
often charged with delicate political and diplomatic missions,
foremost among them that of effecting a reconciliation
between England and Spain in the interest of what we would
call today a 'reactionary' bloc. Meanwhile he remained in
touch with the scholars of his age, and engaged in learned
Latin correspondence on questions of archaeology and art. His
self-portrait with the nobleman's sword, figure 258, shows
that he was very conscious of his unique position. Yet there is
nothing pompous or vain in the shrewd look of his eyes.
He remained a true artist. All the while, pictures of dazzling

mastery poured out from his Antwerp studios on a stupendous scale. Under his hand, the classical fables and allegorical inventions became as convincingly alive as the picture of his own daughter.

Allegorical pictures are usually regarded as rather boring and abstract, but for the age of Rubens they were a convenient means of expressing ideas. Figure 259 is such a picture, which Rubens is said to have presented as a gift to Charles I, when he tried to induce him to make peace with Spain. The painting contrasts the blessings of peace with the horrors of war. Minerva, the goddess of wisdom and the civilizing arts, drives away Mars, who is about to withdraw – his dreadful companion, the Fury of war, having already turned back. And under the protection of Minerva the joys of peace are spread out before our eyes, symbols of fruitfulness and plenty as only Rubens could conceive them: Peace offering her breast to a child, a faun blissfully eyeing the gorgeous fruits, figure 260, the other companions of Bacchus, dancing maenads with gold and treasures, and the panther playing peacefully like a big cat; on the other side three children with anxious eyes, fleeing from the terror of war to the haven of peace and plenty, crowned by a young genius. No one who loses himself in the rich details of this picture, with its vivid contrasts and glowing colours, can fail to see that these ideas were to Rubens not pale abstractions but forceful realities. Perhaps it is because of this quality that some people must first get accustomed to Rubens before they begin to love and understand him. He had no use for the 'ideal' forms of classical beauty. They were too remote and abstract for him. His men and women are living beings such as he saw and liked. And so, since slenderness was not the fashion in the Flanders of his day, some people object to the 'fat women' in his pictures. This criticism, of course, has little to do with art and we need not, therefore, take it too seriously. But, since it is so often made, it may be well to realize that joy in exuberant and almost boisterous life in all its manifestations saved Rubens from becoming a mere virtuoso of his art. It turned his paintings from mere Baroque decorations of festive halls into masterpieces which retain their vitality even within the chilling atmosphere of museums.

Among Rubens's many famous pupils and assistants, the greatest and most independent was Anthony van Dyck (1599-1641), who was twenty-two years his junior, and belonged to the generation of Poussin and Claude Lorrain. He soon acquired all the virtuosity of Rubens in rendering the texture and surface of things, whether it were silk or human flesh, but he differed widely from his master in temperament and mood. It seems that Van Dyck was not a healthy man, and in his paintings a languid and slightly melancholy mood often prevails. It may have been this quality that appealed to the austere noblemen of Genoa and to the cavaliers of Charles I's entourage. In 1632 he had become the Court Painter of Charles I, and his name was anglicized into Sir Anthony Vandyke. It is to him that we owe an artistic record of this society with its defiantly aristocratic bearing and its cult of courtly refinement. His portrait of Charles I, figure 261, just dismounted from his horse on a hunting expedition, showed the Stuart monarch as he would have wished to live in history: a figure of matchless elegance, of unquestioned authority and high culture, the patron of the arts, and the upholder of the divine right of kings, a man who needed no outward trappings of power to enhance his natural dignity. No wonder that a painter who could bring out these qualities in his portraits with such perfection was eagerly sought after by society. In fact, Van Dyck was so overburdened with commissions for portraits that he, like his master Rubens, was unable to cope with them all himself. He had a number of assistants, who painted the

costumes of his sitters arranged on dummies, and he did
not always paint even the whole of the head. Some of these
portraits are uncomfortably near the flattering fashion-
dummies of later periods, and there is no doubt that Van Dyck
established a dangerous precedent which did much harm to
portrait painting. But all this cannot detract from the greatness
of his best portraits. Nor should it make us forget that it was
he, more than anyone else, who helped to crystallize the ideals
of blue-blooded nobility and gentlemanly ease, figure 262,
which enrich our vision of man no less than do Rubens's
robust and sturdy figures of over-brimming life.

On one of his journeys to Spain, Rubens had met a
young painter who was born in the same year as his pupil Van
Dyck, and who filled a position at the court of King Philip IV
in Madrid similar to that of Van Dyck at the court of Charles I.
He was Diego Velázquez (1599-1660). Though he had not yet
been to Italy, Velázquez had been profoundly impressed by
the discoveries and the manner of Caravaggio, which he got to
know through the work of imitators. He had absorbed the
programme of 'naturalism', and devoted his art to the
dispassionate observation of nature regardless of conventions.
Figure 263 shows one of his early works, an old man selling
water in the streets of Seville. It is a genre picture of the type
the Netherlanders invented to display their skill, but it is done
with all the intensity and penetration of Caravaggio's
'Doubting Thomas', figure 252. The old man with his worn and
wrinkly face and his ragged cloak, the big earthenware flask
with its rounded shape, the surface of the glazed jug and the
play of light on the transparent glass, all this is painted so
convincingly that we feel we could touch the objects. No one
who stands before this picture feels inclined to ask whether
the objects represented are beautiful or ugly, or whether the
scene it represents is important or trivial. Not even the colours

are strictly beautiful by themselves. Brown, grey, greenish
tones prevail. And yet, the whole is joined together in such a
rich and mellow harmony that the picture remains quite
unforgettable to anyone who has ever paused in front of it.

On the advice of Rubens, Velázquez obtained leave to
go to Rome to study the paintings of the great masters. He
went there in 1630 but soon returned to Madrid where, apart
from a second Italian journey, he remained as a famous and
respected member of the court of Philip IV. His main task was
to paint the portraits of the King and the members of the royal
family. While few of them had attractive, or even interesting,
faces, they certainly insisted on their dignity, and dressed
in a stiff and unbecoming fashion. Not a very inviting task for
a painter, it would seem. But Velázquez transformed these
portraits, as if by magic, into some of the most fascinating
pieces of painting the world has ever seen. He had long given
up too close an adherence to Caravaggio's manner. He had
studied the brushwork of Rubens and of Titian, but there is
nothing 'secondhand' in his mode of approaching nature.
Figure 264 shows Velázquez's portrait of Pope Innocent X,
painted in Rome in 1649-50, a little more than a hundred
years after Titian's Paul III, figure 214; it reminds us that in the
history of art the passage of time need not always lead to a
change in outlook. Velázquez surely felt the challenge of that
masterpiece, much as Titian had been stimulated by Raphael's
group, figure 206. But for all his mastery of Titian's means, the
way his brush renders the sheen of the material and the
sureness of touch with which he seizes the Pope's expression,
we do not doubt for a moment that this is the man himself
and not a well-rehearsed formula. Nobody who goes to Rome
should miss the great experience of seeing this masterpiece in
the Palazzo Doria Pamphilj. Indeed, Velázquez's mature works
rely to such an extent on the effect of the brushwork, and on

the delicate harmony of the colours, that illustrations can give only very little idea of what the originals are like. Most of all this applies to his enormous canvas (some ten feet high) which goes under the name *Las Meninas* (the maids of honour), figure 266. We see Velázquez himself at work on a large painting and if we look more carefully we also discover what it is he is painting. The mirror on the back wall of the studio reflects the figures of the King and Queen, figure 265, who are sitting for their portrait. We therefore see what they see – a crowd of people who have come into the studio. It is their little daughter, the Infanta Margarita, flanked by two maids of honour, one of them serving her refreshments while the other curtsies to the royal couple. We know their names as we also know about the two dwarfs (the ugly female and the boy teasing a dog), who were kept for amusement. The grave adults in the background seem to make sure that the visitors behave.

What exactly does it all signify? We may never know, but I should like to fancy that Velázquez has arrested a real moment of time long before the invention of the camera. Perhaps the princess was brought into the royal presence to relieve the boredom of the sitting and the King or Queen remarked to Velázquez that here was a worthy subject for his brush. The words spoken by the sovereign are always treated as a command and so we may owe this masterpiece to a passing wish which only Velázquez was able to turn into reality.

But of course Velázquez did not usually rely on such incidents to transform his records of reality into great paintings. There is nothing unconventional in a portrait such as his picture of the two-year-old Prince Philip Prosper of Spain, figure 267, nothing, perhaps, that strikes us at first glance. But in the original, the various shades of red (from the rich Persian carpet to the velvet chair, the curtain, the sleeves and the rosy cheeks of the child), combined with the cool and silvery tones of white and grey which shade into the background, result in a unique harmony. Even a little motif like the small dog on the red chair reveals an unobtrusive mastery which is truly miraculous. If we look back at the little dog in Jan van Eyck's portrait of the Arnolfini couple, figure 160, we see with what different means great artists can achieve their effects. Van Eyck took pains to copy every curly hair of the little creature – Velázquez, two hundred years later, tried only to catch its characteristic impression. Like Leonardo, only more so, he relied on our imagination to follow his guidance and to supplement what he had left out. Though he did not paint one separate hair, his little dog looks, in effect, more furry and natural than Van Eyck's. It was for effects like these that the founders of Impressionism in nineteenth-century Paris admired Velázquez above all other painters of the past.

To see and observe nature with ever-fresh eyes, to discover and enjoy ever-new harmonies of colours and lights, had become the essential task of the painter. In this new zeal, the great masters of Catholic Europe found themselves at one with the painters on the other side of the political barrier, the great artists of the Protestant Netherlands.

The Mirror of Nature

Holland, seventeenth century

The division of Europe into a Catholic and a Protestant camp affected even the art of small countries like the Netherlands. The southern Netherlands, which today we call Belgium, had remained Catholic, and we have seen how Rubens in Antwerp received innumerable commissions from churches, princes and kings to paint vast canvases for the glorification of their power. The northern provinces of the Netherlands, however, had risen against their Catholic overlords, the Spaniards, and most of the inhabitants of their rich merchant towns adhered to the Protestant faith. The taste of these Protestant merchants of Holland was very different from that prevailing across the border. These men were rather comparable in their outlook to the Puritans in England: devout, hard-working, parsimonious men, most of whom disliked the exuberant pomp of the southern manner. Though their outlook mellowed as their security increased and their wealth grew, these Dutch burghers of the seventeenth century never accepted the full Baroque style which held sway in Catholic Europe. Even in architecture they preferred a certain sober restraint. When, in the middle of the seventeenth century, at the peak of Holland's successes, the citizens of Amsterdam decided to erect a large town hall which was to reflect the pride and achievement of their new-born nation, they chose a model which, for all its grandeur, looks simple in outline and sparing in decoration, figure 268.

We have seen that the effect on painting of the victory of Protestantism was even more marked page 283. We know that the catastrophe was so great that in both England and Germany, where the arts had flourished as much as anywhere during the Middle Ages, the career of a painter or a sculptor ceased to attract native talents. We remember that in the Netherlands, where the tradition of good craftsmanship was so strong, painters had to concentrate on certain branches of painting to which there was no objection on religious grounds.

The most important of these branches that could continue in a Protestant community, as Holbein had experienced in his day, was portrait painting. Many a successful merchant wanted to hand down his likeness to those after him, many a worthy burgher who had been elected alderman or burgomaster desired to be painted with the insignia of his office. Moreover, there were many local committees and governing boards, prominent in the life of Dutch cities, which followed the praiseworthy custom of having their group portraits painted for the board-rooms and meeting-places of their worshipful companies. An artist whose manner appealed to this public could therefore hope for a reasonably steady income. Once his manner ceased to be fashionable, however, he might face ruin.

The first outstanding master of free Holland, Frans Hals (1580?-1666), was forced to lead such a precarious existence. Hals belonged to the same generation as Rubens. His parents had left the southern Netherlands because they were Protestants and had settled in the prosperous Dutch city of Haarlem. We know little about his life except that he frequently owed money to his baker or shoemaker. In his old age – he lived to be over eighty – he was granted a small pittance by the municipal almshouse, whose board of governors he painted. Figure 269, which dates from near the beginning of his career, shows the brilliance and originality with which he approached this kind of task. The citizens of the proudly independent towns of the Netherlands had to do their turn in serving as militia-men, usually under the command of the most prosperous inhabitants. It was the custom in the city of Haarlem to honour the officers of these units after their stint of duty with a sumptuous banquet, and it had also become a tradition to commemorate these happy events in a large painting. It was surely no easy matter for an artist to record the likenesses of

so many men within one frame without the result looking stiff
or contrived – as earlier such efforts invariably did.

Hals understood from the beginning how to convey
the spirit of the jolly occasion and how to bring life into such
a ceremonial group without neglecting the purpose of
showing each of the twelve members present so convincingly
that we feel we must have met them: from the portly colonel
who presides at the end of the table, raising his glass, to the
young ensign on the opposite side who is not accorded a seat,
but proudly looks out of the picture as if he wants us to
admire his splendid outfit.

Perhaps we can admire his mastery even more when
we look at one of the many individual portraits that brought
so little money to Hals and his family, figure 270. Compared
to earlier portraits, it looks almost like a snapshot. We seem to
know this Pieter van den Broecke, a true merchant-adventurer
of the seventeenth century. Let us think back to Holbein's
painting of Sir Richard Southwell, figure 242, painted less than
a century earlier, or even to the portraits which Rubens,
Van Dyck or Velázquez painted at that time in Catholic Europe.
For all their liveliness and truth to nature one feels that the
painters had carefully arranged the sitter's pose so as to convey
the idea of dignified aristocratic breeding. The portraits of Hals
give us the impression that the painter has 'caught' his sitter at
a characteristic moment and fixed it for ever on the canvas.
It is difficult for us to imagine how bold and unconventional
these paintings must have looked to the public. The very way
in which Hals handled paint and brush suggests that he quickly
seized a fleeting impression. Earlier portraits are painted with
visible patience – we sometimes feel that the subject must have
sat still for many a session while the painter carefully recorded
detail upon detail. Hals never allowed his model to get tired or
stale. We seem to witness his quick and deft handling of the

brush through which he conjures up the image of tousled hair or of a crumpled sleeve with a few touches of light and dark paint. Of course, the impression that Hals gives us, the impression of a casual glimpse of the sitter in a characteristic movement and mood, could never have been achieved without a very calculated effort. What looks at first like a happy-go-lucky approach is really the result of a carefully thought-out effect. Though the portrait is not symmetrical, as earlier portraits often were, it is not lopsided. Like other masters of the Baroque period, Hals knew how to attain the impression of balance without appearing to follow any rule.

The painters of Protestant Holland who had no inclination or talent for portrait painting had to give up the idea of relying chiefly on commissions. Unlike the masters of the Middle Ages and of the Renaissance, they had to paint their picture first, and then try to find a buyer. We are now so used to this state of affairs, we take it so much for granted that an artist is a man painting away in his studio, which is packed full of pictures he is desperately trying to sell, that we can hardly imagine the change this situation brought about. In one respect, artists may possibly have been glad to be rid of patrons who interfered with their work and who may sometimes have bullied them. But this freedom was dearly bought. For, instead of a single patron, the artist had now to cope with an even more tyrannical master – the buying public. He had either to go to the market-place and to public fairs, there to peddle his wares, or to rely on middlemen, picture dealers who relieved him of this burden but who wanted to buy as cheaply as possible in order to be able to sell at a profit. Moreover, competition was very stiff; there were many artists in each Dutch town exhibiting their paintings on the stalls, and the only chance for the minor masters to make a reputation lay in specializing in one particular branch or genre of painting. Then, as now, the public liked to know what it was getting. Once a painter had made a name as a master of battle-pieces, it was battle-pieces he would be most likely to sell. If he had had success with landscapes in moonlight, it might be safer to stick to that, and to paint more landscapes in moonlight. Thus it came about that the trend towards specialization which had begun in the northern countries in the sixteenth century, *pages 286-7*, was carried to even greater extremes in the seventeenth. Some of the weaker painters became content to turn out the same kind of picture over and over again. It is true that in doing so they sometimes carried their trade to a pitch of perfection which commands our admiration. These specialists were real specialists. The painters of fish knew how to render the silvery hue of wet scales with a virtuosity which puts many a more universal master to shame; and the painters of seascapes not only became proficient in the painting of waves and clouds, but were such experts in the accurate portrayal of ships and their tackle that their paintings are still considered valuable historical documents of the period of England's and Holland's naval expansion. *Figure 271* shows a painting by one of the oldest of these specialists in seascapes, Simon de Vlieger (1601-53). It shows how these Dutch artists could convey the atmosphere of the sea by wonderfully simple and unpretentious means. These Dutchmen were the first in the history of art to discover the beauty of the sky. They needed nothing dramatic or striking to make their pictures interesting. They simply represented a piece of the world as it appeared to them, and discovered that it could make just as satisfying a picture as any illustration of a heroic tale or a comic theme.

One of these discoverers was Jan van Goyen (1596-1656), from The Hague, who was roughly of the same generation as the landscape painter Claude Lorrain. It is

interesting to compare one of the famous landscapes of
Claude, figure 255, a nostalgic vision of a land of serene beauty,
with the simple and straightforward painting by Jan van Goyen,
figure 272. The differences are too obvious to need labouring.
Instead of lofty temples, the Dutchman paints a homely
windmill; instead of alluring glades, a featureless stretch of
his native land. But Van Goyen knows how to transform the
commonplace scene into a vision of restful beauty. He
transfigures familiar motifs, and leads our eyes into the hazy
distance, so that we feel as if we were ourselves standing at
a point of vantage and looking into the light of the evening.
We have seen how the inventions of Claude so captured the
imagination of his admirers in England that they tried to
transform the actual scenery of their native land, and make it
conform to the creations of the painter. A landscape or a
garden which made them think of Claude, they called
'picturesque', like a picture. We have since become used to
applying this word not only to ruined castles and sunsets, but
also to such simple things as sailing boats and windmills.
When we come to consider it, we do so because such motifs
remind us of pictures not by Claude, but by masters like de
Vlieger or Van Goyen. It is they who have taught us to see the
'picturesque' in a simple scene. Many a rambler in the
countryside who delights in what he sees may, without
knowing it, owe his joy to those humble masters who first
opened our eyes to unpretentious natural beauty.

   The greatest painter of Holland, and one of the greatest
painters who ever lived, was Rembrandt van Rijn (1606-69),
who was a generation younger than Frans Hals and Rubens,
and seven years younger than Van Dyck and Velázquez.
Rembrandt did not write down his observations as Leonardo
and Dürer did; he was no admired genius as Michelangelo
was, whose sayings were handed down to posterity; he was no

diplomatic letter-writer like Rubens, who exchanged ideas with the leading scholars of his age. Yet we feel that we know Rembrandt perhaps more intimately than any of these great masters, because he left us an amazing record of his life in a series of self-portraits ranging from the time of his youth, when he was a successful and even fashionable master, to his lonely old age when his face reflected the tragedy of bankruptcy and the unbroken will of a truly great man. These portraits combine into a unique autobiography.

Rembrandt was born in 1606, the son of a well-to-do miller in the university town of Leiden. He matriculated at the University, but soon abandoned his studies to become a painter. Some of his earliest works were greatly praised by contemporary scholars, and at the age of twenty-five Rembrandt left Leiden for the teeming commercial centre of Amsterdam. There he made a rapid career as a portrait painter, married a wealthy girl, bought a house, collected works of art and curios and worked incessantly. When his first wife died, in 1642, she left him a considerable fortune, but Rembrandt's popularity with the public declined, he got into debt, and fourteen years later his creditors sold his house and put his collection up for auction. Only the help of his loyal mistress and his son saved him from utter ruin. They made an arrangement by which he was formally an employee of their art-dealing firm, and, as such, he painted his last great masterpieces. But these faithful companions died before him, and when his life came to an end in 1669, he left no other property than some old clothes and his painting utensils. Figure 273 shows us Rembrandt's face during the later years of his life. It was not a beautiful face, and Rembrandt certainly never tried to conceal its ugliness. He observed himself in a mirror with complete sincerity. It is because of this sincerity that we soon forget to ask about beauty or looks. This is the face

of a real human being. There is no trace of a pose, no trace
of vanity, just the penetrating gaze of a painter who scrutinizes
his own features, ever ready to learn more and more about
the secrets of the human face. Without this profound
understanding Rembrandt could not have created his great
portraits, such as the likeness of his patron and friend, Jan Six,
who later became burgomaster of Amsterdam, figure 274.
It is almost unfair to compare it with the lively portrait by
Frans Hals, for where Hals gives us something like a
convincing snapshot, Rembrandt always seems to show us the
whole person. Like Hals, he enjoyed his virtuosity, the skill
with which he could suggest the sheen of the gold braid or
the play of light on the ruff. He claimed the artist's right to
declare a picture finished – as he said – 'when he had achieved
his purpose', and thus he left the hand in the glove as a mere
sketch. But all this only enhances the sense of life that
emanates from his figure. We feel we know this man. We have
seen other portraits by great masters which are memorable for
the way they sum up a person's character and role. But even
the greatest of them may remind us of characters in fiction or
actors on the stage. They are convincing and impressive, but
we sense that they can only represent one side of a complex
human being. Not even the Mona Lisa can always have smiled.
But in Rembrandt's great portraits we feel face to face with real
people, we sense their warmth, their need for sympathy and
also their loneliness and their suffering. Those keen and steady
eyes that we know so well from Rembrandt's self-portraits
must have been able to look straight into the human heart.

  I realize that such an expression may sound
sentimental, but I know no other way of describing the almost
uncanny knowledge Rembrandt appears to have had of what
the Greeks called the 'workings of the soul', page 77. Like
Shakespeare, he seems to have been able to get into the skin of

all types of men, and to know how they would behave in any given situation. It is this gift that makes Rembrandt's illustrations of biblical stories so different from anything that had been done before. As a devout Protestant, Rembrandt must have read the Bible again and again. He entered into the spirit of its episodes, and attempted to visualize exactly what the situation must have been like, and how people would have moved and borne themselves at such a moment. Figure 275 shows a drawing in which Rembrandt illustrated the parable of the Merciless Servant (Matthew XVIII. 21-35). There is no need to explain the drawing. It explains itself. We see the lord on the day of reckoning, with his steward looking up the servant's debts in a big ledger. We see from the way the servant stands, his head lowered, his hand fumbling deep in his pocket, that he is unable to pay. The relationship of these three people to each other, the busy steward, the dignified lord and the guilty servant, is expressed with a few strokes of the pen.

Rembrandt needs hardly any gestures or movements to express the inner meaning of a scene. He is never theatrical. Figure 276 shows one of the paintings in which he visualized another incident from the Bible which had hardly ever been illustrated before – the reconciliation between King David and his wicked son Absalom. When Rembrandt was reading the Old Testament, and tried to see the kings and patriarchs of the Holy Land in his mind's eye, he thought of the Orientals he had seen in the busy port of Amsterdam. That is why he dressed David like an Indian or Turk with a big turban, and gave Absalom a curved Oriental sword. His painter's eye was attracted by the splendour of these costumes, and by the chance they gave him of showing the play of light on the precious fabric, and the sparkle of gold and jewellery. We can see that Rembrandt was as great a master in conjuring up the effect of these shining textures as Rubens or Velázquez.

Rembrandt used less bright colour than either of them. The first impression of many of his paintings is that of a rather dark brown. But these dark tones give even more power and force to the contrast of a few bright and brilliant colours. The result is that the light on some of Rembrandt's pictures looks almost dazzling. But Rembrandt never used these magic effects of light and shade for their own sake. They always served to enhance the drama of the scene. What could be more moving than the gesture of the young prince in his proud array, burying his face on his father's breast, or King David in his quiet and sorrowful acceptance of his son's submission? Though we do not see Absalom's face, we feel what he must feel.

Like Dürer before him, Rembrandt was great not only as a painter but also as a graphic artist. The technique he used was no longer that of woodcuts or copper-engraving, *page* 210, but a method which allowed him to work more freely and more quickly than was possible with the burin. This technique is called etching. Its principle is quite simple. Instead of laboriously scratching the surface of the copper plate, the artist covers the plate with wax and draws on it with a needle. Wherever his needle goes, the wax is removed and the copper laid bare. All he has to do afterwards is to put his plate into an acid which bites into the copper where the wax has gone, and thus transfer the drawing on to the copper plate. The plate can then be printed in the same way as an engraving. The only means of telling an etching from an engraving is by judging the character of the lines. There is a visible difference between the laborious and slow work of the burin and the free and easy play of the etcher's needle. *Figure* 277 shows one of Rembrandt's etchings – another biblical scene. Christ is preaching, and the poor and humble have gathered round Him to listen. This time Rembrandt has turned to his own city for models. He lived for a long time in the Jewish quarter of

Amsterdam, and he studied the appearance and dresses of the
Jews so as to introduce them into his sacred stories. Here they
stand and sit, huddled together, some listening, enraptured,
others pondering the words of Jesus, some, like the fat man
behind, perhaps scandalized by Christ's attack on the Pharisees.
People who are used to the beautiful figures of Italian art are
sometimes shocked when they first see Rembrandt's pictures
because he seems to care nothing for beauty, and not even to
shrink from outright ugliness. That is true, in a sense. Like
other artists of his time, Rembrandt had absorbed the message
of Caravaggio, whose work he came to know through
Dutchmen who had fallen under his influence. Like
Caravaggio, he valued truth and sincerity above harmony and
beauty. Christ had preached to the poor, the hungry and the
sad, and poverty, hunger and tears are not beautiful. Of course
much depends on what we agree to call beauty. A child often
finds the kind, wrinkled face of his grandmother more
beautiful than the regular features of a film star, and why
should he not? In the same way, one might say that the
haggard old man in the right-hand corner of the etching,
cowering, one hand before his face, and looking up,
completely absorbed, is one of the most beautiful figures ever
drawn. But perhaps it is really not very important what words
we use to express our admiration.

Rembrandt's unconventional approach sometimes
makes us forget how much artistic wisdom and skill he uses in
the arrangement of his groups. Nothing could be more
carefully balanced than the crowd forming a circle round
Jesus, and yet standing at a respectful distance. In this art of
distributing a mass of people, in apparently casual and yet
perfectly harmonious groups, Rembrandt owed much to the
tradition of Italian art, which he by no means despised.
Nothing would be farther from the truth than to imagine that

this great master was a lonely rebel whose greatness went unrecognized by contemporary Europe. It is true that his popularity as a portrait painter decreased as his art became more profound and uncompromising. But whatever the reasons for his personal tragedy and bankruptcy, his fame as an artist stood very high. The real tragedy, then as now, is that fame alone does not suffice to make a living.

The figure of Rembrandt is so important in all branches of Dutch art that no other painter of the period can bear comparison with him. That is not to say, however, that there were not many masters in the Protestant Netherlands who deserve to be studied and enjoyed in their own right. Many of them followed the tradition of northern art in reproducing the life of the people in gay and unsophisticated paintings. We remember that this tradition reaches back to such examples of medieval miniatures as, figure 140, and figure 177. We remember how it was taken up by Bruegel, figure 246, who displayed his skill as a painter and his knowledge of human nature in humorous scenes from the lives of peasants. The seventeenth-century artist who brought this vein to perfection was Jan Steen (1626-79), Jan van Goyen's son-in-law. Like many other artists of his time, Steen could not support himself with his brush, and he kept an inn to earn money. One might almost imagine that he enjoyed this sideline, because it gave him an opportunity of watching the people in their revellings, and of adding to his store of comic types. Figure 278 shows a gay scene from the life of the people – a christening feast. We look into a comfortable room with a recess for the bed in which the mother lies, while friends and relations crowd round the father who holds the baby. It is well worth looking at these various types and their forms of merrymaking, but when we have examined all the detail we should not forget to admire the skill with which the artist has blended the various incidents into a picture. The figure in the foreground, seen from behind, is a wonderful piece of painting, whose gay colours have a warmth and mellowness one does not easily forget when one has seen the original.

One often associates Dutch seventeenth-century art with the mood of gaiety and good living we find in Jan Steen's pictures, but there are other artists in Holland who represent a very different mood, one which comes much nearer to the spirit of Rembrandt. The outstanding example is another 'specialist', the landscape painter Jacob van Ruisdael (1628?-82). Ruisdael was about the same age as Jan Steen, which means that he belonged to the second generation of great Dutch painters. When he grew up the works of Jan van Goyen and even of Rembrandt were already famous and were bound to influence his taste and choice of themes. During the first half of his life he lived in the beautiful town of Haarlem, which is separated from the sea by a range of wooded dunes. He loved to study the effect of light and shade on these tracts and specialized more and more in picturesque forest scenes, figure 279. Ruisdael became a master in the painting of dark and sombre clouds, of evening light when the shadows grow, of ruined castles and rushing brooks; in short it was he who discovered the poetry of the northern landscape much as Claude had discovered the poetry of Italian scenery. Perhaps no artist before him had contrived to express so much of his own feelings and moods through their reflection in nature.

When I called this chapter 'The Mirror of Nature', I did not only want to say that Dutch art had learned to reproduce nature as faithfully as a mirror. Neither art nor nature is ever as smooth and cold as a glass. Nature reflected in art always reflects the artist's own mind, his predilections, his enjoyments and therefore his moods. It is this fact above all which renders the most 'specialized' branch of Dutch painting so interesting, the branch of still-life painting. These still lifes usually show beautiful vessels filled with wine and appetizing fruit, or other dainties invitingly arranged on lovely china. These were pictures which would go well into a dining-room and would be sure to find a buyer. But they are more than mere reminders of the joys of the table. In such still lifes, artists could freely pick up any objects they liked to paint, and arrange them on the table to suit their fancy. Thus they became a wonderful field of experiment for the painters' special problems. Willem Kalf (1619-93), for instance, liked to study the way in which light is reflected and broken by coloured glass. He studied the contrasts and harmonies of colours and textures, and tried to achieve ever-new harmonies between rich Persian carpets, gleaming china, brilliantly coloured fruit and polished metals, figure 280. Without knowing it themselves, these specialists began to demonstrate that the subject of a painting is much less important than might have been thought. Just as trivial words may provide the text for a beautiful song, so trivial objects can make a perfect picture.

This may seem a strange remark to make after the stress I have just laid on the subject-matter of Rembrandt's painting. But actually I do not think that there is a contradiction. A composer who sets to music not a trivial text but a great poem wants us to understand the poem, so that we may appreciate his musical interpretation. In the same way, a painter painting a biblical scene wants us to understand the scene to appreciate his conception. But just as there is great music without words, so there is great painting without an important subject-matter. It was this invention towards which the seventeenth-century artists had been groping when they discovered the sheer beauty of the visible world, figure 4. And the Dutch specialists who spent their lives painting the same kind of subject-matter ended by proving that the subject-matter was of secondary importance.

The greatest of these masters was born a generation after Rembrandt. He was Jan Vermeer van Delft (1632-75). Vermeer seems to have been a slow and a careful worker. He did not paint very many pictures in his life. Few of them represent any important scenes. Most of them show simple figures standing in a room of a typically Dutch house. Some show nothing but a single figure engaged in a simple task, such as a woman pouring out milk, figure 281. With Vermeer, genre painting has lost the last trace of humorous illustration. His paintings are really still lifes with human beings. It is hard to argue the reasons that make such a simple and unassuming picture one of the greatest masterpieces of all time. But few who have been lucky enough to see the original will disagree with me that it is something of a miracle. One of its miraculous features can perhaps be described, though hardly explained. It is the way in which Vermeer achieves complete and painstaking precision in the rendering of textures, colours and forms without the picture ever looking laboured or harsh. Like a photographer who deliberately softens the strong contrasts of the picture without blurring the forms, Vermeer mellowed the outlines and yet retained the effect of solidity and firmness. It is this strange and unique combination of mellowness and precision which makes his best paintings so unforgettable. They make us see the quiet beauty of a simple scene with fresh eyes and give us an idea of what the artist felt when he watched the light flooding through the window and heightening the colour of a piece of cloth.

21

Power and Glory: I

Italy, later seventeenth and eighteenth centuries

We remember the beginning of the Baroque manner of building in such works of late sixteenth-century art as Della Porta's church of the Jesuit Order, figure 250. Della Porta disregarded the so-called rules of classical architecture for the sake of greater variety and more imposing effects. It is in the nature of things that once art has taken this road it must keep to it. If variety and striking effects are considered important, each subsequent artist has to produce more complex decorations and more astounding ideas so as to remain impressive. During the first half of the seventeenth century, this process of piling up more and more dazzling new ideas for buildings and their decorations had gone on in Italy, and by the middle of the seventeenth century the style we call Baroque was fully developed.

Figure 282 shows a typical Baroque church built by the famous architect Francesco Borromini (1599-1667) and his assistants. It is easy to see that even the forms which Borromini applied are really Renaissance forms. Like Della Porta, he used the form of a temple front to frame the central entrance and, like him, he doubled the pilasters on the sides to gain a richer effect. But by comparison with Borromini's façade, Della Porta's looks almost severe and restrained. Borromini was no longer content with decorating a wall with the orders taken from classical architecture. He composed his church through a grouping of different forms – the vast cupola, the flanking towers and the façade. And this façade is curved as if it had been modelled in clay. If we look at the detail we find even more surprising effects. The first storey of the towers is square, but the second is round and the relation between the two storeys is brought about by a strangely broken entablature which would have horrified every orthodox teacher of architecture, but which does the job assigned to it extremely well. The frames of the doors flanking

the main porch are even more astonishing. The way in which
the pediment over the entrance is made to frame an oval
window has no parallel in any earlier building. The scrolls and
curves of the Baroque style had come to dominate both the
general layout and the decorative details. It has been said of
such Baroque buildings that they are over-ornate and
theatrical. Borromini himself would hardly have understood
why this should be a reproach. He wanted a church to look
festive and to be a building full of splendour and movement.
If it is the aim of the theatre to delight us with a vision of a
fairy world of light and pageantry, why should not the
architect designing a church have a right to give us an idea of
even greater pomp and glory to remind us of Heaven?

When we enter these churches we understand even
better how the pomp and display of precious stones, of gold
and stucco, were used deliberately to conjure up a vision
of heavenly glory much more concretely than the medieval
cathedrals do. Figure 283 shows the interior of Borromini's
church. To those of us who are used to the church interiors of
northern countries, this dazzling pageantry may well look too
worldly for our taste. But the Catholic Church of the period
thought differently. The more the Protestants preached against
outward show in the churches, the more eager was the Roman
Church to enlist the power of the artist. Thus the Reformation
and the whole vexed issue of images and their worship, which
had influenced the course of art so often in the past, also had
an indirect effect on the development of Baroque. The Catholic
world had discovered that art could serve religion in ways that
went beyond the simple task assigned to it in the early Middle
Ages – the task of teaching the Doctrine to people who could
not read. It could help to persuade and convert those who
had, perhaps, read too much. Architects, painters and sculptors
were called upon to transform churches into grand show-

pieces whose splendour and vision nearly swept you off your feet. It is not so much the details that matter in these interiors as the general effect of the whole. We cannot hope to understand them, or to judge them correctly, unless we visualize them as the framework for the splendid ritual of the Roman Church, unless we have seen them during High Mass, when the candles are alight on the altar, when the smell of incense fills the nave, and when the sound of the organ and the choir transports us into a different world.

This supreme art of theatrical decoration had mainly been developed by one artist, Gian Lorenzo Bernini (1598-1680). Bernini belonged to the same generation as Borromini. He was one year older than Van Dyck and Velázquez, and eight years older than Rembrandt. Like these masters, he was a consummate portraitist. Figure 284 shows his portrait bust of a young woman which has all the freshness and unconventionality of Bernini's best work. When I saw it last in the museum in Florence, a ray of sunlight was playing on the bust and the whole figure seemed to breathe and come to life. Bernini has caught a transient expression which we are sure must have been most characteristic of his sitter. In the rendering of facial expression, Bernini was perhaps unsurpassed. He used it, as Rembrandt used his profound knowledge of human behaviour, to give visual form to his religious experience.

Figure 285 shows an altar of Bernini's for a side chapel in a small Roman church. It is dedicated to the Spanish Saint Teresa, a nun of the sixteenth century who had described her mystic visions in a famous book. In it she tells of a moment of heavenly rapture, when an angel of the Lord pierced her heart with a golden flaming arrow, filling her with pain and yet with immeasurable bliss. It is this vision that Bernini has dared to represent. We see the saint carried heavenwards on a cloud, towards streams of light which pour down from above in the form of golden rays. We see the angel gently approaching her, and the saint swooning in ecstasy. The group is so placed that it seems to hover without support in the magnificent frame provided by the altar, and to receive its light from an invisible window above. A northern visitor may again be inclined, at first, to find the whole arrangement too reminiscent of stage effects, and the group over-emotional. This, of course, is a matter of taste and upbringing about which it is useless to argue. But if we grant that a work of religious art like Bernini's altar may legitimately be used to arouse those feelings of fervid exultation and mystic transport at which the artists of the Baroque were aiming, we must admit that Bernini has achieved this aim in a masterly fashion. He has deliberately cast aside all restraint, and carried us to a pitch of emotion which artists had so far shunned. If we compare the face of his swooning saint with any work done in previous centuries, we find that he achieved an intensity of facial expression which until then was never attempted in art. Looking from figure 286 to the head of Laocoön, figure 69, or of Michelangelo's 'Dying slave', figure 201, we realize the difference. Even Bernini's handling of draperies was at the time completely new. Instead of letting them fall in dignified folds in the approved classical manner, he made them writhe and whirl to add to the effect of excitement and movement. In all these effects he was soon imitated all over Europe.

If it is true of sculptures like Bernini's 'St Teresa' that they can only be judged in the setting for which they were made, the same applies even more to the painted decorations of Baroque churches. Figure 287 shows the decoration of the ceiling of the Jesuit church in Rome by a painter of Bernini's following, Giovanni Battista Gaulli (1639-1709). The artist wants to give us the illusion that the vault of the church has opened, and that we look straight into the glories of Heaven.

Correggio before him had the idea of painting the heavens on the ceiling, figure 217, but Gaulli's effects are incomparably more theatrical. The theme is the worship of the Holy Name of Jesus, which is inscribed in radiant letters in the centre of His church. It is surrounded by infinite multitudes of cherubs, angels, and saints, each gazing in rapture into the light, while whole legions of demons or fallen angels are driven out of the heavenly regions, expressing their despair. The crowded scene seems to burst the frame of the ceiling, which brims over with clouds carrying saints and sinners right down into the church. In letting the picture thus break the frame, the artist wants to confuse and overwhelm us, so that we no longer know what is real and what illusion. A painting like this has no meaning outside the place for which it was made. Perhaps it is no coincidence, therefore, that, after the development of the full Baroque style, in which all artists collaborated in the achievement of one effect, painting and sculpture as independent arts declined in Italy and throughout Catholic Europe.

In the eighteenth century Italian artists were mainly superb internal decorators, famous throughout Europe for their skill in stucco work and for their great frescoes, which could transform any hall of a castle or monastery into a setting for pageantry. One of the most famous of these masters was the Venetian Giovanni Battista Tiepolo (1696-1770), who worked not only in Italy but also in Germany and Spain. Figure 288 shows part of his decoration of a Venetian palace, painted about 1750. It represents a subject which gave Tiepolo every opportunity to display gay colours and sumptuous costumes: the banquet of Cleopatra. The story goes that Mark Antony gave a feast in honour of the Egyptian queen which was to be the *ne plus ultra* of luxury. The most costly dishes followed each other in endless succession. The queen was not impressed. She wagered her proud host that she would produce a dish much more costly than anything he had offered yet – took a famous pearl from her ear-ring, dissolved it in vinegar and drank the brew. In Tiepolo's fresco we see her showing Mark Antony the pearl while a black servant offers her a glass.

Frescoes like these must have been fun to paint and they are a pleasure to look at. And yet some may feel that these fireworks are of less permanent value than the more sober creations of earlier periods. The great age of Italian art was ending.

Only in one specialized branch did Italian art create new ideas in the early eighteenth century. That was, characteristically enough, the painting and engraving of views. The travellers who came to Italy from all over Europe to admire the glories of her past greatness often wanted to take souvenirs with them. In Venice, in particular, whose scenery is so fascinating to the artist, there developed a school of painters who catered for this demand. Figure 290 shows a view of Venice by one of these painters, Francesco Guardi (1712-93). Like Tiepolo's fresco, it shows that Venetian art had not lost its sense of pageantry, of light and of colour. It is interesting to compare Guardi's views of the Venetian lagoon with the sober and faithful seascapes of Simon de Vlieger, figure 271, painted a century earlier. We realize that the spirit of Baroque, the taste for movement and bold effects, can express itself even in a simple view of a city. Guardi has completely mastered the effects that had been studied by seventeenth-century painters. He has learned that once we are given the general impression of a scene we are quite ready to supply and supplement the details ourselves. If we look closely at his gondoliers we discover, to our surprise, that they are made up simply of a few deftly placed coloured patches – yet if we step back the illusion becomes completely effective. The tradition of Baroque discoveries which lives in these late fruits of Italian art was to gain new importance in subsequent periods.

22

Power and Glory: II

France, Germany and Austria, late seventeenth and
early eighteenth centuries

It was not only the Roman Church that had discovered the power of art to impress and overwhelm. The kings and princes of seventeenth-century Europe were equally anxious to display their might and thus to increase their hold on the minds of the people. They, too, wanted to appear as beings of a different kind, lifted by divine right above the common run of men. This applies particularly to the most powerful ruler of the latter part of the seventeenth century, Louis XIV of France, in whose political programme the display and splendour of royalty was deliberately used. It is surely no accident that Louis XIV invited Bernini to Paris to help with the designing of his palace. This grandiose project never materialized, but another of Louis XIV's palaces became the very symbol of his immense power. This was the palace of Versailles, which was built round about 1660-80, figure 291. Versailles is so huge that no photograph can give an adequate idea of its appearance. There are no fewer than one hundred and twenty-three windows looking towards the park in each storey. The park itself, with its avenues of clipped trees, its urns and statuary, figure 292, and its terraces and lakes, extends over miles of countryside.

It is in its immensity rather than in its decorative detail that Versailles is Baroque. Its architects were mainly intent on grouping the enormous masses of the building into clearly distinct wings, and giving each wing the appearance of nobility and grandeur. They accentuated the middle of the main storey by a row of Ionic columns carrying an entablature with rows of statues on top, and flanked this effective centre-piece with decorations of a similar kind. With a simple combination of pure Renaissance forms, they would hardly have succeeded in breaking the monotony of so vast a façade, but with the help of statues, urns and trophies they produced a certain amount of variety. It is in buildings like these, therefore, that one can best appreciate the true function and purpose of Baroque forms. Had the designers of Versailles been a little more daring than they were, and used more unorthodox means of articulating and grouping the enormous building, they might have been even more successful.

It was only in the next generation that this lesson was completely absorbed by the architects of the period. For the Roman churches and French castles of the Baroque style fired the imagination of the age. Every minor princeling in southern Germany wanted to have his Versailles; every small monastery in Austria or in Spain wanted to compete with the impressive splendour of Borromini's and Bernini's designs. The period round about 1700 is one of the greatest periods of architecture; and not of architecture alone. These castles and churches were not simply planned as buildings – all the arts had to contribute to the effect of a fantastic and artificial world. Whole towns were used like stage settings, stretches of country were transformed into gardens, brooks into cascades. Artists were given free rein to plan to their hearts' content, and to translate their most unlikely visions into stone and gilt stucco. Often the money ran out before their plans became reality, but what was completed of this outburst of extravagant creation transformed the face of many a town and landscape of Catholic Europe. It was particularly in Austria, Bohemia and southern Germany that the ideas of the Italian and French Baroque were fused into the boldest and most consistent style. Figure 293 shows the palace which the Austrian architect, Lucas von Hildebrandt (1668-1745), built in Vienna for Marlborough's ally, Prince Eugene of Savoy. The palace stands on a hill, and seems to hover lightly over a terraced garden with fountains and clipped hedges. Hildebrandt has grouped it clearly into seven different parts, reminiscent of garden pavilions: a five-windowed centre-piece bulging forward, flanked by two wings of only slightly lesser height, and this group in turn flanked by a lower part and four turret-like corner pavilions, which frame the whole building. The central pavilion and the corner-pieces are the most richly decorated parts, and the building forms an intricate pattern, which is nevertheless completely clear and lucid in its outline. This lucidity is not at all disturbed by the freakish and grotesque ornament that Hildebrandt employed in the details of the decoration, the pilasters tapering off downwards, the broken and scrolly pediments over the windows, and the statues and trophies lining the roof.

It is only when we enter the building that we feel the full impact of this fantastic style of decoration. Figure 294 shows the entrance hall of Prince Eugene's palace, and figure 295 a staircase of a German castle designed by Hildebrandt. We cannot do justice to these interiors unless we visualize them in use – on a day when the owner was giving a feast or holding a reception, when the lamps were lit and men and women in the gay and stately fashions of the time arrived to mount these stairs. At such a moment, the contrast between the dark, unlit streets of the time, reeking of dirt and squalor, and the radiant fairy world of the nobleman's dwelling must have been overwhelming.

The buildings of the Church made use of similar striking effects. Figure 296 shows the Austrian monastery of Melk, on the Danube. As one comes down the river, this monastery, with its cupola and its strangely shaped towers, stands on the hill like some unreal apparition. It was built by a local builder called Jakob Prandtauer (died 1726) and decorated by some of the Italian travelling *virtuosi* who were ever ready with new ideas and designs from the vast store of Baroque patterns. How well these humble artists had learnt the difficult art of grouping and organizing a building to give the appearance of stateliness without monotony! They were also careful to graduate the decoration, and to use the more extravagant forms sparingly, but all the more effectively, in the parts of the building they wanted to throw into relief.

In the interior, however, they cast off all restraint. Even Bernini or Borromini in their most exuberant moods would never have gone quite so far. Once more we must imagine what it meant for a simple Austrian peasant to leave his farmhouse and enter this strange wonderland, figure 297. There are clouds everywhere, with angels making music and gesticulating in the bliss of Paradise. Some have settled on the pulpit, everything seems to move and dance, and the architecture framing the sumptuous high altar appears to sway in the rhythm of jubilation. Nothing is 'natural' or 'normal' in such a church – it is not meant to be. It is intended to give us a foretaste of the glory of Paradise. Perhaps it is not everybody's idea of Paradise, but when you are in the midst of it all it envelops you and stops all questioning. You feel you are in a world where our rules and standards simply do not apply.

One can understand that north of the Alps, no less than in Italy, the individual arts were swept into this orgy of decoration and lost much of their independent importance. There were, of course, painters and sculptors of distinction in the period round about 1700, but perhaps there was only one master whose art compares with the great leading painters of the first half of the seventeenth century. This master was Antoine Watteau (1684-1721). Watteau came from a part of Flanders which had been conquered by France a few years before his birth, and he settled in Paris, where he died at the age of thirty-seven. He, too, designed interior decorations for the castles of the nobility, to provide the appropriate background for the festivals and pageantries of court society. But it would seem as if the actual festivities had not satisfied the imagination of the artist. He began to paint his own

visions of a life divorced from all hardship and triviality,
a dream-life of gay picnics in fairy parks where it never rains,
of musical parties where all ladies are beautiful and all lovers
graceful, a society in which all are dressed in sparkling silk
without looking showy, and where the life of the shepherds
and shepherdesses seems to be a succession of minuets. From
such a description one might get the impression that the art
of Watteau is over-precious and artificial. For many, it has
come to reflect the taste of the French aristocracy of the early
eighteenth century which is known as Rococo: the fashion for
dainty colours and delicate decoration which succeeded the
more robust taste of the Baroque period, and which expressed
itself in gay frivolity. But Watteau was far too great an artist to
be a mere exponent of the fashions of his time. Rather it
was he whose dreams and ideals helped to mould the fashion
we call Rococo. Just as Van Dyck had helped to create the idea
of the gentlemanly ease we associate with the Cavaliers,
figure 262, so Watteau has enriched our store of imagination
by his vision of graceful gallantry.

Figure 298 shows his picture of a gathering in a park.
There is nothing of the noisy gaiety of Jan Steen's revelries,
figure 278, in this scene; a sweet and almost melancholy calm
prevails. These young men and women just sit and dream, play
with flowers or gaze at each other. The light dances on their
shimmering dresses, and transfigures the copse into an earthly
paradise. The qualities of Watteau's art, the delicacy of his
brushwork and the refinement of his colour harmonies are
not easily revealed in reproductions. His immensely sensitive
paintings and drawings must really be seen and enjoyed in
the original. Like Rubens, whom he admired, Watteau could
convey the impression of living, palpitating flesh through
a mere whiff of chalk or colour. But the mood of his studies
is as different from Rubens's as his paintings are from Jan

Steen's. There is a touch of sadness in these visions of beauty which is difficult to describe or define, but which lifts Watteau's art beyond the sphere of mere skill and prettiness. Watteau was a sick man, who died of consumption at an early age. Perhaps it was his awareness of the transience of beauty which gave to his art that intensity which none of his many admirers and imitators could equal.

The Age of Reason

England and France, eighteenth century

The period round about 1700 had seen the culmination of the Baroque movement in Catholic Europe. The Protestant countries could not help being impressed by this all-pervading fashion but, nevertheless, they did not actually adopt it. This even applies to England during the Restoration period, when the Stuart court looked towards France and abhorred the taste and outlook of the Puritans. It was during this period that England produced her greatest architect, Sir Christopher Wren (1632-1723), who was given the task of rebuilding London's churches after the disastrous fire of 1666. It is interesting to compare his St Paul's Cathedral, figure 299, with a church of the Roman Baroque, built only some twenty years earlier, figure 282. We see that Wren was definitely influenced by the groupings and effects of the Baroque architect, although he himself had never been to Rome. Like Borromini's church, Wren's cathedral, which is much larger in scale, consists of a central cupola, flanking towers, and the suggestion of a temple façade to frame the main entrance. There is even a definite similarity between Borromini's Baroque towers and Wren's, particularly in the second storey. Nevertheless, the general impression of the two façades is very different. St Paul's is not curved. There is no suggestion of movement, rather of strength and stability. The way in which the paired columns are used to give stateliness and nobility to the façade recalls Versailles, figure 291, rather than the Roman Baroque. Looking at the details, we may even wonder whether or not to call Wren's style Baroque. There is nothing of the freakish or fantastic in his decoration. All his forms adhere strictly to the best models of the Italian Renaissance. Each form and each part of the building can be viewed by itself without losing its intrinsic meaning. Compared with the exuberance of Borromini, or of the architect of Melk, Wren impresses us as being restrained and sober.

The contrast between Protestant and Catholic architecture is even more marked when we consider the interiors of Wren's churches – for instance that of St Stephen Walbrook in London, figure 300. A church like this is designed mainly as a hall where the faithful meet for worship. Its aim is not to conjure up a vision of another world, but rather to allow us to collect our thoughts. In the many churches he designed, Wren endeavoured to give ever-new variations on the theme of such a hall, which would be both dignified and simple.

As with churches, so with castles. No king of England could have raised the prodigious sums to build a Versailles, and no English peer would have cared to compete with the German princelings in luxury and extravagance. It is true that the building craze reached England. The Duke of Marlborough's Blenheim Palace is even larger in scale than Prince Eugene's Belvedere. But these were exceptions. The ideal of the English eighteenth century was not the palace but the country house.

The architects of these country houses usually rejected the extravagances of the Baroque style. It was their ambition not to infringe any rule of what they considered 'good taste', and so they were anxious to keep as closely as possible to the real or pretended laws of classical architecture. Architects of the Italian Renaissance who had studied and measured the ruins of classical buildings with scientific care had published their findings in textbooks to provide builders and craftsmen with patterns. The most famous of these books was written by Andrea Palladio, page 275. This book of Palladio's came to be considered the ultimate authority on all rules of taste in architecture in eighteenth-century England. To build one's villa in the 'Palladian manner' was considered the last word in fashion. Figure 301 shows such a Palladian villa, Chiswick House. Designed for his own use by the great leader of taste and fashion, Lord Burlington (1695-1753), and decorated by his friend, William Kent (1685-1748), it is indeed a close imitation of Palladio's Villa Rotonda, *figure 232*. Unlike Hildebrandt and the other architects of Catholic Europe, *page 340*, the designers of the British villa nowhere offend against the strict rules of the classical style. The stately portico has the correct form of an antique temple front built in the Corinthian order, *page 87*, *figure 67*. The walls of the building are simple and plain, there are no curves and volutes, no statues to crown the roof, and no grotesque decorations.

For the rule of taste in the England of Lord Burlington and Alexander Pope was also the rule of reason. The whole temper of the country was opposed to the flights of fancy of Baroque designs, and to an art that aimed at overwhelming the emotions. The formal parks in the style of Versailles, whose endless clipped hedges and alleyways had extended the architects' design beyond the actual building far into the surrounding country, were condemned as absurd and artificial. A garden or park should reflect the beauties of nature, it should be a collection of fine scenery such as might charm the painter's eye. It was men such as Kent who invented the English 'landscape garden' as the ideal surroundings for their Palladian villas. Just as they had appealed to the authority of an Italian architect for the rules of reason and taste in building, so they turned to a southern painter for a standard of beauty in scenery. Their idea of what nature should look like was largely derived from the paintings of Claude Lorrain. It is interesting to compare the view of the lovely grounds of Stourhead in Wiltshire, *figure 302*, which were laid out before the middle of the eighteenth century, with works by these two masters. The 'temple' in the background again recalls Palladio's Villa Rotonda (which was, in its turn, modelled on the Roman Pantheon), while the whole vista with its lake, its bridge and

its evocation of Roman buildings confirms my remarks on
the influence which the paintings of Claude Lorrain, figure 255,
were to have on the beauty of the English landscape.

The position of English painters and sculptors under
the rule of taste and reason was not always enviable. We have
seen that the victory of Protestantism in England, and the
Puritan hostility to images and to luxury, had dealt the
tradition of art in England a severe blow. Almost the only
purpose for which painting was still in demand was that of
supplying likenesses, and even this function had largely been
met by foreign artists such as Holbein, pages 283-4, and
Van Dyck, page 309, who were called to England after they had
established their reputations abroad.

The fashionable gentlemen of Lord Burlington's days
had no objection to paintings or sculptures on puritan
grounds, but they were not eager to place commissions with
native artists who had not yet made a name in the outside
world. If they wanted a painting for their mansions they
would much rather buy one which bore the name of some
famous Italian master. They prided themselves on being
connoisseurs, and some of them assembled the most
admirable collections of old masters, without, however, giving
much employment to the painters of their time.

This state of affairs greatly irritated a young English
engraver, who had to make his living by illustrating books. His
name was William Hogarth (1697-1764). He felt that he had
it in him to be as good a painter as those whose works were
bought for hundreds of pounds from abroad, but he knew that
there was no public for contemporary art in England. He
therefore set out deliberately to create a new type of painting
which should appeal to his countrymen. He knew that they
were likely to ask 'What is the use of a painting?' and he
decided that, in order to impress people brought up in the

puritan tradition, art must have an obvious purpose.
Accordingly, he planned a number of paintings which should
teach the people the rewards of virtue and the wages of sin.
He would show a 'Rake's progress' from profligacy and idleness
to crime and death, or 'The four stages of cruelty' from a boy
teasing a cat to a grown-up's brutal murder. He would paint
these edifying stories and warning examples in such a way
that anyone who saw the series of pictures would understand
all the incidents and the lessons they taught. His paintings,
in fact, should resemble a kind of dumb show, in which all the
characters have their appointed task and make its meaning
clear through gestures and the use of stage properties. Hogarth
himself compared this new type of painting to the art of
the playwright and the theatrical producer. He did everything
to bring out what he called the 'character' of each figure, not
only through his face but also through his dress and behaviour.
Each of his picture sequences can be read like a story or,
rather, like a sermon. In this respect, this type of art was not
perhaps quite as new as Hogarth thought. We know that
medieval art used images to impart a lesson, and this tradition
of the picture sermon had lived on in popular art up to the time
of Hogarth. Crude prints had been sold at fairs to show the fate
of the drunkard or the perils of gambling, and the ballad-
mongers sold pamphlets with similar tales. Hogarth, however,
was no popular artist in this sense. He had made a careful study
of the masters of the past and of their way of achieving pictorial
effects. He knew the Dutch masters, such as Jan Steen, who
filled their pictures with humorous episodes from the life of
the people and excelled in bringing out the characteristic
expression of a type, figure 278. He also knew the methods of the
Italian artists of his time, of Venetian painters of the type of
Guardi, figure 290, who had taught him the trick of conjuring up
the idea of a figure with a few spirited touches of the brush.

Figure 303 shows an episode from the 'Rake's progress' in which the poor rake comes to his end as a raving maniac in Bedlam. It is a crude scene of horror with all types of madmen represented: the religious fanatic in the first cell writhing on his bed of straw like the parody of a Baroque picture of a saint, the megalomaniac with his royal crown seen in the next cell, the idiot who scrawls the picture of the world on to the wall of Bedlam, the blind man with his paper telescope, the grotesque trio grouped round the staircase – the grinning fiddler, the foolish singer, and the touching figure of the apathetic man who just sits and stares – and, finally, the group of the dying rake, who is mourned by none but the servant girl he once left in the lurch. As he collapses, they take off his irons, the cruel equivalent of the strait-jacket. They are no longer needed. It is a tragic scene, made even more tragic by the grotesque dwarf, who mocks it, and by the contrast with the two elegant visitors, who had known the rake in the days of his prosperity.

Each figure and each episode in the picture has its place in the story Hogarth tells, but that alone would not suffice to make it a good painting. What is remarkable in Hogarth is that, for all his preoccupation with his subject-matter, he still remained a painter, not only in the way he used his brush and distributed light and colour, but also in the considerable skill he showed in arranging his groups. The group round the rake, for all its grotesque horror, is as carefully composed as any Italian painting of the classical tradition. Hogarth, in fact, was very proud of his understanding of this tradition. He was sure that he had found the law which governed beauty. He wrote a book, which he called *The Analysis of Beauty*, to explain the idea that an undulating line will always be more beautiful than an angular one. Hogarth, too, belonged to the age of reason and believed in teachable rules of taste, but he did not succeed in converting his compatriots from their bias for the old masters. It is true that his picture-series earned him great fame and a considerable sum of money, but his reputation was due less to the actual paintings than to reproductions he made of them in engravings which were bought by an eager public. As a painter, the connoisseurs of the period did not take him seriously and, throughout his life, he waged a grim campaign against fashionable taste.

It was only a generation later that an English painter was born whose art satisfied the elegant society of eighteenth-century England – Sir Joshua Reynolds (1723-92). Unlike Hogarth, Reynolds had been to Italy and had come to agree with the connoisseurs of his time that the great masters of the Italian Renaissance – Raphael, Michelangelo, Correggio and Titian – were the unrivalled exemplars of true art. He had absorbed the teaching attributed to the Carracci, *pages 297-8*, that the only hope for an artist lay in the careful study and imitation of what were called the excellences of the ancient masters – the draughtsmanship of Raphael, the colouring of Titian, and so on. Later in his life, when Reynolds had made a career as an artist in England and had become the first president of the newly founded Royal Academy of Art, he expounded this 'academic' doctrine in a series of discourses, which still make interesting reading. They show that Reynolds, like his contemporaries (such as Dr Johnson), believed in the rules of taste and the importance of authority in art. He believed that the right procedure in art could, to a large extent, be taught, if students were given facilities for studying the recognized masterpieces of Italian painting. His lectures are full of exhortations to strive after lofty and dignified subjects, because Reynolds believed that only the grand and impressive was worthy of the name of Great Art. 'Instead of endeavouring to amuse mankind with the minute neatness of his imitations, the genuine painter', Reynolds wrote in his third *Discourse*, 'must endeavour to improve them by the grandeur of his ideas.'

From such a quotation it might easily appear that Reynolds was rather pompous and boring, but if we read his *Discourses* and look at his pictures, we soon get rid of this prejudice. The fact is that he accepted the opinions about art which he found in the writings of the influential critics of the seventeenth century, all of whom were much concerned with the dignity of what was called 'history painting'. We have seen how hard artists had to struggle against social snobbery which made people look down on painters and sculptors because they worked with their hands, *page 216*. We know how artists had to insist that their real work was not handiwork but brain work, and that they were no less fit to be received into polite society than poets or scholars. It was through these discussions that artists were led to stress the importance of poetic invention in art, and to emphasize the elevated subjects with which their minds were concerned. 'Granted,' they argued, 'that there may be something menial in painting a portrait or a landscape from nature where the hand merely copies what the eye sees, but surely it requires more than mere craftsmanship: it requires erudition and imagination to paint a subject like Reni's "Aurora" or Poussin's "Et in Arcadia ego"?', *figures 253, 254*. We know today that there is a fallacy in this argument. We know that there is nothing undignified in any kind of handiwork and that, moreover, it needs more than a good eye and a sure hand to paint a good portrait or landscape. But every period and every society has its own prejudices in matters of art and of taste – ours, of course, not excluded. Indeed, what makes it so interesting to examine these ideas, which highly intelligent people in the past took so much for granted, is precisely that we learn in this way also to examine ourselves.

Reynolds was an intellectual, a friend of Dr Johnson and his circle, but equally welcome in the elegant country houses and town mansions of the powerful and the wealthy. And though he sincerely believed in the superiority of history painting, and hoped for its revival in England, he accepted the fact that the only kind of art really in demand in these circles was that of portraiture. Van Dyck had established a standard of society portraits that all fashionable painters of subsequent generations had tried to reach. Reynolds could be as flattering and as elegant as the best of them, but he liked to add an extra interest to his paintings of people to bring out their character and their role in society. Thus figure 304 represents an intellectual from Dr Johnson's circle, the Italian scholar Joseph Baretti, who had compiled an English-Italian dictionary and later translated Reynolds's *Discourses* into Italian. It is a perfect record, intimate without being impertinent, and a good painting into the bargain.

Even when he had to paint a child, Reynolds tried to make the picture into more than a mere portrait by carefully choosing his setting. Figure 305 shows his portrait of 'Miss Bowles with her dog'. We remember that Velázquez, too, had painted the portrait of a child and dog, figure 267. But Velázquez had been interested in the texture and colour of what he saw. Reynolds wants to show us the touching love of the little girl for her pet. We are told what trouble he took to gain the child's confidence, before he set out to paint her. He was asked to the house and sat beside her at dinner 'where he amused her so much with stories and tricks, that she thought him the most charming man in the world. He made her look at something distant from the table and stole her plate; then he pretended to look for it, then he contrived it should come back to her without her knowing how. The next day she was delighted to be taken to his house, where she sat down with an expression full of glee, the expression of which he at once caught and never lost.' No wonder that the outcome is more self-conscious, and much more thought out, than Velázquez's straightforward arrangement. It is true that, if we compare his handling of paint and his treatment of the living skin and the fluffy fur with that of Velázquez, we may find Reynolds disappointing. But it would hardly be fair to expect of him an effect at which he was not aiming. He wanted to bring out the character of the sweet child, and to make her tenderness and her charm live for us. Today, when photographers have so accustomed us to the trick of observing a child in a similar situation, we may find it difficult fully to appreciate the originality of Reynolds's treatment. But we must not blame a master for the imitations which have spoilt his effects. Reynolds never allowed the interest of the subject-matter to upset the harmony of the painting.

In the Wallace Collection in London, where Reynolds's portrait of Miss Bowles hangs, there is also the portrait of a girl of roughly the same age by his greatest rival in the field of portrait painting, Thomas Gainsborough (1727-88), who only four years his junior. It is the portrait of Miss Haverfield, figure 306. Gainsborough painted the little lady as she was tying the bow of her cape. There is nothing particularly moving or interesting in her action. She is just dressing, we fancy, to go for a walk. But Gainsborough knew how to invest the simple movement with such grace and charm that we find it as satisfying as Reynolds's invention of a girl hugging her pet. Gainsborough was much less interested in 'invention' than Reynolds. He was born in rural Suffolk, had a natural gift for painting, and never found it necessary to go to Italy to study the great masters. In comparison with Reynolds and all his theories about the importance of tradition, Gainsborough was almost a self-made man. There is something in the relationship

of the two which recalls the contrast between the learned
Annibale Carracci, *pages* 296-7, who wanted to revive the
manner of Raphael, and the revolutionary Caravaggio, *pages*
298-9, who wanted to acknowledge no teacher except nature.
Reynolds, at any rate, saw Gainsborough somewhat in this
light, as a genius who refused to copy the masters, and, much
as he admired his rival's skill, he felt bound to warn his
students against his principles. Today, after the passage of
almost two centuries, the two masters do not seem to us so
very different. We realize, perhaps more clearly than they did,
how much they both owed to the tradition of Van Dyck, and
to the fashion of their time. But, if we return to the portrait of
Miss Haverfield with this contrast in mind, we understand the
particular qualities which distinguish Gainsborough's fresh
and unsophisticated approach from Reynolds's more laboured
style. Gainsborough, we now see, had no intention of being
'highbrow'; he wanted to paint straightforward
unconventional portraits in which he could display his
brilliant brushwork and his sure eye. And so he succeeds best
where Reynolds disappointed us. His rendering of the fresh
complexion of the child and the shining material of the cape,
his treatment of the frills and ribbons of the hat, all this shows
his consummate skill in rendering the texture and surfaces of
visible objects. The rapid and impatient strokes of the brush
almost remind us of the work of Frans Hals, figure 270. But
Gainsborough was a less robust artist. There are, in many of
his portraits, a delicacy of shades and a refinement of touch
which rather recall the visions of Watteau, figure 298.

   Both Reynolds and Gainsborough were rather unhappy
to be smothered with commissions for portraits when they
wanted to paint other things. But while Reynolds longed for
time and leisure to paint ambitious mythological scenes or
episodes from ancient history, Gainsborough wanted to paint

the very subjects which his rival despised. He wanted to
paint landscapes. For, unlike Reynolds, who was a man about
town, Gainsborough loved the quiet countryside, and among
the few entertainments he really enjoyed was chamber
music. Unfortunately Gainsborough could not find many
buyers for his landscapes, and so a large number of his
pictures remained mere sketches done for his own
enjoyment, figure 307. In these he arranged the trees and hills
of the English countryside into picturesque scenes which
remind us that this was the age of the landscape gardener.
For Gainsborough's sketches are no views drawn direct from
nature. They are landscape 'compositions', designed to evoke
and reflect a mood.

In the eighteenth century, English institutions and
English taste became the admired models for all people in
Europe who longed for the rule of reason. For in England art
had not been used to enhance the power and glory of god-like
rulers. The public for which Hogarth catered, even the people
who posed for Reynolds's and Gainsborough's portraits, were
ordinary mortals. We remember that in France, too, the heavy
Baroque grandeur of Versailles had gone out of fashion in the
early eighteenth century in favour of the more delicate and
intimate effects of Watteau's Rococo, figure 298. Now this whole
aristocratic dream-world began to recede. Painters began to
look at the life of the ordinary men and women of their time,
to draw moving or amusing episodes which could be spun
out into a story. The greatest of these was Jean-Baptiste-Siméon
Chardin (1699-1779), a painter two years younger than
Hogarth. Figure 308 shows one of his charming paintings – a
simple room with a woman setting dinner on the table and
asking two children to say grace. Chardin liked these quiet
glimpses of the life of ordinary people. He resembles the Dutch
painter Vermeer, figure 281, in the way in which he feels and

preserves the poetry of a domestic scene, without looking for striking effects or pointed allusions. Even his colour is calm and restrained and, by comparison with the scintillating paintings of Watteau, his works may seem to lack brilliance. But if we study them in the original, we soon discover in them an unobtrusive mastery in the subtle gradation of tones and the seemingly artless arrangement of the scene that makes him one of the most lovable painters of the eighteenth century.

In France, as in England, the new interest in ordinary human beings rather than the trappings of power benefited the art of portraiture. Perhaps the greatest of the French portraitists was not a painter but a sculptor, Jean-Antoine Houdon (1741-1828). In his wonderful portrait busts, Houdon carried on the tradition which had been started by Bernini more than a hundred years earlier, *page 333*, figure 284. Figure 309 shows Houdon's bust of Voltaire and allows us to *see*, in the face of this great champion of reason, the biting wit, the penetrating intelligence, and also the deep compassion of a great mind.

The taste for the 'picturesque' aspects of nature, finally, which inspired Gainsborough's sketches in England, is also found in eighteenth-century France. Figure 310 shows a drawing by Jean-Honoré Fragonard (1732-1806), who belonged to the generation of Gainsborough. Fragonard, too, was a painter of great charm who followed the tradition of Watteau in his themes from high life. In his landscape drawings he was a master of striking effects. The view from the Villa d'Este in Tivoli, near Rome, proves how he could find grandeur and charm in a piece of actual scenery.

24

The Break in Tradition

*England, America and France, late eighteenth and
early nineteenth centuries*

In history books modern times begin with the discovery of America by Columbus in 1492. We remember the importance of that period in art. It was the time of the Renaissance, the time when being a painter or a sculptor ceased to be an occupation like any other and became a calling set apart. It was also the period during which the Reformation, through its fight against images in churches, put an end to the most frequent use of pictures and sculptures in large parts of Europe, and forced the artists to look for a new market. But however important all these events were, they did not result in a sudden break. The large mass of artists were still organized in guilds and companies, they still had apprentices like other artisans, and they still relied for commissions largely on the wealthy aristocracy, who needed artists to decorate their castles and country seats and to add their portraits to the ancestral galleries. Even after 1492, in other words, art retained a natural place in the life of people of leisure, and was generally taken for granted as something one could not well do without. Even though fashions changed and artists set themselves different problems, some being more interested in the harmonious arrangement of figures, others in the matching of colours or the achievement of dramatic expression, the purpose of painting or sculpture remained in general the same, and no one seriously questioned it. This purpose was to supply beautiful things to people who wanted them and enjoyed them. There were, it is true, various schools of thought which quarrelled among themselves over what 'beauty' meant and whether it was enough to enjoy the skilful imitation of nature for which Caravaggio, the Dutch painters, or men like Gainsborough, had become famous, or whether true beauty did not depend on the capacity of the artist to 'idealize' nature as Raphael, Carracci, Reni or Reynolds were supposed to have done. But these disputes need not make us forget how much common ground there was among the disputants, and how much between the artists whom they chose as their favourites. Even the 'idealists' agreed that the artists must study nature and learn to draw from the nude, even the 'naturalists' agreed that the works of classical antiquity were unsurpassed in beauty.

Towards the end of the eighteenth century this common ground seemed gradually to give way. We have reached the really modern times which dawned when the French Revolution of 1789 put an end to so many assumptions that had been taken for granted for hundreds, if not for thousands, of years. Just as the Great Revolution has its roots in the Age of Reason, so have the changes in man's ideas about art. The first of these changes concerns the artist's attitude to what is called 'style'. There is a character in one of Molière's comedies who is greatly astonished when he is told that he has spoken prose all his life without knowing it. Something a little similar happened to the artists of the eighteenth century. In former times, the style of the period was simply the way in which things were done; it was practised because people thought it was the best way of achieving certain desired effects. In the Age of Reason, people began to become self-conscious about style and styles. Many architects were still convinced, as we have seen, that the rules laid down in the books by Palladio guaranteed the 'right' style for elegant buildings. But once you turn to textbooks for such questions it is almost inevitable that there will be others who say: 'Why must it be just Palladio's style?' This is what happened in England in the course of the eighteenth century. Among the most sophisticated connoisseurs there were some who wanted to be different from the others. The most characteristic of these English gentlemen of leisure who spent their time thinking about style and the rules of taste was the famous

Horace Walpole, son of the first Prime Minister of England. It was Walpole who decided that it was boring to have his country house on Strawberry Hill built just like any other correct Palladian villa. He had a taste for the quaint and romantic, and was notorious for his whimsicality. It was quite in keeping with his character that he decided to have Strawberry Hill built in the Gothic style like a castle from the romantic past, figure 311. At the time, about 1770, Walpole's Gothic villa passed for the oddity of a man who wanted to show off his antiquarian interests; but seen in the light of what came later, it was really more than that. It was one of the first signs of that self-consciousness which made people select the style of their building as one selects the pattern of a wallpaper.

There were several symptoms of this kind. While Walpole selected the Gothic style for his country house, the architect William Chambers (1726-96) studied the Chinese style of buildings and of gardening, and built his Chinese Pagoda in Kew Gardens. The majority of architects, it is true, still kept to the classical forms of Renaissance building, but even they were increasingly worried about the right style. They looked with some misgivings on the practice and tradition of architecture which had grown up since the Renaissance. They found that many of these practices had no real sanction in the buildings of classical Greece. They realized, with a shock, that what had passed as the rules of classical architecture since the fifteenth century were taken from a few Roman ruins of a more or less decadent period. Now the temples of Periclean Athens were rediscovered and engraved by zealous travellers, and they looked strikingly different from the classical designs to be found in Palladio's book. Thus these architects became preoccupied with correct style. Walpole's 'Gothic revival' was matched by a 'Greek revival' which culminated in the Regency period (1810-20). This is the period in which many of the principal spas in England enjoyed their greatest prosperity, and it is in these towns that one can best study the forms of the Greek revival. Figure 312 shows a house in Cheltenham Spa which is successfully modelled on the pure Ionic style of Greek temples, figure 60. Figure 313 gives an example of the revival of the Doric order in its original form such as we know it from the Parthenon, figure 50. It is a design for a villa by the famous architect Sir John Soane (1752-1837). If we compare it with the Palladian villa built by William Kent some eighty years earlier, figure 301, the superficial similarity only brings out the difference. Kent used the forms he found in tradition freely to compose his building. Soane's project, by comparison, looks like an exercise in the correct use of the elements of Greek style.

This conception of architecture as an application of strict and simple rules was bound to appeal to the champions of Reason, whose power and influence continued to grow all over the world. Thus it is not surprising that a man such as Thomas Jefferson (1743-1826), one of the founders of the United States and its third President, designed his own residence, Monticello, in this lucid, neo-classical style, figure 314, and that the city of Washington, with its public buildings, was planned in the forms of the Greek revival. In France, too, the victory of this style was assured after the French Revolution. The old happy-go-lucky tradition of Baroque and Rococo builders and decorators was identified with the past which had just been swept away; it had been the style of the castles of royalty and of the aristocracy, while the men of the Revolution liked to think of themselves as the free citizens of a new-born Athens. When Napoleon, posing as the champion of the ideas of the Revolution, rose to power in Europe, the neo-classical style of architecture became the style of the Empire. On the Continent, too, a Gothic revival existed side by side with this new revival of the pure Greek style.

It appealed particularly to those Romantic minds who
despaired of the power of Reason to reform the world and
longed for a return to what they called the Age of Faith.

In painting and sculpture, the break in the chain of
tradition was perhaps less immediately perceptible than it
was in architecture, but it was possibly of even greater
consequence. Here, too, the roots of the trouble reach back
far into the eighteenth century. We have seen how dissatisfied
Hogarth was with the tradition of art as he found it, *pages*
350-1, and how deliberately he set out to create a new kind of
painting for a new public. We remember how Reynolds, on
the other hand, was anxious to preserve that tradition as if he
realized that it was in danger. The danger lay in the fact,
mentioned before, that painting had ceased to be an ordinary
trade the knowledge of which was handed down from master
to apprentice. Instead, it had become a subject like philosophy
to be taught in academies. The very word 'academy' suggests
this new approach. It is derived from the name of the grove
in which the Greek philosopher Plato taught his disciples, and
was gradually applied to gatherings of learned men in search
of wisdom. Sixteenth-century Italian artists at first called their
meeting-places 'academies' to stress that equality with scholars
on which they set such great store; but it was only in the
eighteenth century that these academies gradually took over
the function of teaching art to students. Thus the old methods,
by which the great masters of the past had learned their trade
by grinding colours and assisting their elders, had fallen into
decline. No wonder that academic teachers like Reynolds felt
compelled to urge young students to study diligently the
masterpieces of the past and to assimilate their technical skill.
The academies of the eighteenth century were under royal
patronage, to manifest the interest which the King took in the
arts in his realm. But for the arts to flourish, it is less

important that they should be taught in Royal Institutions than that there should be enough people willing to buy paintings or sculptures by living artists.

It was here that the main difficulties arose, because the very emphasis on the greatness of the masters of the past, which was favoured by the academies, made patrons inclined to buy old masters rather than to commission paintings from the living. As a remedy, the academies, first in Paris, then in London, began to arrange annual exhibitions of the works of their members. We may find it hard to realize what a momentous change this was, since we are so used to the idea of artists painting and sculptors modelling their work mainly with the idea of sending it to an exhibition to attract the attention of art critics and to find buyers. These annual exhibitions became social events that formed the topic of conversation in polite society, and made and unmade reputations. Instead of working for individual patrons whose wishes they understood, or for the general public, whose taste they could gauge, artists had now to work for success in a show where there was always a danger of the spectacular and pretentious outshining the simple and sincere. The temptation was indeed great for artists to attract attention by selecting melodramatic subjects for their paintings, and by relying on size and loud colour effects to impress the public. Thus it is not surprising that some artists despised the 'official' art of the academies, and that the clash of opinions, between those whose gifts allowed them to appeal to the public taste and those who found themselves excluded, threatened to destroy the common ground on which all art had so far developed.

Perhaps the most immediate and visible effect of this profound crisis was that artists everywhere looked for new types of subject-matter. In the past, the subject-matter of paintings had been very much taken for granted. If we walk round our galleries and museums we soon discover how many of the paintings illustrate identical topics. The majority of the older pictures, of course, represent religious subjects taken from the Bible, and the legends of the saints. But even those that are secular in character are mostly confined to a few selected themes. There are the mythologies of ancient Greece with their stories of the loves and quarrels of the gods; there are the heroic tales from Rome with their examples of valour and self-sacrifice; and there are, finally, the allegorical subjects illustrating some general truth by means of personifications. It is curious how rarely artists before the middle of the eighteenth century strayed from these narrow limits of illustration, how rarely they painted a scene from a romance, or an episode of medieval or contemporary history. All this changed very rapidly during the period of the French Revolution. Suddenly artists felt free to choose as their subjects anything from a Shakespearean scene to a topical event, anything, in fact, that appealed to the imagination and aroused interest. This disregard for the traditional subject-matter of art may have been the only thing the successful artists of the period and the lonely rebels had in common.

It is hardly an accident that this breakaway from the established traditions of European art was partly accomplished by artists who had come to Europe from across the ocean – Americans who worked in England. Obviously these men felt less bound to the hallowed customs of the Old World and were readier to try new experiments. The American John Singleton Copley (1737-1815) is a typical artist of this group. Figure 315 shows one of his large paintings, which caused a sensation when it was first exhibited in 1785. The subject was indeed an unusual one. The Shakespearean scholar Malone, a friend of the politician Edmund Burke, had suggested it to the painter and provided him with all the historical information necessary. He was to paint the famous incident when Charles I demanded from the House of Commons the arrest of five impeached members, and when the Speaker challenged the King's authority and declined to surrender them. Such an episode from comparatively recent history had never been made the subject of a large painting before, and the method which Copley selected for the task was equally unprecedented. It was his intention to reconstruct the scene as accurately as possible – as it would have presented itself to the eyes of a contemporary witness. He spared no pains in getting the historical facts. He consulted antiquarians and historians about the actual shape of the chamber in the seventeenth century and the costumes people wore; he travelled from country house to country house to collect portraits of as many men as possible who were known to have been Members of Parliament at that critical moment. In short, he acted as a conscientious producer might act today when he has to reconstruct such a scene for a historical film or play. We may or may not find these efforts well spent. But it is a fact that, for more than a hundred years afterwards, many artists great and small saw their task in exactly this type of antiquarian research, which should help people to visualize decisive moments of history.

In Copley's case, this attempt to re-evoke the dramatic clash between the King and the representatives of the people was certainly not only the work of a disinterested antiquarian. Only two years before, George III had had to submit to the challenge of the colonists and had signed the peace with the United States. Burke, from whose circle the suggestion for the subject had come, had been a consistent opponent of the war, which he considered unjust and disastrous. The meaning of Copley's evocation of the previous rebuff to royal pretensions was perfectly understood by all. The story is told that when the Queen saw the painting she turned away in pained surprise, and after a long and ominous silence said to the young American: 'You have chosen, Mr Copley, a most unfortunate subject for the exercise of your pencil.' She could not know *how* unfortunate the reminiscence was going to prove. Those who remember the history of these years will be struck by the fact that, hardly four years later, the scene of the picture was to be re-enacted in France. This time, it was Mirabeau who denied the King's right to interfere with the representatives of the people, and thus gave the starting signal for the French Revolution of 1789.

The French Revolution gave an enormous impulse to this type of interest in history, and to the painting of heroic subjects. Copley had looked for examples in England's national past. There was a Romantic strain in his historical painting which may be compared to the Gothic revival in architecture. The French revolutionaries loved to think of themselves as Greeks and Romans reborn, and their painting, no less than their architecture, reflected this taste for what was called Roman grandeur. The leading artist of this neo-classical style was the painter Jacques-Louis David (1748-1825), who was the 'official artist' of the Revolutionary Government, and designed the costumes and settings for such propagandist pageantries as the 'Festival of the Supreme Being' in which Robespierre officiated as a self-appointed High Priest. These people felt that they were living in heroic times, and that the events of their own years were just as worthy of the painter's attention as the episodes of Greek and Roman history. When one of the leaders of the French Revolution, Marat, was killed in his bath by a fanatical young woman, David painted him as a martyr who had died for his cause, figure 316. Marat was apparently in the habit of working in his bath, and his bath tub was fitted with a simple desk. His assailant had handed him a petition, which he was about to sign when she struck him down. The situation does not seem to lend itself easily to a picture of dignity and grandeur, but David succeeded in making it seem heroic, while yet keeping to the actual details of a police record. He had learned from the study of Greek and Roman sculpture how to model the muscles and sinews of the body, and give it the appearance of noble beauty; he had also learned from classical art to leave out all details which are not essential to the main effect, and to aim at simplicity. There are no motley colours and no complicated foreshortening in the painting. Compared to Copley's great showpiece, David's painting looks austere. It is an impressive commemoration of a humble 'friend of the people' – as Marat had styled himself – who had suffered the fate of a martyr while working for the common weal.

Among the artists of David's generation who discarded the old type of subject-matter was the great Spanish painter, Francisco Goya (1746-1828). Goya was well versed in the best tradition of Spanish painting, which had produced El Greco, figure 238, and Velázquez, figure 264, and his group on a balcony, figure 317, shows that unlike David he did not renounce this mastery in favour of classical grandeur. The great Venetian painter of the eighteenth century, Giovanni Battista Tiepolo, figure 288, had ended his days as a court painter in Madrid, and there is something of his radiance in Goya's painting. And yet Goya's figures belong to a different world. The two women who eye the passer-by provokingly, while two rather sinister gallants keep in the background, may be closer to the world of Hogarth. Goya's portraits which secured him a place at the Spanish court, figure 318, look superficially like the traditional state portraits of Van Dyck, figure 261, or of Reynolds. The skill with which he conjured up the glitter of silk and gold recalls Titian or Velázquez. But he also looks at his sitters with a different eye. Not that these masters had flattered the mighty, but Goya seems to have known no pity. He made their features reveal all their vanity and ugliness, their greed and emptiness, figure 319. No court painter before or after has ever left such a record of his patrons.

It was not only as a painter that Goya asserted his independence of the conventions of the past. Like Rembrandt, he produced a great number of etchings, most of them in a new technique called aquatint, which allows not only etched lines but also shaded patches. The most striking fact about Goya's prints is that they are not illustrations of any known subject, either biblical, historical or genre. Most of them are fantastic visions of witches and uncanny apparitions. Some are meant as accusations against the powers of stupidity and reaction, of cruelty and oppression, which Goya had witnessed in Spain, others seem just to give shape to the artist's nightmares. Figure 320 represents one of the most haunting of his dreams – the figure of a giant sitting on the edge of the world. We can gauge his colossal size from the tiny landscape in the foreground, and we can see how he dwarfs houses and castles into mere specks. We can make our imagination play around this dreadful apparition, which is drawn with a clarity of outline as if it were a study from life. The monster sits in the moonlit landscape like some evil incubus. Was Goya thinking of the fate of his country, of its oppression by wars and human folly? Or was he simply creating an image like a poem? For this was the most outstanding effect of the break in tradition – that artists felt free to put their private visions on paper as hitherto only the poets had done.

The most outstanding example of this new approach to art was the English poet and mystic William Blake (1757-1827), who was eleven years younger than Goya. Blake was a deeply religious man, who lived in a world of his own. He despised the official art of the academies, and declined to accept its standards. Some thought he was completely mad;

others dismissed him as a harmless crank, and only a very few of his contemporaries believed in his art and saved him from starvation. He lived by making prints, sometimes for others, sometimes to illustrate his own poems. Figure 321 represents one of Blake's illustrations to his poem, *Europe, a Prophecy*. It is said that Blake had seen this enigmatic figure of an old man, bending down to measure the globe with a compass, in a vision which hovered over his head at the top of a staircase when he was living in Lambeth. There is a passage in the Bible (Proverbs VIII. 22-7), in which Wisdom speaks and says:

> The Lord possessed me in the beginning of His way, before His works of old ... before the mountains were settled, before the hills was I brought forth ... when He prepared the Heavens, I was there: when He set a compass on the face of the depths: when He established the clouds above: when He strengthened the fountains of the deep.

It is this grandiose vision of the Lord setting a compass upon the face of the depths that Blake illustrated. There is something of Michelangelo's figure of the Lord, figure 200, in this image of the Creation, and Blake admired Michelangelo. But in his hands the figure has become dream-like and fantastic. In fact, Blake had formed a mythology of his own, and the figure of the vision was not strictly speaking the Lord Himself, but a being of Blake's imagination whom he called Urizen. Though Blake conceived of Urizen as the creator of the world, he thought of the world as bad and therefore of its creator as of an evil spirit. Hence the uncanny nightmare character of the vision, in which the compass appears like a flash of lightning in a dark and stormy night.

Blake was so wrapped up in his visions that he refused to draw from life and relied entirely on his inner eye. It is easy to point to faults in his draughtsmanship, but to do so would be to miss the point of his art. Like the medieval artists, he did not care for accurate representation, because the significance of each figure of his dreams was of such overwhelming importance to him that questions of mere correctness seemed to him irrelevant. He was the first artist after the Renaissance who thus consciously revolted against the accepted standards of tradition, and we can hardly blame his contemporaries who found him shocking. It was almost a century before he was generally recognized as one of the most important figures in English art.

There was one branch of painting that profited much by the artist's new freedom in his choice of subject-matter – this was landscape painting. So far, it had been looked upon as a minor branch of art. The painters, in particular, who had earned their living painting 'views' of country houses, parks or picturesque scenery, were not taken seriously as artists. This attitude changed somewhat through the romantic spirit of the late eighteenth century, and great artists saw it as their purpose in life to raise this type of painting to new dignity. Here, too, tradition could serve both as a help and a hindrance, and it is fascinating to see how differently two English landscape painters of the same generation approached this question. One was J.M.W. Turner (1775-1851), the other John Constable (1776-1837). There is something in the contrast of these two men which recalls the contrast between Reynolds and Gainsborough, but, in the fifty years which separate their generations, the gulf between the approaches of the two rivals had very much widened. Turner, like Reynolds, was an immensely successful artist whose pictures often caused a sensation at the Royal Academy. Like Reynolds, he was obsessed with the problem of tradition. It was his ambition in life to reach, if not surpass, the celebrated landscape paintings

of Claude Lorrain, figure 255. When he left his pictures and
sketches to the nation, he did so on the express condition that
one of them, figure 322, must always be shown side by side
with a work by Claude Lorrain. Turner hardly did himself
justice by inviting this comparison. The beauty of Claude's
pictures lies in their serene simplicity and calm, in the clarity
and concreteness of his dream-world, and in the absence of
any loud effects. Turner, too, had visions of a fantastic world
bathed in light and resplendent with beauty, but it was a
world not of calm but of movement, not of simple harmonies
but of dazzling pageantries. He crowded into his pictures
every effect which could make them more striking and more
dramatic, and, had he been a lesser artist than he was, this
desire to impress the public might well have had a disastrous
result. Yet he was such a superb stage-manager, he worked
with such gusto and skill, that he carried it off and the best of
his pictures do, in fact, give us a conception of the grandeur
of nature at its most romantic and sublime. Figure 323 shows
one of Turner's most daring paintings – a steamer in a
blizzard. If we compare this whirling composition with the
seascape of de Vlieger, figure 271, we gain a measure of the
boldness of Turner's approach. The Dutch artist of the
seventeenth century did not only paint what he saw at a
glance, but also, to some extent, what he knew was there. He
knew how a ship was built and how it was rigged, and,
looking at his painting, we might be able to reconstruct these
vessels. Nobody could reconstruct a nineteenth-century
steamer from Turner's seascape. All he gives us is the
impression of the dark hull, of the flag flying bravely from the
mast – of a battle with the raging seas and threatening squalls.
We almost feel the rush of the wind and the impact of the
waves. We have no time to look for details. They are swallowed
up by the dazzling light and the dark shadows of the storm

cloud. I do not know whether a blizzard at sea really looks like this. But I do know that it is a storm of this awe-inspiring and overwhelming kind that we imagine when reading a romantic poem or listening to romantic music. In Turner, nature always reflects and expresses man's emotions. We feel small and overwhelmed in the face of the powers we cannot control, and are compelled to admire the artist who had nature's forces at his command.

Constable's ideas were very different. To him the tradition which Turner wanted to rival and surpass was not much more than a nuisance. Not that he failed to admire the great masters of the past. But he wanted to paint what he saw with his own eyes – not with those of Claude Lorrain. It might be said that he continued where Gainsborough had left off, figure 307. But even Gainsborough had still selected motifs which were 'picturesque' by traditional standards. He had still looked at nature as a pleasing setting for idyllic scenes. To Constable all these ideas were unimportant. He wanted nothing but the truth. 'There is room enough for a natural painter,' he wrote to a friend in 1802; 'the great vice of the present day is *bravura*, an attempt to do something beyond the truth.' The fashionable landscape painters who still took Claude as their model had developed a number of easy tricks by which any amateur could compose an effective and pleasing picture. An impressive tree in the foreground would serve as a striking contrast to the distant view that opened up in the centre. The colour scheme was neatly worked out. Warm colours, preferably brown and golden tones, should be in the foreground. The background should fade into pale blue tints. There were recipes for painting clouds, and special tricks for imitating the bark of gnarled oaks. Constable despised all these set-pieces. The story goes that a friend remonstrated with him for not giving his foreground the requisite mellow brown of an old violin, and

that Constable thereupon took a violin and put it before him
on the grass to show the friend the difference between the
fresh green as we see it and the warm tones demanded
by convention. But Constable had no wish to shock people by
daring innovations. All he wanted was to be faithful to his
own vision. He went out to the countryside to make sketches
from nature, and then elaborated them in his studio. His
sketches, figure 324, are often bolder than his finished pictures,
but the time had not yet come when the public would accept
the record of a rapid impression as a work worthy to be
shown at an exhibition. Even so, his finished pictures caused
uneasiness when they were first exhibited. Figure 325 shows the
painting which made Constable famous in Paris when he
sent it there in 1824. It represents a simple rural scene, a
haywain fording a river. We must lose ourselves in the picture,
watch the patches of sunlight on the meadows in the
background and look at the drifting clouds; we must follow
the course of the mill-stream, and linger by the cottage, which
is painted with such restraint and simplicity, to appreciate the
artist's absolute sincerity, his refusal to be more impressive
than nature, and his complete lack of pose or pretentiousness.

The break with tradition had left artists with the two
possibilities which were embodied in Turner and Constable.
They could become poets in painting, and seek moving and
dramatic effects, or they could decide to keep to the motif in
front of them, and explore it with all the insistence and
honesty at their command. There were certainly great artists
among the Romantic painters of Europe, men such as Turner's
contemporary, the German Caspar David Friedrich (1774-
1840), whose landscape pictures reflect the mood of the
Romantic lyrical poetry of his time which is more familiar to
us through Schubert's songs. His painting of a bleak mountain
scene, figure 326, may even remind us of the spirit of Chinese

landscape paintings, figure 98, which also comes so close to the ideas of poetry. But however great and deserved was the popular success which some of these Romantic painters achieved in their day, I believe that those who followed Constable's path and tried to explore the visible world rather than to conjure up poetic moods achieved something of more lasting importance.

Permanent Revolution

The nineteenth century

What I have called the break in tradition, which marks the period of the Great Revolution in France, was bound to change the whole situation in which artists lived and worked. The academies and exhibitions, the critics and connoisseurs, had done their best to introduce a distinction between Art with a capital A and the mere exercise of a craft, be it that of the painter or the builder. Now the foundations on which art had rested throughout its existence were being undermined from another side. The Industrial Revolution began to destroy the very traditions of solid craftsmanship; handiwork gave way to machine production, the workshop to the factory.

The most immediate results of this change were visible in architecture. The lack of solid craftsmanship, combined with a strange insistence on 'style' and 'beauty', nearly killed it. The amount of building done in the nineteenth century was probably greater than in all former periods taken together. It was the time of the vast expansion of cities in England and America that turned whole tracts of country into 'built-up areas'. But this time of unlimited building activity had no natural style of its own. The rules of thumb and the pattern books, which had so admirably served their turn up to the Georgian period, were generally discarded as too simple and too 'inartistic'. The businessman or town committee that planned a new factory, railway station, school building or museum, wanted Art for their money. Accordingly, when the other specifications had been fulfilled, the architect was commissioned to provide a façade in the Gothic style, or to turn the building into the semblance of a Norman castle, a Renaissance palace, or even an Oriental mosque. Certain conventions were more or less accepted, but they did not help much to improve matters. Churches were more often than not built in the Gothic style because this had been prevalent

in what was called the Age of Faith. For theatres and opera
houses the theatrical Baroque style was often considered
suitable, while palaces and ministries were thought to look
most dignified in the stately forms of the Italian Renaissance.

It would be unfair to assume that there were no gifted
architects in the nineteenth century. There certainly were.
But the situation of their art was all against them. The more
conscientiously they studied to imitate the bygone styles, the
less their designs were likely to be adapted to the purpose
for which they were intended. And if they decided to be
ruthless with the conventions of the style they had to adopt,
the result was usually not too happy either. Some nineteenth-
century architects succeeded in finding a way between these
two unpleasant alternatives, and in creating works which
are neither sham antiques nor mere freak inventions. Their
buildings have become landmarks of the cities in which they
stand, and we have come to accept them almost as if they
were part of the natural scenery. This is true, for instance, of
the Houses of Parliament in London, figure 327, whose history
is characteristic of the difficulties under which architects of
the period had to work. When the old chamber burned
down in 1834, a competition was organized, and the jury's
choice fell on the design of Sir Charles Barry (1795-1860),
an expert on the Renaissance style. It was felt, however, that
England's civil liberties rested on the achievements of the
Middle Ages, and that it was right and proper to erect the
shrine of British Freedom in the Gothic style – a point of
view, by the way, which was still universally accepted when
the restoration of the chamber after its destruction by
German bombers was discussed after the Second World
War. Accordingly, Barry had to seek the advice of an expert
on Gothic details, A.W.N. Pugin (1812-52), one of the most
uncompromising champions of the Gothic revival.

The collaboration amounted more or less to this – that Barry was allowed to determine the overall shape and grouping of the building, while Pugin looked after the decoration of the façade and the interior. To us this would hardly seem a very satisfactory procedure, but the outcome was not too bad. Seen from the distance, through the London mists, Barry's outlines do not lack a certain dignity; and, seen at close quarters, the Gothic details still retain something of their Romantic appeal.

In painting or sculpture, the conventions of 'style' play a less prominent part, and it might thus be thought that the break in tradition affected these arts less; but this was not the case. The life of an artist had never been without its troubles and anxieties, but there was one thing to be said for the 'good old days' – no artist needed to ask himself why he had come into the world at all. In some ways his work had been as well defined as that of any other calling. There were always altar-paintings to be done, portraits to be painted; people wanted to buy pictures for their best parlours, or commissioned murals for their villas. In all these jobs he could work on more or less pre-established lines. He delivered the goods which the patron expected. True, he could produce indifferent work, or do it so superlatively well that the job in hand was no more than the starting point for a transcendent masterpiece. But his position in life was more or less secure. It was just this feeling of security that artists lost in the nineteenth century. The break in tradition had thrown open to them an unlimited field of choice. It was for them to decide whether they wanted to paint landscapes or dramatic scenes from the past, whether they chose subjects from Milton or the classics, whether they adopted the restrained manner of David's classical revival or the fantastic manner of the Romantic masters. But the greater the range of choice had become, the less likely was it that the artist's taste would coincide with that of his public. Those who buy pictures usually have a certain idea in mind. They want to get something very similar to what they have seen elsewhere. In the past, this demand was easily met by the artists because, even though their work differed greatly in artistic merit, the works of a period resembled each other in many respects. Now that this unity of tradition had disappeared, the artist's relations with his patron were only too often strained. The patron's taste was fixed in one way: the artist did not feel it in him to satisfy that demand. If he was forced to do so for want of money, he felt he was making 'concessions', and lost his self-respect and the esteem of others. If he decided to follow only his inner voice, and to reject any commission which he could not reconcile with his idea of art, he was in danger of starvation. Thus a deep cleavage developed in the nineteenth century between those artists whose temperament or convictions allowed them to follow conventions and to satisfy the public's demand, and those who gloried in their self-chosen isolation. What made matters worse was that the Industrial Revolution and the decline of craftsmanship, the rise of a new middle class which often lacked tradition, and the production of cheap and shoddy goods which masqueraded as 'Art', had brought about a deterioration of public taste.

The distrust between artists and the public was generally mutual. To the successful businessman, an artist was little better than an impostor who demanded ridiculous prices for something that could hardly be called honest work. Among the artists, on the other hand, it became an acknowledged pastime to 'shock the bourgeois' out of his complacency and to leave him bewildered and bemused. Artists began to see themselves as a race apart, they grew long hair and beards, they dressed in velvet or corduroy, wore broad-brimmed hats and loose ties, and generally stressed their contempt for the conventions of the 'respectable'. This state of affairs was hardly sound, but it was perhaps inevitable. And it must be acknowledged that, though the career of an artist was beset with the most dangerous pitfalls, the new conditions also had their compensations. The pitfalls are obvious. The artist who sold his soul and pandered to the taste of those who lacked taste was lost. So was the artist who dramatized his situation, who thought of himself as a genius for no other reason than that he found no buyers. But the situation was only desperate for weak characters. For the wide range of choice, and independence of the patron's whim, which had been acquired at such high cost, also held their advantages. For the first time, perhaps, it became true that art was a perfect means of expressing individuality – provided the artist had an individuality to express.

To many this may sound like a paradox. They think of all art as a means of 'expression', and to some extent they are right. But the matter is not quite so simple as it is sometimes thought to be. It is obvious that an Egyptian artist had little opportunity of expressing his personality. The rules and conventions of his style were so strict that there was very little scope for choice. It really comes to this – that where there is no choice there is no expression. A simple example will make this clear. If we say that a woman 'expresses her individuality' in the way she dresses, we mean that the choice she makes indicates her fancies and preferences. We need only watch an acquaintance buying a hat and try to find out why she rejects this and selects the other. It always has something to do with the way she sees herself and wants others to see her, and every such act of choice can teach us something about her personality. If she had to wear a uniform there might still remain some scope for 'expression', but obviously much less. Style is such a uniform. True, we know that as time went on the scope it afforded the individual artist increased, and with it the artist's means of expressing his personality. Everyone can see that Fra Angelico was a different character from Vermeer van Delft. Yet none of these artists was deliberately making his choice in order to express his personality. He did it only incidentally, as we express ourselves in everything we do – whether we light a pipe or run after a bus. The idea that the true purpose of art was to express personality could only gain ground when art had lost every other purpose. Nevertheless, as things had developed, it was a true and valuable statement. For what people who cared about art came to look for in exhibitions and studios was no longer the display of ordinary skill – that had become too common to warrant attention – they wanted art to bring them into contact with men with whom it would be worth while to converse: men whose work gave evidence of an incorruptible sincerity, artists who were not content with borrowed effects and who would not make a single stroke of the brush without asking themselves whether it satisfied their artistic conscience. In this respect the history of painting in the nineteenth century differs very considerably from the history of art as we have encountered it so far. In earlier periods it was usually the leading masters, artists whose skill was supreme, who also received the most important commissions and therefore became very famous. Think of Giotto, Michelangelo, Holbein, Rubens or even Goya. This does not mean that tragedies could never occur or that no painter was ever insufficiently honoured in his country, but by and large the artists and their public shared certain assumptions and therefore also agreed on standards of excellence. It was only in the nineteenth century that the real gulf opened between the successful artists – who contributed to 'official art' – and the nonconformists, who were mainly appreciated after their death. The result is a strange paradox. Even today there are few specialists who know much about the 'official art' of the nineteenth century. Admittedly most of us are familiar with some of its products, the monuments to great men in public squares, murals in town halls and stained-glass windows in churches or colleges, but for most of us these have acquired such a musty look that we pay no more attention to them than we do to the engravings after once famous exhibition pieces we still encounter in old-fashioned hotel lounges.

Maybe there is a reason for this frequent neglect. In discussing Copley's painting of Charles I confronting Parliament, *pages 367-8, figure 315*, I mentioned that his effort to visualize a dramatic moment of history as exactly as possible made a lasting impression, and that for a whole century many artists expended much labour on such historical costume pictures showing famous men of the past – Dante, Napoleon or George Washington – at some dramatic turning point in their lives. I might have added that such theatrical pictures generally scored a great success in exhibitions but that they soon lost their appeal. Our ideas of the past tend to change very quickly. The elaborate costumes and settings soon look unconvincing and the heroic gestures look like 'hamming'. It is quite likely that the time will come when these works will be rediscovered and when it will be possible again to discriminate between the really bad and the meritorious. For obviously not all of that art was as hollow and conventional as we tend to think today. And yet, it will possibly always remain true that since the Great Revolution the word Art has acquired a different meaning for us and that the history of art in the nineteenth century can never become the history of the most successful and best-paid masters of that time. We see it rather as the history of a handful of lonely men who had the courage and the persistence to think for themselves, to examine conventions fearlessly and critically and thus to create new possibilities for their art.

The most dramatic episodes in this development took place in Paris. For it was Paris that became the artistic capital of Europe in the nineteenth century much as Florence had been in the fifteenth century and Rome in the seventeenth. Artists from all over the world came to Paris to study with the leading masters and, most of all, to join in the discussion about the nature of art that never ended in the cafés of Montmartre, where the new conception of art was painfully hammered out.

The leading conservative painter in the first half of the nineteenth century was Jean-Auguste-Dominique Ingres (1780-1867). He had been a pupil and follower of David, *page 369*, and like him admired the heroic art of classical antiquity. In his teaching he insisted on the discipline of absolute precision in the life-class and despised improvisation and messiness. Figure 328 shows his own mastery in the rendering of forms and the cool clarity of his composition. It is easy to understand why many artists envied Ingres his technical assurance and respected his authority even where they disagreed with his views. But it is also easy to understand why his more passionate contemporaries found such smooth perfection unbearable.

The rallying-point for his opponents was the art of Eugène Delacroix (1798-1863). Delacroix belonged to the long line of great revolutionaries produced in the country of revolutions. He himself was a complex character with wide and varied sympathies, and his beautiful diaries show that he would not have enjoyed being typed as the fanatical rebel. If he was cast in this role it was because he could not accept the standards of the Academy. He had no patience with all the talk about the Greeks and Romans, with the insistence on correct drawing, and the constant imitation of classical statues. He believed that, in painting, colour was much more important than draughtsmanship, and imagination than knowledge. While Ingres and his school cultivated the Grand Manner and admired Poussin and Raphael, Delacroix shocked the connoisseurs by preferring the Venetians and Rubens. He was tired of the learned subjects the Academy wanted painters to illustrate, and went to North Africa in 1832 to study the glowing colours and romantic trappings of the Arab world. When he saw horses fighting in Tangier, he noted in his diary: 'From the very beginning they reared up and fought with a fury that made me tremble for their riders, but magnificent for painting. I am sure that I have witnessed a scene as extraordinary and fantastic as anything that ... Rubens could have imagined.' Figure 329 shows one of the fruits of his journey. Everything in the picture is a denial of the teachings of David and Ingres. There is no clarity of outline here, no modelling of the nude in carefully graded tones of light and shade, no pose and restraint in the composition, not even a patriotic or edifying subject. All the painter wants is to make us partake in an intensely exciting moment, and to share his joy in the movement and romance of the scene, with the Arab cavalry sweeping past, and the fine thoroughbred rearing in the foreground. It was Delacroix who acclaimed Constable's picture in Paris, page 376, figure 325, though in his personality and choice of romantic subjects he is perhaps more akin to Turner.

Be that as it may, we know that Delacroix really admired a French landscape painter of his own generation whose art may be said to form a bridge between these contrasting approaches to nature. He was Jean-Baptiste Camille Corot (1796-1875). Like Constable, Corot started out with the determination to render reality as truthfully as possible, but the truth he wished to capture was somewhat different.

Figure 330 shows that he concentrated less on details than on the general form and tone of his motifs, to convey the heat and stillness of a summer day in the South.

It so happens that about a hundred years earlier Fragonard had also selected a motif from the park of the Villa d'Este near Rome, figure 310, and it may be worth pausing for a moment to compare these and other images, all the more as landscape painting was increasingly to become the most important branch of nineteenth-century art. Fragonard clearly looked for variety, while Corot sought for a clarity and balance that may remind us remotely of Poussin, figure 254, and of Claude Lorrain, figure 255, but the radiant light and atmosphere that fill Corot's picture are achieved with very different means. Here the comparison with Fragonard can help us again, because Fragonard's medium had compelled him to concentrate on the careful gradation of tone. As a draughtsman, all he had at his disposal was the white of the paper and various intensities of brown; but look, for instance, at the wall in the foreground to see how these sufficed to convey the contrast between shadow and sunlight. Corot achieved similar effects by the use of his palette, and painters know that this is no minor achievement. The reason is that colour often comes into conflict with the gradations of tone on which Fragonard could rely.

We may recall the advice which Constable received and rejected, to paint the foreground a mellow brown, as Claude and other painters had done. This conventional wisdom rested on the observation that strong greens tend to clash with other colours. However faithful a photograph (such as figure 302) may look to us, its intense colours would surely have a disruptive effect on that gentle gradation of tones that also served Caspar David Friedrich, figure 326, to achieve the impression of distance. Indeed, if we look at Constable's 'Haywain', figure 325, we shall notice that he also muted the colour of the foreground and of the foliage to remain within a unified tonal range. Corot appears to have captured the radiant light and luminous haze of the scene with his palette by novel means. He worked within a key of silvery grey that does not quite swallow up the colours but maintains them in harmony without departing from the visual truth. True, like Claude and like Turner, he never hesitated to people his stage with figures from the classical or biblical past, and in fact it was this poetic bent that finally secured him international fame.

Much as Corot's quiet mastery was loved and admired also by his younger colleagues, they did not wish to follow him along this path. In fact the next revolution was mainly concerned with the conventions governing subject-matter. In the academies the idea was still prevalent that dignified paintings must represent dignified personages, and that workers or peasants provided suitable subjects only for genre scenes in the tradition of the Dutch masters, *pages* 288, 326. During the time of the Revolution of *1848*, a group of artists gathered in the French village of Barbizon to follow the programme of Constable and look at nature with fresh eyes. One of them, Jean-François Millet (1814-75), decided to extend this programme from landscapes to figures. He wanted to paint scenes from peasant life as it really was, to paint men and women at work in the fields. It is curious to reflect that this should have been considered revolutionary, but in the art of the past peasants were generally seen as comic yokels as Bruegel had painted them, *figure 246*. Figure *331* represents Millet's famous picture 'The gleaners'. There is no dramatic incident represented here, nothing in the way of an anecdote. Just three hard-working people in a flat field where harvesting is in progress. They are neither beautiful nor graceful. There is no suggestion of the country idyll in the picture. These peasant women move slowly and heavily. They

are all intent on their work. Millet had done everything to
emphasize their square and solid build and their deliberate
movements. He modelled them firmly and in simple outlines
against the bright sunlit plain. Thus his three peasant women
assumed a dignity more natural and more convincing than
that of academic heroes. The arrangement, which looks casual
at first sight, supports this impression of tranquil poise.
There is a calculated rhythm in the movement and distribution
of the figures which gives stability to the whole design and
makes us feel that the painter looked at the work of harvesting
as a scene of solemn significance.

The painter who gave a name to this movement was
Gustave Courbet (1819-77). When he opened a one-man show
in a shack in Paris in the year 1855, he called it *Le Réalisme,
G. Courbet*. His 'realism' was to mark a revolution in art.
Courbet wanted to be the pupil of no one but nature. To some
extent, his character and programme resembled that of
Caravaggio, *pages 298-9, figure 252*. He wanted not prettiness but
truth. He represented himself walking across country with his
painter's tackle on his back, respectfully greeted by his friend
and patron, *figure 332*. He called the picture 'Bonjour, Monsieur
Courbet'. To anyone used to the show-pieces of academic
art, this picture must have seemed downright childish. There
are no graceful poses here, no flowing lines, no impressive
colours. Compared with its artless arrangement, even the
composition of Millet's 'The gleaners' looks calculated. The
whole idea of a painter representing himself in shirtsleeves as
a kind of tramp must have appeared as an outrage to the
'respectable' artists and their admirers. This, at any rate, was
the impression Courbet wanted to make. He wanted his
pictures to be a protest against the accepted conventions of
his day, to 'shock the bourgeois' out of his complacency, and
to proclaim the value of uncompromising artistic sincerity

as against the deft handling of traditional clichés. Sincere
Courbet's pictures undoubtedly are. 'I hope', he wrote in a
characteristic letter in 1854, 'always to earn my living by my
art without having ever deviated by even a hair's breadth
from my principles, without having lied to my conscience
for a single moment, without painting even as much as can
be covered by a hand only to please anyone or to sell more
easily.' Courbet's deliberate renunciation of easy effects,
and his determination to render the world as he saw it,
encouraged many others to flout convention and to follow
nothing but their own artistic conscience.

The same concern for sincerity, the same impatience
with the theatrical pretentiousness of official art, that led the
group of the Barbizon painters and Courbet towards 'Realism',
caused a group of English painters to take a very different
path. They pondered on the reasons which had led art into
such a dangerous rut. They knew that the academies claimed
to represent the tradition of Raphael and what was known as
the 'Grand Manner'. If that was true, then art had obviously
taken a wrong turning with, and through, Raphael. It was he
and his followers who had exalted the methods of 'idealizing'
nature, page 244, and of striving for beauty at the expense of
truth. If art was to be reformed, it was therefore necessary to
go further back than Raphael, to the time when artists were
still 'honest to God' craftsmen, who did their best to copy
nature, while thinking not of earthly glory, but of the glory
of God. Believing, as they did, that art had become insincere
through Raphael and that it behoved them to return to
the 'Age of Faith', this group of friends called themselves
the 'Pre-Raphaelite Brotherhood'. One of its most gifted
members was the son of an Italian refugee, Dante Gabriel
Rossetti (1828-82). Figure 333 shows Rossetti's painting of
the Annunciation. Usually, this theme was represented on the

pattern of the medieval representations such as figure 141.
Rossetti's intention to return to the spirit of the medieval
masters did not mean that he wanted to copy their
pictures. What he desired to do was to emulate their attitude,
to read the biblical narrative with a devout heart, and to
visualize the scene when the angel came to the Virgin and
saluted her: 'And when she saw him, she was troubled at his
saying and cast in her mind what manner of salutation
this should be' (Luke 1. 29). We can see how Rossetti strove
for simplicity and sincerity in his new rendering, and how
much he wanted to let us see the ancient story with a fresh
mind. But for all his intention to render nature as faithfully
as the admired Florentines of the *Quattrocento* had done,
some will feel that the Pre-Raphaelite Brotherhood set itself
an unattainable goal. It is one thing to admire the naïve and
unselfconscious outlook of the 'primitives' (as the painters
of the fifteenth century were then oddly called); it is quite
another thing to strive for it oneself. For this is the one virtue
which the best will in the world cannot help us to attain. Thus,
while their starting point was similar to that of Millet and
Courbet, I think that their honest endeavour landed them in a
blind alley. The longing of Victorian masters for innocence was
too self-contradictory to succeed. The hope of their French
contemporaries to make progress in the exploration of the
visible world proved more fruitful for the next generation.

The third wave of revolution in France (after the first
wave of Delacroix and the second wave of Courbet) was
started by Édouard Manet (1832-83) and his friends. These
artists took Courbet's programme very seriously. They looked
out for conventions in painting which had become stale and
meaningless. They found that the whole claim of traditional art
to have discovered the way to represent nature, as we see it,
was based on a misconception. At the most, they would

concede that traditional art had found a means of representing men or objects under very artificial conditions. Painters let their models pose in their studios, where the light falls through the window, and made use of the slow transition from light to shade to give the impression of roundness and solidity. The art students at the academies were trained from the beginning to base their pictures on this interplay between light and shade. At first, they usually drew from the plaster casts taken from antique statues, hatching their drawings carefully to achieve different densities of shading. Once they acquired this habit, they applied it to all objects. The public had become so accustomed to seeing things represented in this manner that they had forgotten that in the open air we do not usually perceive such even gradations from dark to light. There are harsh contrasts in the sunlight. Objects taken out of the artificial conditions of the artist's studio do not look so round or so much modelled as plaster casts from the antique. The parts which are lit appear much brighter than in the studio, and even the shadows are not uniformly grey or black, because the reflections of light from surrounding objects affect the colour of these unlit parts. If we trust our eyes, and not our preconceived ideas of what things *ought* to look like according to academic rules, we shall make the most exciting discoveries.

That such ideas were first considered extravagant heresies is hardly surprising. We have seen throughout this story of art how much we are all inclined to judge pictures by what we *know* rather than by what we *see*. We remember how the Egyptian artists found it inconceivable to represent a figure without showing each part from its most characteristic angle, *pages 52-3*. They knew what a foot, an eye, or a hand 'looked like', and they fitted these parts together to form a complete man. To represent a figure with one arm hidden from view, or one foot distorted by foreshortening, would have seemed outrageous. We remember that it was the Greeks who succeeded in breaking down this prejudice, and allowed foreshortening in pictures, *pages 67-8, figure 49*. We remember how the importance of knowledge came to the fore again in early Christian and medieval art, *pages 106-7, figure 87*, and remained so till the Renaissance. Even then the importance of theoretical knowledge of what the world *ought* to look like was enhanced rather than diminished through the discoveries of scientific perspective and the emphasis on anatomy, *pages 170-3*. The great artists of subsequent periods had made one discovery after another which allowed them to conjure up a convincing picture of the visible world, but none of them had seriously challenged the conviction that each object in nature has its definite fixed form and colour which must be easily recognizable in a painting. It may be said, therefore, that Manet and his followers brought about a revolution in the rendering of colours which is almost comparable with the revolution in the representation of forms brought about by the Greeks. They discovered that, if we look at nature in the open, we do not see individual objects each with its own colour but rather a bright medley of tints which blend in our eye or really in our mind.

These discoveries were not made all at once or all by one man. But even Manet's first paintings in which he abandoned the traditional method of mellow shading in favour of strong and harsh contrasts caused an outcry among the conservative artists. In 1863 the academic painters refused to show his works in the official exhibition called the Salon. An agitation followed which prompted the authorities to show all works condemned by the jury in a special show called the 'Salon of the Rejected'. The public went there mainly to laugh at the poor deluded tyros who had refused to accept the verdict of their betters. This episode marks the first stage of a battle which was to rage for nearly thirty years. It is difficult for us to conceive the violence of these quarrels between the artists and the critics, all the more since the paintings of Manet strike us today as being essentially akin to the great paintings of earlier periods, such as those by Frans Hals, figure 270. Indeed, Manet violently denied that he wanted to be a revolutionary. He quite deliberately looked for inspiration in the great tradition of the masters of the brush whom the Pre-Raphaelites had rejected, the tradition initiated by the great Venetians Giorgione and Titian, and carried on triumphantly in Spain by Velázquez, figures 264-7, and down to the nineteenth century by Goya. It was clearly one of Goya's paintings, figure 317, that had challenged him to paint a similar group on a balcony and to explore the contrast between the full light of the open air and the dark which swallows up the forms in the interior, figure 334. But Manet in 1869 carried this exploration much further than Goya had done sixty years earlier. Unlike Goya's, the heads of Manet's ladies are not modelled in the traditional manner, as we shall discover if we compare both with Leonardo's 'Mona Lisa', figure 193, Rubens's portrait of his child, figure 257, or Gainsborough's 'Miss Haverfield', figure 306. However different these painters were in their methods, they all wanted to create the impression of solid bodies, and did so through the interplay of shadow and light. Compared with theirs, Manet's heads look flat. The lady in the background has not even got a proper nose. We can well imagine why this treatment looked like sheer ignorance to those not acquainted with Manet's intentions. But the fact is that in the open air, and in the full light of day, round forms sometimes *do* look flat, like mere coloured patches. It was this effect which Manet wanted to explore. The consequence is that as we stand before one of his pictures it looks more immediately real than any old master. We have the illusion that we really stand face to face with this group on the balcony. The general impression of the whole is not flat but, on the contrary, that of real depth. One of the reasons for this striking effect is the bold colour of the balcony railing. It is painted in a bright green which cuts across the composition regardless of the traditional rules of colour harmonies. The result is that this railing seems to stand out boldly in front of the scene, which thus recedes behind it.

The new theories did not concern only the treatment of colours in the open air (*plein air*), but also that of forms in movement. Figure 335 shows one of Manet's lithographs – a method of reproducing drawings made directly on stone, which had been invented early in the nineteenth century. At first sight, we may see nothing but a confused scrawl. It is the picture of a horse-race. Manet wants us to gain the impression of light, speed and movement by giving nothing but a bare hint of the forms emerging out of the confusion. The horses are racing towards us at full speed and the stands are packed with excited crowds. The example shows more clearly than any other how Manet refused to be influenced in his representation of form by his knowledge. None of his horses has four legs. We simply do not see the four legs at a momentary glance at such a scene. Nor can we take in the details of the spectators. Some fourteen years earlier the English painter William Powell Frith (1819-1909) had painted his 'Derby Day', figure 336, which was very popular in Victorian times for the Dickensian humour with which he depicted the types and incidents of the event. Such pictures are indeed best enjoyed by studying the gay variety of these situations one by one at our leisure. But in actual life we can only focus on one spot with our eyes – all the rest looks to us like a jumble of disconnected forms. We may know what they are, but we do not see them. In this sense, Manet's lithograph of a racecourse is really much more 'true' than that of the Victorian humorist.

It transports us for an instant to the bustle and excitement of the scene which the artist witnessed, and of which he recorded only as much as he could vouch for having seen in an instant.

Among the painters who joined Manet and helped to develop these ideas was a poor and dogged young man from Le Havre, Claude Monet (1840-1926). It was Monet who urged his friends to abandon the studio altogether and never to paint a single stroke except in front of the 'motif'. He had a little boat fitted out as a studio to allow him to explore the moods and effects of the river scenery. Manet, who came to visit him, became convinced of the soundness of the younger man's method and paid him a tribute by painting his portrait while at work in this open-air studio, figure 337. It is at the same time an exercise in the new manner advocated by Monet. For Monet's idea that all painting of nature must actually be finished 'on the spot' not only demanded a change of habits and a disregard of comfort, it was bound to result in new technical methods. 'Nature' or the 'motif' changes from minute to minute as a cloud passes over the sun or the wind breaks the reflection in the water. The painter who hopes to catch a characteristic aspect has no leisure to mix and match his colours, let alone to apply them in layers on a brown foundation as the old masters had done. He must fix them straight on to his canvas in rapid strokes, caring less for detail than for the general effect of the whole. It was this lack of finish, this apparently slapdash approach, which frequently enraged the critics. Even after Manet himself had gained a certain amount of public recognition through his portraits and figure compositions, the younger landscape painters round Monet found it exceedingly difficult to have their unorthodox paintings accepted for the Salon. Accordingly they banded together in 1874 and arranged a show in the studio of a photographer. It contained a picture by Monet which the catalogue described as 'Impression: sunrise' – it was the picture of a harbour seen through the morning mists. One of the critics found this title particularly ridiculous, and he referred to the whole group of artists as 'The Impressionists'. He wanted to convey that these painters did not proceed by sound knowledge, and thought that the impression of a moment was sufficient to be called a picture. The label stuck. Its mocking undertone was soon forgotten, just as the derogatory meaning of terms like 'Gothic', 'Baroque' or 'Mannerism' is now forgotten. After a time the group of friends themselves accepted the name Impressionists, and as such they have been known ever since.

It is interesting to read some of the press notices with which the first exhibitions of the Impressionists were received. A humorous weekly wrote in 1876:

> The rue le Peletier is a road of disasters. After the fire at the Opéra, there is now yet another disaster there. An exhibition has just been opened at Durand-Ruel which allegedly contains paintings. I enter and my horrified eyes behold something terrible. Five or six lunatics, among them a woman, have joined together and exhibited their works. I have seen people rock with laughter in front of these pictures, but my heart bled when I saw them. These would-be artists call themselves revolutionaries, "Impressionists". They take a piece of canvas, colour and brush, daub a few patches of paint on it at random, and sign the whole thing with their name. It is a delusion of the same kind as if the inmates of Bedlam picked up stones from the wayside and imagined they had found diamonds.

It was not only the technique of painting which so outraged the critics. It was also the motifs these painters chose. In the past, painters were expected to look for a corner of nature which was by general consent 'picturesque'. Few people realize that this demand was somewhat unreasonable. We call 'picturesque' such motifs as we have seen in pictures before. If painters were to keep to those they would have to repeat each other endlessly. It was Claude Lorrain who made Roman ruins 'picturesque', figure 255, and Jan van Goyen who turned Dutch windmills into 'motifs', figure 272. Constable and Turner in England, each in his own way, had discovered new motifs for art. Turner's 'Steamer in a snowstorm', figure 323, was as new in subject as it was in manner. Claude Monet knew Turner's works. He had seen them in London, where he stayed during the Franco-Prussian war (1870-1), and they had confirmed him in his conviction that the magic effects of light and air counted for more than the subject of a painting. Nevertheless, a painting such as figure 338, which represents a Paris railway station, struck the critics as sheer impudence. Here is a real 'impression' of a scene from everyday life. Monet is not interested in the railway station as a place where human beings meet or take leave – he is fascinated by the effect of light streaming through the glass roof on to the clouds of steam, and by the forms of engines and carriages emerging from the confusion. Yet there is nothing casual in this eye-witness account by a painter. Monet balanced his tones and colours as deliberately as any landscape painter of the past.

The painters of this young group of Impressionists applied their new principles not only to landscape painting but to any scene of real life. Figure 339 shows a painting by Pierre Auguste Renoir (1841-1919) which represents an open-air dance in Paris, painted in 1876. When Jan Steen, figure 278, represented such a scene of revelry, he was eager to depict the various humorous types of the people. Watteau, in his dream scenes of aristocratic festivals, figure 298, wanted to capture the

mood of a carefree existence. There is something of both in
Renoir. He, too, has an eye for the behaviour of the gay crowd
and he, too, is enchanted by festive beauty. But his main
interest lies elsewhere. He wants to conjure up the gay medley
of bright colours and to study the effect of sunlight on
the whirling throng. Even compared to Manet's painting of
Monet's boat, the picture looks 'sketchy' and unfinished.
Only the heads of some figures in the foreground are shown
with a certain amount of detail, but even they are painted in
the most unconventional and daring manner. The eyes and
forehead of the sitting lady lie in the shadow while the sun
plays on her mouth and chin. Her bright dress is painted with
loose strokes of the brush, bolder even than those used by
Frans Hals, figure 270, or Velázquez, figure 267. But these are the
figures we focus on. Beyond, the forms are increasingly
dissolved in sunlight and air. We are reminded of the way
in which Francesco Guardi, figure 290, conjured up the figures
of his Venetian oarsmen with a few patches of colour. After
the lapse of a century it is hard for us to understand why these
pictures aroused such a storm of derision and indignation.
We realize without difficulty that the apparent sketchiness has
nothing whatever to do with carelessness but is the outcome
of great artistic wisdom. If Renoir had painted in every detail,
the picture would look dull and lifeless. We remember that
a similar conflict had faced artists once before, in the fifteenth
century, when they had first discovered how to mirror nature.
We remember that the very triumphs of naturalism and of
perspective had led to their figures looking somewhat rigid
and wooden, and that it was only the genius of Leonardo that
overcame this difficulty by letting the forms intentionally
merge into dark shadows – the device that was called 'sfumato',
figures 193-4. It was their discovery that dark shadows of the
kind Leonardo used for modelling do not occur in sunlight

and open air, which barred this traditional way out to the Impressionists. Hence, they had to go farther in the intentional blurring of outlines than any previous generation had gone. They knew that the human eye is a marvellous instrument. You need only give it the right hint and it builds up for you the whole form which it knows to be there. But one must know how to look at such paintings. The people who first visited the Impressionist exhibition obviously poked their noses into the pictures and saw nothing but a confusion of casual brushstrokes. That is why they thought these painters must be mad.

Faced with such paintings as figure 340, in which one of the oldest and most methodical champions of the movement, Camille Pissarro (1830 - 1903), evoked the 'impression' of a Paris boulevard in sunshine, these outraged people would ask: 'If I walk along the boulevard – do I look like this? Do I lose my legs, my eyes and my nose and turn into a shapeless blob?' Once more it was their knowledge of what 'belongs' to a man which interfered with their judgement of what we really see.

It took some time before the public learned that to appreciate an Impressionist painting one has to step back a few yards, and enjoy the miracle of seeing these puzzling patches suddenly fall into place and come to life before our eyes. To achieve this miracle, and to transfer the actual visual experience of the painter to the beholder, was the true aim of the Impressionists.

The feeling of a new freedom and a new power which these artists had must have been truly exhilarating; it must have compensated them for much of the derision and hostility they encountered. Suddenly the whole world offered fit subjects for the painter's brush. Wherever he discovered a beautiful combination of tones, an interesting configuration of colours and forms, a satisfying and gay patchwork of sunlight and coloured shades, he could set down his easel and try to transfer his impression on to the canvas. All the old bogeys of 'dignified subject-matter', of 'balanced compositions', of 'correct drawing', were laid to rest. The artist was responsible to no one but his own sensibilities for what he painted and how he painted it. Looking back at this struggle it is perhaps less surprising that the views of these young artists encountered resistance than that they were so soon to be taken for granted. For bitter as was the fight and hard as it was for the artists concerned, the triumph of Impressionism was complete. Some of these young rebels at least, notably Monet and Renoir, luckily lived long enough to enjoy the fruits of this victory and to become famous and respected all over Europe. They witnessed their works entering public collections and being coveted possessions of the wealthy. This transformation moreover made a lasting impression on artists and critics alike. The critics who had laughed had proved very fallible indeed. Had they bought these canvases rather than mocked them they would have become rich. Criticism therefore suffered a loss of prestige from which it never recovered. The struggle of the Impressionists became the treasured legend of all innovators in art, who could always point to this conspicuous failure of the public to recognize novel methods. In a sense this notorious failure is as important in the history of art as was the ultimate victory of the Impressionist programme.

Perhaps this victory would not have been so quick and so thorough had it not been for two allies which helped people of the nineteenth century to see the world with different eyes. One of these allies was photography. In the early days this invention had mainly been used for portraits. Very long exposures were necessary, and people who sat for their photographs had to be propped up in a rigid posture to be able to keep still so long. The development of the portable camera, and of the snapshot, began during the same years which also saw the rise of Impressionist painting. The camera helped to discover the charm of the fortuitous view and of the unexpected angle. Moreover, the development of photography was bound to push artists further on their way of exploration and experiment. There was no need for painting to perform a task which a mechanical device could perform better and more cheaply. We must not forget that in the past the art of painting served a number of utilitarian ends. It was used to record the likeness of a notable person or the view of a country house. The painter was a man who could defeat the transitory nature of things and preserve the aspect of any object for posterity. We would not know what the dodo looked like, had not a Dutch seventeenth-century painter used his skill in portraying a specimen shortly before these birds became extinct. Photography in the nineteenth century was about to take over this function of pictorial art. It was a blow to the position of artists, as serious as had been the abolition of religious images by Protestantism, *page 283*. Before that invention nearly every self-respecting person sat for his portrait at least once in his lifetime. Now people rarely underwent this ordeal unless they wanted to oblige and help a painter-friend. So it came about that artists were increasingly compelled to explore regions where photography could not follow them. In fact, modern art would hardly have become what it is without the impact of this invention.

The second ally which the Impressionists found in their adventurous quest for new motifs and new colour schemes was the Japanese colour-print. The art of Japan had developed out of Chinese art, *page 116*, and had continued along these lines for nearly a thousand years. In the eighteenth century, however, perhaps under the influence of European prints, Japanese artists had abandoned the traditional motifs of Far Eastern art, and had chosen scenes from low life as a subject for colour woodcuts, which combined great boldness of invention with masterly technical perfection. Japanese connoisseurs did not think very highly of these cheap products. They preferred the austere traditional manner. When Japan was forced, in the middle of the nineteenth century, to enter into trade relations with Europe and America, these prints were often used as wrappings and padding, and could be picked up cheaply in tea-shops. Artists of Manet's circle were among the first to appreciate their beauty, and to collect them eagerly. Here they found a tradition unspoilt by those academic rules and clichés which the French painters strove to get rid of. The Japanese prints helped them to see how much of the European conventions still remained with them without their having noticed it. The Japanese relished every unexpected and unconventional aspect of the world. Their master, Hokusai (1760-1849), would represent Mount Fuji seen as by chance behind a scaffolding, figure 341; Utamaro (1753-1806) would not hesitate to show some of his figures cut off by the margin of a print or a bamboo curtain, figure 342. It was this daring disregard of an elementary rule of European painting that struck the Impressionists. They discovered in this rule a last hide-out of the ancient domination of knowledge over vision. Why should a painting always show the whole or a relevant part of each figure in a scene?

The painter who was most deeply impressed by these possibilities was Edgar Degas (1834-1917). Degas was a little older than Monet and Renoir. He belonged to the generation of Manet and, like him, kept somewhat aloof from the Impressionist group though he was in sympathy with most of their aims. Degas was passionately interested in design and draughtsmanship and greatly admired Ingres. In his portraits, figure 343, he wanted to bring out the impression of space and of solid forms seen from the most unexpected angles. That is also why he liked to take his subjects from the ballet rather than from out-door scenes. Watching rehearsals, Degas had an opportunity of seeing bodies from all sides in the most varied attitudes. Looking down on to the stage from above, he would see the girls dancing, or resting, and would study the intricate foreshortening and the effect of stage-lighting on the modelling of the human form. Figure 344 shows one of the pastel sketches made by Degas. The arrangement could not be more casual in appearance. Of some of the dancers we see only the legs, of some only the body. Only one figure is seen complete, and that in a posture which is intricate and difficult to read. We see her from above, her head bent forward, her left hand clasping her ankle, in a state of deliberate relaxation. There is no story in Degas's pictures. He was not interested in the ballerinas because they were pretty girls. He did not seem to care for their moods. He looked at them with the dispassionate objectivity with which the Impressionists looked at the landscape around them. What mattered to him was the interplay of light and shade on the human form, and the way in which he could suggest movement or space. He proved to the academic world that, far from being incompatible with perfect draughtsmanship, the new principles of the young artists were posing new problems which only the most consummate master of design could solve.

The main principles of the new movement could find full expression only in painting, but sculpture, too, was soon drawn into the battle for or against 'modernism'. The great French sculptor Auguste Rodin (1840-1917) was born in the same year as Monet. Since he was an ardent student of classical statues and of Michelangelo there need have been no fundamental conflict between him and traditional art. In fact,

Rodin soon became an acknowledged master, and enjoyed a public fame as great as, if not greater than, that of any other artist of his time. But even his works were the object of violent quarrels among the critics, and were often lumped together with those of the Impressionist rebels. The reason may become clear if we look at one of his portraits, figure 345. Like the Impressionists, Rodin despised the outward appearance of 'finish'. Like them, he preferred to leave something to the imagination of the beholder. Sometimes he even left part of the stone standing to give the impression that his figure was just emerging and taking shape. To the average public this seemed to be an irritating eccentricity if not sheer laziness. Their objections were the same as those which had been raised against Tintoretto, pages 280-1. To them artistic perfection still meant that everything should be neat and polished. In disregarding these petty conventions to express his vision of the divine act of Creation, figure 346, Rodin helped to assert what Rembrandt had claimed as his right, page 322 – to declare his work finished when he had reached his artistic aim. As no one could say that his procedure resulted from ignorance, his influence did much to pave the way for the acceptance of Impressionism outside the narrow circle of its French admirers.

Artists from all over the world came into contact with Impressionism in Paris, and carried away with them the new discoveries, and also the new attitude of the artist as a rebel against the prejudices and conventions of the bourgeois world. One of the most influential apostles of this gospel outside France was the American James Abbott McNeill Whistler (1834-1903). Whistler had taken part in the first battle of the new movement; he had exhibited with Manet in the Salon of the Rejected in 1863, and he shared the enthusiasm of his painter-colleagues for Japanese prints. He was not an

Impressionist in the strict sense of the word, any more than was Degas or Rodin, for his main concern was not with the effects of light and colour but rather with the composition of delicate patterns. What he had in common with the Paris painters was his contempt for the interest the public showed in sentimental anecdotes. He stressed the point that what mattered in painting was not the subject but the way in which it was translated into colours and forms. One of Whistler's most famous paintings, perhaps one of the most popular paintings ever made, is the portrait of his mother, figure 347. It is characteristic that the title under which Whistler exhibited this painting in 1872 was 'Arrangement in grey and black'. He shrank from any suggestion of 'literary' interest or sentimentality. Actually the harmony of forms and colours at which he aimed is in no contradiction with the feeling of the subject-matter. It is the careful balance of simple forms that gives the picture its restful quality, and the subdued tones of its 'grey and black', ranging from the lady's hair and dress to the wall and setting, enhance the expression of resigned loneliness which gives the painting its wide appeal. It is strange to realize that the painter of this sensitive and gentle picture was notorious for his provocative manner and his exercises in what he called 'the gentle art of making enemies'. He had settled in London and felt called upon to fight the battle for modern art almost single-handed. His habit of giving paintings names which struck people as eccentric, his disregard of academic convention, brought upon him the wrath of John Ruskin (1819-1900), the great critic who had championed Turner and the Pre-Raphaelites. In 1877 Whistler exhibited night-pieces in the Japanese manner which he called 'Nocturnes', figure 348, asking 200 guineas for each. Ruskin wrote: 'I have never expected to hear a coxcomb ask two hundred guineas for flinging a pot of paint in the public's face.' Whistler sued him for libel, and the case once more brought out the deep cleavage that separated the public's point of view from that of the artist. The question of 'finish' was promptly trotted out, and Whistler was cross-examined as to whether he really asked that enormous sum 'for two days' work', to which he replied: 'No, I ask it for the knowledge of a lifetime.'

It is strange how much the opponents in this unfortunate law-suit really had in common. Both were deeply dissatisfied with the ugliness and squalor of their surroundings. But while Ruskin, the older man, hoped to lead his countrymen to a greater awareness of beauty by an appeal to their moral sense, Whistler became a leading figure in the so-called 'aesthetic movement', which tried to make out that artistic sensibility is the only thing in life worth taking seriously. Both these views gained in importance as the nineteenth century drew to its close.

In Search of
New Standards

The late nineteenth century

Superficially, the end of the nineteenth century was a period of great prosperity and even complacency. But the artists and writers who felt themselves outsiders were increasingly dissatisfied with the aims and methods of the art that pleased the public. Architecture provided the easiest target for their attacks. Building had developed into an empty routine. We remember how the large blocks of flats, factories and public buildings of the vastly expanding cities were erected in a motley of styles which lacked any relation to the purpose of the buildings. Often it seemed as if the engineers had first erected a structure to suit the natural requirements of the building, and a bit of 'Art' had then been pasted on the façade in the form of ornament taken from one of the pattern books on 'historical styles'. It is strange how long the majority of architects were satisfied with this procedure. This public demanded these columns, pilasters, cornices and mouldings, so these architects provided them. But towards the end of the nineteenth century an increasing number of people became aware of the absurdity of this fashion. In England in particular, critics and artists were unhappy about the general decline in craftsmanship caused by the Industrial Revolution, and hated the very sight of these cheap and tawdry machine-made imitations of ornament which had once had a meaning and a nobility of its own. Men like John Ruskin and William Morris dreamt of a thorough reform of the arts and crafts, and the replacement of cheap mass-production by conscientious and meaningful handiwork. The influence of their criticism was very widespread even though the humble handicrafts which they advocated proved, under modern conditions, to be the greatest of luxuries. Their propaganda could not possibly abolish industrial mass-production, but it helped to open people's eyes to the problems this had raised, and to spread a taste for the genuine, simple and 'homespun'.

Ruskin and Morris had still hoped that the regeneration
of art could be brought about by a return to medieval conditions. But many artists saw that this was an impossibility. They
longed for a 'New Art' based on a new feeling for design and
for the possibilities inherent in each material. This banner
of a new art or *Art Nouveau* was raised in the 1890s. Architects
experimented with new types of material and new types of
ornament. The Greek orders had been developed from primitive
timber structures, *page 64*, and had provided the stock-in-trade
of architectural decoration since the Renaissance, *pages 168-9,
186-7*. Was it not high time that the new architecture of iron
and glass that had grown up almost unobserved in railway
stations, *page 399*, and industrial structures should develop an
ornamental style of its own? And if the Western tradition was
too much wedded to the old building methods, would the
East perhaps provide a new set of patterns and new ideas?

This must have been the reasoning behind the designs
of the Belgian architect Victor Horta (1861-1947) that made
an immediate hit. Horta had learned from Japan to discard
symmetry and to relish the effect of swerving curves that we
remember from Eastern art, *page 113*. But he was no mere
imitator. He transposed these lines into iron structures that
went well with modern requirements, *figure 349*. For the first
time since Brunelleschi, European builders were offered an
entirely new style. No wonder that these inventions became
identified with *Art Nouveau*.

For this self-consciousness about 'style' and this hope
that Japan might help Europe to get out of the impasse were
not confined to architecture, but the feeling of uneasiness and
dissatisfaction with the achievements of nineteenth-century
painting which took hold of young artists towards the end of
the period is less easy to explain. Yet it is important that we
should understand its roots, because it was out of this feeling

that there grew the various movements which are now usually called 'Modern Art'. Some people may consider the Impressionists the first of the moderns, because they defied certain rules of painting as taught in the academies. But it is well to remember that the Impressionists did not differ in their aims from the traditions of art that had developed since the discovery of nature in the Renaissance. They, too, wanted to paint nature as we see it, and their quarrel with the conservative masters was not so much over the aim as over the means of achieving it. Their exploration of colour reflexes, their experiments with the effect of loose brushwork, aimed at creating an even more perfect replica of the visual impression. It was only in Impressionism, in fact, that the conquest of nature had become complete, that everything that presented itself to the painter's eye could become the motif of a picture, and that the real world in all its aspects became a worthy object of the artist's study. Perhaps it was just this complete triumph of their methods which made some artists hesitate to accept them. It seemed, for a moment, as if all the problems of an art aiming at the imitation of the visual impression had been solved, and as if nothing was to be gained by pursuing these aims any further.

But we know that in art one problem need only be solved for a host of new ones to appear in its stead. Perhaps the first who had a clear feeling of the nature of these new problems was an artist who still belonged to the same generation as the Impressionist masters. He was Paul Cézanne (1839-1906), who was only seven years younger than Manet, and even two years older than Renoir. In his youth Cézanne took part in the Impressionist exhibitions, but was so disgusted by the reception accorded them that he withdrew to his native town of Aix-en-Provence, where he studied the problems of his art, undisturbed by the clamour of the critics.

He was a man of independent means and regular habits, and was not dependent on finding buyers for his pictures. Thus he could dedicate his whole life to the solution of the artistic problems he had set himself, and could apply the most exacting standards to his own work. Outwardly, he lived a life of tranquillity and leisure, but he was constantly engaged in a passionate struggle to achieve in his painting that ideal of artistic perfection after which he strove. He was no friend of theoretical talk, but as his fame among his few admirers grew he did sometimes try to explain to them in a few words what he wanted to do. One of his reported remarks was that he aimed at painting 'Poussin from nature'. What he wanted to say was that the old classical masters such as Poussin had achieved a wonderful balance and perfection in their work. A painting like Poussin's 'Et in Arcadia ego', figure 254, presents a beautifully harmonious pattern in which one shape seems to answer the other. We feel that everything is in its place, and nothing is casual or vague. Each form stands out clearly and one can visualize it as a firm, solid body. The whole has a natural simplicity which looks restful and calm. Cézanne aimed at an art which had something of this grandeur and serenity. But he did not think that it could be achieved any longer by the methods of Poussin. The old masters, after all, had accomplished that balance and solidity at a price. They did not feel bound to respect nature as they saw it. Their pictures are rather arrangements of forms they had learned from the study of classical antiquity. Even the impression of space and solidity was achieved through the application of firm traditional rules rather than through looking at each object anew. Cézanne agreed with his friends among the Impressionists that these methods of academic art were contrary to nature. He admired the new discoveries in the field of colour and modelling. He, too, wanted to surrender to his impressions, to paint the forms and colours he saw, not those he knew about or had learned about. But he felt uneasy about the direction painting had taken. The Impressionists were true masters in painting 'nature'. But was that really enough? Where was that striving for a harmonious design, the achievement of solid simplicity and perfect balance which had marked the greatest paintings of the past? The task was to paint 'from nature', to make use of the discoveries of the Impressionist masters, and yet to recapture the sense of order and necessity that distinguished the art of Poussin.

In itself the problem was not new to art. We remember that the conquest of nature and the invention of perspective in the Italian *Quattrocento* had endangered the lucid arrangements of medieval paintings, and had created a problem which only Raphael's generation had been able to solve, *pages 195-6, 242*. Now the same question was repeated on a different plane. The dissolution of firm outlines in flickering light and the discovery of coloured shadows by the Impressionists had once again posed a new problem: how could these achievements be preserved without leading to a loss of clarity and order? To put it into simpler language: Impressionist pictures tended to be brilliant but messy. Cézanne abhorred messiness. Yet he did not want to return to the academic conventions of drawing and shading to create the illusion of solidity any more than he wanted to return to 'composed' landscapes to achieve harmonious designs. He was faced with an even more urgent issue when he pondered the right use of colour. Cézanne longed for strong, intense colours as much as he longed for lucid patterns. Medieval artists, we remember, *pages 135-6*, were able to satisfy this same desire freely because they were not bound to respect the actual appearance of things. As art had returned to the observation of nature, however, the pure and shining colours of medieval stained glass or book illuminations had given way to those mellow mixtures of tones with which the greatest painters among the Venetians, *page 248*, and the Dutch, *pages 323-4*, contrived to suggest light and atmosphere. The Impressionists had given up mixing the pigments on the palette and had applied them separately on to the canvas in small dabs and dashes to render the flickering reflections of an 'open-air' scene. Their pictures were much brighter in tone than any of their predecessors but the result did not yet satisfy Cézanne. He wanted to convey the rich and unbroken tones that belong to nature under southern skies, but he found that a simple return to the painting of whole areas in pure primary colours endangered the illusion of reality. Pictures painted in this manner resemble flat patterns and fail to give the impression of depth. Thus Cézanne seemed to be caught up in contradictions all round. His wish to be absolutely faithful to his sense impressions in front of nature seemed to clash with his desire to turn — as he said — 'Impressionism into something more solid and enduring, like the art of the museums'. No wonder that he was often near despair, that he slaved at his canvas and never ceased to experiment. The real wonder is that he succeeded, that he achieved the apparently impossible in his pictures. If art were a matter of calculation it could not have been done; but of course it is not. This balance and harmony about which artists worry so much is not the same as the balance of machines. It suddenly 'happens', and no one quite knows how or why. Much has been written about the secret of Cézanne's art. All kinds of explanations have been suggested of what he wanted and what he achieved. But these explanations remain crude; sometimes they even sound self-contradictory. But even if we get impatient with the critics, there are always the pictures to convince us. And the best advice here and always is 'go and look at the pictures in the original'.

Even our illustrations, however, should at least convey something of the greatness of Cézanne's triumph. The landscape with Mont Sainte-Victoire in southern France, figure 350, is bathed in light and yet firm and solid. It presents a lucid pattern and yet gives the impression of great depth and distance. There is a sense of order and repose in the way Cézanne marked the horizontal of the viaduct and road in the centre and the verticals of the house in the foreground, but nowhere do we feel that it is an order which Cézanne has imposed on nature. Even his brushstrokes are so arranged as to fall in with the main lines of the design and to strengthen the feeling of natural harmony. The way in which Cézanne altered the direction of his brushstroke without ever resorting to outline drawing can also be seen in figure 351, which shows how deliberately the artist counteracted the effect of the flat pattern which might have resulted in the upper half by emphasizing the solid tangible forms of the rocks in the foreground. His wonderful portrait of his wife, figure 352, shows how greatly Cézanne's concentration on simple, clear-cut forms contributes to the impression of poise and tranquillity. Compared with such calm masterpieces, the works of the Impressionists such as Manet's portrait of Monet, figure 337, often look like merely witty improvisations.

Admittedly there are paintings by Cézanne which are not so easily understood. In an illustration, a still life such as figure 353 may not look too promising. How awkward it seems if we compare it with the assured treatment of a similar subject by the Dutch seventeenth-century master Kalf, figure 280! The fruit-bowl is so clumsily drawn that its foot does not even rest in the middle. The table not only slopes from left to right, it also looks as if it were tilted forward. Where the Dutch master excelled in the rendering of soft and fluffy surfaces Cézanne gives us a patchwork of colour dabs which

make the napkin look as if it were made of tinfoil. Small
wonder that Cézanne's paintings were at first derided
as pathetic daubs. But the reason for this apparent clumsiness
is not far to seek. Cézanne had ceased to take any of the
traditional methods of painting for granted. He had decided to
start from scratch as if no painting had been done before him.
The Dutch master had painted his still life to display his
stupendous virtuosity. Cézanne had chosen his motifs to study
some specific problems that he wanted to solve. We know that
he was fascinated by the relation of colour to modelling.
A brightly coloured round solid such as an apple was an ideal
motif to explore this question. We know that he was interested
in the achievement of a balanced design. That is why he
stretched the bowl to the left so as to fill a void. As he wanted
to study all the shapes on the table in their relationships he
simply tilted it forward to make them come into view. Perhaps
the example shows how it happened that Cézanne became the
father of 'modern art'. In his tremendous effort to achieve a
sense of depth without sacrificing the brightness of colours, to
achieve an orderly arrangement without sacrificing the sense
of depth – in all the struggles and gropings there was one
thing he was prepared to sacrifice if need be: the conventional
'correctness' of outline. He was not out to distort nature; but
he did not mind very much if it became distorted in some
minor detail provided this helped him to obtain the desired
effect. Brunelleschi's invention of 'linear perspective', *page 170*,
did not interest him overmuch. He threw it overboard
when he found that it hampered him in his work. After all,
this scientific perspective had been invented to help painters
create the illusion of space – as Masaccio had done in his
fresco in Sta Maria Novella, *figure 149*. Cézanne did not aim at
creating an illusion. He wanted rather to convey the feeling
of solidity and depth, and he found he could do that without

conventional draughtsmanship. He hardly realized that this example of indifference to 'correct drawing' would start a landslide in art.

While Cézanne was groping for a conciliation of the methods of Impressionism and the need for order, a much younger artist, Georges Seurat (1859-91), set out to tackle this question almost like a mathematical equation. Using the Impressionist painting method as a starting point, he studied the scientific theory of colour vision and decided to build up his pictures by means of small regular dabs of unbroken colour like a mosaic. This, he hoped, would lead to the colours blending in the eye (or rather in the mind) without their losing in intensity and luminosity. But this extreme technique, which became known as pointillism, naturally endangered the legibility of his paintings by avoiding all contours and breaking up every form into areas of multicoloured dots. Seurat was thus driven to compensate for the complexity of his painting technique by an even more radical simplification of forms than anything Cézanne had ever contemplated, figure 354. There is something almost Egyptian in Seurat's emphasis on verticals and horizontals which led him increasingly further away from the faithful rendering of natural appearances and towards an exploration of interesting and expressive patterns.

In the winter of 1888, while Seurat was attracting attention in Paris and Cézanne was working in his seclusion in Aix, an earnest young Dutchman left Paris for southern France in search of the intense light and colour of the South. He was Vincent van Gogh. Van Gogh was born in Holland in 1853, the son of a pastor. He was a deeply religious man who had worked as a lay preacher in England and among Belgian miners. He had been deeply impressed by the art of Millet, pages 389-90, and its social message, and decided to become a painter himself. His younger brother, Theo, who worked in

an art-dealer's shop, introduced him to Impressionist painters.
This brother was a remarkable man. Though he was poor
himself, he always gave ungrudgingly to the older Vincent and
even financed his journey to Arles in southern France. Vincent
hoped that if he could work there undisturbed for a number
of years he might one day be able to sell his pictures and repay
his generous brother. In his self-chosen solitude in Arles,
Vincent set down all his ideas and hopes in his letters to Theo,
which read like a continuous diary. These letters, by a humble
and almost self-taught artist who had no idea of the fame he
was to achieve, are among the most moving and exciting in all
literature. In them we can feel the artist's sense of mission, his
struggle and triumphs, his desperate loneliness and longing
for companionship, and we become aware of the immense
strain under which he worked with feverish energy. After less
than a year, in December 1888, he broke down and had an
attack of insanity. In May 1889 he went into a mental asylum,
but he still had lucid intervals during which he continued to
paint. The agony lasted for another fourteen months. In July
1890 Van Gogh put an end to his life – he was thirty-seven like
Raphael, and his career as a painter had not lasted more than
ten years; the paintings on which his fame rests were all
painted during three years which were interrupted by crises
and despair. Most people nowadays know some of these
paintings; the sunflowers, the empty chair, the cypresses and
some of the portraits have become popular in coloured
reproductions and can be seen in many a simple room. That
is exactly what Van Gogh wanted. He wanted his pictures
to have the direct and strong effect of the coloured Japanese
prints, *pages* 403-4, he admired so much. He longed for
an unsophisticated art which would not only appeal to rich
connoisseurs but give joy and consolation to every human
being. Nevertheless this is not quite the whole story.

No reproduction is perfect. The cheaper ones make Van Gogh's pictures look cruder than they really are, and one may sometimes tire of them. Whenever that happens, it is quite a revelation to return to Van Gogh's original works and to discover how subtle and deliberate he could be even in his strongest effects.

For Van Gogh, too, had absorbed the lessons of Impressionism and of Seurat's pointillism. He liked the technique of painting in dots and strokes of pure colour, but under his hands it became something rather different from what these Paris artists had meant it to be. Van Gogh used the individual brushstrokes not only to break up the colour but also to convey his own excitement. In one of his letters from Arles he describes his state of inspiration when 'the emotions are sometimes so strong that one works without being aware of working ... and the strokes come with a sequence and coherence like words in a speech or a letter'. The comparison could not be clearer. In such moments he painted as other men write. Just as the appearance of a handwritten page, the traces left by the pen on the paper, impart something of the gestures of the writer, so that we feel instinctively when a letter was written under great stress of emotion – so the brushstrokes of Van Gogh tell us something of the state of his mind. No artist before him had ever used this means with such consistency and effect. We remember that there is bold and loose brushwork in earlier paintings, in works by Tintoretto, figure 237, by Hals, figure 270, and by Manet, figure 337, but in these it rather conveys the artist's sovereign mastery, his quick perception and magic capacity for conjuring up a vision. In Van Gogh it helps to convey the exaltation of the artist's mind. Van Gogh liked to paint objects and scenes which gave this new means full scope – motifs in which he could draw as well as paint with his brush, and lay on the colour

thick just like a writer who underlines his words. That is
why he was the first painter to discover the beauty of stubble,
hedgerows and cornfields, of the gnarled branches of olive
trees and the dark, flamelike shapes of the cypress, figure 355.

Van Gogh was in such a frenzy of creation that he felt
the urge not only to draw the radiant sun itself, figure 356,
but also to paint humble, restful and homely things which
no one had ever thought of as being worthy of the artist's
attention. He painted his narrow lodgings in Arles, figure 357,
and what he wrote about this painting to his brother explains
his intentions wonderfully well:

> I had a new idea in my head and here is the sketch to it ...
> this time it's just simply my bedroom, only here colour is to do
> everything, and, giving by its simplification a grander style to
> things, is to be suggestive here of rest or of sleep in general. In a
> word, to look at the picture ought to rest the brain or rather
> the imagination.
> The walls are pale violet. The ground is of red tiles.
> The wood of the bed and chairs is the yellow of fresh butter, the
> sheets and pillows very light greenish lemon. The coverlet scarlet.
> The window green. The toilet-table orange, the basin blue. The
> doors lilac. And that is all — there is nothing in this room with
> closed shutters. The broad lines of the furniture, again, must
> express absolute rest. Portraits on the walls, and a mirror and a
> towel and some clothes.
> The frame — as there is no white in the picture — will be
> white. This by way of revenge for the enforced rest I was obliged
> to take.
> I shall work at it again all day, but you see how simple the
> conception is. The shading and the cast shadows are suppressed, it
> is painted in free flat washes like the Japanese prints ...

It is clear that Van Gogh was not mainly concerned with correct representation. He used colours and forms to convey what he felt about the things he painted, and what he wished others to feel. He did not care much for what he called 'stereoscopic reality', that is to say, the photographically exact picture of nature. He would exaggerate and even change the appearance of things if this suited his aim. Thus he had arrived by a different road at a juncture similar to that at which Cézanne found himself during these same years. Both took the momentous step of deliberately abandoning the aim of painting as an 'imitation of nature'. Their reasons, of course, were different. When Cézanne painted a still life, he wanted to explore the relationship of forms and colours, and took in only so much of 'correct perspective' as he happened to need for his particular experiment. Van Gogh wanted his paintings to express what he felt, and if distortion helped him to achieve this aim he would use distortion. Both of them had arrived at this point without wanting to overthrow the old standards of art. They did not pose as 'revolutionaries'; they did not want to shock the complacent critics. Both of them, in fact, had almost given up hope of anybody paying attention to their pictures – they just worked on because they had to.

It was rather different with a third artist who was also to be found in southern France in 1888 – Paul Gauguin (1848-1903). Van Gogh had a great desire for companionship; he dreamed of a brotherhood of artists such as the Pre-Raphaelites had founded in England, *pages 391-2*, and he persuaded Gauguin, who was five years older, to join him in Arles. As a man, Gauguin was very different from Van Gogh. He had none of his humility and sense of mission. On the contrary, he was proud and ambitious. But there were some points of contact between the two. Like Van Gogh, Gauguin had started painting comparatively late in life (he had been a well-to-do

stockbroker); like him, he was almost self-taught. The companionship of the two, however, ended in disaster. Van Gogh, in
a fit of madness, attacked Gauguin, who fled to Paris. Two
years later, Gauguin left Europe altogether and went to one of
the proverbial 'South Sea Islands', Tahiti, in search of the
simple life. For he had more and more become convinced that
art was in danger of becoming slick and superficial, that all
the cleverness and knowledge which had been accumulated in
Europe had deprived men of the greatest gift – strength and
intensity of feeling, and a direct way of expressing it.

Gauguin, of course, was not the first artist to have these
qualms about civilization. Ever since artists had become self-
conscious about 'style' they felt distrustful of conventions and
impatient of mere skill. They longed for an art which did
not consist of tricks which can be learned, for a style which
was no mere style, but something strong and powerful
like human passion. Delacroix had gone to Algiers to look for
more intense colours and a life of less restraint, *page 387*.
The Pre-Raphaelites in England hoped to find this directness
and simplicity in the unspoilt art of the 'Age of Faith'.
The Impressionists admired the Japanese, but theirs was
a sophisticated art compared with the intensity and simplicity
for which Gauguin longed. At first he studied peasant art, but
it did not hold him for long. He needs must get away from
Europe and live among the natives of the South Seas as one of
them, to work out his own salvation. The works he brought
back from there puzzled even some of his former friends. They
seemed so savage and primitive. That was just what Gauguin
wanted. He was proud to be called 'barbarian'. Even his colour
and draughtsmanship should be 'barbaric' to do justice to the
unspoilt children of nature he had come to admire during his
stay in Tahiti. Looking at one of these pictures today, *figure 358*,
we may not quite succeed in recapturing this mood. We have

become used to much greater 'savagery' in art. And yet it is not difficult to realize that Gauguin struck a new note. It is not only the subject-matter of his pictures that is strange and exotic. He tried to enter into the spirit of the natives and to look at things as they did. He studied the methods of native craftsmen and often included representations of their works in his pictures. He strove to bring his own portraits of the natives into harmony with this 'primitive' art. So he simplified the outlines of forms and did not shrink from using large patches of strong colour. Unlike Cézanne, he did not mind if these simplified forms and colour-schemes made his pictures look flat. He gladly ignored the centuries-old problems of Western art when he thought that this helped him to render the unspoilt intensity of nature's children. He may not always have fully succeeded in his aim of achieving directness and simplicity. But his longing for it was as passionate and sincere as that of Cézanne for a new harmony, and that of Van Gogh for a new message; for Gauguin, too, sacrificed his life to his ideal. He felt himself misunderstood in Europe and decided to return to the South Sea Islands for good. After years of loneliness and disappointment, he died there of ill-health and privation.

Cézanne, Van Gogh and Gauguin were three desperately lonely men, who worked on with little hope of ever being understood. But the problems of their art about which they felt so strongly were seen by more and more artists of the younger generation who found no satisfaction in the skills they acquired at the art schools. They had learned how to represent nature, how to draw correctly and how to use paint and brush; they had even absorbed the lessons of the Impressionist Revolution and became deft in conveying the flicker of sunlight and air. Some great artists indeed persevered along this path, and championed these new methods in countries where resistance against Impressionism was still strong, but many painters of the younger generation searched for new methods to solve, or at least to bypass, the difficulties that Cézanne had felt. Basically these difficulties arose from that clash (discussed earlier, *pages 375-6*) between the need for tonal gradation to suggest depth and the desire to preserve the beauty of the colours we see. The art of the Japanese had convinced them that a picture could make a much stronger impression if modelling and other details were sacrificed to bold simplification. Both Van Gogh and Gauguin had gone a certain way along this road, enhancing their colours and disregarding the impression of depth, and Seurat had gone even further in his experiments with pointillism. Pierre Bonnard (1867-1947) showed particular skill and sensitivity in suggesting a sense of light and colour flickering on the canvas as if it were a tapestry. His painting of a spread table, *figure 359*, illustrates how he avoided a stress on perspective and depth in order to make us enjoy a colourful pattern. The Swiss painter Ferdinand Hodler (1853-1918) boldly simplified his native scenery even further to achieve a poster-like clarity, *figure 360*.

It is no accident that this painting reminds us of posters, for it turned out that the approach which Europe had learned from the Japanese proved particularly suited to the art of advertising. It was before the turn of the century that the gifted follower of Degas, *pages 404-5*, Henri de Toulouse-Lautrec (1864-1901), resorted to such an economy of means for the new art of the poster, *figure 361*.

The art of illustration profited equally from the development of such effects. Remembering the love and care which earlier ages had bestowed on the production of books, men such as William Morris, *page 411*, would not want to tolerate badly produced books or illustrations that merely told a story regardless of their effect on the printed page. Inspired

by Whistler and the Japanese, the young prodigy Aubrey
Beardsley (1872-1898) rose to immediate fame all over Europe
with his sophisticated black and white illustrations, figure 362.

The word of praise much used in this period of *Art
Nouveau* was 'decorative'. Paintings and prints should present a
pleasing pattern to the eye long before we can see what they
represent. Slowly, but surely, this fashion for the decorative
thus paved the way for a new approach to art. Fidelity to the
motif or the telling of a moving story no longer mattered
so much, provided the picture or print made a pleasing effect.
And yet, some artists felt increasingly that in all this search
something had gone out of art – something they desperately
tried to retrieve. We remember that Cézanne had felt that
what had been lost was the sense of order and balance; that
the Impressionist preoccupation with the fleeting moment had
made them neglect the solid and enduring forms of nature.
Van Gogh had felt that by surrendering to visual impressions,
and by exploring nothing but the optical qualities of light and
colour, art was in danger of losing that intensity and passion
through which alone the artist can express his feeling to his
fellow men. Gauguin, finally, was altogether dissatisfied with
life and art as he found them. He longed for something
much simpler and more direct and hoped to find it among
the primitives. What we call modern art grew out of these
feelings of dissatisfaction; and the various solutions after which
these three painters had been groping became the ideals of
three movements in modern art. Cézanne's solution ultimately
led to Cubism, which originated in France; Van Gogh's to
Expressionism, which found its main response in Germany;
and Gauguin's to the various forms of Primitivism. However
'mad' these movements may have seemed at first, today it
is not difficult to show that they were consistent attempts to
escape from a deadlock in which artists found themselves.

27

Experimental Art

The first half of the twentieth century

When people talk about 'Modern Art', they usually think of a type of art which has completely broken with the traditions of the past and tries to do things no artist would have dreamed of before. Some like the idea of progress and believe that art, too, must keep in step with the times. Others prefer the slogan of 'the good old days', and think that modern art is all wrong. But we have seen that the situation is really more complex, and that modern art no less than old art came into existence in response to certain definite problems. Those who deplore the break in tradition would have to go back beyond the French Revolution of 1789, and few would think this possible. It was then, as we know, that artists had become self-conscious about style, and had begun to experiment and to launch new movements which usually raised a new 'ism' as a battle-cry. Strangely enough, it was that branch of art which had suffered most from the general confusion of tongues that succeeded best in creating a new and lasting style; modern architecture was slow in coming, but its principles are now so firmly established that few would still want to challenge them seriously. We remember how the groping for a new style in building and ornament led to the experiments of *Art Nouveau* in which the new technical possibilities of iron construction were still combined with playful ornaments, figure 349. But it was not from such exercises in inventiveness that the architecture of the twentieth century was to arise. The future belonged to those who decided to begin afresh and to rid themselves of this preoccupation with style or ornament, were it old or new. Instead of clinging to the idea of architecture as a 'fine art', the youngest architects rejected decoration altogether and proposed to look at their task afresh in the light of its purpose.

This fresh approach made itself felt in several parts of the world, but nowhere more consistently than in America, where technological progress was much less hampered by the weight of traditions. The incongruity of building skyscrapers in Chicago and covering them with decorations from European pattern books was apparent. But it needed a forceful mind and a clear conviction for an architect to persuade his clients to accept an entirely unorthodox house. The most successful of these was the American Frank Lloyd Wright (1869-1959). He saw that what mattered in a house was the rooms, and not the façade. If it was commodious and well planned inside, and suited to the requirements of the owners, it was sure also to present an acceptable view from the outside. To us this may not seem a very revolutionary point of view, but in fact it was, for it led Wright to discard all the old shibboleths of building, especially the traditional demand for strict symmetry. Figure 363 shows one of Wright's first houses, in a wealthy suburb of Chicago. He has swept away all the usual trimmings, the mouldings and cornices, and built the house entirely to suit the plan. Yet Wright did not look upon himself as an engineer. He believed in what he called 'Organic Architecture', by which he meant that a house must grow out of the needs of the people and the character of the country like a living organism.

One can appreciate Wright's reluctance to accept the claims of the engineer all the more as these claims began to be advanced at that moment with great force and persuasiveness. For, if Morris had been right in thinking that the machine could never successfully emulate the work of human hands, the solution was obviously to find out what the machine could do and to regulate our designs accordingly.

To some, this principle seemed to be an outrage against taste and decency. In doing away with all ornaments, the modern architects did, in fact, break with the tradition of many centuries. The whole system of fictitious 'orders',

developed since the time of Brunelleschi, was swept aside and
all the cobwebs of false mouldings, scrolls and pilasters
brushed away. When people first saw these houses they looked
to them intolerably bare and naked. But we have all become
accustomed to their appearance and have learned to enjoy the
clean outlines and simple forms of modern engineering styles,
figure 364. We owe this revolution in taste to a few pioneers
whose first experiments in the use of modern building
materials were often greeted with ridicule and hostility. Figure
365 shows one of the experimental buildings which became
a storm-centre of propaganda for and against modern architecture. It is the Bauhaus in Dessau, a school of architecture
founded by the German Walter Gropius (1883-1969), which
was closed and abolished by the Nazi dictatorship. It was built
to prove that art and engineering need not remain estranged
from each other as they had been in the nineteenth century;
that, on the contrary, each could benefit the other. The students
at the school took part in the designing of buildings and
fittings. They were encouraged to use their imagination and to
experiment boldly yet never to lose sight of the purpose which
their design should serve. It was at this school that tubular
steel chairs and similar furnishings of our daily use were first
invented. The theories for which the Bauhaus stood are
sometimes condensed in the slogan of 'functionalism' – the
belief that if something is only designed to fit its purpose
we can let beauty look after itself. There is certainly much
truth in this belief. At any rate it has helped us to get rid of
much unnecessary and tasteless knick-knackery with which
the nineteenth-century ideas of Art had cluttered up our
cities and our rooms. But like all slogans it really rests on an
oversimplification. Surely there are things which are
functionally correct and yet rather ugly, or at least indifferent.
The best works of this style are beautiful not only because they

happen to fit the function for which they are built, but because they were designed by men of tact and taste who knew how to make a building fit for its purpose and yet 'right' for the eye. To discover these secret harmonies a great deal of trial and error is needed. Architects must be free to experiment with different proportions and different materials. Some of these experiments may lead them into a blind alley, but the experience gained need not be in vain for all that. No artist can always 'play safe', and nothing is more important than to recognize the role that even apparently extravagant or eccentric experiments have played in the development of new designs which we have now come to take almost for granted.

In architecture, the value of bold inventions and innovations is fairly widely recognized, but few people realize that the situation is similar in painting and sculpture. Many who have no use for what they call 'this ultra-modern stuff' would be surprised to learn how much of it has entered their lives already, and has helped to mould their taste and their preferences. Forms and colour-schemes which were developed by ultra-modern rebels in painting have become the common stock-in-trade of commercial art; and when we meet them on posters, magazine covers or fabrics, they look quite normal to us. It might even be said that modern art has found a new function in serving as testing-ground for new ways of combining shapes and patterns.

But what should a painter experiment with and why can he not be content to sit down before nature and paint it to the best of his abilities? The answer seems to be that art has lost its bearings because artists have discovered that the simple demand that they should 'paint what they see' is self-contradictory. This sounds like one of the paradoxes with which modern artists and critics like to tease the long-suffering public; but to those who have followed this book from the beginning it should not be difficult to understand. We remember how the primitive artist used to build up, say, a face out of simple forms rather than copy a real face, figure 25; we have often looked back to the Egyptians and their methods of representing in a picture what they knew rather than what they saw. Greek and Roman art breathed life into these schematic forms; medieval art used them in turn for telling the sacred story; Chinese art for contemplation. Neither was urging the artist to 'paint what he saw'. This idea dawned only during the age of the Renaissance. At first all seemed to go well. Scientific perspective, 'sfumato', Venetian colours, movement and expression, were added to the artist's means of representing the world around him; but every generation discovered that there were still unsuspected 'pockets of resistance', strongholds of conventions which made artists apply forms they had learned rather than paint what they really saw. The nineteenth-century rebels proposed to make a clean sweep of all these conventions; one after another was tackled, till the Impressionists proclaimed that their methods allowed them to render on the canvas the act of vision with 'scientific accuracy'.

The paintings that resulted from this theory were very fascinating works of art, but this should not blind us to the fact that the idea on which they were based was only half true. We have come to realize more and more, since those days, that we can never neatly separate what we see from what we know. A person who is born blind, and who gains eyesight later on, must learn to see. With some self-discipline and self-observation we can all find out for ourselves that what we call seeing is invariably coloured and shaped by our knowledge (or belief) of what we see. This becomes clear enough whenever the two are at variance. It happens that we make mistakes in seeing. For example, we sometimes see a small object which is close to our eyes as if it were a big mountain on the horizon, or a fluttering paper as if it were a bird. Once we know we have made a mistake, we can no longer see it as we did before. If we had to paint the objects concerned, we should certainly use different shapes and colours to represent them before and after our discovery. In fact, as soon as we start to take a pencil and draw, the whole idea of surrendering passively to what is called our sense impressions becomes really an absurdity. If we look out of the window we can see the view in a thousand different ways. Which of them is our sense impression? But we must choose; we must start somewhere; we must build up some picture of the house across the road and of the trees in front of it. Do what we may, we shall always have to make a beginning with something like 'conventional' lines or forms. The 'Egyptian' in us can be suppressed, but he can never be quite defeated.

This, I think, is the difficulty which was dimly felt by the generation that wanted to follow and surpass the Impressionists and which ultimately led them to a rejection of the whole Western tradition. For if the 'Egyptian' or the child in us remains stubbornly there, why not face the basic facts of image-making honestly? The experiments of Art Nouveau had called in Japanese prints to help solve the crisis, page 414. But why only such late and sophisticated products? Was it not better to begin again at the beginning and search out the art of the true 'primitives', the fetishes of cannibals and the masks of savage tribes? During the revolution in art that mounted to its climax before the First World War, an admiration of Negro sculpture was indeed one of the enthusiasms that bound together young artists of the most varied tendencies. Such objects could be picked up in curio shops for very little money, and so some tribal mask from Africa would replace the cast from the 'Apollo Belvedere', figure 64, that had adorned the

studio of the academic artist. It is easy to see when we look
at one of the masterpieces of African sculpture, figure 366, why
such an image could appeal so strongly to a generation that
looked for a way out of the impasse of Western art. Neither
that 'truth to nature' nor that 'ideal beauty' that were the twin
themes of European art seemed to have troubled the minds of
these craftsmen, but their works possessed precisely what
European art seemed to have lost in that long pursuit – intense
expressiveness, clarity of structure and a forthright simplicity
of technique.

We know today that the traditions of tribal art are more
complex and less 'primitive' than its discoverers believed;
we have even seen that the imitation of nature is by no means
excluded from its aims, figure 23. But the style of these
ritualistic objects could still serve as a common focus for that
search for expressiveness, structure and simplicity that the new
movements had inherited from the experiments of the three
lonely rebels, Van Gogh, Cézanne and Gauguin.

For good or ill, these artists of the twentieth century
had to become inventors. To secure attention they had to
strive for originality rather than for that mastery we admire
in the great artists of the past. Any departure from tradition
that interested the critics and attracted a following was
greeted as a new 'ism' to which the future would belong.
That future did not always last long, and yet the history of
twentieth-century art must take note of this restless
experimentation because many of the most gifted artists of
the period joined in these efforts.

The experiments of Expressionism are, perhaps, the
easiest to explain in words. The term itself may not be happily
chosen, for we know that we are all expressing ourselves in
everything we do or leave undone, but the word became a
convenient label because of its easily remembered contrast to

Impressionism, and as a label it is quite useful. In one of his letters, Van Gogh had explained how he set about painting the portrait of a friend who was very dear to him. The conventional likeness was only the first stage. Having painted a 'correct' portrait, he proceeded to change the colours and the setting:

> I exaggerate the fair colour of the hair, I take orange, chrome, lemon colour, and behind the head I do not paint the trivial wall of the room but the Infinite. I make a simple background out of the most intense and richest blue the palette will yield. The blond luminous head stands out against this strong blue background mysteriously like a star in the azure. Alas, my dear friend, the public will see nothing but caricature in this exaggeration, but what does that matter to us?

Van Gogh was right in saying that the method he had chosen could be compared to that of the caricaturist. Caricature had always been 'expressionist', for the caricaturist plays with the likeness of his victim, and distorts it to express just what he feels about his fellow man. As long as these distortions of nature sailed under the flag of humour nobody seemed to find them difficult to understand. Humorous art was a field in which everything was permitted, because people did not approach it with the prejudices they reserved for Art with a capital A. But the idea of a serious caricature, of an art which deliberately changed the appearance of things not to express a sense of superiority, but maybe love, or admiration, or fear, proved indeed a stumbling block as Van Gogh had predicted. Yet there is nothing inconsistent about it. It is the sober truth that our feelings about things do colour the way in which we see them and, even more, the forms which we remember. Everyone must have experienced how different the same place may look when we are happy and when we are sad.

Among the first artists to explore these possibilities even further than Van Gogh was the Norwegian painter Edvard Munch (1863-1944). Figure 367 shows a lithograph he made in 1895 which he called 'The scream'. It aims at expressing how a sudden excitement transforms all our sense impressions. All the lines seem to lead towards the one focus of the print – the shouting head. It looks as if all the scenery shared in the anguish and excitement of that scream. The face of the shouting person is indeed distorted like that of a caricature. The staring eyes and hollow cheeks recall a death's head. Something terrible must have happened, and the print is all the more disquieting because we shall never know what the scream meant.

What upset the public about Expressionist art was, perhaps, not so much the fact that nature had been distorted as that the result led away from beauty. That the caricaturist may show up the ugliness of man was granted – it was his job. But that men who claimed to be serious artists should forget that if they must change the appearance of things they should idealize them rather than make them ugly was strongly resented. But Munch might have retorted that a shout of anguish is not beautiful, and that it would be insincere to look only at the pleasing side of life. For the Expressionists felt so strongly about human suffering, poverty, violence and passion, that they were inclined to think that the insistence on harmony and beauty in art was only born out of a refusal to be honest. The art of the classical masters, of a Raphael or Correggio, seemed to them insincere and hypocritical. They wanted to face the stark facts of our existence, and to express their compassion for the disinherited and the ugly. It became almost a point of honour with them to avoid anything which smelt of prettiness and polish, and to shock the 'bourgeois' out of his real or imagined complacency.

Not that the German artist Käthe Kollwitz (1867-1945) created her moving prints and drawings mainly for the sake of creating a sensation. She felt very deeply with the poor and the down-trodden, whose cause she wished to champion. Figure 368 forms part of a series of illustrations from the 1890s inspired by a play dealing with the plight of Silesian textile workers in a period of unemployment and social revolt. Actually the scene of the dying child does not occur in the play but it adds to the poignancy of the composition. When the series was voted to receive a gold medal the responsible minister advised the Emperor against accepting this recommendation 'in view of the subject of the work and of its naturalistic execution, entirely lacking in mitigating or conciliatory elements'. This was, of course, precisely what Käthe Kollwitz intended. Unlike Millet, figure 331, who in his 'Gleaners' wanted us to sense the dignity of labour, she saw no other way out but that of revolution. No wonder her work inspired many artists and propagandists in the Communist East where it became much better known than in the West.

In Germany too the call for a radical change was frequently heard. In 1906 a group of German painters founded a society they called Die Brücke (the Bridge) to make a complete break with the past and fight for a new dawn. Their aims were shared by Emil Nolde (1867-1956), though he did not belong to the society for long. Figure 369 shows one of his impressive woodcuts, 'The prophet', that well illustrates the strong, almost poster-like effects at which these artists aimed. But now it was no longer the decorative impression they were after. Their simplification was to stand entirely in the service of enhanced expression, and thus everything is concentrated in the ecstatic gaze of the man of God.

The Expressionist movement found its most fertile soil in Germany, where it succeeded, in fact, in arousing the anger

and vindictiveness of the 'little man'. When the Nazis came to
power in 1933, modern art was banned and the greatest
leaders of the movement were exiled or forbidden to work.
This was the fate of the Expressionist sculptor Ernst Barlach
(1870-1938), whose sculpture 'Have pity!' is shown in
figure 370. There is a great intensity of expression in the simple
gesture of the old and bony hands of this beggar woman, and
nothing is allowed to divert our attention from this dominating
theme. The woman has drawn her cloak over her face, and
the simplified form of her covered head increases the appeal
to our feelings. The question whether we should call such a
work ugly or beautiful is as irrelevant here as it was in the case
of Rembrandt, *page 325*, of Grünewald, *pages 265-6*, or of those
'primitive' works which the Expressionists most admired.

Among the painters who shocked the public by
refusing to see only the bright side of things was the Austrian
Oskar Kokoschka (1886-1980), whose first works caused a
storm of indignation when they were exhibited in Vienna in
1909. Figure 371 shows one of these early paintings, a group
of children at play. To us it looks amazingly lifelike and
convincing, but it is not hard to understand why this type of
portrait aroused such opposition. If we think back to the
children's portraits by such great artists as Rubens, *figure 257*,
Velázquez, *figure 267*, Reynolds, *figure 305*, or Gainsborough,
figure 306, we realize the reason for the shock. In the past, a
child in a painting had to look pretty and contented. Grown-
ups did not want to know about the sorrows and agonies of
childhood, and they resented it if this subject was brought
home to them. But Kokoschka would not fall in with these
demands of convention. We feel that he has looked at these
children with a deep sympathy and compassion. He has
caught their wistfulness and dreaminess, the awkwardness
of their movements and the disharmonies of their growing

bodies. To bring all this out he could not rely on the accepted stock-in-trade of correct draughtsmanship, but his work is all the more true to life for what it lacks in conventional accuracy.

The art of Barlach or of Kokoschka can hardly be called 'experimental'. But the doctrine of Expressionism as such certainly encouraged experimentation if it was to be put to the test. If the doctrine was right that what mattered in art was not the imitation of nature but the expression of feelings through the choice of colours and lines, it was legitimate to ask whether art could not be made more pure by doing away with all subject-matter and relying exclusively on the effects of tones and shapes. The example of music which gets on so well without the crutch of words had often suggested to artists and critics the dream of a pure visual music. It will be remembered that Whistler had gone some way in this direction by giving his paintings musical names, figure 348. But it is one thing to talk about such possibilities in general terms, another really to exhibit a painting without any recognizable object. It appears that the first artist to do this was the Russian painter Wassily Kandinsky (1866-1944), who lived at that time in Munich. Kandinsky, like many of his German painter friends, was really a mystic who disliked the values of progress and of science and longed for a regeneration of the world through a new art of pure 'inwardness'. In his somewhat confused and passionate book *Concerning the Spiritual in Art* (1912) he stressed the psychological effects of pure colour, the way in which a bright red can affect us like the call of a trumpet. His conviction that it was possible and necessary to bring about in this way a communion from mind to mind gave him the courage to exhibit these first attempts at colour music, figure 372, which really inaugurated what came to be known as 'abstract art'.

It has often been remarked that the word 'abstract' is not very happily chosen, and substitutes such as 'non-objective' or 'non-figurative' have been suggested instead. But most labels current in the history of art are fortuitous, *page 398*. What matters is the work of art and not its tag. One may doubt whether Kandinsky's first experiments at colour music were a complete success, but it is easy to understand the interest they aroused. Even so it is unlikely that 'abstract art' could have become a movement through Expressionism alone. To understand its success and the whole transformation of the artistic scene in these years before the First World War we must again turn to Paris. For it was in Paris that Cubism originated – a movement which led to much more radical departures from the Western tradition of painting than even Kandinsky's Expressionist colour chords.

Yet Cubism did not set out to abolish representation, only to reform it. To understand the problems which the Cubist experiments tried to solve we have to think back to the symptoms of ferment and crisis discussed in the last chapter. We remember the feeling of uneasiness created by the brilliant messiness of Impressionist 'snapshots' of fleeting sights, the longing for more order, structure and pattern that had animated the illustrators of *Art Nouveau* with their emphasis on 'decorative' simplification no less than such masters as Seurat and Cézanne.

There was one problem in particular that this search had revealed – the conflict between pattern and solidity. The impression of solidity in art, as we all know, is achieved through what we call shading, the indication of the fall of light. Thus a radical simplification of the pattern could look striking enough in the posters of Toulouse-Lautrec or the illustrations of Beardsley, *figures 361-2*, but in the absence of shading the effect is flat. We have seen that artists such as

Hodler, figure 360, or Bonnard, figure 359, might have welcomed this quality, because it placed a new emphasis on the shapes of their compositions, but in thus ignoring the impression of solidity, they inevitably came up against the kind of problem that had arisen in the Renaissance through the introduction of perspective: the need to reconcile the rendering of reality with a lucid design, *page 196*.

Now the problem was reversed: in giving priority to the decorative pattern, they sacrificed the age-old practice of modelling all forms in light and shade. True, this sacrifice could also be experienced as a liberation. At last the beauty and purity of luminous colours that had once contributed to the glory of medieval stained-glass windows, figure 121, and miniatures, were no longer dimmed by shadows. It was here that the influence of Van Gogh and of Gauguin made itself felt when their works began to attract attention. Both had encouraged artists to abandon the slickness of an over-refined art and to be forthright and direct in their forms and colour-schemes. They made artists impatient of subtlety and look for intense colours and daring 'barbaric' harmonies. In 1905 a group of young painters exhibited in Paris who were to become known as *Les Fauves*, which means 'the wild beasts' or 'the savages'. They owed their name to their open disregard for the forms of nature and their enjoyment of violent colours. Actually there was little savagery in them. The most famous of the group, Henri Matisse (1869-1954), was two years older than Beardsley and had a similar talent for decorative simplification. He studied the colour-schemes of Oriental carpets and of North African scenery and developed a style that has exerted a great influence on modern design. Figure 373 shows one of his paintings from the year 1908, called 'La Desserte'. We can see that Matisse continued along the lines which Bonnard had explored, but while Bonnard still wanted to

preserve the impression of light and glitter, Matisse went
much further in the transformation of the sight before him
into a decorative pattern. The interplay of the wallpaper
design and the fabric of the tablecloth with the objects on
the table forms the main motif of the picture. Even the human
figure and the landscape seen through the window have
become part of this pattern, making it appear quite consistent
that the woman and the trees are much simplified in their
outlines and even distorted in their form to fit in with the
flowers of the wallpaper. In fact the artist called the painting
a 'harmony in red', reminding us of Whistler's titles, *pages
407-8*. There is something of the decorative effect of children's
drawings in the bright colours and simple outlines of these
paintings, though Matisse himself did not for a moment
renounce sophistication. This was his strength, but also his
weakness, because he failed to show a way out of the impasse.
It was an impasse that could only be overcome when the
example of Cézanne became known and studied as happened
after the master's death in 1906, when a large retrospective
exhibition was arranged in Paris.

No other artist was more impressed by this revelation
than a young painter from Spain, Pablo Picasso (1881-1973).
Picasso was the son of a drawing master, and had been
something of an infant prodigy in the Barcelona Art School.
At the age of nineteen he had come to Paris, where he painted
subjects that would have pleased the Expressionists: beggars,
outcasts, strollers and circus people. But he evidently found no
satisfaction in this, and began to study primitive art, to which
Gauguin and perhaps also Matisse had drawn attention. We can
imagine what he learned from these works: he learned how
it is possible to build up an image of a face or an object out
of a few very simple elements, *pages 43-4*. This was something
different from the simplification of the visual impression

which the earlier artists had practised. They had reduced the forms of nature to a flat pattern. Perhaps there were means of avoiding that flatness, of building up the picture of simple objects and yet retaining a sense of solidity and depth? It was this problem which led Picasso back to Cézanne. In one of his letters to a young painter, Cézanne had advised him to look at nature in terms of spheres, cones and cylinders. He presumably meant that he should always keep these basic solid shapes in mind when organizing his pictures. But Picasso and his friends decided to take this advice literally. I suppose they reasoned somewhat like this: 'We have long given up claiming that we represent things as they appear to our eyes. That was a will-o'-the-wisp which it is useless to pursue. We do not want to fix on the canvas the imaginary impression of a fleeting moment. Let us follow Cézanne's example, and build up the picture of our motifs as solidly and enduringly as we can. Why not be consistent and accept the fact that our real aim is rather to construct something than to copy something? If we think of an object, let us say a violin, it does not appear before the eye of our mind as we would see it with our bodily eyes. We can, and in fact do, think of its various aspects at the same time. Some of them stand out so clearly that we feel that we can touch and handle them; other are somehow blurred. And yet this strange medley of images represents more of the "real" violin than any single snapshot or meticulous painting could ever contain.' This, I suppose, was the reasoning which led to such paintings as Picasso's still life of a violin, figure 374. In some respects it represents a return to what we have called the Egyptian principles, in which an object was drawn from the angle from which its characteristic form came out most clearly, page 52. The scroll and one peg are seen from the side as we imagine them when we think of a violin. The sound-holes, on the other hand, are seen as from in front –

they would not be visible from the side. The curve of the rim is greatly exaggerated, as we are apt to over-estimate the steepness of such curves when thinking of the feeling it gives us to run our hand along the sides of such an instrument. The bow and the strings float somewhere in space; the strings even occur twice, once related to the front view, once towards the volute. Despite this apparent jumble of disconnected forms – and there are more than I have enumerated – the picture does not really look messy. The reason is that the artist has constructed his picture out of more or less uniform parts so that the whole presents an appearance of consistency comparable to such works of primitive art as the American totem pole, figure 26.

Of course, there is one drawback in this method of building up the image of an object, of which the originators of Cubism were very well aware. It can be done only with more or less familiar forms. Those who look at the picture must know what a violin looks like to be able to relate the various fragments in the picture to each other. That is the reason why the Cubist painters usually chose familiar motifs – guitars, bottles, fruit-bowls, or occasionally a human figure – where we can easily pick our way through the paintings and understand the relationship of the various parts. Not all people enjoy this game, and there is no reason why they should. But there is every reason why they should not misunderstand the artist's purpose. Critics considered it an insult to their intelligence to be expected to believe that a violin 'looks like that'. But there never was any question of an insult. If anything, the artist paid them a compliment. He assumed that they knew what a violin was like, and that they did not come to his pictures to receive this elementary information. He invited them to share with him in this sophisticated game of building up the idea of a tangible solid object out of the few

flat fragments on his canvas. We know that artists of all periods
have tried to put forward their solution of the essential
paradox of painting, which is that it represents depth on a
surface. Cubism was an attempt not to gloss over this paradox
but rather to exploit it for new effects. But while the Fauves
had sacrificed the device of shading to the pleasure of colour,
the Cubists took the opposite road: they renounced that
pleasure and rather played their game of hide-and-seek with
the traditional device of 'formal' modelling.

Picasso never pretended that the methods of Cubism
could replace all other ways of representing the visible world.
On the contrary. He was ever ready to change his methods
and to return once in a while from the boldest experiments in
image-making to various traditional forms of art, figures 11, 12.
It may be hard to believe that figure 375 and figure 376 both
represent a human head as drawn by the same artist. To understand the second we must go back to our experiments in
'doodling', pages 43-4, to the primitive fetish of figure 24 or the
mask of figure 25. Apparently Picasso wanted to find out
how far the idea of constructing the image of a head out of
the most unlikely materials and forms could be carried. He cut
out the shape of the 'head' of rough material, pasted it on his
drawing surface and then put the schematic eyes on its
margins as far from each other as possible. He let a broken
line stand for the mouth with its row of teeth and he
somehow added an undulating shape to suggest the contour
of the face. But from these adventures on the borderline of the
impossible he returned to such firm, convincing and moving
images as figure 375. No method and no technique satisfied
him for long. At times he abandoned painting for handmade
pottery. Few people might guess at first sight that the plate,
figure 377, was made by one of the most sophisticated masters
of the age. Maybe it was precisely his amazing facility in

draughtsmanship, his technical virtuosity, which made Picasso long for the simple and uncomplicated. It must have given him a peculiar satisfaction to throw all his cunning and cleverness overboard and to make something with his own hands which recalls the works of peasants or children.

Picasso himself denied that he was making experiments. He said he did not search, he found. He mocked at those who wanted to understand his art. 'Everyone wants to understand art. Why not try to understand the song of a bird?' Of course, he was right. No painting can be fully 'explained' in words. But words are sometimes useful pointers, they help to clear away misunderstandings and can give us at least an inkling of the situation in which the artist finds himself. I believe that the situation which led Picasso to his different 'finds' is very typical of twentieth-century art.

The best way, perhaps, of understanding this situation is by looking once more at its origin. To the artists of the 'good old days' the subject had come first. They received a commission to paint, say, a Madonna or a portrait and they then set to work to carry it out as best they could. When commissions of this kind became rarer, artists had to choose their own subjects. Some concentrated on themes which would attract prospective buyers. They painted carousing monks, or lovers in the moonlight, or a dramatic event from patriotic history. Other artists refused to become illustrators of this kind. If they had to choose a subject themselves they would choose one which allowed them to study some definite problem of their craft. Thus the Impressionists, who were interested in the effects of light in the open, shocked the public by painting suburban streets or haystacks rather than scenes with a 'literary' appeal. By calling the portrait of his mother, figure 347, 'Arrangement in grey and black' Whistler flaunted his conviction that to an artist any subject is but an

opportunity for studying the balance of colour and design.
A master such as Cézanne did not even have to proclaim this
fact. We remember that his still life, *figure 353*, could only
be understood as a painter's attempt to study various problems
of his art. The Cubists continued where Cézanne had left off.
Henceforward an increasing number of artists took it for
granted that what matters in art is to find new solutions for
what are called problems of 'form'. To these artists, then,
'form' always comes first and the 'subject' second.

The best description of this procedure was given by the
Swiss painter and musician Paul Klee (1879-1940), who was
a friend of Kandinsky's but had also been deeply impressed by
the experiments of the Cubists which he got to know in Paris
in 1912. To him these experiments showed not so much the
way to new methods of representing reality as to new
possibilities of playing with forms. In a lecture at the Bauhaus,
page 431, Klee tells us how he began by relating lines, shades
and colours to each other, adding a stress here, removing
a weight there, to achieve the feeling of balance or 'rightness'
after which every artist strives. He described how the forms
emerging under his hands gradually suggested some real or
fantastic subject to his imagination and how he followed these
hints when he felt he would help and not hinder his
harmonies by completing the image that he had 'found'. It
was his conviction that this way of creating images was more
'true to nature' than any slavish copy could ever be. For
nature herself, he argued, creates through the artist; it is the
same mysterious power that formed the weird shapes of
prehistoric animals, and the fantastic fairyland of the deep-sea
fauna, which is still active in the artist's mind and makes
his creatures grow. Like Picasso, Klee enjoyed the variety of
images that could be produced in this way. Indeed it is
difficult to appreciate the wealth of his fantasies from one of

his pictures alone. But figure 378 gives at least an idea of his wit and sophistication. He called it 'A tiny tale of a tiny dwarf' and we can watch the fairy-tale transformation of the gnome, for the head of the little man can also be seen as the lower part of the larger face on top.

It is most unlikely that Klee had thought out this trick before he began to paint the picture. But the dream-like freedom of his play with shapes had led him to this invention which he then completed. Of course we may be sure that even artists of the past had sometimes trusted to the inspiration and the luck of the moment. But though they may have welcomed some such happy accident, they always tried to stay in control. Many modern artists who share Klee's faith in creative nature think it wrong even to aim at such deliberate control. They believe that the work should be allowed to 'grow' according to its own laws. This method again recalls our doodles, *pages* 43-4, when we let ourselves be surprised by the outcome of our idle pen games, except that to the artist this can become a serious matter.

Needless to say it was and remained very much a matter of temperament and of taste how far an artist wanted this play with forms to lead him into such fantasies. The paintings of the American Lyonel Feininger (1871-1956), who also worked at the Bauhaus, provide a good example of the way in which an artist selects his subjects mainly in order to demonstrate certain problems of form. Like Klee, Feininger had been to Paris in 1912 and found the world of art there 'agog with Cubism'. He saw that this movement had developed new solutions to the age-old puzzle of painting, the problem of how to represent space on a flat surface without thereby destroying the lucid design, *pages* 417, 443-4. He developed an ingenious device of his own, that of building his pictures out of overlapping triangles which look as if they

were transparent and thus suggest a succession of layers –
much like the transparent curtains one sometimes sees on the
stage. As these shapes appear to lie one behind the other
they convey the idea of depth and allow the artist to simplify
the outlines of his objects without the picture looking flat.
Feininger liked to select motifs such as the gabled streets of
medieval cities or groups of sailing boats which gave scope
to his triangles and diagonals. His picture of a sailing regatta,
figure 379, shows that the method enabled him to convey not
only a feeling of space but also a sense of movement.

The same interest in what I called formal problems
could lead a sculptor such as the Romanian Constantin
Brancusi (1876-1957) to abandon the skills he had acquired at
art school and as an assistant to Rodin, pages 407-8, in order to
strive for extremes of simplification. For several years he
worked on his conception of a group representing a kiss in
the form of a cube, figure 380. Though his solution was so
radical that it again may remind us of caricature, the problem
he wanted to tackle was not entirely new. We remember that
Michelangelo's idea of sculpture was to bring out the form
that seems to slumber in the marble block, page 237-8, and
to give life and movement to his figures while yet preserving
the simple outline of the stone. Brancusi must have decided
to approach the problem from the other end. He wanted to
find out how much the sculptor could retain of the original
stone while still transforming it into the suggestion of a
human group.

It was almost inevitable that this increasing concern
with problems of form should impart a new interest to the
experiments in 'abstract painting' which Kandinsky had
launched in Germany. We remember that his ideas had grown
out of Expressionism and aimed at a kind of painting that
would rival music in expressiveness. The interest in structure

aroused by Cubism raised the question among painters in Paris, in Russia and soon also in Holland, whether painting could not be turned into a kind of construction like architecture. The Dutchman Piet Mondrian (1872-1944) wanted to build up his pictures out of the simplest elements: straight lines and pure colours, figure 381. He longed for an art of clarity and discipline that somehow reflected the objective laws of the universe. For Mondrian, like Kandinsky and Klee, was something of a mystic and wanted his art to reveal immutable realities behind the ever-changing forms of subjective appearance.

In a similar frame of mind the English artist Ben Nicholson (1894-1982) absorbed himself in the problems of his choice. But where Mondrian was exploring the relationships of elementary colours, Nicholson concentrated on that of simple shapes such as the circle and the rectangle, which he often carved into white boards, giving each a slightly different depth, figure 382. He too expressed his conviction that what he was searching for was 'Reality' and that for him art and religious experience were the same thing.

Whatever we may think of this philosophy, it is easy to imagine a frame of mind in which an artist may get completely engrossed in the mysterious problem of relating a few shapes and tones till they appear right, pages 28-30. It is quite possible that a picture which contains nothing but two squares may have caused its maker more worry than it caused an artist of the past to paint a Madonna. For the painter of the Madonna knew what he was aiming at. He had tradition as his guide and the number of decisions with which he was confronted was limited. The abstract painter with his two squares is in a less enviable position. He may shift them about on his canvas, try an infinite number of possibilities and may never know when and where to stop.

Even if we do not share his interest we need not scoff at his self-imposed labours.

There was one artist who found a very individual way out of this situation. He was the American sculptor Alexander Calder (1898-1976). Calder had been trained as an engineer, and had been much impressed by the art of Mondrian, whose studio he visited in Paris in 1930. Like him, he longed for an art that reflected the mathematical laws of the universe, but for him such an art could not be rigid and static. The universe is in constant motion but held together by mysterious balancing forces, and it was this idea of balance that first inspired Calder to construct his mobiles, figure 383. He suspended forms of various shapes and colours and made them circle and sway in space. Here the word 'balance' is no longer a mere figure of speech. Much thought and experience had to go into the creation of this delicate poise. Of course once the trick was invented it could also be used for the creation of fashionable toys. Few people who enjoy a mobile still think of the universe, any more than those who have applied Mondrian's rectangular compositions to cover-designs still think of his philosophy. Yet this preoccupation with puzzles of balance and method, however subtle and absorbing, left them with a feeling of emptiness which they tried almost desperately to overcome. Like Picasso they groped for something less sophisticated, less arbitrary. But if the interest should lie neither in the 'subject' – as of old – nor in the 'form' – as recently – what are these works meant to stand for?

The answer is more easily felt than given, for such explanations so easily deteriorate into sham profundity or downright nonsense. Still, if it must be said, I suppose the true reply is that the modern artist wants to create things. The stress is on create and on things. He wants to feel that he has made something which had no existence before. Not just a copy of a real object, however skilful, not just a piece of decoration, however clever, but something more relevant and lasting than either, something that he feels to be more real than the shoddy objects of our humdrum existence. If we want to understand this frame of mind, we must go back to our own childhood, to a time when we still felt able to make things out of bricks or sand, when we turned a broomstick into a magic wand, and a few stones into an enchanted castle. Sometimes these self-made things acquired an immense significance for us – perhaps as much as the image may have for the primitive. I believe it is this intense feeling for the uniqueness of a thing made by the magic of human hands that the sculptor Henry Moore (1898 - 1986) wanted us to have in front of his creations, figure 384. Moore did not start by looking at his model. He started by looking at his stone. He wanted to 'make something' out of it. Not by smashing it to bits, but by feeling his way, and by trying to find out what the stone 'wanted'. If it turned into a suggestion of a human figure, well and good. But even in this figure he wanted to preserve something of the solidity and simplicity of a rock. He did not try to make a woman of stone but a stone which suggests a woman. It is this attitude which has given the artists of the twentieth century a new feeling for the values of the arts of the primitives. Indeed, some of them almost envy the tribal craftsman whose images are felt to be charged with magic power and are destined to play a part in the most sacred rituals of the tribe. The mystery of ancient idols and remote fetishes arouses their romantic longing to flee from a civilization that seems to be tainted by commercialism. The primitive may be savage and cruel, but at least he seems to lack the burden of hypocrisy. It was this romantic longing that had taken Delacroix to North Africa, page 387, and Gauguin to the South Seas, pages 424 - 5.

In one of his letters from Tahiti, Gauguin had written that he felt he had to go back beyond the horses of the Parthenon, back to the rocking-horse of his childhood. It is easy to smile at this preoccupation of modern artists with the simple and childlike, and yet it should not be hard to understand it. For artists feel that this directness and simplicity is the one thing that cannot be learnt. Every other trick of the trade can be acquired. Every effect becomes easy to imitate after it has been shown that it can be done. Many artists feel that the museums and exhibitions are full of works of such amazing facility and skill that nothing is gained by continuing along these lines; that they are in danger of losing their souls and becoming slick manufacturers of paintings or sculptures unless they become as little children.

This Primitivism advocated by Gauguin became perhaps an even more lasting influence on modern art than either Van Gogh's Expressionism or Cézanne's way to Cubism. It heralded a complete revolution in taste which began round about 1905, the year of the first exhibition of the 'Fauves', *page 442*. It was only through this revolution that critics began to discover the beauty of the works of the early Middle Ages such as *figure 106*, or *figure 119*. It was then, as we have seen, that artists began to study the works of native tribesmen with the same zeal with which academic artists studied Greek sculpture. It was this change of taste, too, which led young painters in Paris at the beginning of the twentieth century to discover the art of an amateur painter, a customs official who led a quiet and unobtrusive life in the suburbs. This painter, Henri Rousseau (1844-1910), proved to them that, far from being a way to salvation, the training of the professional painter may spoil his chances. For Rousseau knew nothing of correct draughtsmanship, nothing of the tricks of Impressionism. He painted with simple, pure colours and clear outlines, every

single leaf of a tree and every blade of grass on a lawn,
figure 385. And yet there is in his pictures, however awkward
they may seem to the sophisticated mind, something so
vigorous, simple and poetic that one must acknowledge him
as a master.

In the strange race after the naïve and unsophisticated
which now began, those artists who, like Rousseau himself,
had had first-hand experience of the simple life enjoyed
a natural advantage. Marc Chagall (1887-1985), for instance,
a painter who came to Paris from a small provincial ghetto
in Russia shortly before the First World War, did not allow
his acquaintance with modern experiments to blot out his
childhood memories. His paintings of village scenes and types,
such as his musician who has become one with his
instrument, figure 386, succeed in preserving something of the
zest and childlike wonder of real folk art.

The admiration for Rousseau and the naïve self-taught
manner of 'Sunday painters' led other artists to renounce
the complicated theories of Expressionism and of Cubism as
unnecessary ballast. They wanted to conform to the ideal
of the 'man in the street', and paint clear and straightforward
pictures in which every leaf on the trees and every furrow
in the fields could be counted. It was their pride to be 'down
to earth' and 'matter of fact' and also to paint subjects which
the plain man can like and understand. Both in Nazi Germany
and in Communist Russia this attitude found eager support
from the politicians, but this need prove nothing for or against
it. The American Grant Wood (1892-1942), who had been
to Paris and Munich, celebrated the beauty of his native Iowa
with this deliberate simplicity. For his painting of 'Spring
turning', figure 387, he even made a clay model which enabled
him to study the scenery from an unexpected angle and
impart to his work something of the charm of a toy landscape.

One may well sympathize with the taste of twentieth-century artists for all that is direct and genuine and yet feel that their efforts to become deliberately naïve and unsophisticated were bound to land them in self-contradiction. One cannot become 'primitive' at will. Their frantic wish to become childlike drove some of the artists merely to exercises in calculated silliness.

But there was one way that had only rarely been explored in the past: the creation of fantastic and dream-like images. True, there had been pictures of demons and devils such as the ones in which Hieronymus Bosch had excelled, figures 229, 230, and also grotesques such as the window by Zuccaro, figure 231, but perhaps only Goya had succeeded in making his mysterious vision of a giant sitting at the edge of the world, figure 320, wholly convincing.

It was the ambition of Giorgio de Chirico (1888-1978), a Greek born of Italian parents, to capture the feeling of strangeness that can overcome us when we encounter the unexpected and wholly enigmatic. Using the traditional skills of representation he put together a monumental classical head and a large rubber glove in a deserted city, calling it 'The song of love', figure 388.

We hear that when the Belgian painter René Magritte (1898-1967) first saw a reproduction of this painting he felt, as he later wrote, 'that it represented a complete break with the mental habits of artists who are prisoners of talent, virtuosity and all the little aesthetic specialities: it was a new vision ...' He followed this lead throughout most of his life, and many of his dream-like images, painted with meticulous accuracy and exhibited with puzzling titles, are memorable precisely because they are inexplicable. Figure 389, painted in 1928, is called 'Attempting the impossible'. It might almost serve as a motto to this chapter. After all, we have seen, pages 434-5, that it was the feeling that there was a catch in the demand that artists should simply paint what they saw that drove them to ever fresh experimentation. Magritte's artist (and it is a self-portrait) attempts the standard task of the academies, the painting of a nude, but he realizes that what he does is not copying reality but rather creating a new reality, much as we do in our dreams. How we do it we do not know.

Magritte was a prominent member of a group of artists who called themselves 'Surrealists'. The name was coined in 1924 to express the longing of many young artists I mentioned before, to create something more real than reality itself, *page 451*. One of the early members of the group was the young Italian-Swiss sculptor Alberto Giacometti (1901-66), whose sculpture of a head, *figure 390*, may remind us of the work of Brancusi, though what he was after was not so much simplification as the achievement of expression by minimal means. Though all that is visible on the slab are two dells, one vertical and one horizontal, it still gazes at us much as do those works of tribal art discussed in the first chapter, *figure 24*.

Many of the Surrealists were greatly impressed by the writings of Sigmund Freud, who had shown that when our wakening thoughts are numbed the child and the savage in us takes over. It was this idea which made the Surrealists proclaim that art can never be produced by wide-awake reason. They might admit that reason can give us science but would say that only unreason can give us art. Even this theory is not quite as new as it may sound. The ancients spoke of poetry as a kind of 'divine madness', and Romantic writers like Coleridge and De Quincey deliberately experimented with opium and other drugs to drive out reason and let imagination take sway. The Surrealists, too, hankered after mental states in which what is deep down in our minds may come to the surface. They agreed with Klee that an artist cannot plan his work but must let it grow. The result may look monstrous to an outsider, but if he discards his prejudice and lets his fancy play he may come to share the artist's strange dream.

I do not think that this theory is right; nor does it really correspond to the ideas of Freud. Nevertheless, the experiment of painting dream-pictures was certainly worth making. In dreams we often experience the strange feeling that people and objects merge and exchange places. Our cat may at the same time be our aunt, and our garden Africa. One of the leading Surrealist painters, the Spaniard Salvador Dali (1904-89), who spent many years in the United States, tried to imitate this weird confusion of our dream-life. In some of his pictures he mixed surprising and incoherent fragments of the real world – painted with the same detailed accuracy with which Grant Wood painted his landscapes – and gives us the haunting feeling that there must be some sense in this apparent madness. As we look more closely at figure 391, for instance, we discover that the dream-landscape in the upper right-hand corner, the bay with its waves, the mountain with its tunnel, represents at the same time the head of a dog, whose collar is also a railway viaduct across the sea. The dog hovers in mid-air – the middle part of its body is formed by a fruit-bowl with pears, which in its turn merges into the face of a girl whose eyes are formed by some strange seashells on a beach crowded with puzzling apparitions. As in a dream, some things, like the rope and the cloth, stand out with unexpected clarity while other shapes remain vague and elusive.

A painting such as this brings it home to us for the last time why twentieth-century artists have not been satisfied in simply representing 'what they see'. They have become too much aware of the many problems which are hidden in this demand. They know that the artist who wants to 'represent' a real (or imagined) thing does not start by opening his eyes and looking about him but by taking colours and forms and building up the required image. The reason why we often forget this simple truth is that in most pictures of the past each form and each colour happened to signify only one thing in nature – the brown strokes stood for tree trunks, the green dots for leaves. Dali's way of letting each form represent several things at the same time may focus our attention on the many possible meanings of each colour and form – much in the way in which a successful pun may make us aware of the function of words and their meanings. Dali's seashell, which is also an eye, his fruit-bowl, which is also a girl's forehead and nose, may send our thoughts back to the first chapter of this book, to the Aztec rain-god Tlaloc, whose features were composed of rattlesnakes, figure 30.

And yet, if we really take the trouble to look at the ancient idol we may receive something of a shock – how great is the difference in spirit for all possible similarity of method! Both images may have emerged from a dream, but Tlaloc, we feel, was the dream of a whole people, the nightmare figure of the dire power that held sway over their fate; Dali's dog and fruit-bowl reflect the elusive dream of a private person to which we hold no key. It would clearly be unfair to blame the artist for this difference. It arises out of the totally different circumstances in which the two works were created.

To produce a perfect pearl the oyster needs some piece of matter, a sandcorn or a small splinter round which the pearl can form. Without such a hard core it may grow into a shapeless mass. If the artist's feelings for forms and colours are to crystallize in a perfect work, he, too, needs such a hard core – a definite task on which he can bring his gifts to bear.

We know that in the more distant past all works of art gained shape round such a vital core. It was the community which set the artists their tasks – be it the making of ritual

masks or the building of cathedrals, the painting of portraits
or the illustration of books. It matters comparatively little
whether we happen to be in sympathy with all these tasks or
not; one need not approve of bison-hunting by magic, or the
glorification of criminal wars or the ostentation of wealth and
power to admire the works of art which were once created
to serve such ends. The pearl completely covers the core. It is
the secret of the artist that he does his work so superlatively
well that we all but forget to ask what his work was supposed
to be, for sheer admiration of the way he did it. We are all
familiar with this shift of emphasis in more trivial instances. If
we say of a schoolboy that he is an artist in boasting or that he
has turned shirking into a fine art, we mean precisely this –
that he displays such ingenuity and imagination in the
pursuance of his unworthy ends that we are forced to admire
his skill however much we may disapprove of his motives. It
was a fateful moment in the story of art when people's
attention became so riveted on the way in which artists had
developed painting or sculpting into a fine art that they forgot
to give artists more definite tasks. We know that the first step
in this direction was taken in Hellenistic times, *pages 87-9*,
another in the Renaissance, *pages 215-7*. But however surprising
this may sound, this step did not yet deprive painters and
sculptors of that vital core of a task which alone could fire
their imagination. Even when definite jobs became rarer there
remained a host of problems for the artist in the solution
of which he could display his mastery. Where these problems
were not set by the community they were set by tradition. It
was the tradition of image-making which carried in its stream,
as it were, those indispensable sandcorns of tasks. We know
that it was a matter of tradition rather than any inherent
necessity that art should reproduce nature. The importance of
this demand in the history of art from Giotto, *page 150*, to the

Impressionists, *pages* 398-9, does not lie in the fact – as is
sometimes thought – that it is the 'essence' or 'duty' of art to
imitate the real world. Nor is it true, I believe, that this
demand is entirely irrelevant. For it provided, as we have seen,
just the type of insoluble problem which challenges the artist's
ingenuity and makes him do the impossible. We have
frequently seen, moreover, how each solution of one of these
problems, however breath-taking, gave rise to new problems
elsewhere which gave younger men the opportunity of
showing what they could do with colours and forms. For even
the artist who is in revolt against tradition depends on it for
that stimulus which gives direction to his efforts.

It is for this reason that I have tried to tell the story of
art as the story of a continuous weaving and changing of
traditions in which each work refers to the past and points to
the future. For there is no aspect of this story more wonderful
than this – that a living chain of tradition still links the art
of our own days with that of the Pyramid age. The heresies of
Akhnaten, *page* 56, the turmoil of the Dark Ages, *page* 119, the
crisis of art in the Reformation period, *page* 283, and the break
in tradition at the time of the French Revolution, *page* 362-3,
each threatened this continuity. The danger was often very real.
After all, the arts have been known to die out in whole
countries and civilizations when the last link snapped. But
somehow and somewhere the final disaster was always
averted. When old tasks disappeared new ones turned up
which gave artists that sense of direction and sense of purpose
without which they cannot create great works. In architecture,
I believe, this miracle has happened once more. After the
fumblings and hesitations of the nineteenth century modern
architects have found their bearings. They know what they
want to do and the public has begun to accept their work as a
matter of course. For painting and sculpture the crisis has not

yet passed the danger point. Despite some promising experiments there still remains an unhappy cleavage between what is called 'applied' or 'commercial' art, which surrounds us in daily life, and the 'pure' art of exhibitions and galleries, which many of us find hard to understand.

It is just as thoughtless to be 'for modern art' as it is to be 'against it'. The situation in which it grew is just as much our own doing as that of the artists. There are certainly painters and sculptors alive today who would have done honour to any age. If we do not ask them to do anything in particular, what right have we to blame them if their work appears to be obscure and aimless?

The general public has settled down to the notion that an artist is a fellow who should produce Art much in the way a bootmaker produces boots. By this they mean that he should produce the kind of paintings or sculptures they have seen labelled as Art before. One can understand this vague demand, but, alas, it is the one job the artist cannot do. What has been done before presents no problem any more. There is no task in it that could put the artist on his mettle. But critics and 'highbrows', too, are sometimes guilty of a similar misunderstanding. They, too, tell the artist to produce Art; they, too, are inclined to think of pictures and statues as specimens for future museums. The only task they set the artist is that of creating 'something new' – if they had their way, each work would represent a new style, a new 'ism'. In the absence of any more concrete jobs even the most gifted modern artists sometimes fall in with these demands. Their solutions of the problem of how to be original are sometimes of a wit and brilliance not to be despised, but in the long run this is hardly a task worth pursuing. That, I believe, is the ultimate reason why modern artists so often turn to various theories, new and old, about the nature of art. It is probably no more true to say that 'art is expression' or that 'art is construction' than it was to say that 'art is the imitation of nature'. But any such theory, even the most obscure one, may contain that proverbial grain of truth which might do for the pearl.

Here, at last, we are back at our starting point. There really is no such thing as Art. There are only artists – men and women, that is, who are favoured with the wonderful gift of balancing shapes and colours till they are 'right', and, rarer still, who possess that integrity of character which never rests content with half-solutions but is ready to forgo all easy effects, all superficial success for the toil and agony of sincere work. Artists, we trust, will always be born. But whether there will also be art depends to no small extent on ourselves, their public. By our indifference or our interest, by our prejudice or our understanding we may yet decide the issue. It is we who must see to it that the thread of tradition does not break and that there remain opportunities for the artist to add to the precious string of pearls that is our heirloom from the past.

28

A Story without End

The triumph of Modernism

This book was written shortly after the end of the Second World War, and first published in 1950. At that time most of the artists mentioned in its final chapter were still alive, and a few of the works I illustrated were of quite recent date. No wonder, that with the passage of time there arose a demand for me to add a further chapter, devoted to current developments. The pages now before the reader were in fact largely added to the eleventh edition, and originally headed 'Postscript 1966'. But as that date, in its turn, receded into the past, I changed that title to 'A story without end'.

I confess that I now regret this decision, because I have found that it invites a confusion between the story of art, as here conceived, and a chronicle of fashions. Not that such a confusion is in any way surprising. After all, we need only turn the pages of this book, to be reminded of the many times when works of art reflected the elegance and refinement of current fashions – whether we turn to the dainty ladies of the Limbourg Book of Hours celebrating the coming of May, figure 144, or to the dream-world of Antoine Watteau's 'Rococo', figure 298. But in appreciating these works, we must not forget how quickly the fashions they reflected became obsolete while the paintings have retained their appeal: the Arnolfini couple in their finery, as painted by Jan van Eyck, figure 158, would have cut funny figures at the Spanish court as painted by Diego Velázquez, figure 266, and his tightly laced Infanta, in her turn, might have been mercilessly mocked by the children portrayed by Sir Joshua Reynolds, figure 305.

What has been called the 'whirlygig of fashion' is indeed likely to keep turning, as long as there are people around with sufficient money and leisure to seek to impress society with novel eccentricities, and this may really be a 'story without end'. But fashion journals which tell those who want to remain in the swim what is worn today are purveyors of news much as our daily papers are. The day's events only turn into a 'story' when we have gained sufficient distance, to know what effect (if any) they have had on later developments.

The application of these reflections to the story of art as it has been told in these pages hardly needs spelling out: the story of artists can only be told when it has become clear, after a certain lapse of time, what influence their work had on others and what contributions they have made to the story of art as such. Thus I tried to select, from the mass of buildings, sculptures and paintings still known to us after thousands of years, a very small number that could figure in a story that dealt first and foremost with the solution of certain artistic problems, solutions, that is, that determined the course of future developments.

The nearer we come to our own time, the harder it inevitably becomes to distinguish passing fashions from lasting achievements. The search for alternatives to that contest with natural appearances that I had described in the preceding pages was bound to lead to eccentricities, designed to catch attention, but it also opened up a vast field for experimentation with colour and form which remains to be explored. With what results we do not yet know.

It is for this reason that I feel uncomfortable about the idea that one can write the story of art 'up to the present day'. True, one can record and discuss the latest fashions, the figures who happen to have caught the limelight at the time of writing. But only a prophet could tell whether these artists will really 'make history', and on the whole critics have proved poor prophets. Imagine an open-minded and eager critic in 1890 trying to bring the history of art 'up to date'. With the best will in the world he could not have known that the three figures who were making history at that time were Van Gogh, Cézanne and Gauguin; the first, a crazy middle-aged

Dutchman working away in southern France, the second a retiring gentleman of independent means, who had long ceased to send his paintings to exhibitions, and the third a stockbroker who had become a painter late in life and was soon off to the South Seas. The question is not so much whether our critic could have appreciated the works of these men as whether he could have known of them at all.

Any historian who has lived long enough to experience what happens as the present becomes the past has a story to tell about the way the outlines change with increasing distance. The last chapter of this book is a case in point. At the time when I wrote the account of Surrealism I was not aware of the fact that an elderly refugee, whose work would prove of greater influence in the subsequent years, was then still living in England in the Lake District. I am referring to Kurt Schwitters (1887-1948), whom I regarded as one of the amiable eccentrics of the early 1920s. Schwitters used discarded bus tickets, newspaper cuttings, rags and other odds and ends, and glued them together to form quite tasteful and amusing bouquets, figure 392. In refusing to use conventional paint and conventional canvas his attitude was connected with an extremist movement that had started in Zürich during the First World War. I could have discussed this group of 'Dada' in the section of my last chapter which is concerned with Primitivism. I quoted there, pages 454, the letter by Gauguin according to which he felt he had to go back beyond the horses of the Parthenon to the rocking-horse of his childhood; and the childish syllables Da-da can stand for such a toy. It was certainly the wish of these artists to become as little children and to cock a snook at the solemnity and pomposity of Art with a capital A. It is not difficult to understand these sentiments, but it has always seemed to me a little incongruous to record, analyse and teach such gestures of 'anti-art' with the very solemnity, not to say pomposity, they had set out to ridicule and abolish. Even so, I cannot accuse myself of having dismissed or ignored the sentiments which have animated this movement. I tried to describe the frame of mind in which the everyday things in the world of a child may acquire a vivid significance, *page 453*. True, I had not foreseen to what an extent this return to the mentality of children would come to blur the difference between works of art and other man-made objects. The French artist Marcel Duchamp (1887-1968) acquired fame and notoriety for taking any such object (which he called a 'ready-made') and signing it with his name, and a much younger artist, Joseph Beuys (1921-86), in Germany followed him, claiming that he had widened or extended the notion of 'art'.

I sincerely hope that I did not contribute to this fashion – for it became a fashion – when I opened these pages with the remark that 'there really is no such thing as Art', *page 21*. What I meant, of course, was that the word 'art' has meant different things at different times. In the Far East, for instance, calligraphy is the most respected of the 'arts'. But I have also argued, *page 460*, that we speak of art whenever anything is done so superlatively well that we all but forget to ask what the work is supposed to be, for sheer admiration of the way it is done. I have suggested that this had happened to painting to an increasing extent. Developments after the Second World War have borne me out. If by painting we mean simply the application of paint to canvas, you can have connoisseurs who admire the way this is done to the exclusion of everything else. Even in the past an artist's handling of paint, the energy of his brushstrokes or the subtlety of his touch, had been prized, but generally in the larger context of the effect thus achieved. Turn back to figure 213, to admire how Titian handled the paint in the indication of the ruff, to figure 260 to enjoy the

sure touch of Rubens's brush as he painted the beard of the
Faun. Or look at the virtuosity with which Chinese painters,
figure 98, applied their brush to the silk in the most subtle
gradation and yet without a trace of fussiness. It was in China
in particular that the sheer mastery of brushwork was most
discussed and appreciated. We remember that it was the
ambition of Chinese masters to acquire such a facility in the
handling of brush and ink that they could write down their
vision while their inspiration was still fresh, much as the poet
jots down his verse. Indeed for the Chinese, writing and
painting have much in common. I just mentioned the Chinese
art of 'calligraphy', but really it is not the formal beauty of the
characters that the Chinese admire so much as that feeling
of mastery and inspiration that must inform every stroke.

Here, then, was an aspect of painting that still appeared
to be unexplored – the sheer handling of paint regardless of
any ulterior motive or purpose. In France this concentration
on the mark or blot left by the brush was called *tachisme*, from
tache (blot). Most of all it was the American artist Jackson
Pollock (1912-56) who aroused interest with his novel ways of
applying paint. Pollock had been captivated by Surrealism, but
he gradually discarded the weird images that had haunted
his paintings for exercises in abstract art. Becoming impatient
of conventional methods, he put his canvas on the floor and
dripped, poured or threw his paint to form surprising
configurations, figure 393. He probably remembered stories of
Chinese painters who had used such unorthodox methods and
also the practice of American Indians who make pictures in
the sand for magic purposes. The resulting tangle of lines
satisfies two opposing standards of twentieth-century art: the
longing for childlike simplicity and spontaneity that evokes
the memory of childish scrawls at the time of life before
children even start to form images; and, at the opposite end,

the sophisticated interest in the problems of 'pure painting'.
Pollock has thus been hailed as one of the initiators of a new
style known as 'action painting' or Abstract Expressionism.
Not all his followers used Pollock's extreme methods but
all of them believed in the need to surrender to spontaneous
impulse. Like Chinese calligraphy these paintings must be
done rapidly. They should not be premeditated but rather
resemble a spontaneous outburst. There is little doubt that,
in advocating this approach, artists and critics were in fact
influenced not only by Chinese art but altogether by Far
Eastern mysticism, particularly in the form that has become
fashionable in the West under the name of Zen Buddhism.
In this respect, too, the new movement continued the earlier
tradition of twentieth-century art. We remember that
Kandinsky, Klee and Mondrian were mystics who wanted to
break through the veil of appearances to a higher truth,
pages 444, 452-3, 455, and that the Surrealists courted 'divine
madness', *page 461.* It is part of the doctrine of Zen
(though not its most important part) that no one who has
not been shocked out of his rational habits of thought can
become enlightened.

I made a point in the previous chapter that one need
not necessarily accept the artist's theories to appreciate his
work. If one has the patience and the interest to look at many
paintings of this kind one will certainly come to like some
better than others and gradually appreciate the problems these
artists are after. Even to compare a painting by the American
artist Franz Kline (1910-62) with one by the French *tachiste*
Pierre Soulages (born 1919) is not uninstructive, figures 394,
395. It is characteristic that Kline called his paintings 'White
forms'. He obviously wanted us to pay attention not only to
his lines but also to the canvas which they somehow
transform. For, simple as are his strokes, they do result in some

impression of a spatial arrangement, as if the lower half were receding towards the centre. To me, though, the painting by Soulages looks more interesting. The gradation of his energetic brushstrokes also results in the impression of three dimensions, but at the same time the quality of the paint looks more pleasant to me – though these differences hardly come through in illustration. It may even be that this resistance to photographic reproduction is precisely what attracts some contemporary artists. They want to feel that their work really remains unique, the product of their hands, in a world in which so much is machine-made and standardized. Some went in for canvases of enormous size where it is the scale alone that makes an impact, and this scale, too, loses its point in an illustration. Most of all, however, many artists are fascinated by what they call 'texture', the feel of a substance, its smoothness or roughness, its transparency or density. They therefore discard ordinary paint for other media, such as mud, sawdust or sand.

Here is one of the reasons for the revival of interest in the paste-ups of Schwitters and the other Dadaists. The coarseness of sacking, the polish of plastics, the grain of rusty iron, can all be exploited in novel ways. These products stand somewhere between painting and sculpture. Thus the Hungarian Zoltan Kemeny (1907-65), who lived in Switzerland, composed his abstracts with metal, figure 396. In making us aware of the variety and surprise that our urban surroundings offer to our sense of sight and touch, works of this kind may claim to do for us what landscape painting did for the connoisseurs of the eighteenth century by preparing them for the discovery of the 'picturesque' beauties of nature in the raw, pages 302-3.

I trust no reader will think, however, that these few examples exhaust the possibilities and the range of variations

likely to be encountered in any collection of recent art.
There are artists, for instance, who have become particularly
interested in the optical effects of shapes and colours, the
way they can be made to interact on the canvas to produce
an unexpected dazzle or flicker – a movement which has
been dubbed 'Op Art'. But it would be misleading to present
the contemporary scene as if it were entirely dominated by
experiments with paint, texture or shapes alone. It is true
that to command respect among the younger generation an
artist has to master these media in an interesting and
personal way. But some of the painters who have attracted
most attention in the post-war period have from time to
time returned from their exploration of abstract art to the
making of images. I am thinking in particular of the Russian
émigré Nicolas de Staël (1914-55), whose simple yet subtle
brushstrokes often compose themselves into convincing
evocations of landscapes which miraculously give us a sense
of light and distance without making us forget the quality of
the paint, *figure 397*. They continue the explorations of image-
making discussed in the previous chapter, *pages 432-3*.

Other artists of this post-war period have been
engrossed by one image which haunted and obsessed their
mind. The Italian sculptor Marino Marini (1901-80) became
famous for his many variations on a motif that impressed
itself on his mind during the war – the sight of stocky Italian
peasants fleeing from their villages on farm-horses during air-
raids, *figure 398*. It is the contrast between these anxious
creatures and the traditional image of the heroic horseman
such as Verrocchio's Colleoni, *figure 188*, that lends a special
pathos to these works.

The reader may well wonder whether these disparate
examples add up to the continuation of the story of art, or
whether what was once a mighty river has meanwhile broken

up into many branches and rivulets. We cannot tell, but we may take comfort from the very multiplicity of efforts. Indeed in this respect there is no cause for pessimism. I expressed my conviction at the conclusion of the previous chapter, *page 463*, that there will always be artists, 'men and women, that is, who are favoured with the wonderful gift of balancing shapes and colours till they are "right", and, rarer still, who possess that integrity of character which never rests content with half-solutions, but is ready to forgo all lazy effects, all superficial success for the toil and agony of sincere work.'

One such artist who meets that description admirably was another Italian, Giorgio Morandi (1890-1964). Morandi had been briefly impressed by the paintings of de Chirico, *figure 388*, but soon came to reject all associations with fashionable movements in order to concentrate doggedly on the basic problems of his craft. He liked to paint or etch simple still lifes representing a number of vases and vessels he had in his studio from different angles and in different light, *figure 399*. He did so with such sensitivity that slowly but surely he gained the respect of his fellow artists, of the critics and of the public for his single-minded pursuit of perfection.

There is no reason to think that Morandi was the only master of this century thus to devote himself to the problems he had set himself regardless of the 'isms' that clamoured for attention. But it is hardly surprising that others of our contemporaries were tempted to follow, or better still, to launch a novel fashion.

Take the movement known as 'Pop Art'. The ideas behind it are not hard to understand. I hinted at them when I spoke of the 'unhappy cleavage between what is called "applied" or "commercial" art, which surrounds us in daily life, and the "pure" art of exhibitions and galleries, which many of us find hard to understand', *page 462*. It is natural that this rift presented a challenge to the art students for whom it has become a matter of course that one must always side with what is despised by people of 'taste'. All the other forms of anti-art had by now become a matter for highbrows. They shared with the hated idea of Art its exclusiveness and its mystical pretensions. Why was this not so in music? There was a kind of new music that had conquered the masses and engaged their interest to the point of hysterical devotion. This was Pop Music. Could we not have Pop Art as well and could it not be achieved by simply using the images familiar to everyone from comic strips or advertising?

It is the job of the historian to make intelligible what actually happens. It is the job of the critic to criticize what happens. One of the most serious problems in trying to write the history of the present is that the two functions get mixed up. Luckily I have already announced in the Preface that I intended 'to cut out anything which might merely be interesting as a specimen of taste or fashion'. I have not yet seen a result of these experiments which I would not consider as falling under this rule. It should not be difficult for the reader, however, to make up his or her mind, for exhibitions of these latest trends are now organized in many places. This too is a new development and a very welcome one.

No revolution in art has been more successful than that which started before the First World War. Those of us who knew some of the first champions of these movements and recall their courage, and also their bitterness as they defied a hostile press and a mocking public, can hardly trust our eyes when we see exhibitions of one-time rebels arranged with official backing and beleaguered by earnest crowds anxious to learn and absorb the new idioms. This is a piece of history I have experienced, and in a way this book itself testifies to this change. When I first conceived and wrote the Introduction

and the chapter on Experimental Art I took it for granted that
it was the duty of the critic and of the historian to explain and
to justify all artistic experiments in the face of hostile criticism.
Today the problem is rather that the shock has worn off
and that almost anything experimental seems acceptable to the
press and the public. If anybody needs a champion today it
is the artist who shuns rebellious gestures. I believe that it is
this dramatic transformation rather than any particular new
movement that represents the most important event in the
history of art which I have witnessed since this book was first
published in 1950. Observers from very different quarters have
commented on this unexpected turn in the tide of fashion.

Here is Professor Quentin Bell writing on 'The Fine
Arts' in a book on The Crisis in the Humanities (edited by J.H.
Plumb) in 1964:

> In 1914, when he was referred to indiscriminately as 'cubist',
> 'futurist' or 'modernist', the post-Impressionist artist was regarded
> as a crank or a charlatan. The painters and sculptors who the
> public knew and admired were bitterly opposed to radical
> innovations. The money, the influence, and the patronage were all
> on their side. Today, it is almost true to say the situation is
> reversed. Public Bodies such as the Arts Council and the British
> Council and Broadcasting House, Big Business, the Press, the
> Churches, the Cinema, and the advertisers are all on the side of
> what, to use a misnomer, is called nonconformist art ...
> the public can take anything, or at least there is a very large
> and influential section of it that can do so ... there is no form
> of pictorial eccentricity which can provoke or even astonish
> the critics. ...

And here is the influential champion of contemporary
American painting, Mr Harold Rosenberg, who coined the

term 'action painting', commenting on the scene on the other side of the Atlantic. In an article in the New Yorker of 6 April 1963, he reflected on the difference between the reaction of the public to the first exhibition of avant-garde art in New York in 1913 – The Armory Show – and that of a new kind of public which he describes as the 'Vanguard Audience':

> The Vanguard Audience is open to anything. Its eager representatives – curators, museum directors, art educators, dealers – rush to organize exhibitions and provide explanatory labels before the paint has dried on the canvas or the plastic has hardened. Co-operating critics comb the studios like big-league scouts, prepared to spot the art of the future and to take the lead in establishing reputations. Art historians stand ready with cameras and notebooks to make sure every novel detail is safe for the record. The tradition of the new has reduced all other traditions to triviality ...

Mr Rosenberg may well be right when he implies that we art historians have contributed to this change in the situation. Indeed I think any author who now writes a history of art, and particularly of contemporary art, has the duty to draw attention to this unintended effect of his activities. In my Introduction, pages 33-4, I touched on the harm which a book of this kind might do. I mentioned the temptation of indulging in clever talk about art. But this danger is trivial compared to the misleading impression which such a panorama may give that all that matters in art is change and novelty. It is the interest in change that has accelerated change to its giddy pace. Of course it would not be fair to lay all the undesirable consequences – as well as the desirable ones – at the door of art history. In a certain sense the new interest in the history of art is in itself a consequence of a great many factors which have changed the

position of art and artists in our society and made art more
fashionable than it had ever been in the past. I should like in
conclusion to list some of these factors.

1

The first is no doubt connected with everybody's experience
of progress and change. It has made us see human history in
terms of successive periods leading onwards to our own age
and beyond into the future. We know of the Stone Age and the
Iron Age, we know of the Feudal Age and the Industrial
Revolution. Our view of this process may have ceased to be
optimistic. We may be aware of losses as well as of gains in
these successive transformations, which have carried us
into the Space Age. But ever since the nineteenth century the
conviction has taken root that this march of the Ages is
irresistible. It is felt that art no less than economics or
literature is swept along by this irreversible process. Indeed art
is regarded as the main 'expression of the age'. Here in
particular the development of art history (and even a book
such as this) has its share in spreading this belief. Have we not
all the feeling, as we turn back its pages, that a Greek temple,
a Roman theatre, a Gothic cathedral or a modern skyscraper
'express' a different mentality and symbolize a different type
of society? There is some truth in this conviction, if it is
simply taken to mean that the Greeks could not have built the
Rockefeller Center and might not have wanted to build Notre-
Dame. But too often it is implied that the condition of
their Age, or what it is called its spirit, was bound to blossom
forth in the Parthenon, that the Feudal Age could not help
creating cathedrals and that we are destined to build
skyscrapers. On this view, which I do not share, it is of course
both futile and foolish not to accept the art of one's age.
It thus becomes sufficient for any style or experiment to be

proclaimed 'contemporary' for the critic to feel the obligation to understand and promote it. It is through this philosophy of change that critics have lost the courage to criticize and have become chroniclers of events instead. They have justified this change of attitude by pointing to the notorious failures of earlier critics to recognize and accept the rise of new styles. It was in particular the hostile reception first accorded to the Impressionists, *page* 398, who later rose to such fame and commanded such high prices, that led to this loss of nerve. The legend has sprung up that all great artists were always rejected and derided in their time and so the public now makes the laudable effort no longer to reject or deride anything. The idea that artists represent the vanguard of the future, and that it is we and not they who will look funny if we fail to appreciate them, has taken hold at least of a large minority.

2

A second element that has contributed to this situation is also connected with the development of science and technology. Everybody knows that the ideas of modern science often look extremely abstruse and unintelligible but that they still prove their worth. The most striking example, of which most people are by now aware, is of course Einstein's theory of relativity, which appeared to contradict all common-sense notions about time and space, but led to the equation of mass and energy that resulted in the atom bomb. Both artists and critics were and are immensely impressed by the power and prestige of science and derive from it not only a healthy belief in experiments but also a less healthy faith in anything that looks abstruse. But, alas, science differs from art because the scientist can sort out the abstruse from the absurd by rational methods. The critic of art has no such clear-cut tests.

And yet he feels that it is no longer possible to ask for time to consider whether a new experiment makes sense or not. If he does, he may fall behind. This might not have mattered all that much to critics of the past, but today the conviction is almost universal that those who stick to obsolete beliefs and who refuse to change will go to the wall. In economics we are constantly told that we must adapt or die. We must keep an open mind and give a chance to new methods which have been proposed. No industrialist could risk the stigma of conservatism. He must not only go with the times, he must be seen to go with the times, and one way of ensuring this is to decorate his board-room with works of the latest fashion, the more revolutionary the better.

3

The third element in the present situation may seem at first blush to contradict what has gone before. For art not only wants to keep step with science and technology, it also wants to provide an escape from these monsters. It is for this reason, as we have seen, that artists have come to shun what is rational and mechanical and that so many of them embrace some mystical faith that stresses the value of spontaneity and individuality. It is indeed easy to understand how people may feel threatened by mechanization and automation, by the over-organization and standardization of our lives and the dull conformism that they demand. Art seems the only haven where capriciousness and personal quirks are still permitted and even treasured. Since the nineteenth century many an artist has claimed that he fought the good fight against stuffy conventionalism by baiting the bourgeois, *pages 390-1*. Alas, the bourgeois has meanwhile found out that it is quite fun to be baited. Do we not all feel some kind of pleasure in the spectacle of people who refuse to grow up and still find a niche in the contemporary world? And is it not an added asset if we can advertise our lack of prejudice by refusing to be shocked or bemused? And so the world of technical efficiency and that of art have reached a *modus vivendi*. The artist can withdraw into his private world and concern himself with the mysteries of his craft and with the dreams of his childhood, provided, at least, he lives up to the public's notion of what art is about.

4

These notions are very much coloured by certain psychological assumptions about art and artists of which we have seen the growth in the course of this book. There is the idea of self-expression that goes back to the Romantic era, *pages 383-4*; and the profound impression made by the discoveries of Freud, *page 457*, which were taken to imply a more immediate connection between art and mental distress than Freud himself would have accepted. Combined with the increasing belief that art is the 'expression of the age' these convictions could lead to the conclusion that the artist has not only the right but the duty to abandon all self-control. If the resulting outbursts are not pretty to contemplate, this is because our age is not pretty either. What matters is to face these stark realities that help us to diagnose our predicament. The opposite idea, that art alone might give us a glimpse of perfection in this very imperfect world, is generally dismissed as 'escapism'. The interests aroused by psychology have certainly driven both the artists and their public to explore regions of the human mind which were formerly considered repellent or taboo. The desire to escape the stigma of escapism has prevented many from averting their eyes from spectacles which former generations would have shunned.

5

The four factors so far enumerated have influenced the
situation in literature and music no less than in painting and
sculpture. The remaining five I should like to consider are
more or less peculiar to the practice of art. For art differs from
other forms of creation in being less dependent on
intermediaries. Books must be printed and published, plays
and compositions must be performed; and this need of
an apparatus applies a certain brake to extreme experiment.
Painting has therefore proved of all the arts the most
responsive to radical innovations. You don't have to use
a brush if you prefer to pour your paint, and if you are a neo-
Dadaist you can also send some piece of rubbish to an
exhibition and dare the organizers to reject it. Whatever they
do, you may have your fun. It is true that ultimately the artist
also needs an intermediary, the dealer who shows and
promotes his works. Needless to say, this remains a problem;
but all the influences discussed so far are likely to work on the
dealer even more than they work on the critic or the artist.
If anyone it is he who must keep his eye on the barometer of
change, watch trends and look out for rising talents. If he
backs the right horse not only can he make a fortune, but
his clients will remain grateful to him. Conservative critics of
the last generation used to grumble that 'this modern art' was
all a dealers' racket. But dealers have always wanted to make a
profit. They are not the masters but the servants of the market.
There may have been moments when a correct guess gave
an individual dealer the power and prestige for a time to make
or break reputations, but dealers do not cause the winds of
change any more than windmills cause the wind.

6

It may be different with teachers. Art teaching seems to me to
be the sixth element and a very important one in the contemporary situation. It was in the teaching of art to children
that the revolution in modern education made itself first felt.
At the beginning of this century art teachers began to discover
how much more they could get out of children if they abandoned the soul-destroying drill of traditional methods.

It was the time, of course, when these methods had anyhow
become suspect through the success of Impressionism and the
experiments of *Art Nouveau, page* 412. The pioneers of this
movement of liberation, notably Franz Cizek (1865-1946) in
Vienna, wanted the children's talent to unfold in freedom till
they were ready for the appreciation of artistic standards.
The results he achieved were so spectacular that the originality
and charm of children's work became the envy of trained
artists, *page* 443. In addition psychologists came to value the
sheer pleasure which children experience in messing about
with paint and plasticine. It was in the art class that the ideal
of 'self-expression' was first appreciated by large numbers.
Today we use the term 'child art' as a matter of course without
even realizing that it contradicts all the notions of art held by
previous generations. Most members of the public have been
conditioned by this education, which has taught them a
new tolerance. Many of them have tasted the satisfaction of
free creativity and practise painting as a relaxation. This rapid
increase in the number of amateurs must affect art in many
different ways. While it has fostered an interest that artists
must welcome, many professionals are also eager to stress the
difference between an artist's handling of paint and an
amateur's. The mystique of the expert brushstroke may have
something to do with this.

7

It is here that we may conveniently list the seventh factor, which could also have been listed as the first – the spread of photography as a rival to painting. Not that the painting of the past ever aimed entirely and exclusively at the imitation of reality. But as we have seen, *pages 464-5*, the link with nature provided some kind of anchorage, a challenging problem that kept the best minds among artists busy for centuries and provided for the critics at least a superficial standard. It is true that photography dates back to the early nineteenth century. There are many millions of camera owners in every country and the number of colour photographs produced during every vacation period must run into billions. There are bound to be many lucky shots among these which may be as beautiful and as evocative as many average landscape paintings, and as telling and memorable as many a painted portrait. No wonder therefore that 'photographic' has become a dirty word among painters and teachers of art appreciation. The reason they sometimes give for their rejection may be fanciful and unjust, but the argument that art must now explore alternatives to the representation of nature is plausible to many.

8

We must not forget here, as our eighth element in the situation, that there are large parts of the world where artists are forbidden to explore alternatives. The theories of Marxism as they were interpreted in the former Soviet Union regarded all the experimentation of twentieth-century art as a mere symptom of the decay of capitalist society. The symptom of a healthy communist society was an art that celebrated the joys of productive work by painting cheerful tractor drivers or sturdy miners. Naturally this attempt to control the arts from above has made us all aware of the real blessings we owe to

our freedom. It also, unfortunately, drew the arts into the
political arena and turned them into a weapon in the Cold War.
Official sponsorship of extremist rebels in the Western camp
might not have been so eager had it not been for the
opportunity to drive home this very real contrast between
a free society and a dictatorship.

9

Here we come to the ninth element in the new situation.
There is indeed a lesson to be drawn from the contrast
between the drab uniformity of totalitarian countries and the
gay variety of a free society. Everybody who watches the
contemporary scene with sympathy and understanding must
acknowledge that even the eagerness of the public for novelty
and its responsiveness to the whims of fashion add zest to our
lives. It has stimulated inventiveness and an adventurous gaiety
in art and design for which the older generation may well
envy the young. We may sometimes be tempted to dismiss the
latest success in abstract painting as 'pleasant curtain material',
but we should not forget how exhilarating the rich and
varied curtain materials have become through the stimulus
of these abstract experiments. The new tolerance, the
readiness of critics and manufacturers to give new ideas and
new colour combinations a chance, has certainly enriched
our surroundings, and even the rapid turnover of fashions
contributes to the fun. It is in this spirit, I believe, that many
young people look at what they feel to be the art of their
own time without worrying overmuch about the mystical
obscurities contained in the preface to the exhibition
catalogue. This is as it should be. Provided the enjoyment is
genuine we can be glad if some ballast is being discarded.

The danger in these surrenders to fashion, on the
other hand, need hardly be emphasized. It lies in the threat to

that very freedom we enjoy. Not from the police, to be sure, and that is something to be grateful for; but from the pressures of conformism, the fear of falling behind, the fear of being considered 'square' or whatever the latest equivalent label may be. Only recently a newspaper told its readers to take note of a current one-man show if they wanted to 'stay in the art race'. There is no such race, but if there were we should do well to remember the fable of the tortoise and the hare.

It is indeed astonishing to what extent the attitude we saw Harold Rosenberg describe as 'the tradition of the new', *pages 475-6*, has come to be taken for granted in contemporary art. Anyone who questions it is considered a 'flat earther' who denies the obvious. Yet is is well to remember that this idea that artists must be in the vanguard of progress is by no means shared by all cultures. Many ages and many parts of the globe knew nothing of this obsession. The craftsman who made the beautiful rug, *figure 91*, would have been surprised to be asked to invent a new pattern never seen before. All he wished to do, no doubt, was to produce a fine rug. Would it not be a blessing if this attitude also became more widespread among us?

It is true that the Western world owes a great deal to the ambition of artists to surpass each other. Without this ambition there would have been no 'story of art'. And yet it is more than ever necessary to remember that art differs from science and technology. It is true that the history of art can sometimes trace the steps in the solution of certain artistic problems, and this book has tried to make these intelligible. But it has also tried to show that in art we cannot speak of 'progress' as such, because every gain in one respect is likely to be offset by a loss in another, *pages 195-6, 412-5*. This is as true of the present as it was of the past. It stands to reason, for instance, that the welcome gain in tolerance will also result in a loss of standards and that the search for new thrills must also endanger that patience that made art-lovers of the past woo the acknowledged masterpieces till they yielded something of their secret. Granted that this respect for the past had its drawbacks where it led to a neglect of living artists. We have no guarantee that our new responsiveness will not lead us to neglect a real genius among us who forges ahead regardless of fashion and publicity. Moreover, the absorption in the present could easily cut us off from our heritage if we came to regard the art of the past as the mere foil against which the new conquests acquire meaning. Paradoxically, both museums and books on art history may increase this danger, for by grouping totem poles, Greek statues, cathedral windows, Rembrandts and Jackson Pollocks together we too easily give the impression that all this is Art with a capital A though dating from different periods. The history of art only begins to make sense when we see why it is not; and why painters and sculptors responded to different situations, institutions and fashions in very different ways. It is for this reason that I have concentrated in this chapter on the situation, institutions and beliefs to which artists today are likely to respond. As for the future – who can tell?

Another turning of the tide

Since I concluded the preceding section in 1966 with a question, it was felt that I should also give an answer after the future had once again turned into the past and another edition of this book was in preparation in 1989. Certainly the 'tradition of the new' that had maintained such a firm hold on twentieth-century art had not weakened in the intervening period. But for that very reason it was sensed that the Modern Movement had become so universally accepted and so respectable that it was by now 'old hat'. Surely it was time for another turning of the tide. It was this expectation that crystallized in the new slogan of 'Post-Modernism'. Nobody claims that this is a good term. After all, it says nothing more than that the adherents of this trend consider 'Modernism' to be a thing of the past.

Having quoted the opinions of respected critics in the preceding section so as to document the unquestioned victory of the Modern Movement, *pages 475-6*, I should like here to cite a few passages from the Editorial of December 1987 of the journal published by the National Museum of Modern Art in Paris (*Les Cahiers du Musée National d'Art Moderne*, editor Yves Michaud):

> The symptoms of a post-modern period are not difficult
> to perceive. The menacing cubes of the modern suburban housing
> projects tend to transform themselves into constructions which
> may still be cubes, but are now covered with stylized ornaments.
> The puritan or simply boring asceticism of the various forms of
> abstract painting ('hard-edged' or 'colour field' or 'post-painterly')
> has been replaced by allegorical or mannerist paintings, frequently
> figurative ... full of allusions to tradition and mythology. In
> sculpture composite objects, 'high-tech' or mocking, have replaced
> the works which searched for the truth of material or questioned
> three-dimensionality. Artists no longer recoil from narration, from
> preaching or moralizing ... At the same time the administrators
> and bureaucrats of art, museum people, art historians and critics
> have lost or abandoned their firm belief in the history of forms
> which they had recently identified with abstract American
> painting. They have become open, for good or for ill, to a diversity
> which no longer cares for avant-gardes.

On 11 October 1988, John Russell Taylor wrote in *The Times*:

> Fifteen or twenty years ago we did know fairly clearly what we
> meant by 'modern' and what sort of thing, very roughly, we might
> expect to see if we went to a show which advertised its allegiance
> to the avant-garde. But now, of course, we live in a pluralist world
> where often the most advanced, being probably Post-Modern, is
> likely to look the most traditional and retrograde.

It would be easy to quote texts by other distinguished critics
which read like speeches at the graveside of Modern Art. True,
we may recall Mark Twain's notorious quip that the news of
his death was much exaggerated, but there is no denying that
the old certainties have been somewhat shaken.

The attentive reader of this book will not be too
surprised at this development. I remarked in the Preface that
'each generation is at some point in revolt against the
standards of its fathers; each work of art derives its appeal to
contemporaries not only from what it does but also from what
it leaves undone', *page 11*. If that was true at the time it could
only mean that the triumph of Modernism which I described
could not last for ever. The very idea of progress, of the avant-
garde, would seem a little trivial and boring to newcomers
to the scene, and who knows whether this book has not also
contributed to this altered mood?

The term Post-Modernism was introduced into the
discussion in 1975 by Charles Jencks, a young architect who
was tired of the doctrine of functionalism, which was
identified with modern architecture and which I discussed
and criticized on *pages 431-2*. I then said that the doctrine
'has helped us to get rid of much unnecessary and tasteless
knick-knackery with which the nineteenth-century ideas of
Art had cluttered up our cities' but that, like all slogans,

it rested on an over-simplification. Admittedly decoration can be trivial and tasteless, but it can also give us pleasure, a pleasure which the 'puritans' of the Modern Movement wished to deny the public. If such decoration now shocked the older critics, so much the better, for to be 'shocking' had, after all, been accepted by them as a sign of originality. It is in the nature of things that, like Functionalism, the application of playful forms can be sensible or frivolous, according to the talents of the designer.

In any case, if the reader looks back from figure 400 to figure 364, it will come as no surprise that the 1976 design for a skyscraper in New York by Philip Johnson (1906-2005) caused quite a stir, not only among critics but even in the daily press. Instead of the usual square boxes with flat roofs, the design harks back to the ancient device of the pediment, faintly reminiscent of Leon Battista Alberti's façade of about 1460, figure 162. This defiant departure from pure functionalism appealed to the industrialists I mentioned in the preceding section who want to demonstrate that they are going with the times, *pages 478-9*, and for obvious reasons this is also true of museum directors. The Clore Gallery by James Stirling (1926-92) housing the Turner Collection of the London Tate Gallery, figure 401, is a case in point. The architect has rejected the austere and forbidding aspect of buildings like the Bauhaus, figure 365, in favour of something lighter, more colourful and more inviting.

It is not only the external aspect of many museums that has changed, but also the exhibits on view. A short time ago all forms of nineteenth-century art against which the Modern Movement rebelled were condemned unseen; in particular the official art of the Salon was banished to the cellars of museums. I ventured to suggest on *page 385* that this attitude was unlikely to last and that the time would come when these works would be rediscovered. Even so it came as a surprise to most of us when a new museum was recently opened in Paris, the Musée d'Orsay, housed in a former Art Nouveau railway station, in which conservative and modern paintings are shown side by side to enable visitors to make up their own minds and to revise old prejudices. Many found to their surprise that it was no disgrace for a painting to illustrate an anecdote or to celebrate an incident of history. It could be done well or badly.

It was only to be expected that this new tolerance should also affect the outlook of practising artists. In 1966 I ended the preceding section with a tailpiece I took from the New Yorker magazine, figure 402. In a way the question which the exasperated woman is seen asking the bearded painter foreshadows the altered mood of today, and no wonder. It has been obvious for some time that what I called the triumph of modernism landed the non-conformists in a contradiction. It was quite understandable that young art students felt provoked by conventional views of art to produce 'anti-art', but as soon as anti-art received official backing, it became art with a capital A and what was left to be defied?

Architects, as we have seen, might still hope to make an impact by departing from functionalism, but what is loosely called 'modern painting' never adopted such a single principle. All that the movements and trends that rose to prominence in the twentieth century had in common was their rejection of the study of natural appearances. Not that all artists of the period were willing to make this break, but the majority of critics were convinced that only the most radical departures from tradition could lead to progress. The quotations from recent comments on the present situation in art with which I opened this section indicate precisely that this conviction has lost ground. It is a pleasant side effect of this increase in tolerance that the sharp contrasts between Western and Eastern societies in their attitude to art, *pages 483-4*, have markedly mellowed. There is a much greater diversity of critical opinion today which gives many more artists a chance of recognition. Some of them have returned to figurative art and (as the preceding extract says) 'no longer recoil from narration, from preaching or moralizing'. It was this also which John Russell Taylor meant, *page 488*, when he spoke of a 'pluralist world where often the most advanced … is likely to look the most traditional …'

Not all of the artists today who enjoy this new-found right to diversity would accept the label of 'Post-Modern'. It is for this reason that I have preferred to speak of 'an altered mood' rather than of a new style. It is always misleading to think of styles as following each other like soldiers on parade. Admittedly readers and writers of books on art history might prefer such a tidy arrangement, but it is now more generally recognized that artists have a right to go their own way. Thus it is no longer as true as it was in 1966 that 'if anybody needs a champion today it is the artist who shuns rebellious gestures', *page 475*. A notable example is the painter Lucian Freud (born 1922), who never rejected the study of natural appearances. His painting of 'Two plants', *figure 403*, may make one think of Albrecht Dürer's 'Great piece of turf' of 1502, *figure 221*. Both show the artist engrossed in the beauty of ordinary plants, but while Dürer's watercolour was a study for his private use, Freud's large oil painting is a work in its own right that now hangs in the Tate Gallery in London.

I also mentioned in the previous section that to teachers of art appreciation the word 'photographic' had become a term of abuse, *page 483*. Meanwhile, interest in photography has grown enormously and collectors vie with each other to obtain prints of the works of the leading photographers, past and

present. Indeed it may be argued that a photographer such
as Henri Cartier-Bresson (1908-2004) enjoyed as much esteem
in his later years as any painter of his time. Many a tourist
may have snapped a view of a picturesque Italian village but it
is most unlikely that any of them succeeded in producing
such a convincing image as Cartier-Bresson did of Aquila degli
Abruzzi, figure 404. With his miniature camera at the ready,
Cartier-Bresson experienced the excitement of the huntsman
lying in wait, finger on the trigger, for the precise moment to
'shoot'. But he has also confessed to a 'passion for geometry',
which made him carefully compose any scene within his
viewfinder. The result is that we feel we are in the picture,
that we sense the coming and going of the women carrying
loaves up the steep incline, and remain captivated by the
composition – of the railings and the steps, the church
and the distant houses – which rivals in interest many more
contrived paintings.

In recent years artists have also taken up the medium of
photography for the creation of novel effects that had previously
been the preserve of painters. Thus David Hockney (born 1937)
has enjoyed using his camera for multiple images somewhat
reminiscent of Cubist paintings such as Picasso's picture of
'Violin and grapes' of 1912, figure 374. His portrait of his mother,
figure 405, is a mosaic of various shots taken from slightly
different angles and also records the movement of her head.
One might expect such a combination to result in an incoherent
jumble but the portrait is certainly evocative. After all, when we
look at a person our eyes never stand still for any length of time
and the image we form in our minds when we think of a
person is always composite. It is this experience which Hockney
has somehow captured in his photographic experiments.

It looks at the present moment as if this conciliation
between the photographer and the artist will increase in

importance in years to come. To be sure, even painters of the nineteenth century made a good deal of use of photographs, but now the practice is acknowledged and widespread in the search for novel effects.

What these recent developments have brought home to us again is that there are tides of taste in art no less than there are tides of fashion in clothing or decoration. It is undeniable that many of the old masters whom we admire and indeed many styles of the past failed to be appreciated by very sensitive and knowledgeable critics of former generations. This is certainly true. No critic and no historian can be entirely unbiased, but I think it is wrong to draw the conclusion that artistic values are altogether relative. Granted that we rarely stop to look for the objective merits of works or styles that have failed immediately to appeal to us, this does not prove that our appreciations are entirely subjective. I still remain convinced that we can recognize mastery in art, and this recognition has little to do with our personal likes and dislikes. One reader of this book may like Raphael and dislike Rubens or the other way round, but the book would have failed in its purpose if its readers did not also recognize that both of them were towering masters.

The changing past

Our knowledge of history is always incomplete. There are always new facts to be discovered which may change our image of the past. The story of art which is in the reader's hands was never meant to be anything other than selective, but as I originally said in my note on art books, 'even a simple book like this may be described as a report on the work of a large team of historians, living and dead, who have helped to clarify the outlines of periods, styles and personalities.'

It may indeed be worth while briefly to ask when the
works on which I based this story came to our knowledge. It
was in the Renaissance that lovers of antiquity began to search
systematically for relics of classical art; the discovery of the
Laocoön, figure 69, in 1506 and of the Apollo Belvedere, page
104, figure 64, in the same period made a deep impression on
artists and art-lovers. In the seventeenth century the early
Christian catacombs, figure 84, were systematically explored for
the first time in the wake of the new religious fervour of the
Counter Reformation. Then there followed in the eighteenth
century the discovery of Herculaneum (1719), Pompeii (1748)
and the other cities which had been buried under the ashes
of Vesuvius and which yielded over the years so many fine
paintings, figures 70-1. Strangely enough, it was not until the
eighteenth century that the beauty of Greek vase paintings was
first appreciated, many of which were discovered in tombs
on Italian soil, figures 48-9, 58.

Napoleon's campaign in Egypt (1801) opened up that
country to archaeologists who succeeded in deciphering
the hieroglyphic script, enabling scholars gradually to
understand the meaning and function of these monuments
which became the object of eager search by many nations,
figures 31-7. Greece in the early nineteenth century was still part
of the Turkish empire and not easily accessible to travellers.
A mosque had been erected inside the Parthenon on the
Acropolis and the classical carvings had long been neglected
when the British Ambassador to Constantinople, Lord Elgin,
obtained permission to take some of the sculptures to
England, figures 56-7. Shortly afterwards, in 1820, the Venus of
Milo, figure 65, was found by accident on the Island of Melos
and taken to the Louvre in Paris, where it acquired instant
fame. In the middle of the century the British diplomat and
archaeologist Sir Austen Layard played a leading part in

exploring the sands of Mesopotamia, figure 45. In 1870 a German amateur, Heinrich Schliemann, set out to look for the places celebrated in the Homeric poems and discovered the tombs of Mycenae, figure 41. By that time archaeologists no longer liked to leave this work to non-professionals. Governments and national academies parcelled out the available sites and organized systematic excavations, often still on the principle that finders would be keepers. It was then that German teams began to uncover the remains of Olympia, where there had been only unsystematic digs by the French before, figure 52, and found the famous statue of Hermes in 1875, figures 62-3. Four years later another German mission uncovered the altar of Pergamon, figure 68, and took it to Berlin; in 1892 the French began to excavate ancient Delphi, figures 47, 53-4, having had to remove a whole Greek village for the purpose.

Even more exciting is the story of the first discovery of prehistoric cave paintings in the late nineteenth century, for when those of Altamira, figure 19, were first published in 1880 only a minority of scholars were prepared to admit that the history of art had to be pushed back by many thousand years. It goes without saying that our knowledge of the art of Mexico and South America, figures 27, 29-30, Northern India, figures 80-1, and ancient China, figures 93-4, is no less due to men of great enterprise and learning than were the discoveries in 1905 of the Viking tombs at Oseberg, figure 101.

Among finds subsequently made in the Middle East and illustrated in this book, I would like to mention the Victory Monument, figure 44, found by the French in Persia around 1900, the Hellenistic portraits found in Egypt, figure 79, the discoveries at Tell-el-Amarna made by English and German teams, figures 39-40, and, of course, the sensational treasure trove from the tomb of Tutankhamun, found by Lord Carnarvon and Howard Carter in 1922, figure 42. The ancient

Sumerian burial grounds at Ur, *figure 43*, were explored by
Leonard Woolley beginning in 1926. The most recent
discoveries I was able to include when I wrote this book were
the murals of the synagogue of Dura-Europos, unearthed
in 1932-3, *figure 82*, the caves of Lascaux, found accidentally in
1940, *figures 20-1*, and at least one of the wonderful bronze
heads from Nigeria, *figure 23*, of which more examples have
meanwhile come to light.

Incomplete as is this list, it contains one deliberate
omission: the finds made by Sir Arthur Evans around 1900
on the island of Crete. The attentive reader may have noticed
that these great discoveries are indeed mentioned in my text,
page 57, but that for once I departed from the principle of
illustrating what I discussed. Those who have visited Crete may
well have resented this apparent lapse, for they would surely
have been impressed there by the palace of Knossos and the
great murals on its walls. I, too, was impressed by them, but I
hesitated to illustrate them in this book because I could not
help wondering how much of what we saw was also seen by
the ancient Cretans. No blame attaches to their discoverer
who, intent on evoking the lost splendours of the palace, asked
the Swiss painter Émile Gilliéron and his son to reconstruct
the murals from the fragments that had been found. These
paintings certainly give more pleasure to most visitors in their
present form than if they had been left in the state in which
they were found, but nagging doubts persist.

Hence it was particularly welcome that in excavations
begun in 1967 by the Greek archaeologist Spyros Marinatos
similar murals were found in the ruins on the island of
Santorini (ancient Thera) which are much better preserved.
The figure of a fisherman, *figure 406*, fits in well with
the impression I had derived from the earlier finds, when I
mentioned their free and graceful style, which is much less

rigid than that of Egyptian art. These artists were obviously less bound by religious conventions and though they did not anticipate the systematic explorations of the Greeks in the rendering of foreshortening, let alone of light and shade, their pleasing creations should not now be omitted from the story of art.

In discussing that great period of discovery in ancient Greece I was anxious to remind the reader that our picture of Greek art is somewhat distorted because we have so largely to rely for our knowledge of the famous bronze statues made by such masters as Myron on later copies produced in marble for Roman collectors, figure 55. It was for this reason that I selected the Delphi charioteer with its inset eyes, figures 53-4, rather than more famous works, to counter any impression on the part of the reader that there was something bland in the beauty of Greek statuary. Meanwhile in August 1972 a pair of figures, dating no doubt from the fifth century BC, were fished out of the sea near the village of Riace, not far from the southern tip of Italy, and they can help to make this point even more forcefully, figures 408-9. The life-size bronzes of two heroes or athletes must have been carried off from Greece on a ship by Romans and were probably jettisoned during a storm. Archaeologists have not yet given their final verdict about their likely date or place of origin, but their appearance suffices to convince us of their artistic quality and their impressive vigour. There is no mistaking the mastery in the modelling of these muscular bodies and these virile bearded heads. The care with which the artist has rendered the eyes, lips and even teeth in other materials, figure 407, might have shocked those lovers of Greek art who always looked for what they called the 'ideal', but like all great works of art these new finds refute the dogmas of critics, pages 31-2, and show triumphantly that the more we generalize about art the more likely we are to go wrong.

There is one gap in our knowledge which every lover
of Greek art feels most keenly. We do not know the works
of their great painters about which the ancient authors wrote
with such enthusiasm. The name of Apelles, who lived at the
time of Alexander the Great, for instance, remained proverbial,
but we have no work by his hand. All we used to know of
Greek paintings are their reflections on Greek pottery,
figures 46, 48-9, 58, and the copies or variants found on Roman
or Egyptian soil, figures 70-2, 79. This situation has now been
dramatically changed thanks to the discovery of a royal tomb
at Vergina in northern Greece in what was once Macedonia,
the homeland of Alexander the Great. There is every indication,
in fact, that the body found in the main tomb chamber is
that of Alexander's father, King Philip II, who was murdered in
336 BC. The precious finds made by Professor Manolis
Andronikos in the 1970s include not only furnishings,
jewellery and even fabrics, but also murals evidently made by
real masters. One of the murals, on the outer wall of a smaller
side chamber, represents the ancient myth of the Rape of
Persephone (or Proserpina, as the Romans called her).
According to the story, Pluto, the ruler of the Underworld,
during one of his rare visits to the upper regions, saw a girl
picking spring flowers with her companions. He desired
and seized her and carried her off to his nether kingdom,
where she ruled as his spouse, though permitted to return to
her grieving mother Demeter (or Ceres) during the months
of spring and summer. This theme, which is evidently
fitting for the decoration of a tomb, is the subject of the wall-
painting of which figure 410 shows the central section.
The whole is described by Professor Andronikos in a lecture
on 'The Royal Tombs at Vergina' which he gave at the British
Academy in November 1979:

The composition is developed on one surface, 3.5 metres long and
1.01 high, with exceptional freedom, daring and ease of design.
In the top left corner something like lightning can be discerned
[Zeus's thunderbolt]: Hermes runs in front of the chariot with his
caduceus [wand] in his hand. The chariot, which is drawn by four
white steeds, is red; Pluto, holding the sceptre and reins in his
right hand, has seized Persephone by the waist with his left one.
She stretches out her arms and throws back her body in despair.
The god has his right foot inside the chariot while the sole of the
left one still touches the ground, where one can see the flowers
which Persephone and her friend Kyane were gathering … Behind
the chariot Kyane is portrayed on her knees, terrified.

The detail shown here may not be very easy to make out at
first, except for the beautifully painted head of Pluto, the
foreshortened wheel of his chariot and the fluttering drapery
of his victim's garment; but after a while we also see
Proserpina's half-naked body gripped by Pluto's left hand,
with her arms stretched out in a gesture of despair. The group
gives us at least an inkling of the power and passion of which
these masters of the fourth century BC were capable.

While we were thus learning about the tomb of the
powerful King of Macedonia who really laid the foundations
through his policy for the vast empire of his son Alexander the
Great, archaeologists in the north of China near the city of
Sian (Hsian) made a most startling discovery close to the tomb
of an even more powerful ruler – the first Emperor of China,
whose name is sometimes spelt Shi Hwang-ti but whom
the Chinese now prefer us to call Qin Shi Huangdi. This
formidable warlord, who ruled from 221 to 210 BC (about
a hundred years after Alexander the Great), is known to
historians as the man who first united China and who built
the Great Wall in order to protect his domains against the

incursions of nomads from the West. We say 'he' built it, but we should really say that he made his subjects erect this enormous line of fortifications – the remark is relevant because the new finds show that there must still have been enough hands to spare to toil on an even more extraordinary enterprise, the creation of what has become known as his 'terracotta army', formation after formation of life-sized soldiers of baked clay, arrayed around his tomb, which has not yet been opened, figure 411.

Writing of the Egyptian pyramids, figure 31, in this volume, I reminded the reader of the enormous demands these burials must have made on the population, and of the religious beliefs which must have prompted these incredible enterprises. I mentioned that one Egyptian word for sculptor was 'he who keeps alive', and that the statuary in the tombs were perhaps substitutes for the servants and slaves who were once sacrificed to accompany their powerful masters to the land of the dead. I even mentioned in discussing Chinese tombs of the Han period (the one following the rule of Shi Huangdi) that here burial customs were somewhat reminiscent of those of the Egyptians; but nobody could have imagined a single man commanding his craftsmen to fashion an army of some seven thousand men complete with their horses, weapons, uniforms and trappings. Nor could anyone have known that the vivid portrayal we admired in the head of a Lohan, figure 96, was here practised twelve hundred years earlier on this astounding scale. Like the newly discovered Greek statues, these images of soldiers were also made more lifelike by the application of colour, traces of which are still visible, figure 412. Yet all this skill was not intended to arouse the admiration of us mortals. It was to serve the purpose of that self-appointed superman who probably could not bear the thought that there was one enemy whose power he could not break – Death.

It so happens that the last of the new discoveries I wish
to introduce also has connections with that universal belief
in the power of images, to which I alluded in the first chapter,
called 'Strange beginnings'. I am referring to the irrational
hatred images can provoke if they are believed to embody
hostile forces. Much of the statuary of the Cathedral of Notre-
Dame in Paris, figures 122, 125, fell victim to this kind of hatred
during the time of the French Revolution, pages 369-70. Looking
at the picture of the Cathedral's façade, figure 125, we can
discern the horizontal row of figures over the three porches.
These were meant to represent kings of the Old Testament,
and thus they were shown with crowns on their heads. Alas,
they were later believed to portray kings of France and
inevitably incurred the wrath of the revolutionaries – they
were decapitated like Louis XVI. What we see on the building
today is the work of a nineteenth-century restorer, Viollet-
le-Duc, who devoted his life and energies to returning
the medieval buildings of France to their pristine form, from
motives not unlike those of Sir Arthur Evans, who had the
damaged murals of Knossos restored.

Clearly the loss of these statues made for the Cathedral
of Paris around 1230 was and remains a serious gap in our
knowledge – and so art historians have had reason to rejoice
at the find made in April 1977 when workmen digging
foundations for a bank in the centre of Paris came across a
buried heap of no fewer than 364 fragments which had
obviously been dumped there after their destruction in the
eighteenth century, figure 413. Sadly damaged as are the heads
of these figures, they still merit study and contemplation for
the traces of their craftsmanship and their air of dignity and
repose, which is reminiscent of the earlier statuary at Chartres,
figure 127, and that of the roughly contemporary cathedral
of Strasbourg, figure 129. Strangely enough, their destruction

has helped to preserve a feature we have remarked on in two other cases – they, too, showed traces of colour and gilding at the time of their discovery, traces which may not survive further exposure to the light. It is indeed probable that other monuments of medieval sculpture, no less than much of medieval architecture, figure 124, was originally coloured, and that like our ideas about Greek sculpture, those about the appearance of medieval works may well be in need of adjustment. But is not this constant need for revision one of the thrills of the study of the past?

Plates

1

Peter Paul Rubens
Portrait of his son Nicholas,
c.1620

2

Albrecht Dürer
Portrait of his mother, 1514

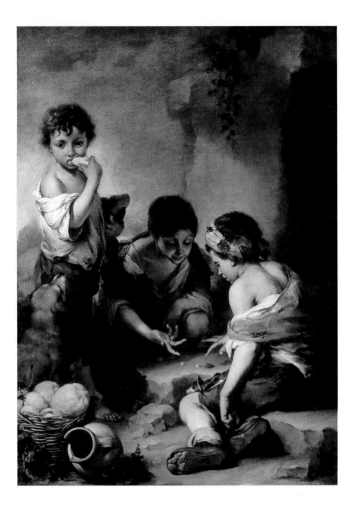

3

Bartolomé Esteban Murillo
Street arabs, c. 1670-5

4

Pieter de Hooch
*Interior with a woman
peeling apples,* 1663

5

6

Melozzo da Forlì
Angel, c. 1480

Hans Memling
Angel, c. 1490

7

Guido Reni
Christ crowned with thorns,
c. 1639-40

8

Tuscan master
Head of Christ, c. 1175 - 1225

9

Albrecht Dürer
Hare, 1502

10

Rembrandt van Rijn
Elephant, 1637

11

Pablo Picasso
Hen with chicks,
1941-2

233.38.

Pablo Picasso
Cockerel, 1938

13

Théodore Géricault
Horse-racing at Epsom, 1821

14

Eadweard Muybridge
Galloping horse in motion,
1872

15

Caravaggio
Saint Matthew, 1602

16

Caravaggio
Saint Matthew, 1602

17

Raphael
Virgin in the meadow, 1505-6

18

Raphael
*Four studies for the 'Virgin
in the meadow', 1505-6*

19

Bison, c. 15,000 – 10,000 BC

20

Horse, c. 15,000 - 10,000 BC

21

Cave at Lascaux, France,
c. 15,000 - 10,000 BC

22

Lintel from a Maori chieftain's
house, early 19th century

23

*Head of a Negro, probably
representing a ruler (Oni),
from Ife, Nigeria,
12th-14th century*

24

Oro, God of War, from Tahiti
18th century

25

Ritual mask from the Papuan
Gulf region, New Guinea,
c. 1880

26

Model of a nineteenth-century
Haida chieftain's house,
north-west coast Indians

27

*Head of the death-god,
from a stone Mayan altar
found at Copan, Honduras,
c. 500-600 AD*

28

Inuit dance mask from *Alaska*,
c. 1880

29

Vessel in the form of a one-eyed man, found in the Chicanná Valley, Peru, c.250–550 AD

30

Tlaloc, the Aztec rain-god,
14th-15th century

31

The Pyramids of Giza,
c. 2613-2563 BC

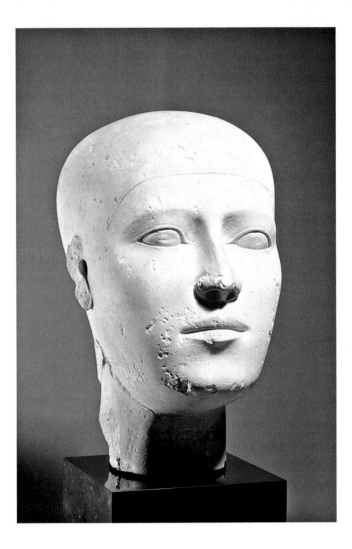

32

Portrait head,
c.2551-2528 BC

33

The garden of Nebamun,
c. 1400 BC

34

Portrait of Hesire, from
a wooden door in his tomb,
c.2778–2723 BC

35

Wall-painting from
the tomb of Khnumhotep,
c.1900 BC

36

Detail of figure 35

37

Birds in an acacia bush
Detail of figure 35

The jackal-faced god Anubis
supervising the weighing
of a dead man's heart, while
the ibis-headed messenger-god
Thoth on the right records
the result, c. 1285 BC

39

Amenophis IV (Akhnaten),
c. 1360 BC

Akhnaten and Nefertiti with
their children, c. 1345 BC

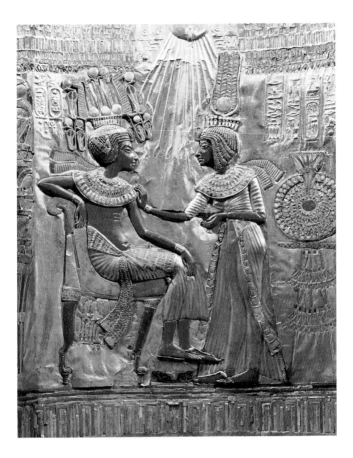

41

Dagger, c. 1600 BC

42

Tutankhamun and his wife,
c. 1330 BC

43

Fragment of a harp,
c. 2600 BC

44

Monument of King Naramsin,
c. 2270 BC

45

*Assyrian army besieging
a fortress*, c.883–859 BC

46

The mourning of the dead,
c.700 BC

47

Polymedes of Argos
The brothers Cleobis and Biton,
c.615-590 BC

48

*Achilles and Ajax playing
draughts*, c.540 BC

49

The warrior's leave-taking,
c. 510–500 BC

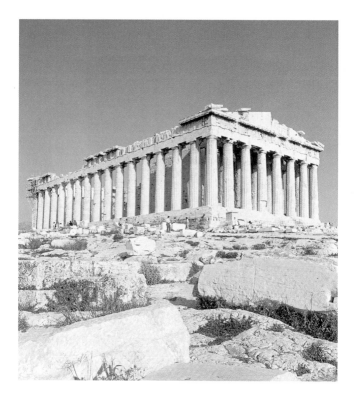

50

Iktinos
The Parthenon, Acropolis,
Athens, 447-432 BC

51

Athena Parthenos,
c.447-432 BC

52

Hercules carrying the heavens,
c.470-460 BC

53

Charioteer, c.475 BC

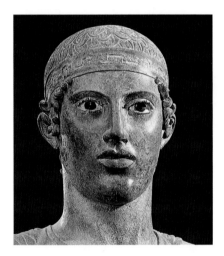

54

Detail of figure 53

55

Discobolos, c.450 BC

56

Charioteer, c.440 BC

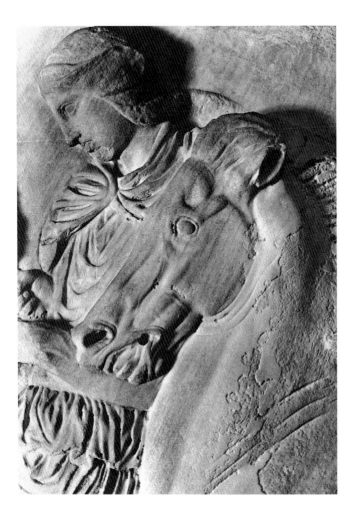

57

Horse and horseman,
c.440 BC

58

*Ulysses recognized by his old
nurse, 5th century* BC

59

Tombstone of Hegeso,
c.400 BC

60

The Erechtheion, Acropolis,
Athens, c.420-405 BC

61

Goddess of victory, 408 BC

62

Praxiteles
Hermes with the young Dionysus,
c.340 BC

63

Detail of figure 62

64

Apollo Belvedere, c. 350 BC

65

Venus of Milo, c. 200 BC

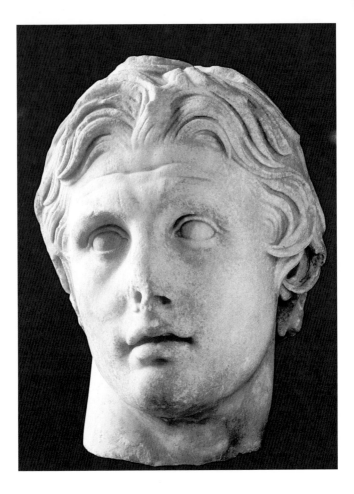

66

Head of Alexander the Great,
c. 325-300 BC

67

'Corinthian' capital,
c. 300 BC

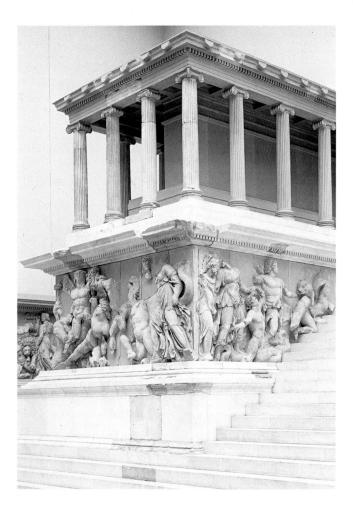

68

The altar of Zeus from
Pergamon, c. 164–156 BC

69

Hagesandros, Athenodoros
and Polydoros of Rhodes
Laocoön and his sons,
c. 175–50 BC

70

Maiden gathering flowers,
1st century AD

71

Head of a faun,
2nd century BC

72

Landscape, 1st century AD

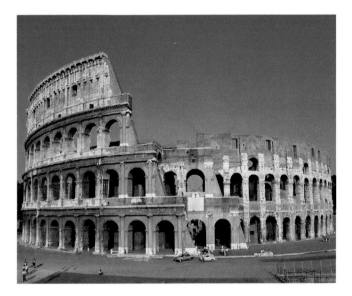

73

The Colosseum, Rome,
c.80 AD

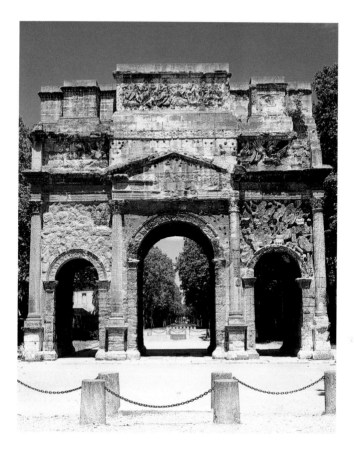

74

Triumphal arch of Tiberius,
Orange, Southern France,
C. 14-37 AD

75

Interior of the Pantheon, Rome,
c. 130 AD

76

Emperor Vespasian, c. 70 AD

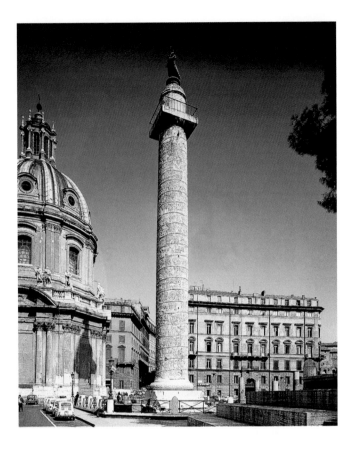

77

Trajan's Column, Rome,
c. 114 AD

78

Detail of figure 77; scenes
showing the fall of a town
(top), a battle against
the Dacians (centre) and
soldiers cutting corn
outside a fort (bottom)

79

Portrait of a man, c. 100 AD

80

Gautama (Buddha) leaving his
home, c. 2nd century AD

81

Head of the Buddha,
4th-5th century AD

82

Moses striking water from
the rock, 245-56 AD

83

*Christ with St Peter
and St Paul, c.389 AD*

84

The three men in the fiery
furnace, 3rd century AD

85

Portrait of an official from
Aphrodisias, c.400 AD

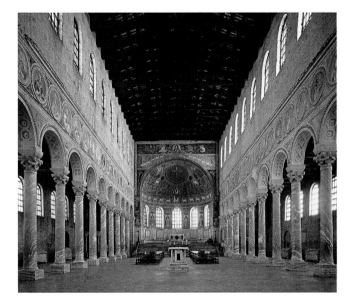

Basilica of S. Apollinare in
Classe, Ravenna, c. 530 AD

87

The Miracle of the Loaves
and Fishes, c. 520 AD

88

Madonna and Child on
a curved throne, c. 1280

89

Christ as Ruler of the
Universe, the Virgin and Child,
and saints, c. 1190

90

Court of Lions, Alhambra,
Granada, Spain, 1377

91

Persian carpet,
17th century

92

The Persian Prince Humay
meets the Chinese Princess
Humayun in her garden,
c. 1430-40

93

A reception, c. 150 AD

94

Winged beast, c.523 AD

故曰翼翼矜矜福所以興靜恭基自思榮顯所期

此之由

95

Husband reproving his wife,
c.400 AD

Head of a Lohan, c. 1000

玄
靄
雨
歇
澍
房
山

克
恭
為
茲
歡
畫
雨
山
禹
畫
克
恭
兩
小
斡
疎
本
也

97

Ma Yüan
Landscape in moonlight,
c.1200

98

Attributed to Kao K'o-kung
Landscape after rain, c.1300

99

Attributed to Liu Ts'ai
Three fishes, c. 1068-85

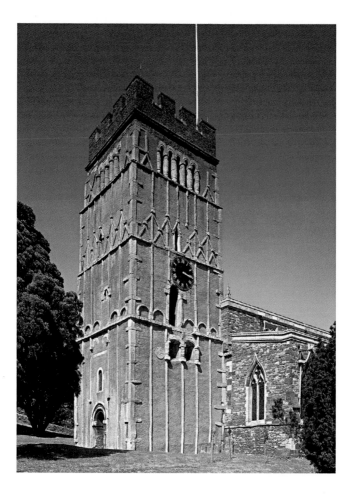

100

*Church of All Saints, Earls
Barton, Northamptonshire,*
c. 1000

101

Dragon's head, c.820 AD

St Luke, c. 750 AD

103

Page from the Lindisfarne
Gospels, c.698 AD

104

Aachen Cathedral,
consecrated in 805 AD

105

St Matthew, c.800 AD

106

St Matthew, c.830 AD

107

Christ washing the apostles'
feet, c. 1000

108

Adam and Eve after the Fall,
c.1015

109, 110

The Bayeux Tapestry, c. 1080

III

Benedictine church of
Murbach, Alsace, c. 1160

112

Tournai Cathedral, Belgium,
1171-1213

113, 114

Nave and west front of Durham
Cathedral, 1093-1128

115

Façade of the church of
St-Trophime, Arles, c. 1180

116

Christ in glory
Detail of figure 115

The Gloucester Candlestick,
c. 1104-13

118

Reiner van Huy
Font, 1107-18

119

The Annunciation, c. 1150

120

Saints Gereon, Willimarus,
Gall and the martyrdom of
St Ursula with her 11,000
maidens, 1137-47

121

The Annunciation,
mid-12th century

122

*Cathedral of Notre-Dame
of Paris, 1163-1250*

123

Robert de Luzarches
The nave of Amiens Cathedral,
c. 1218-47

124

Sainte-Chapelle, Paris, 1248

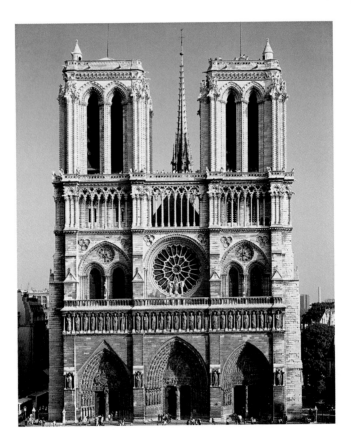

125

Cathedral of Notre-Dame
of Paris, 1163-1250

126

Porch of the north transept
of Chartres Cathedral, 1194

127

*Melchizedek, Abraham
and Moses,* 1194

128

Porch of the south transept
of Strasbourg Cathedral,
c. 1230

129

The Death of the Virgin

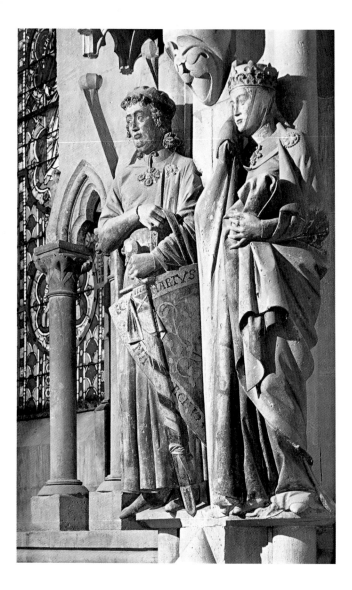

130

Ekkehart and Uta, c. 1260

131

The Entombment of Christ,
c. 1250 – 1300

132

Matthew Paris
An elephant and its keeper,
c. 1255

133

Nicola Pisano
*Annunciation, Nativity
and Shepherds*, 1260

134

Giotto di Bondone
Faith, c. 1305

135

Giotto di Bondone
The Mourning of Christ,
c. 1305

136

Detail of figure 135

137

West front of Exeter Cathedral,
c. 1350-1400

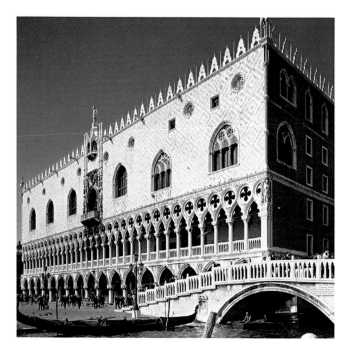

138

Doges' Palace, Venice,
begun in 1309

139

*Virgin and Child, c. 1324-39;
dedicated by Joan of
Evreux in 1339*

140

*Christ in the Temple;
a hawking party, c. 1310*

sūt ī mīquitatībʒ: non est qui fa
ciat bonum ※※※※※
Deus de celo pspexit super filios ho
minū: ut uideat si est intelligens

141

Simone Martini
& Lippo Memmi
The Annunciation, 1333

142

Peter Parler the Younger
Self-portrait, 1379-86

143 overleaf

St John the Baptist, St Edward
the Confessor and St Edmund
commend Richard II to Christ
(the Wilton Diptych), c. 1395

144

Paul and Jean de Limbourg
May, c. 1410

145

Antonio Pisanello
Studies of a monkey, c. 1430

146

Filippo Brunelleschi
Dome of Florence Cathedral,
c. 1420-36

147

Filippo Brunelleschi
Cappella Pazzi, Florence,
c. 1430

148

Filippo Brunelleschi
Interior of the Cappella Pazzi,
Florence, c. 1430

149

Masaccio
Holy Trinity with the Virgin,
St John and donors, c. 1425-8

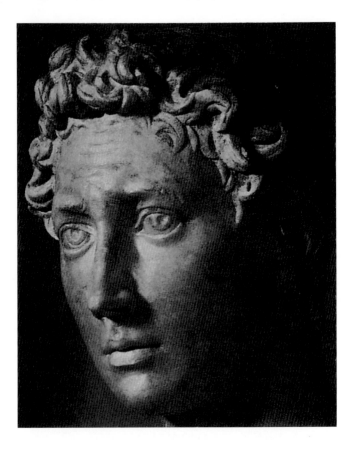

150

Detail of figure 151

151

Donatello
St George, c. 1415-16

152

Donatello
The Feast of Herod, 1423–7

153

Detail of figure 152

154

Claus Sluter
The prophets Daniel and
Isaiah, 1396-1404

Jan van Eyck
*The Ghent altarpiece
with wings folded*, 1432

156

The Ghent altarpiece
with wings open

157

Details of figure 156

158

Jan van Eyck
The betrothal of the Arnolfini,
1434

159, 160

Details of figure 158

161 *overleaf*

Konrad Witz
*The Miraculous Draught
of Fishes,* 1444

162

Leon Battista Alberti
Church of S. Andrea, Mantua,
c. 1460

163

Leon Battista Alberti
Palazzo Rucellai, Florence,
c. 1460

164

Lorenzo Ghiberti
The Baptism of Christ, 1427

165

Fra Angelico
The Annunciation, c. 1440

166

167

Paolo Uccello,
The Battle of San Romano,
c. 1450

Detail of figure 166

168

Benozzo Gozzoli
The Journey of the Magi to Bethlehem, c. 1459-63

169

Andrea Mantegna
*St James on the way to his
execution, c.* 1455

170

Piero della Francesca
Constantine's dream, c. 1460

171

Antonio Pollaiuolo
*The martyrdom of Saint
Sebastian, c. 1475*

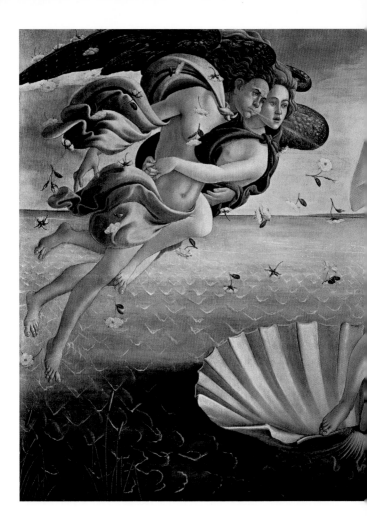

Sandro Botticelli
The birth of Venus, c. 1485

173

Gherardo di Giovanni
*The Annunciation and scenes
from Dante's 'Divine Comedy'*,
c. 1474-6

174

Courtyard of the Palace of
Justice (formerly Treasury),
Rouen, 1482

175

King's College Chapel,
Cambridge, begun in 1446

176

Stefan Lochner
The Virgin in the rose-bower,
c. 1440

Prologue de lacteur.
Et sont des anciens dont
on voulentiers lyre ouyr
et diligentement retenir.
Car ilz peuent valoir et
donner bon exemple aux hardis en armes

Jean Le Tavernier
Dedication page
to 'The Conquests of
Charlemagne', c. 1460

178

Jean Fouquet
Estienne Chevalier, Treasurer
of Charles VII of France,
with St Stephen, c. 1450

179

Rogier van der Weyden
The Descent from the Cross,
c. 1435

180

Hugo van der Goes
The Death of the Virgin,
c. 1480

181

Detail of figure 180

182

Veit Stoss
Altar of the church of
Our Lady, Cracow, 1477-89

183

Veit Stoss
Head of an apostle

184

The good man on his death-bed,
c. 1470

185

Martin Schongauer
The Holy Night, c. 1470-3

186
Caradosso
Foundation medal for the new
St Peter's, showing Bramante's
scheme for a huge dome, 1506

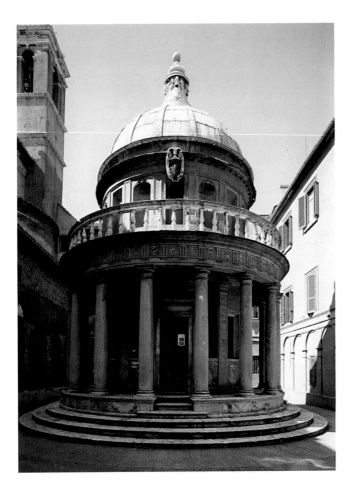

187

Donato Bramante
The Tempietto, church of
S. Pietro in Montorio, Rome,
1502

188

189

Andrea del Verrocchio
Bartolommeo Colleoni, 1479

Detail of figure 188

190

Leonardo da Vinci
Anatomical studies
(larynx and leg), 1510

191

The refectory of the monastery
of Sta Maria delle Grazie, Milan,
with Leonardo da Vinci's
'The Last Supper' on the end wall

192

Leonardo da Vinci
The Last Supper, 1495-8

193

Leonardo da Vinci
Mona Lisa, c. 1502

194

Detail of figure 193

195

Domenico Ghirlandaio
Birth of the Virgin, 1491

DEI GENITRIX VIRGO GAVDIVM ANNVNTIAVIT VNIVERSO · MVNDO ·

196

Sistine Chapel, Vatican

198

Michelangelo
Sistine Chapel ceiling,
1508-12

Michelangelo
Detail of the *Sistine*
Chapel ceiling

199

Michelangelo
*Study for the Libyan Sibyl on
the Sistine Chapel ceiling,*
c. 1510

201

Michelangelo
The dying slave, c. 1513

200

Michelangelo
The creation of Adam
Detail of figure 198

202

Perugino
*The Virgin appearing
to St Bernard*, c. 1490-4

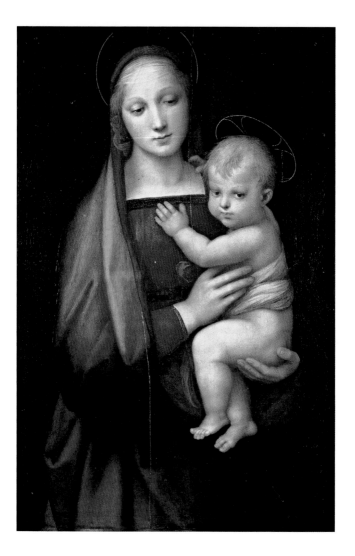

203

Raphael
Madonna del Granduca, c. 1505

204

Raphael
The nymph Galatea, c. 1512-14

205

Detail of figure 204

206

Raphael
*Pope Leo X with two
cardinals, 1518*

207

Jacopo Sansovino
Library of San Marco, Venice,
1536

208

Giovanni Bellini
Madonna with saints, 1505

209

Giorgione
The tempest, c. 1508

210

Titian
*Madonna with saints
and members of the
Pesaro family,* 1519-26

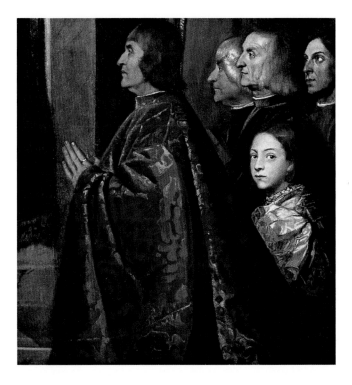

211

Detail of figure 210

212

Titian
Portrait of a man, the so-
called 'Young Englishman',
c. 1540-5

213

Detail of figure 212

214

Titian
*Pope Paul III with Alessandro
and Ottavio Farnese*, 1546

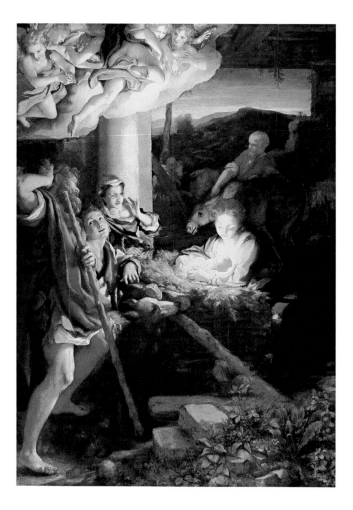

215

Correggio
The Holy Night, c. 1530

216

Correggio
The Assumption of the Virgin:
study for the cupola of Parma
Cathedral, c. 1526

217

Correggio
The *Assumption of the Virgin*

218

Pierre Sohier
Choir of the church of
St-Pierre, Caen, 1518-45

219

Jan Wallot and
Christian Sixdeniers
The Old Chancellery
('Le Greffe'), Bruges, 1535-7

220

Albrecht Dürer
*St Michael's fight against
the dragon*, 1498

221

Albrecht Dürer
Great piece of turf, 1503

222

Albrecht Dürer
The Nativity, 1504

223

Albrecht Dürer
Adam and Eve, 1504

Grünewald
The Crucifixion, 1515

Grünewald
The Resurrection, 1515

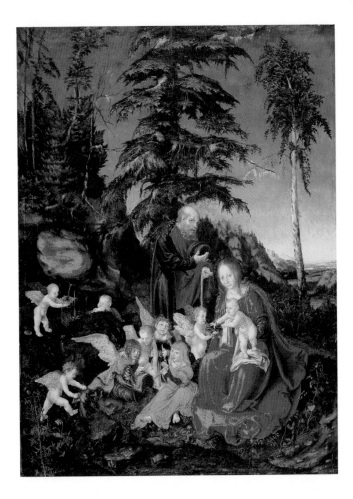

226

Lucas Cranach
*The rest on the Flight
into Egypt,* 1504

227

Albrecht Altdorfer
Landscape, c. 1526-8

228 *overleaf*

Mabuse
St Luke painting the Virgin,
c. 1515

229, 230

Hieronymus Bosch
Paradise and Hell, c. 1510

453.

232

Andrea Palladio
Villa Rotonda, near Vicenza,
1550

231

Federico Zuccaro
Window of the Palazzo Zuccari,
Rome, 1592

233

Benvenuto Cellini
Salt-cellar, 1543

234

Parmigianino
Madonna with the long neck,
1534-40

235

Giambologna
Mercury, 1580

Tintoretto
*The finding of St Mark's
remains*, c. 1562

237

Tintoretto
St George and the dragon,
c. 1555-8

238

El Greco
The opening of the Fifth Seal
of the Apocalypse, c. 1608-14

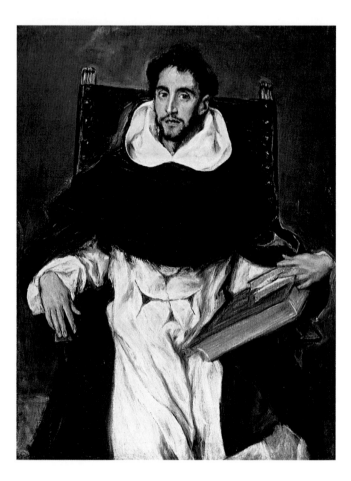

239

El Greco
Brother Hortensio Felix
Paravicino, 1609

240

Hans Holbein the Younger
*The Virgin and Child with the
family of Burgomaster Meyer,*
1528

241

Hans Holbein the Younger
*Anne Cresacre, Sir Thomas
More's daughter-in-law,* 1528

.X°. IVLII. ANNO.
.H. VIII. XXVIII.

ETATIS SVÆ
ANNO XXXIII.

242

Hans Holbein the Younger
Sir Richard Southwell, 1536

243

Hans Holbein the Younger
Georg Gisze, a German
merchant in London, 1532

244

Nicholas Hilliard
Young man among roses,
c. 1587

245

Pieter Bruegel the Elder
The painter and the buyer,
c. 1565

246

Pieter Bruegel the Elder
Peasant wedding, c. 1568

247

Detail of figure 246

248

Jean Goujon
Nymphs from the Fontaine
des Innocents, 1547-9

Cap.º Esgangarato.   Cap.º Cocodrillo

249

Jacques Callot
Two Italian clowns, c. 1622

250

Giacomo della Porta
Church of Il Gesù, Rome,
c. 1575-7

251

Annibale Carracci
The Virgin mourning Christ,
1599-1600

252

Caravaggio
Doubting Thomas, c. 1602-3

253

Guido Reni
Aurora, 1614

254

Nicolas Poussin
'Et in Arcadia ego', 1638-9

255

Claude Lorrain
Landscape with sacrifice
to Apollo, 1662-3

256

Peter Paul Rubens
*Virgin and Child enthroned
with saints, c.* 1627-8

257

Peter Paul Rubens
*Head of a child, probably the
artist's daughter Clara Serena,*
c. 1616

258

Peter Paul Rubens
Self-portrait, c. 1639

259

Peter Paul Rubens
*Allegory on the blessings
of peace*, 1629-30

260

Detail of figure 259

261

Anthony van Dyck
Charles I of England, c. 1635

262

Anthony van Dyck
*Lord John and Lord Bernard
Stuart, c. 1638*

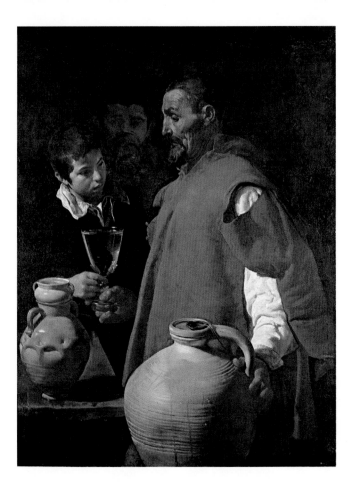

263

Diego Velázquez,
The water-seller of Seville,
c. 1619-20

264

Diego Velázquez
Pope Innocent X, 1649-50

265

Detail of figure 266

266

Diego Velázquez
Las Meninas, 1656

267

Diego Velázquez
Prince Philip Prosper of Spain,
1659

268

Jakob van Campen
*The Royal Palace (former Town
Hall), Amsterdam,* 1648

269
Frans Hals
Banquet of the officers of the
St George Militia Company,
1616

270

Frans Hals
Pieter van den Broecke,
c. 1633

271

Simon de Vlieger
*Dutch man of war and various
vessels in a breeze*, c. 1640-5

272

Jan van Goyen
Windmill by a river, 1642

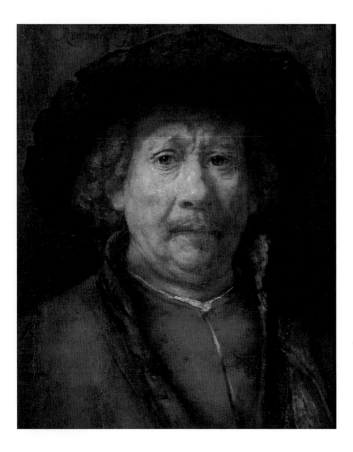

273

Rembrandt van Rijn
Self-portrait, c. 1655-8

Rembrandt van Rijn,
Jan Six, 1654

275

Rembrandt van Rijn
*Parable of the Merciless
Servant, c. 1655*

276

Rembrandt van Rijn
*The reconciliation of David
and Absalom*, 1642

277

Rembrandt van Rijn
Christ preaching, c. 1652

278

Jan Steen
The christening feast, 1664

279

Jacob van Ruisdael
A pool surrounded by trees,
c. 1665-70

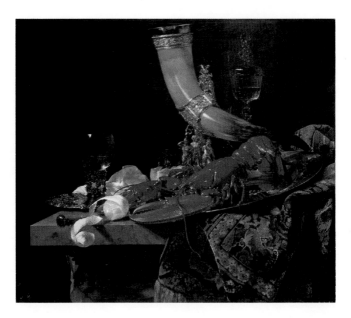

280

Willem Kalf
*Still life with the drinking horn
of the St Sebastian Archers'
Guild, lobster and glasses, c. 1653*

281

Jan Vermeer
The kitchen maid, c. 1660

282

Francesco Borromini
& Carlo Rainaldi
Church of Sta *Agnese*,
Piazza Navona, Rome, 1653

283 *overleaf*

Francesco Borromini
& Carlo Rainaldi
Interior of the church of
Sta Agnese, Piazza Navona,
Rome, c. 1653

284

Gian Lorenzo Bernini
Costanza Buonarelli, c. 1635

285

Gian Lorenzo Bernini
The ecstasy of St Teresa,
1645-52

286

Detail of figure 285

287 *overleaf*

Giovanni Battista Gaulli
*The worship of the Holy Name
of Jesus*, 1670-83

288

Giovanni Battista Tiepolo
The banquet of Cleopatra,
c. 1750

289

Detail of figure 288

290

Francesco Guardi
View of S. Giorgio Maggiore,
Venice, c. 1775-80

291

Louis Le Vau & Jules
Hardouin-Mansart
The palace of Versailles, near
Paris, 1655-82

The gardens at Versailles

293

Lucas von Hildebrandt
Upper Belvedere, Vienna,
1720-4

294

Lucas von Hildebrandt
Upper Belvedere, Vienna,
entrance hall and staircase,
1724

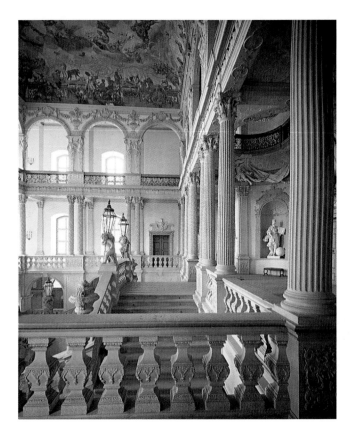

295

Lucas von Hildebrandt
& Johann Dientzenhofer
Staircase of the castle
of Pommersfelden, Germany,
1713-14

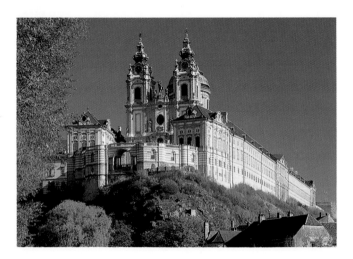

296

Jakob Prandtauer
Melk Monastery, 1702

297

Jakob Prandtauer, Antonio
Beduzzi & Josef Munggenast
*Interior of the church of Melk
Monastery*, c. 1738

298

Antoine Watteau
Fête in a park, c. 1719

299

Sir Christopher Wren
St Paul's Cathedral, London,
1675-1710

300
Sir Christopher Wren
Interior of the church of
St Stephen Walbrook, London,
1672

301

Lord Burlington
& William Kent
Chiswick House, London,
c. 1725

302

The grounds of Stourhead,
Wiltshire, laid out from
1741

303

William Hogarth
*The rake's progress: the rake
in Bedlam, 1735*

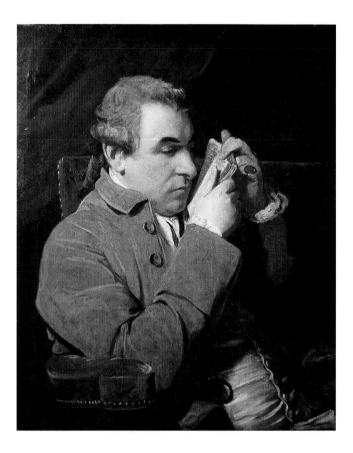

304

Sir Joshua Reynolds
Joseph Baretti, 1773

305

Sir Joshua Reynolds
Miss Bowles with her dog,
1775

306

Thomas Gainsborough
Miss Haverfield, c. 1780

307

Thomas Gainsborough
Rural scene, c. 1780

Jean-Baptiste-Siméon Chardin
Saying grace (*Le Bénédicité*), 1740

309

Jean-Antoine Houdon
Voltaire, 1781

310

Jean-Honoré Fragonard
The park of the Villa d'Este,
Tivoli, c.1760

311

Horace Walpole, Richard
Bentley and John Chute
*Strawberry Hill, Twickenham,
London, c. 1750-75*

312

John Papworth
Dorset House, Cheltenham
c. 1825

313

Sir John Soane
Design for a country house

Thomas Jefferson
Monticello,Virginia, 1796-1806

315

John Singleton Copley
*Charles I demanding the
surrender of the five impeached
members of the House of
Commons, 1641,* 1785

316

Jacques-Louis David
Marat assassinated, 1793

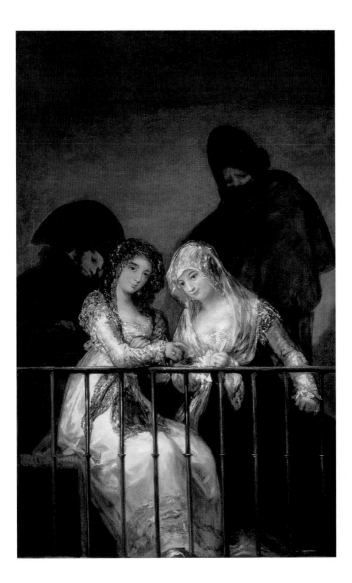

317

Francisco Goya
Group on a balcony,
c. 1810-15

318

Francisco Goya
King Ferdinand VII of Spain,
c. 1814

319

Detail of figure 318

Francisco Goya
The giant, c. 1818

321

William Blake
The Ancient of Days, 1794

322

Joseph Mallord
William Turner
Dido building Carthage,
1815

323

Joseph Mallord
William Turner
Steamer in a snowstorm,
1842

324

John Constable
Study of tree trunks,
c. 1821

325

John Constable
The haywain, 1821

326

Caspar David Friedrich
Landscape in the Silesian
Mountains, c. 1815-20

327

Charles Barry & Augustus
Welby Northmore Pugin
Houses of Parliament, London,
1835

328

Jean-Auguste-
Dominique Ingres
The Valpinçon bather,
1808

329

Eugène Delacroix
*Arab cavalry practising
a charge*, 1832

330

Jean-Baptiste Camille Corot
*Tivoli, the gardens of the Villa
d'Este*, 1843

331

Jean-François Millet
The gleaners, 1857

332

Gustave Courbet
*The meeting, or 'Bonjour
Monsieur Courbet'*, 1854

333

Dante Gabriel Rossetti
'*Ecce Ancilla Domini*',
1849-50

334

Édouard Manet
The balcony,
1868-9

335

Édouard Manet
The races at Longchamp,
1865

336

William Powell Frith
Derby Day, 1856-8

337

Édouard Manet
Monet working in his boat,
1874

338

Claude Monet
Gare St-Lazare,
1877

339

Pierre Auguste Renoir
*Dance at the Moulin
de la Galette*, 1876

340

Camille Pissarro
The boulevard des Italiens,
morning, sunlight, 1897

井戸浚の不二

341

Katsushika Hokusai
Mount Fuji seen behind
a cistern, 1835

342
Kitagawa Utamaro
Rolling up a blind for
the plum-blossom view,
late 1790s

343

Edgar Degas
*Henri Degas and his
niece Lucie, 1876*

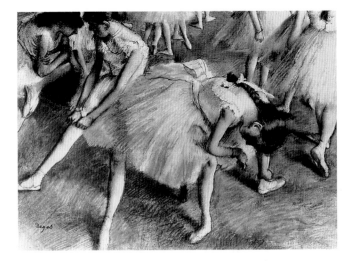

344

Edgar Degas
Awaiting the cue,
1879

345

Auguste Rodin
The sculptor Jules Dalou,
1883

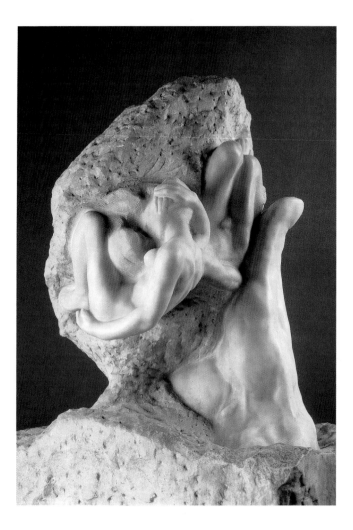

346
Auguste Rodin
The hand of God,
c. 1898

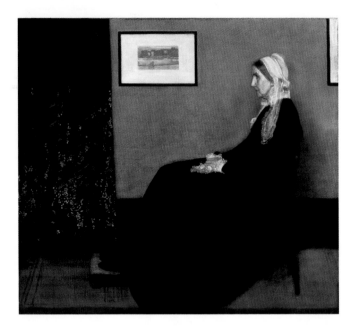

347

James Abbott
McNeill Whistler
*Arrangement in grey
and black: portrait
of the artist's mother,*
1871

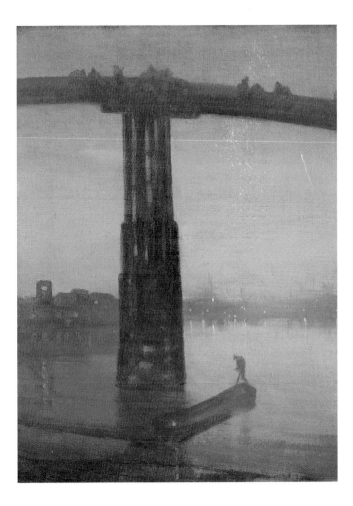

348

James Abbott
McNeill Whistler
*Nocturne in blue
and silver: old Battersea
Bridge*, c. 1872-5

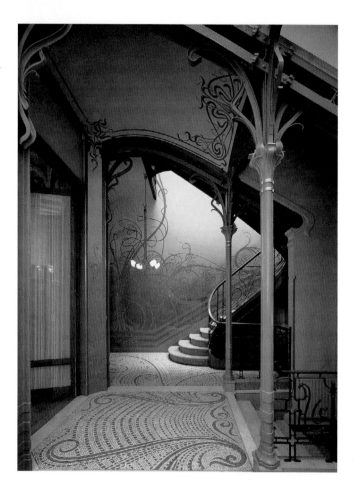

349
Victor Horta
Staircase, Hôtel Tassel,
rue Paul-Émile Janson,
Brussels, 1893

350

Paul Cézanne
*Mont Sainte-Victoire seen
from Bellevue*, c. 1885

351

Paul Cézanne
Mountains in Provence
1886-90

352

Paul Cézanne
Mme Cézanne, 1883-7

353

Paul Cézanne
Still life, c. 1879-82

354

Georges Seurat
The bridge at Courbevoie
1886-7

355 *overleaf*

Vincent van Gogh
Cornfield with cypresses
1889

356

Vincent van Gogh
*View of Les Saintes-Maries-
de-la-Mer,* 1888

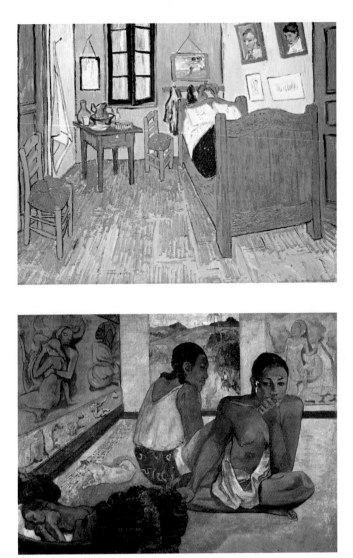

357

Vincent van Gogh
The artist's room in Arles,
1889

358

Paul Gauguin
Te Rerioa (Day-dreaming),
1897

359

Pierre Bonnard
At the table, 1899

360

Ferdinand Hodler
Lake Thun, 1905

361

Henri de Toulouse-Lautrec
Les Ambassadeurs:
Aristide Bruant, 1892

362

Aubrey Beardsley
Illustration to Oscar Wilde's
'Salome', 1894

363

Frank Lloyd Wright
540 Fairoaks Avenue,
Oak Park, Illinois, 1902

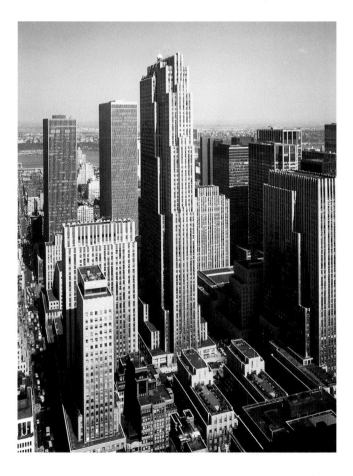

364

Andrew Reinhard, Henry
Hofmeister and others
The Rockefeller Center,
New York, 1931-9

365

Walter Gropius
The Bauhaus, Dessau, 1926

366

Mask of the Dan tribe,
West Africa, c. 1910-20

367

Edvard Munch
The scream, 1895

368

Käthe Kollwitz
Need, 1893-1901

369

Emil Nolde
The prophet, 1912

370

Ernst Barlach
'Have pity!', 1919

371

Oskar Kokoschka
Children playing, 1909

372

Wassily Kandinsky
Cossacks, 1910-11

373
Henri Matisse
La Desserte (*The dinner table*),
1908

374

Pablo Picasso
Violin and grapes,
1912

375

Pablo Picasso
Head of a young boy, 1945

376

Pablo Picasso
Head, 1928

377

Pablo Picasso
Bird, 1948

378

Paul Klee
A tiny tale of a tiny dwarf,
1925

379

Lyonel Feininger
Sailing boats, 1929

380

Constantin Brancusi
The kiss, 1907

381

Piet Mondrian
Composition with red, black,
blue, yellow and grey, 1920

382

Ben Nicholson
1934 (relief), 1934

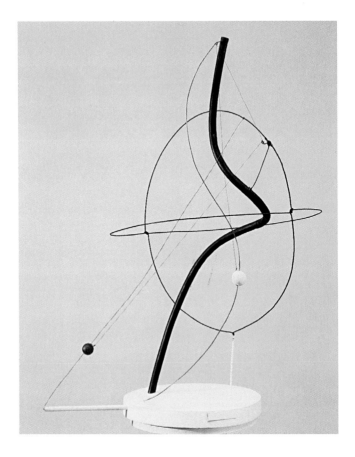

383

Alexander Calder
A universe, 1934

384

Henry Moore
Recumbent figure,
1938

385

Henri Rousseau
Portrait of Joseph Brummer,
1909

386

Marc Chagall
The cellist, 1939

387

Grant Wood
Spring turning, 1936

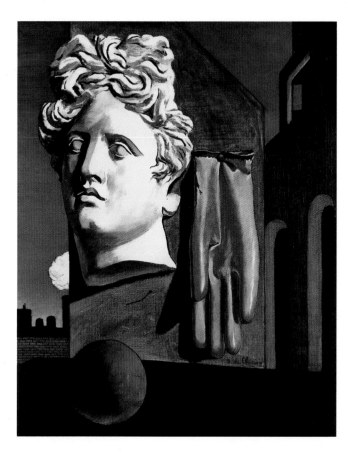

388

Giorgio de Chirico
The song of love, 1914

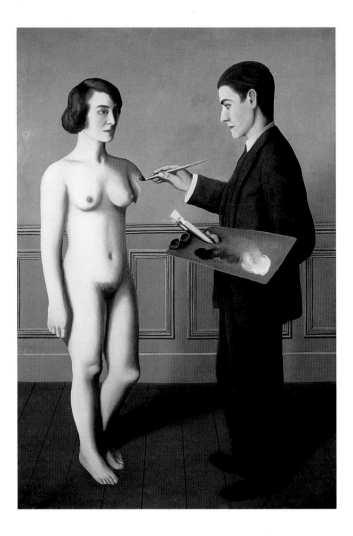

389

René Magritte
Attempting the impossible,
1928

390

Alberto Giacometti
Head, 1927

391

Salvador Dali
*Apparition of face and
fruit-bowl on a beach,*
1938

392

Kurt Schwitters
Invisible ink, 1947

393
Jackson Pollock
One (number 31, 1950),
1950

394

Franz Kline
White forms, 1955

395

Pierre Soulages
3 April 1954, 1954

396

Zoltan Kemeny
Fluctuations, 1959

397

Nicolas de Staël
Agrigento, 1953

398

Marino Marini
Horseman, 1947

399

Giorgio Morandi
Still life, 1960

400

Philip Johnson
& John Burgee
The AT&T building
New York, 1978-82

401

James Stirling &
Michael Wilford
Entrance to the Clore Gallery
Tate Britain, London, 1982-6

402

Stan Hunt
'Why do you have to be
nonconformist like
everybody else?', 1958

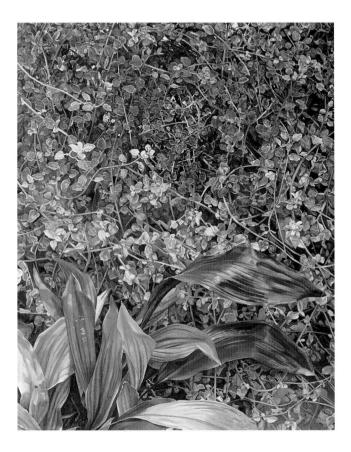

403

Lucian Freud
Two plants, 1977-80

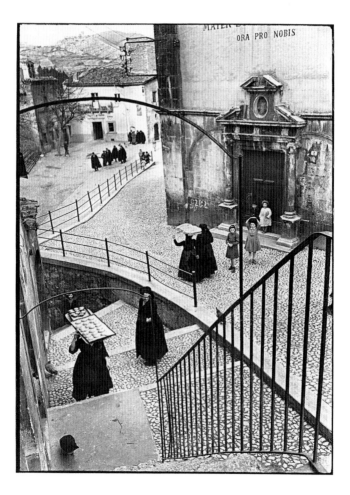

404

Henri Cartier-Bresson
Aquila degli Abruzzi,
1952

405

David Hockney
My mother, Bradford, Yorkshire,
4th May 1982, 1982

406

Fisherman, c. 1500 BC

407

Detail of figure 409

408, 409

Heroes or athletes,
5th century BC

410

The rape of Persephone,
c.366 BC

411

Part of the 'terracotta army'
of the emperor Qin Shi Huangdi,
c.210 BC

412

Head of a soldier from the
'terracotta army', c.210 BC

413

Head of an Old Testament king,
c. 1230

A note on art books

I have made it a rule in the main body of the text not to irritate the reader with repeated reminders of the many things that lack of space prevented me from showing or discussing. I must break this rule here and say with emphasis, and with regret, that it is quite impossible for me to acknowledge all the authorities to whom I am indebted in the foregoing pages. Our ideas about the past are the results of an immense co-operative effort, and even a simple book like this may be described as a report on the work of a large team of historians, living and dead, who have helped to clarify the outlines of periods, styles and personalities. And how many facts, formulations and opinions one may have taken from others without knowing it! I happen to remember that I owe my remarks on the religious roots of Greek games (p. 89) to a broadcast by Gilbert Murray at the time of the London Olympic Games in 1948, but it was only on re-reading D.F. Tovey's book *The Integrity of Music* (London: Oxford U.P., 1941) that I realized how many of its ideas I had used in my introduction.

But, while I cannot hope to list all the writings I may have read or consulted, I did express the hope, in my preface, that this volume might equip newcomers for consulting more specialized books to greater advantage. It therefore remains to show the way to these books. It must be added, though, that the situation here has radically changed since *The Story of Art* was first published. The number of titles has greatly increased, and with it the need to be selective.

It may be useful to start with some rough and ready divisions to distinguish the many kinds of art books which crowd the shelves of our libraries and bookshops. There are books for reading, books for reference and books to look at. By the first group I mean books we enjoy for the sake of their authors. These are works which cannot 'date' because, even when the views and interpretations they offer are no longer in fashion, they remain valuable as documents of their time and as expressions of a personality. For obvious reasons I have listed here only books in English, but those who can read the original texts are sure to realize that translations can never be more than poor substitutes. To those who want to deepen their acquaintance with the world of art in general, without wanting to become specialists in any particular field, it is books for reading I would recommend first of all. Among these, I would single out the source books of the past, books by artists or writers who were in close touch with the things they describe. Not all of them make easy reading, but any effort it may take to get acquainted with a world of ideas so different from our own will be richly rewarded through a better and more intimate understanding of the past.

It has been decided to divide these notes into five sections. Books relating to individual periods or artists are listed in the fifth section under the relevant chapter heading (see pp. 646-54). Those concerned with more general topics will be found under the various subheadings of the first four sections. In citing titles I have been guided by purely practical considerations without claiming consistency. Needless to say, there are other good books that could be included in these lists and the omission of a work is not intended to reflect on its quality.

An asterisk (*) indicates that the book is available as a paperback.

Primary Sources

Anthologies

For those who want to dive into the past and read texts written by contemporaries of the artists discussed in this book, there are several excellent anthologies which may serve as the best introduction to this field of study. A large selection of such writings has been compiled by Elizabeth Holt, who has also provided English translations. Her three-volume work *A Documentary History of Art* (new edition, Princeton U.P., 1981-8*) extends from the Middle Ages to the Impressionists. The same author has also collected a large number of texts from newspapers and other sources to document the emerging role of exhibitions and critics in the nineteenth century in a further three-volume work, *The Expanding World of Art 1874-1902*. The first volume is entitled *Universal Exhibitions and State-Sponsored Fine Arts Exhibitions* (New Haven and London: Yale U.P., 1988*). More specialized in character is the series of volumes of sources and documents published by Prentice-Hall (general editor, H.W. Janson). These are anthologies, arranged according to periods and countries and even styles, with material chosen from a wide range of sources – such as contemporary descriptions and criticism, legal documents and letters – which are explained and annotated by the individual compilers. The volumes include *The Art of Greece, 1400-31 BC*, ed. J.J. Pollitt (1965; 2nd edition, 1990); *The Art of Rome, 753 BC-337 AD*, ed. J.J. Pollitt (1966); *The Art of the Byzantine Empire, 312-1453*, ed. Cyril Mango (1972); *Early Medieval Art, 300-1150*, ed. Caecilia Davis-Weyer (1971); *Gothic Art, 1140-c.1450*, ed. Teresa G. Frisch (1971); *Italian Art, 1400-1500*, ed. Creighton Gilbert (1980); *Italian Art, 1500-1600*, ed. Robert Enggass and Henri Zerner (1966); *Northern Renaissance Art, 1400-1600*, ed. Wolfgang Stechow (1966); *Italy and Spain, 1600-1750*, ed. Robert Enggass and Jonathan Brown (1970); *Neoclassicism and Romanticism*, ed. Lorenz Eitner (2 vols., 1970); *Realism and*

Tradition in Art, 1848-1900, ed. Linda Nochlin (1966); and Impressionism and Post-Impressionism, 1874-1904, ed. Linda Nochlin (1966). An anthology of Renaissance source material in translation is provided by D.S. Chambers in Patrons and Artists in the Italian Renaissance (London: Macmillan, 1970). A more wide-ranging selection is Artists on Art, compiled by Robert Goldwater and Marco Treves (London: Routledge & Kegan Paul, 1947).

For the modern period useful anthologies of documents are Nineteenth-Century Theories of Art, ed. Joshua C. Taylor (Berkeley: California U.P., 1987); Theories of Modern Art: A Source Book by Artists and Critics, ed. Herschel B. Chipp (Berkeley: California U.P., 1968; reprinted 1970*); and Art in Theory: An Anthology of Changing Ideas, ed. Charles Harrison and Paul Wood (Oxford: Blackwell, 1992*).

Single Editions

The following is a selection of primary sources available in English:

Vitruvius on Architecture, an immensely influential treatise by an architect of the time of Augustus, is available in a translation by M.H. Morgan (New York: Dover, 1960*). From the classical world, see also the elder Pliny's Chapters on the History of Art, translated by K.J. Bleake, with a commentary by E. Sellers, originally published in 1896, but separately available now as part of the Loeb Classical Library translation of Pliny's Natural History, ed. H. Rackham, vol. IX, books 33-5 (London: Heinemann, 1952). It is our most important source of information on Greek and Roman painting and sculpture, compiled from older texts by the famous scholar who perished in the destruction of Pompeii (p. 113). Pausanias's Description of Greece has been translated and edited by J.G. Frazer (6 vols., London: Macmillan, 1898), and is available in a paperback edition as Guide to Greece, ed. Peter Levi (2 vols., Harmondsworth: Penguin, 1971*). Old Chinese writings on art are most easily accessible in a volume of the 'Wisdom of the East' series, entitled The Spirit of the Brush, translated by Shio Sakanishi (London: John Murray, 1939). The most important document for the outlook of the great medieval cathedral builders (pp. 185-8) is the account by Abbot Suger of the building of the first great Gothic church, which exists in a model edition, Abbot Suger on the Abbey Church of Saint Denis and its Art Treasures, translated, edited and annotated by Erwin Panofsky (Princeton U.P., 1946; revised edition, 1979*). Theophilus's The Various Arts has been translated and edited by C.R. Dodwell (London: Nelson, 1961; 2nd edition, Oxford U.P., 1986*). Those who are interested in the technique and training of late medieval painters can now turn to the equally scholarly edition of Cennino Cennini, The Craftsman's Handbook, by Daniel V. Thompson Jr. (2 vols., New Haven and London: Yale U.P., 1932-3; reprinted New York: Dover, 1954*). The mathematical and classical interests of the first Renaissance generation (pp. 224-30) are exemplified by Leon Battista Alberti's *On Painting and Sculpture*, translated and edited by Cecil Grayson (London: Phaidon, 1972; reprinted Harmondsworth: Penguin, 1991*). The standard edition of Leonardo's principal writings is J.P. Richter, *The Literary Works of Leonardo da Vinci* (Oxford U.P., 1939; reprinted with new illustrations, London: Phaidon, 1970*). Anyone studying Leonardo's writings in depth should also consult Carlo Pedretti's two-volume *Commentary to Richter* (Oxford: Phaidon, 1977). Leonardo's *Treatise on Painting*, translated and annotated by A. Philip McMahon (Princeton U.P., 1956), is based on an important collection of the master's notes made in the sixteenth century, some of which no longer exist in the original. *Leonardo on Painting*, ed. Martin Kemp (New Haven and London: Yale U.P., 1989*), is an extremely useful anthology. The letters of Michelangelo (p. 315), were translated and published in a complete edition by E.H. Ramsden (2 vols., London: Peter Owen, 1964). *The Complete Poems and Selected Letters of Michelangelo*, translated by Creighton Gilbert, are also available (Princeton U.P., 1980*). *The Poetry of Michelangelo*, with the original text and a translation by James M. Saslow (New Haven and London: Yale U.P., 1991*) may also be consulted. For a biography of Michelangelo by one of his contemporaries, see Ascanio Condivi, *The Life of Michelangelo*, translated by Alice Sedgwick Wohl and edited by Hellmut Wohl (Baton Rouge: Louisiana State U.P., 1976).

The writings of Albrecht Dürer (p. 342) were translated and edited by W.M. Conway, with an introduction by Alfred Werner (London: Peter Owen, 1958); there is also an edition of Dürer's *The Painter's Manual* by W.L. Strauss (New York: Abaris, 1977).

By far the most important source book for the art of the Renaissance in Italy is Giorgio Vasari's *Lives of the Painters, Sculptors and Architects*, which exists in Everyman's Library in four volumes, ed. William Gaunt (London: Dent, 1963*); Penguin publish a useful two-volume selection by George Bull (Harmondsworth, 1987*). The original text, first published in 1550, was revised and enlarged in 1568. It can be read for pleasure as a collection of anecdotes and short stories, some of which may even be true. It will be read with even greater profit and enjoyment if we take it as an interesting document of the period of 'Mannerism', when artists became conscious and over-conscious of the great achievements of the past that weighed on them (pp. 361 ff.). The other fascinating book by a Florentine artist of that restless period, Benvenuto

Cellini's autobiography (p. 363), exists in various English editions: for example, by George Bull (Harmondsworth: Penguin, 1956*); John Pope-Hennessy, *The Life of Benvenuto Cellini* (London: Phaidon, 1949; 2nd edition, 1995*); Charles Hope, *The Autobiography of Benvenuto Cellini* (abridged and illustrated; Oxford: Phaidon, 1983). Antonio Manetti's *Life of Brunelleschi* has been translated by Catherine Enggass and edited by Howard Saalman (University Park: Pennsylvania State U.P., 1970). Enggass has also translated Filippo Baldinucci's *Life of Bernini* (University Park: Pennsylvania State U.P., 1966). The lives of other seventeenth-century artists have been recorded by Carel van Mander, *Dutch and Flemish Painters*, translated and edited by Constant van de Wall (New York: McFarlane, 1936; reprinted New York: Arno, 1969); and Antonio Palomino, *Lives of the Eminent Spanish Painters and Sculptors*, translated by Nina Mallory (Cambridge U.P., 1987). The letters of Peter Paul Rubens (p. 397) were translated and edited by Ruth Saunders Magurn (Cambridge, Mass.: Harvard U.P., 1955; new edition, Evanston, Ill.: Northwestern U.P., 1991*).

The academic tradition of the seventeenth and eighteenth centuries, tempered by much wisdom and common sense, is presented in *Sir Joshua Reynolds: Discourses on Art* (p. 464), ed. Robert R. Wark (San Marino, Cal.: Huntington Library, 1959; reprinted New Haven and London: Yale U.P., 1981*). William Hogarth's unorthodox *The Analysis of Beauty* (1753) is available in a facsimile reprint (New York: Garland, 1973). Constable's equally independent attitude towards the academic tradition (pp. 494-5) can best be gauged from his letters and lectures, which are to be found in C.R. Leslie's *Memoirs of the Life of John Constable* (London: Phaidon, 1951; 3rd edition, 1995*). His complete correspondence, in eight volumes, ed. R.B. Beckett, is also available (Ipswich: Suffolk Records Society, 1962-75).

The Romantic point of view is most clearly reflected in the wonderful *Journals of Eugène Delacroix* (p. 504), translated by Lucy Norton (London: Phaidon, 1951; 3rd edition, 1995*). There is also a single-volume edition of his letters, selected and translated by Jean Stewart (London: Eyre & Spottiswode, 1971). Goethe's writings on art are conveniently collected in *Goethe on Art*, translated and edited by John Gage (Berkeley: California U.P., 1980). The letters of the Realist painter Gustave Courbet have recently been translated and edited by Petra ten-Doesschate Chu (Chicago U.P., 1992). A source book on the Impressionists (p. 519) by an art dealer who knew most of them is Théodore Duret's *Manet and the French Impressionists* (London: Lippincott, 1910); but many will find the study of their letters more rewarding. There are English translations of

the letters of Camille Pissarro (p. 522), selected and edited by John
Rewald (London: Kegan Paul, 1944; 4th edition, 1980), of Degas (p. 526)
by Marcel Guérin (Oxford: Cassirer, 1947), of Cézanne (pp. 538, 574) by
John Rewald (London: Cassirer, 1941; 4th edition, 1977). For a personal
account of Renoir (p. 520), see Jean Renoir's *Renoir, my Father*, translated by
Randolph and Dorothy Weaver (London: Collins, 1962; reprinted London:
Columbus, 1988*). *The Complete Letters of Vincent van Gogh* (pp. 544, 563)
were published in English in three volumes (London: Thames & Hudson,
1958). A translation of a selection of Gauguin's letters (pp. 550, 586)
by Bernard Denvir is available (London: Collins & Brown, 1992); for an
edition of Gauguin's semi-autobiographical book *Noa Noa*, see *Noa Noa:
Gauguin's Tahiti, the Original Manuscript*, ed. Nicholas Wadley (Oxford:
Phaidon, 1985). Whistler's *Gentle Art of Making Enemies* (p. 530) was first
published in 1890 (reprinted New York: Dover, 1968*). More recent
autobiographies include one by Oskar Kokoschka (p. 568), *My Life*
(London: Thames & Hudson, 1974), and Salvador Dali's *Diary of a Genius*
(London: Hutchinson, 1966; 2nd edition, 1990*). The *Collected Writings*
of Frank Lloyd Wright (p. 558) have been published recently (2 vols.,
New York: Rizzoli, 1992*). A lecture by Walter Gropius (p. 560) on
The New Architecture and the Bauhaus exists in a translation by P. Morton
Shand (London: Faber, 1965), and a wider selection of documents in *The
Bauhaus: Master and Students by Themselves* (London: Conran Octopus, 1992).

Among modern painters who have explained their artistic creed
in print I may mention Paul Klee (p. 578), *On Modern Art*, translated by
P. Findley (London: Faber, 1948; new edition, 1966*), and Hilaire Hiler,
Why Abstract? (London: Falcon, 1948), which contains a clear and
intelligible account of an American artist's conversion to 'abstract'
painting. The two series directed by Robert Motherwell, 'Documents of
Modern Art' (New York: Wittenborn, 1944-61) and 'Documents of 20th-
Century Art' (London: Thames & Hudson, 1971-3) publish reprints of
essays and utterances (in the original language and in translation) of
many other 'abstract' and Surrealist artists, including Kandinsky (p. 570),
Concerning the Spiritual in Art, which is also published separately (New York:
Dover, 1986*). See also *Matisse on Art*, translated and edited by J. Flam
(London: Phaidon, 1973; 2nd edition, Oxford, 1978; reprinted 1990*)
and *Kandinsky: The Complete Writings on Art*, ed. Kenneth Lindsay and Peter
Vergo (London: Faber, 1982). The 'World of Art' series (London: Thames
& Hudson) includes a volume on *Dada* (p. 601) by H. Richter (1966)
and the manifestos of *Surrealism* (p. 592) by P. Waldberg (1966).
Guillaume Apollinaire's *The Cubist Painters: Aesthetic Meditations*, first

published in 1913, is available in the series 'Documents of Modern Art',
translated by Lionel Abel (New York: Wittenborn, 1949; reprinted 1977*),
while André Breton's *Surrealism and Painting* has been translated by Simon
Watson Taylor (New York: Harper & Row, 1972). Robert L. Herbert's *Modern
Artists on Art* (New York: Prentice-Hall, 1965*) contains ten essays,
including two by Mondrian (p. 582) and several utterances by Henry
Moore (p. 585), for whom see also Philip James, *Henry Moore on Sculpture*
(London: Macdonald, 1966).

Leading Critics

This category of books, which should be read just as much for the
sake of their authors as for the information they contain, also includes
a number of works by the great critics. Opinions about their relative
merits may differ, and the following list should only be taken as a guide.

Those who want to clarify their own views on artistic matters
and to benefit from past enthusiasm might do worse than sample the
voluminous writings of the leading nineteenth-century art critics such
as John Ruskin (p. 530), whose *Modern Painters* is available in an abridged
edition ed. David Barrie (London: Deutsch, 1987), William Morris
(p. 535) or Walter Pater, the representative of the 'aesthetic movement' in
England (p. 533). Pater's most important work, *The Renaissance*, is available
with an introduction and notes by Kenneth Clark (London: Fontana, 1961;
reprinted 1971*), who was also responsible for a stimulating anthology
of Ruskin's copious writings entitled *Ruskin Today* (London: John Murray,
1964; reprinted Harmondsworth: Penguin, 1982*). See also *The Lamp
o Beauty: writings on Art by John Ruskin*, selected and edited by Joan Evans,
(London: Phaidon, 1959; 3rd edition, 1995*). *The Letters of William Morris
to his Family and Friends* have been edited by Philip Henderson (London:
Longman, 1950). The French critics of the period happen to be
a little closer to our present outlook, and the writings on art by Charles
Baudelaire, Eugène Fromentin and the brothers Edmond and Jules de
Goncourt are related to the artistic revolutions of French painting
(p. 512). Two volumes of Baudelaire's writings, translated and edited by
Jonathan Mayne, have been published by Phaidon Press: *The Painter of
Modern Life* (London, 1964; 2nd edition, 1995*) and *Art in Paris* (London,
1965; 3rd edition, 1995*). Phaidon has also published translations of
Fromentin's *The Masters of Past Time* (London, 1948; 3rd edition, 1995*)
and *French Eighteenth-Century Painters* by Edmond and Jules de Goncourt
(London, 1948; 3rd edition, 1995*). A selection from the De Goncourt
brothers' *Journal*, edited, translated and with an introduction by Robert

Baldick, has also been published (Oxford U.P., 1962; reprinted Harmondsworth: Penguin, 1984*). For profiles of these and other great French writers on art, the reader may consult Anita Brookner's *Genius of the Future* (London: Phaidon, 1971; reprinted Ithaca: Cornell U.P., 1988*).

The spokesman for Post-Impressionism in England was Roger Fry – see, for example, his *Vision and Design* (London: Chatto & Windus, 1920; new edition, ed. J.B. Bullen, London: Oxford U.P., 1981*), *Cézanne: a Study of his Development* (London: Hogarth Press, 1927; new edition, Chicago U.P., 1989*), and *Last Lectures* (Cambridge U.P., 1939). The most dedicated champion of 'experimental' art in England from the 1930s to the 1950s was Sir Herbert Read, in such books as *Art Now* (London: Faber, 1933; 5th edition, 1968*) and *The Philosophy of Modern Art* (London: Faber, 1931; reprinted 1964*). The advocates of American 'action painting' (p. 604) were Harold Rosenberg, author of *The Tradition of the New* (New York: Horizon Press, 1959; London: Thames & Hudson, 1962; reprinted London: Paladin, 1970*) and *The Anxious Object: Art Today and its Audience* (New York: Horizon Press, 1964; London: Thames & Hudson, 1965) and Clement Greenberg, author of *Art and Culture* (Boston: Beacon Press, 1961; London: Thames & Hudson, 1973).

The philosophical background

For background reading to help one understand the philosophical arguments behind the classical and academic tradition, the following may be of use: Anthony Blunt, *Artistic Theory in Italy 1450-1600* (Oxford U.P., 1940*); Michael Baxandall, *Giotto and the Orators* (Oxford U.P., 1971; reprinted 1986*); Rudolf Wittkower, *Architectural Principles in the Age of Humanism* (London: Warburg Institute, 1949; new edition, London: Academy, 1988*); Erwin Panofsky, *Idea: A Concept in Art Theory* (New York: Harper & Row, 1975).

Approaches to the History of Art

Art history is a branch of history, a word originally derived from the Greek word for 'inquiry'. What are sometimes described as the various 'methods' of art-historical research should therefore be understood as efforts to answer different questions we may ask about the past. Which of these questions we wish to ask at a given moment depends on us and our interests, while the answer will depend on the evidence the historian can bring to light.

Connoisseurship

In relation to any work of art, we are likely to want to know *when* it was made, *where*, and (if possible) by *whom*. Those who have refined their methods in order to answer these questions are known as *connoisseurs*. This category includes the towering figures of a bygone age whose word on 'attribution' was (or still is) law. Bernard Berenson's *Italian Painters of the Renaissance* (Oxford: Clarendon Press, 1930; 3rd edition, Oxford: Phaidon, 1980*) has become something of a classic. See also his *Drawings of the Florentine Painters* (London: John Murray, 1903; expanded edition, Chicago U.P., 1970). Max J. Friedländer's *Art and Connoisseurship* (London: Cassirer, 1942) provides the best introduction to the approach of this group.

Many of the leading connoisseurs of our own days have placed all of us in their debt by compiling the catalogues of public or private collections and of exhibitions, the best of which permit the user to examine the grounds which led them to their results.

The hidden enemy against which connoisseurship has to fight is the forger. A concise introduction to this field is Otto Kurz, *Fakes* (New York: Dover, 1967*). See also the fascinating catalogue of an exhibiton held at the British Museum ed. Mark Jones, *Fake? The Art of Deception* (London: British Museum, 1990*).

Histories of style

There have always been historians of art who have wished to go beyond the questions asked by connoisseurs, desiring to explain or interpret those changes in style which are also the subject of this book.

The interest in this question came to the fore in Germany in the eighteenth century, when Johann Joachim Winckelmann published the first history of ancient art in 1764. Few readers today wish to tackle this book, but there is available in English his *Reflections on the Imitation of Greek Works in Painting and Sculpture* (London: Orpen, 1987); and an anthology edited by David Irwin, *Writings on Art* (London: Phaidon, 1972).

The tradition he inaugurated was vigorously pursued in German-speaking countries during the nineteenth and twentieth centuries, but few of the works produced have yet been translated into English. A valuable conspectus of these various theories or ideas is Michael Podro, *The Critical Historians of Art* (New Haven and London: Yale U.P., 1982*). The best point of entry into these problems of the history of styles is still the writings of the Swiss historian Heinrich Wölzin, a master of comparative description, most of whose books are now available in translation: *Renaissance and Baroque*, with an informative introduction by

Peter Murray (London: Fontana, 1964*); *Classic Art: an Introduction to the Italian Renaissance* (London: Phaidon, 1952; 5th edition, 1994*); *Principles of Art History* (London: Bell, 1932; reprinted New York: Dover, 1986*) and *The Sense of Form in Art* (New York: Chelsea, 1958). A psychology of style was attempted by Wilhelm Worringer, whose *Abstraction and Empathy* (English translation, London: Routledge & Kegan Paul, 1953) was in tune with the Expressionist movement (p. 567). Among French students of style, Henri Focillon, with his *The Life of Forms in Art*, translated by C.B. Hogan and G. Kubler, (New York: Wittenborn, Schultz, 1948; reprinted New York: Zone Books, 1989), should be mentioned.

The study of subject-matter

The interest in the religious and symbolic content of art started in nineteenth-century France and culminated in the life-work of Emile Mâle. His book *Religious Art in France: the Twelfth Century* was published in an annotated English translation (Princeton U.P., 1978), as was *Religious Art in France: the Thirteenth Century* (Princeton U.P., 1984). Chapters from other volumes are included in *Religious Art from the Twelfth to the Eighteenth Century* (London: Routledge & Kegan Paul, 1949). The best introduction to the study of mythological themes in art, initiated by Aby Warburg and his school, is Jean Seznec, *The Survival of the Pagan Gods* (Princeton U.P., 1953; reprinted 1972*). The interpretation of symbolism in Renaissance art is brilliantly exemplified in Erwin Panofsky's *Studies in Iconology* (New York: Harper & Row, 1972*) and his *Meaning in the Visual Arts* (New York: Doubleday, 1957; reprinted Harmondsworth: Penguin, 1970*), as well as in Fritz Saxl's *A Heritage of Images* (Harmondsworth: Penguin, 1970*). I have also published a volume of essays on this theme: *Symbolic Images* (London: Phaidon, 1972; 3rd edition, Oxford, 1985; reprinted London, 1995*).

There are also a number of dictionaries for those interested in Christian and pagan symbolism, for example James Hall, *Dictionary of Subjects and Symbols in Art* (London: John Murray, 1974*), and G. Ferguson, *Signs and Symbols in Christian Art* (Oxford U.P., 1954).

The study of individual themes or motifs in the history of Western art has been enriched and enlivened by Kenneth Clark, in particular in his *Landscape into Art* (London: John Murray, 1949; revised edition, 1979*) and *The Nude* (London: John Murray, 1956; reprinted Harmondsworth: Penguin, 1985*). Charles Sterling's *Still Life Painting: From Antiquity to the Twentieth Century*, translated by James Emmons (London: Harper & Row, 1981) also belongs in this category.

Social history

Questions about the social conditions that gave rise to particular styles
and movements have been frequently raised by historians of a Marxist
persuasion, the most comprehensive being Arnold Hauser, author of
A Social History of Art (2 vols., London: Routledge & Kegan Paul, 1951; new
edition, 4 vols., 1990*), for which see also my article in *Meditations on a
Hobby Horse* (London: Phaidon, 1963; 4th edition, Oxford, 1985; reprinted
London, 1994*). More specialized studies in this area are: Frederick Antal,
Florentine Painting and its Social Background (London: Routledge & Kegan Paul,
1947); and T.J. Clark, *Image of the People: Gustave Courbet and the Revolution of
1848* (London: Thames & Hudson, 1973*). Among questions more
recently raised is that of the role of women in art – see Germaine Greer,
The Obstacle Race (London: Secker & Warburg, 1979; reprinted London: Pan,
1981*) and Griselda Pollock, *Vision and Difference: Femininity, Feminism and the
Histories of Art* (London: Routledge, 1988). Some recent historians,
stressing the need to concentrate on social aspects, have adopted the label
of the 'New Art History'; see the anthology of that
title ed. A.L. Rees and Frances Borzello (London: Camden, 1986*). It may
be argued that, in their aim of eschewing aesthetic evaluations as too
subjective, they have long been anticipated by archaeologists, who are
used to examining the artefacts of the past for what they tell us of a given
culture. See also the more recent anthology, *Art in Modern Culture*, ed. Francis
Frascina and Jonathan Harris (London: Phaidon, 1992; reprinted 1994*).

Psychological theories

There being several schools of psychology, the questions asked vary
accordingly. I have discussed the theories of Freud and their bearing on
art in various essays: 'Psycho-Analysis and the History of Art', in
Meditations on a Hobby Horse (London: Phaidon, 1963; 4th edition, Oxford,
1985; reprinted London, 1994*), pp. 30-44; 'Freud's Aesthetics', in
Reflections on the History of Art (Oxford: Phaidon, 1987), pp. 221-39; and
'Verbal Wit as a Paradigm of Art: the Aesthetic Theories of Sigmund Freud
(1856-1939)', in *Tributes: Interpreters of our Cultural Tradition* (Oxford:
Phaidon, 1984), pp. 93-115. Peter Fuller, in *Art and Psychoanalysis* (London:
Hogarth Press, 1988), takes a Freudian approach, whereas Richard
Wollheim's *Painting as Art* (London: Thames & Hudson, 1987*) has adopted
the modifications of Freud's theories by Melanie Klein. The work of
Adrian Stokes, belonging to the same school, remains of great interest –
see for example his *Painting and the Inner World* (London: Tavistock, 1963).
The problems of the psychology of visual perception, to which I have

frequently referred in *The Story of Art*, are more fully investigated in my books on *Art and Illusion* (London: Phaidon, 1960; 5th edition, Oxford, 1977; reprinted London, 1994*), *The Sense of Order* (Oxford: Phaidon, 1979; reprinted London, 1994*) and *The Image and the Eye* (Oxford: Phaidon, 1982; reprinted London, 1994*). The book by Rudolf Arnheim, *Art and Visual Perception* (Berkeley: California U.P., 1954*), is based on the Gestalt theory of perception that is concerned with principles of formal balance. David Freedberg's *The Power of Images: Studies in the History and Theory of Response* (Chicago U.P., 1989*) discusses the role of images in ritual, magic and superstition.

Taste and collecting
The last of the questions to be mentioned here concerns the history of collections and of taste, the most comprehensive work on this subject being Joseph Alsop's *The Rare Art Tradition: The History of Art Collecting and its Linked Phenomena* (Princeton U.P., 1981). Francis Haskell and Nicholas Penny, in their *Taste and the Antique* (New Haven and London: Yale U.P., 1981*), trace a particular theme. Individual periods are treated in the following works: Michael Baxandall, *Painting and Experience in Fifteenth-Century Italy* (Oxford U.P., 1972; 2nd edition, 1988*); Martin Wackernagel, *The World of the Florentine Renaissance Artist: Projects and Patrons, Workshop and Art Market*, translated by Alison Luchs (Princeton U.P., 1981); Francis Haskell, *Patrons and Painters* (London: Chatto & Windus, 1963; revised and enlarged edition, New Haven and London: Yale U.P., 1980*) and *Rediscoveries in Art* (London: Phaidon, 1976; reprinted Oxford, 1980*). For the vagaries of the art market, see Gerald Reitlinger, *The Economics of Taste* (3 vols., London: Barrie & Rockliff, 1961-70).

Techniques
Here are a few examples of works dealing with techniques and practical aspects of art: Rudolf Wittkower, *Sculpture* (Harmondsworth: Penguin, 1977*) is the best overall survey; Sheila Adam, *The Techniques of Greek Sculpture* (London: Thames & Hudson, 1966); Ralph Mayer, *The Artist's Handbook of Materials and Techniques* (London: Faber, 1951; 5th edition, 1991*); A.M. Hind, *An Introduction to the History of Woodcut* (2 vols., London: Constable, 1935; reprinted in 1 vol., New York: Dover, 1963*), and by the same author, *A History of Engraving and Etching* (London: Constable, 1927; reprinted New York: Dover, n.d.*); Francis Ames-Lewis and Joanne Wright, *Drawing in the Italian Renaissance Workshop* (London: Victoria & Albert Museum, 1983*); John Fitchen, *The Construction of Gothic Cathedrals*

(Oxford U.P., 1961). The National Gallery in London has mounted three exhibitions in their series 'Art in the Making', dealing with the techniques of painting as revealed by scientific examination: *Rembrandt* (1988*), *Italian Painting before 1400* (1989*) and *Impressionism* (1990*). Their survey *Giotto to Dürer: Early Renaissance Painting in the National Gallery* (1991*) also deals with technical questions, and much besides.

Handbooks and surveys of styles and periods

The way to the books we want to read or to look up when we are in search of information on a particular period, technique or master is easily shown, though it may take a little trouble and practice to walk it to the end. There exist a growing number of excellent handbooks which contain the essential facts and show the way to further reading. The most important of the various series is the 'Pelican History of Art', originally edited by Nikolaus Pevsner, and now published by Yale University Press. Most volumes are available in paperback, and several in revised editions. Some of them offer the best general survey of their subjects that is available. The series is supplemented by the *Oxford History of English Art* edited by T.S.R. Boase, published in 11 volumes. The 'Phaidon Colour Library' offers an authoritative but accessible approach to a wide range of artists and movements, with good-quality colour illustrations, as does Thames & Hudson's 'World of Art' series.

Among the mass of other authoritative handbooks in English, I would list the following publications: Hugh Honour and John Fleming, *A World History of Art* (London: Macmillan, 1982; 3rd edition, London: Laurence King, 1987*); H.W. Janson, *A History of Art* (London: Thames & Hudson; and New York: Abrams, 1962; 4th edition, 1991); Nikolaus Pevsner, *An Outline of European Architecture* (London: Penguin, 1943; 7th edition, 1963*); Patrick Nuttgens, *The Story of Architecture* (Oxford: Phaidon, 1983; reprinted London, 1994*). For sculpture, see John Pope-Hennessy, *An Introduction to Italian Sculpture* (3 vols., London: Phaidon, 1955-63; 2nd edition, 1970-72; reprinted Oxford, 1985*). For oriental art, see *The Heibonsha Survey of Japanese Art* (30 vols., Tokyo: Heibonsha, 1964-9; and New York: Weatherhill, 1972-80).

The student in search of detailed and up-to-date information does not usually turn to books for guidance. His happy hunting grounds are the various periodicals, the yearbooks, quarterlies and monthlies published by various institutions and learned societies all over Europe and America. Among them, the *Burlington Magazine* and the *Art Bulletin* are foremost. In these, specialists write for specialists, and publish the documents and interpretations out of which the mosaic of art history is formed. This type of reading can only be done in one of the major libraries. There, on the open shelves, the student will also be sure to find a number of reference books he needs as constant guides. One is the *Encyclopedia of World Art*, originally an Italian enterprise, published in English by McGraw-Hill, New York, 1959-68. Another is the *Art Index*, a cumulative author and subject index to a selected list of fine art periodicals and museum bulletins, which is published annually. It is complemented by the *International Repertory of the Literature of Art* (RILA), known since 1991 as the *Bibliography of the History of Art*.

Dictionaries

Among useful dictionaries and reference books are: Peter and Linda Murray, *The Penguin Dictionary of Art and Artists* (Harmondsworth: Penguin, 1959; 6th edition, 1989*); John Fleming and Hugh Honour, *The Penguin Dictionary of Decorative Arts* (Harmondsworth: Penguin, 1979; new edition, 1989*) and, with Nikolaus Pevsner, *The Penguin Dictionary of Architecture* (Harmondsworth: Penguin, 1966; 4th edition, 1991*); *The Oxford Companion to Art* and *The Oxford Companion to the Decorative Arts*, both edited by Harold Osborne (Oxford U.P., 1970 and 1975). The forthcoming *Macmillan Dictionary of Art*, planned in over 30 volumes, will bring together an impressive range of up-to-date reference material.

Travel

Needless to say, if there is one field of study that cannot be mastered by reading alone, it is the history of art. Any art lover will seek an opportunity to travel and to spend as much time as possible exploring the monuments and works of art at first hand. It is neither possible nor desirable to list here all the guidebooks, but some may be mentioned: the 'Companion Guides' (published by Collins), 'Blue Guides' (A. & C. Black) and the 'Phaidon Cultural Guides'. Outstanding for English architecture is Nikolaus Pevsner's Penguin series, 'The Buildings of England' (by county).

As for the rest – *bon voyage!*

Bibliography by Chapter

Works are generally listed in the order in which artists
and topics are discussed within each chapter.

1
Strange Beginnings
Prehistoric and primitive peoples; Ancient America

Anthony Forge, *Primitive Art and Society* (London: Oxford U.P., 1973)
Douglas Fraser, *Primitive Art* (London: Thames & Hudson, 1962)
Franz Boas, *Primitive Art* (New York: Peter Smith, 1962)

2
Art for Eternity
Egypt, Mesopotamia, Crete

W. Stevenson Smith, *The Art and Architecture of Ancient Egypt*
     (Harmondsworth: Penguin, 1958; 2nd edition, revised by
     William Kelly Simpson, 1981*)
Heinrich Schäfer, *Principles of Egyptian Art*, translated by J. Baines
     (Oxford U.P., 1974)
Kurt Lange and Max Hirmer, *Egypt: Architecture, Sculpture, Painting*
     (London: Phaidon, 1956; 4th edition, 1968; reprinted 1974)
Henri Frankfort, *The Art and Architecture of the Ancient Orient*
     (Harmondsworth: Penguin, 1954; 4th edition, 1970*)

3
The Great Awakening
Greece, seventh to fifth century BC

Gisela M.A. Richter, *A Handbook of Greek Art* (London: Phaidon, 1959;
     9th edition, Oxford, 1987; reprinted London, 1994*)
Martin Robertson, *A History of Greek Art* (2 vols., Cambridge U.P., 1975)
—, *A Shorter History of Greek Art* (Cambridge U.P., 1981*)
Andrew Stewart, *Greek Sculpture*
     (2 vols., New Haven and London: Yale U.P., 1990)
John Boardman, *The Parthenon and its Sculptures*
     (London: Thames & Hudson, 1985)

Bernard Ashmole, *Architect and Sculptor in Classical Greece*
    (London: Phaidon, 1972)
J.J. Pollitt, *Art and Experience in Classical Greece* (Cambridge U.P., 1972)
R.M. Cook, *Greek Painted Pottery* (London: Methuen, 1960; 2nd edition, 1972)
Claude Rolley, *Greek Bronzes* (London: Sotheby's, 1986)

4
The Realm of Beauty
Greece and the Greek world, fourth century BC to first century AD

Margarete Bieber, *Sculpture of the Hellenistic Age*
    (New York: Columbia U.P., 1955; revised edition, 1961)
J. Onians, *Art and Thought in the Hellenistic Age*
    (London: Thames & Hudson, 1979)
J.J. Pollitt, *Art in the Hellenistic Age* (Cambridge U.P., 1986*)

5
World Conquerors
Romans, Buddhists, Jews and Christians, first to fourth century AD

Martin Henig, ed., *A Handbook of Roman Art*
    (Oxford: Phaidon, 1983; reprinted London, 1992*)
Ranuccio Bianchi Bandinelli, *Rome: the Centre of Power*
    (London: Thames & Hudson, 1970)
—, *Rome: the Late Empire* (London: Thames & Hudson, 1971)
Richard Brilliant, *Roman Art: From the Republic to Constantine*
    (London: Phaidon, 1974)
William Macdonald, *The Pantheon* (Harmondsworth: Penguin, 1976*)
Diana E.E. Kleiner, *Roman Sculpture* (New Haven and London: Yale U.P., 1993)
Roger Ling, *Roman Painting* (Cambridge U.P., 1991*)

6
A Parting of Ways
Rome and Byzantium, fifth to thirteenth century

Richard Krautheimer, *Rome, Profile of a City, 312-1308* (Princeton U.P., 1980)
Otto Demus, *Byzantine Art and the West* (London: Weidenfeld & Nicolson, 1970)
Ernst Kitzinger, *Byzantine Art in the Making* (London: Faber, 1977)
—, *Early Medieval Art in the British Museum* (London: British Museum, 1940*)

John Beckwith, The Art of Constantinople
    (London: Phaidon, 1961; 2nd edition, 1968)
Richard Krautheimer, Early Christian and Byzantine Art and Architecture
    (Harmondsworth: Penguin, 1965; 4th edition, 1986*)

7
Looking Eastwards
Islam, China, second to thirteenth century

Jerrilyn D. Dodds, ed., Al-Andalus: The Art of Islamic Spain
    (New York: Metropolitan Museum of Art, 1992)
Oleg Grabar, The Alhambra (London: Allen Lane, 1978)
—, The Formation of Islamic Art
    (New Haven and London: Yale U.P., 1973; revised edition, 1987*)
Godfrey Goodwin, History of Ottoman Architecture
    (London: Thames & Hudson, 1971; reprinted 1987*)
Basil Gray, Persian Painting (London: Batsford, 1947; reprinted 1961)
R.W. Ferrier, ed., The Arts of Persia
    (New Haven and London: Yale U.P., 1989)
J.C. Harle, Art and Architecture of the Indian Subcontinent
    (Harmondsworth: Penguin, 1986*)
T. Richard Blurton, Hindu Art (London: British Museum, 1992*)
James Cahill, Chinese Painting
    (Geneva: Skira, 1960; reprinted New York: Skira/Rizzoli, 1977*)
W. Willetts, Foundations of Chinese Art (London: Thames & Hudson, 1965)
William Watson, Style in the Arts of China (Harmondsworth: Penguin, 1974*)
Michael Sullivan, Symbols of Eternity (Oxford U.P., 1980)
—, The Arts of China (Berkeley: California U.P., 1967; 3rd edition, 1984*)
Wen C. Fong, Beyond Representation
    (New Haven and London: Yale U.P., 1992)

8
Western Art in the Melting Pot
Europe, sixth to eleventh century

David Wilson, Anglo-Saxon Art (London: Thames & Hudson, 1984)
—, The Bayeux Tapestry (London: Thames & Hudson, 1985)
Janet Backhouse, The Lindisfarne Gospels
    (Oxford: Phaidon, 1981; reprinted London, 1994*)
Jean Hubert et al., Carolingian Art (London: Thames & Hudson, 1970)

9
The Church Militant
The twelfth century

Meyer Schapiro, *Romanesque Art* (London: Chatto & Windus, 1977)

George Zarnecki, ed., *English Romanesque Art 1066-1200*
    (London: Royal Academy, 1984)

Hanns Swarzenski, *Monuments of Romanesque Art: the Art of Church Treasures in
    North-Western Europe* (London: Faber, 1954; 2nd edition, 1967)

Otto Pächt, *Book Illumination in the Middle Ages* (London: Harvey Miller, 1986)

Christopher de Hamel, *A History of Illuminated Manuscripts*
    (Oxford: Phaidon, 1986; 2nd edition, London, 1994)

J.J.G. Alexander, *Medieval Illuminators and their Methods*
    (New Haven and London: Yale U.P., 1992).

10
The Church Triumphant
The thirteenth century

Henri Focillon, *The Art of the West in the Middle Ages*
    (2 vols., London: Phaidon, 1963; 3rd edition, Oxford, 1980*)

Joan Evans, *Art in Mediaeval France* (London: Oxford U.P., 1948)

Robert Branner, *Chartres Cathedral* (London: Thames & Hudson, 1969;
    reprinted New York: W.W. Norton, 1980*)

George Henderson, *Chartres* (Harmondsworth: Penguin, 1968*)

Willibald Sauerländer, *Gothic Sculpture in France 1140-1270*, translated by
    Janet Sondheimer (London: Thames & Hudson, 1972)

Jean Bony, *French Gothic Architecture of the 12th and 13th Centuries*
    (Berkeley: California U.P., 1983*)

James H. Stubblebine, *Giotto, the Arena Chapel Frescoes*
    (London: Thames & Hudson, 1969; 2nd edition, 1993)

Jonathan Alexander and Paul Binski, ed., *Age of Chivalry: Art in Plantagenet
    England 1200-1400* (London: Royal Academy, 1987*)

11
Courtiers and Burghers
The fourteenth century

Jean Bony, *The English Decorated Style* (Oxford: Phaidon, 1979)

Andrew Martindale, *Simone Martini* (Oxford: Phaidon, 1988)

Millard Meiss, French Painting in the Time of Jean de Berry: The Limbourgs and
    their Contemporaries (2 vols., New York: Braziller, 1974)
Jean Longnon et al., The Très Riches Heures of the Duc de Berry
    (London: Thames & Hudson, 1969; reprinted 1989*)

12
The Conquest of Reality
The early fifteenth century

Eugenio Battisti, Brunelleschi: the Complete Work
    (London: Thames & Hudson, 1981)
Bruce Cole, Masaccio and the Art of Early Renaissance Florence
    (Bloomington: Indiana U.P., 1980)
Umberto Baldini & Ornella Casazza, The Brancacci Chapel Frescoes
    (London: Thames & Hudson, 1992)
Paul Joannides, Masaccio and Masolino (London: Phaidon, 1993)
H.W. Janson, The Sculpture of Donatello (Princeton U.P., 1957)
Bonnie A. Bennett and David G. Wilkins, Donatello (Oxford: Phaidon, 1984)
Kathleen Morand, Claus Sluter: Artist of the Court of Burgundy
    (London: Harvey Miller, 1991)
Elizabeth Dhanens, Hubert and Jan van Eyck
    (Antwerp: Fonds Mercator, 1980)
Erwin Panofsky, Early Netherlandish Painting: Its Origin and Character
    (2 vols., Cambridge, Mass.: Harvard U.P., 1953; reprinted New York:
    Harper & Row, 1971*)

13
Tradition and Innovation: I
The later fifteenth century in Italy

Franco Borsi, L.B. Alberti: Complete Edition (Oxford: Phaidon, 1977)
Richard Krautheimer, Lorenzo Ghiberti
    (Princeton U.P., 1956; revised edition, 1970)
John Pope-Hennessy, Fra Angelico
    (London: Phaidon, 1952; 2nd edition, 1974)
—, Uccello (London: Phaidon, 1950; 2nd edition, 1969)
Ronald Lightbown, Mantegna (Oxford: Phaidon-Christie's, 1986)
Jane Martineau, ed., Andrea Mantegna (London: Thames & Hudson, 1992)
Kenneth Clark, Piero della Francesca
    (London: Phaidon, 1951; 2nd edition, 1969)

Ronald Lightbown, *Piero della Francesca* (New York: Abbeville, 1992)

L.D. Ettlinger, *Antonio and Piero Pollaiuolo* (Oxford: Phaidon, 1978)

H. Horne, *Botticelli: Painter of Florence*
(London: Bell, 1908; revised edition, Princeton U.P., 1980)

Ronald Lightbown, *Botticelli* (2 vols., London: Elek, 1978; revised
edition published as *Sandro Botticelli: Life and Work*, London: Thames
& Hudson, 1989)

For *La Primavera* and *The Birth of Venus*, see my essay on Botticelli's
mythologies in *Symbolic Images* (London: Phaidon, 1972; 3rd edition,
Oxford, 1985; reprinted London, 1995*), pp. 31-81

14
Tradition and Innovation: II
The fifteenth century in the North

John Harvey, *The Perpendicular Style* (London: Batsford, 1978)

Martin Davies, *Rogier van der Weyden: An Essay, with a Critical Catalogue of
Paintings ascribed to him and to Robert Campin* (London: Phaidon, 1972)

Michael Baxandall, *The Limewood Sculptors of Renaissance Germany*
(New Haven and London: Yale U.P., 1980*)

Jan Bialastocki, *The Art of the Renaissance in Eastern Europe*
(Oxford: Phaidon, 1976)

15
Harmony Attained
Tuscany and Rome, early sixteenth century

Arnaldo Bruschi, *Bramante*, translated by Peter Murray
(London: Thames & Hudson, 1977)

Kenneth Clark, *Leonardo da Vinci* (Cambridge U.P., 1939; revised edition
by Martin Kemp, Harmondsworth: Penguin, 1988*)

A.E. Popham, ed., *Leonardo da Vinci: Drawings*
(London: Cape, 1946; revised edition, 1973*)

Martin Kemp, *Leonardo da Vinci: The Marvellous Works of Nature and Man*
(London: Dent, 1981*)

See also my essays in *The Heritage of Apelles* (Oxford: Phaidon, 1976;
reprinted London, 1993*), pp. 39-56, and *New Light on Old Masters*
(Oxford: Phaidon, 1986; reprinted London, 1993*), pp. 32-88

Herbert von Einem, *Michelangelo*
(revised English edition, London: Methuen, 1973)

Howard Hibbard, Michelangelo
    (Harmondsworth: Penguin, 1975; 2nd edition, 1985*)
    This and the above work are useful general introductions
Johannes Wilde, Michelangelo: Six Lectures (Oxford U.P., 1978*)
Ludwig Goldscheider, Michelangelo: Paintings, Sculpture, Architecture
    (London: Phaidon, 1953; 6th edition, 1995*)
Michael Hirst, Michelangelo and his Drawings
    (New Haven and London: Yale U.P., 1988*)
For complete catalogues of Michelangelo's work see:
Frederick Hartt, The Paintings of Michelangelo (New York: Abrams, 1964)
—, Michelangelo: The Complete Sculpture (New York: Abrams, 1970)
—, Michelangelo Drawings (New York: Abrams, 1970)
On the Sistine Chapel see:
Charles Seymour, ed., Michelangelo: The Sistine Ceiling
    (New York: W.W. Norton, 1972)
Carlo Pietrangeli, ed., The Sistine Chapel: Michelangelo Rediscovered
    (London: Muller, Blond & White, 1986)
John Pope-Hennessy, Raphael (London: Phaidon, 1970)
Roger Jones and Nicholas Penny, Raphael
    (New Haven and London: Yale U.P., 1983*)
Luitpold Dussler, Raphael: A Critical Catalogue of his Pictures, Wall-Paintings and
    Tapestries (London: Phaidon, 1971)
Paul Joannides, The Drawings of Raphael, with a Complete Catalogue
    (Oxford: Phaidon, 1983)
On the Stanza della Segnatura, see my essay in Symbolic Images
    (London: Phaidon, 1972; 3rd edition, Oxford, 1985; reprinted
    London, 1995*), pp. 85-101; on the Madonna della Sedia, see my essay
    in Norm and Form (London: Phaidon, 1966; 4th edition, Oxford, 1985;
    reprinted London, 1995*), pp. 64-80

16
Light and Colour
Venice and northern Italy, early sixteenth century

Deborah Howard, Jacopo Sansovino (New Haven and London: Yale U.P., 1975*)
Bruce Boucher, The Sculpture of Jacopo Sansovino
    (2 vols., New Haven and London: Yale U.P., 1992)
Johannes Wilde, Venetian Art from Bellini to Titian (Oxford U.P., 1974*)
Giles Robertson, Giovanni Bellini (Oxford U.P., 1968)
Terisio Pignatti, Giorgione: Complete Edition (London: Phaidon, 1971)

Harold Wethey, *The Paintings of Titian* (3 vols., London: Phaidon, 1969-75)
Charles Hope, *Titian* (London: Jupiter, 1980)
Cecil Gould, *The Paintings of Correggio* (London: Faber, 1976)
A.E. Popham, *Correggio's Drawings* (London: British Academy, 1957)

17
The New Learning Spreads
Germany and the Netherlands, early sixteenth century

Erwin Panofsky, *The Life and Art of Albrecht Dürer*
    (Princeton U.P., 1943; 4th edition, 1955; reprinted 1971*)
Nikolaus Pevsner and Michael Meier, *Grünewald*
    (London: Thames & Hudson, 1948)
G. Scheja, *The Isenheim Altarpiece*
    (Cologne: DuMont; and New York: Abrams, 1969)
Max J. Friedländer and Jakob Rosenberg, *The Paintings of Lucas Cranach*,
    translated by Heinz Norden (London: Sotheby's, 1978)
Walter S. Gibson, *Hieronymus Bosch* (London: Thames & Hudson, 1973) –
    see also my essay in *The Heritage of Apelles* (Oxford: Phaidon, 1976;
    reprinted London, 1993*), pp. 79-90
R.H. Marijnissen, *Hieronymus Bosch: The Complete Works* (Antwerp: Tatard, 1987)

18
A Crisis of Art
Europe, later sixteenth century

James Ackerman, *Palladio* (Harmondsworth: Penguin, 1966*)
John Shearman, *Mannerism* (Harmondsworth: Penguin, 1967*)
John Pope-Hennessy, *Cellini* (London: Macmillan, 1985)
Sydney J. Freedberg, *Parmigianino: His Works in Painting*
    (2 vols., Cambridge, Mass.: Harvard U.P., 1950)
A.E. Popham, *Catalogue of the Drawings of Parmigianino*
    (3 vols., New Haven and London, Yale U.P., 1971)
Charles Avery, *Giambologna*
    (Oxford: Phaidon-Christie's, 1987; reprinted London: Phaidon, 1993*)
Hans Tietze, *Tintoretto: The Paintings and Drawings* (London: Phaidon, 1948)
Harold E. Wethey, *El Greco and his School* (2 vols., Princeton U.P., 1962)
John Rowlands, *Holbein: The Paintings of Hans Holbein the Younger*
    (Oxford: Phaidon, 1985)

Roy Strong, *The English Renaissance Miniature*
    (London: Thames & Hudson, 1983*) — contains essays on Nicholas
    Hilliard and Isaac Oliver
F. Grossmann, *Pieter Bruegel: Complete Edition of the Paintings*
    (London: Phaidon, 1955; 3rd edition, 1973)
Ludwig Münz, *Bruegel: The Drawings* (London: Phaidon, 1961)

19
Vision and Visions
Catholic Europe, first half of the seventeenth century

Rudolf Wittkower, *Art and Architecture in Italy 1600-1750*
    (Harmondsworth: Penguin, 1958; 3rd edition, 1973*)
Ellis Waterhouse, *Italian Baroque Painting*
    (London: Phaidon, 1962; 2nd edition, 1969)
Donald Posner, *Annibale Carracci: A Study in the Reform of Italian Painting around*
    1590 (2 vols., London: Phaidon, 1971)
Walter Friedländer, *Caravaggio Studies* (Princeton U.P., 1955*)
Howard Hibbard, *Caravaggio* (London: Thames & Hudson, 1983*)
D. Stephen Pepper, *Guido Reni: A Complete Catalogue of his Works with an*
    Introductory Text (Oxford: Phaidon, 1984)
Anthony Blunt, *The Paintings of Poussin* (3 vols., London: Phaidon, 1966-7)
Marcel Röthlisberger, *Claude Lorrain: The Paintings*
    (2 vols., New Haven and London: Yale U.P., 1961)
Julius S. Held, *Rubens: Selected Drawings* (2 vols., London: Phaidon, 1959;
    2nd edition, in 1 vol., Oxford, 1986)
—, *The Oil Sketches of Peter Paul Rubens: A Critical Catalogue*
    (2 vols., Princeton U.P., 1980)
Corpus Rubenianum Ludwig Burchard (London: Phaidon; and London: Harvey
    Miller, 1968-; 27 parts planned, of which 15 have been published)
Michael Jaffé, *Rubens and Italy* (Oxford: Phaidon, 1977)
Christopher White, *Peter Paul Rubens: Man and Artist*
    (New Haven and London: Yale U.P., 1987)
Christopher Brown, *Van Dyck* (Oxford: Phaidon, 1982)
Jonathan Brown, *Velázquez* (New Haven and London: Yale U.P., 1986*)
Enriqueta Harris, *Velázquez* (Oxford: Phaidon, 1982)
Jonathan Brown, *The Golden Age of Painting in Spain*
    (New Haven and London: Yale U.P., 1991)

20
The Mirror of Nature
Holland, seventeenth century

Katharine Fremantle, *The Baroque Town Hall of Amsterdam*
    (Utrecht: Dekker & Gumbert, 1959)
Bob Haak, *The Golden Age: Dutch Painters of the Seventeenth Century* translated
    by E. Williams-Freeman (London: Thames & Hudson, 1984)
Seymour Slive, *Frans Hals* (3 vols., London: Phaidon, 1970-4)
—, *Jacob van Ruisdael* (New York: Abbeville, 1981)
Gary Schwarz, *Rembrandt: His Life, his Paintings*
    (Harmondsworth: Penguin, 1985*)
Jakob Rosenberg, *Rembrandt: Life and Work* (2 vols., Cambridge, Mass.:
    Harvard U.P., 1948; 4th edition, Oxford: Phaidon, 1980*)
A. Bredius, *Rembrandt: Complete Edition of the Paintings* (Vienna: Phaidon,
    1935; 4th edition, revised by Horst Gerson, London: Phaidon, 1971*)
Otto Benesch, *The Drawings of Rembrandt*
    (6 vols., London: Phaidon, 1954-7; revised edition, 1973)
Christopher White and K.G. Boon, *Rembrandt's Etchings: An Illustrated Critical
    Catalogue* (2 vols., Amsterdam: Van Ghendt, 1969)
Christopher Brown, Jan Kelch and Pieter van Thiel, *Rembrandt: The Master and his
    Workshop* (2 vols., New Haven and London: Yale U.P., 1991*)
Baruch D. Kirschenbaum, *The Religious and Historical Paintings of Jan Steen*
    (Oxford: Phaidon, 1977)
Wolfgang Stechow, *Dutch Landscape Painting of the Seventeenth Century*
    (London: Phaidon, 1966; 3rd edition, Oxford, 1981*)
Svetlana Alpers, *The Art of Describing: Dutch Art in the Seventeenth Century*
    (London: John Murray, 1983*)
Lawrence Gowing, *Vermeer* (London: Faber, 1952)
Albert Blankert, *Vermeer of Delft: Complete Edition of the Paintings*
    (Oxford: Phaidon, 1978)
John Michael Montias, *Vermeer and his Milieu* (Princeton U.P., 1989)

21
Power and Glory: I
Italy, later seventeenth and eighteenth centuries

Anthony Blunt, ed., *Baroque and Rococo Architecture and Decoration*
    (London: Elek, 1978)

—, Borromini (Harmondsworth: Penguin, 1979; new edition, Cambridge,
    Mass.: Harvard U.P., 1990*)

Rudolf Wittkower, Gian Lorenzo Bernini
    (London: Phaidon, 1955; 3rd edition, Oxford, 1981)

Robert Enggass, The Paintings of Baciccio: Giovanni Battista Gaulli 1639-1709
    (University Park: Pennsylvania State U.P., 1964)

Michael Levey, Giambattista Tiepolo (New Haven and London: Yale U.P., 1986)

—, Painting in Eighteenth Century Venice (London: Phaidon, 1959;
    3rd edition, New Haven and London: Yale U.P., 1994)

Julius S. Held and Donald Posner, Seventeenth and Eighteenth Century Art
    (New York and London: Abrams, 1972)

22
Power and Glory: II
France, Germany and Austria, late seventeenth and early eighteenth centuries

G. Walton, Louis XIV and Versailles (Harmondsworth: Penguin, 1986)

Anthony Blunt, Art and Architecture in France 1500-1700
    (Harmondsworth: Penguin, 1953; 4th edition, 1980*)

Henry-Russell Hitchcock, Rococo Architecture in Southern Germany
    (London: Phaidon, 1968)

Eberhard Hempel, Baroque Art and Architecture in Central Europe
    (Harmondsworth: Penguin, 1965*)

Marianne Roland Michel, Watteau: An Artist of the Eighteenth Century
    (London: Trefoil, 1984)

Donald Posner, Antoine Watteau (London: Weidenfeld & Nicolson, 1984)

23
The Age of Reason:
England and France, eighteenth century

Kerry Downes, Sir Christopher Wren (London: Granada, 1982)

Ronald Paulson, Hogarth: His Life, Art and Times (2 vols., New Haven and
    London: Yale U.P., 1971; abridged 1-vol. edition, 1974*)

David Bindman, Hogarth (London: Thames & Hudson, 1981)

Ellis Waterhouse, Reynolds (London: Phaidon, 1973)

Nicholas Penny, ed., Reynolds (London: Royal Academy, 1986*)

John Hayes, Gainsborough: Paintings and Drawings
    (London: Phaidon, 1975, reprinted Oxford, 1978)

—, *The Landscape Paintings of Thomas Gainsborough: A Critical Text and Catalogue Raisonné* (2 vols., London: Sotheby's, 1982)

—, *The Drawings of Thomas Gainsborough* (2 vols., London: Zwemmer, 1970)

—, *Thomas Gainsborough* (London: Tate Gallery, 1980*)

Georges Wildenstein, *Chardin, a Catalogue Raisonné* (Oxford: Cassirer, 1969)

Philip Conisbee, *Chardin* (Oxford: Phaidon, 1986)

H.H. Arnason, *The Sculptures of Houdon* (London: Phaidon, 1975)

Jean-Pierre Cuzin, *Jean-Honoré Fragonard: Life and Work, Complete Catalogue of the Oil Paintings* (New York: Abrams, 1988)

Oliver Millar, *Zoffany and his Tribuna* (London: Routledge & Kegan Paul, 1967)

24
The Break in Tradition
England, America and France, late eighteenth and early nineteenth centuries

J. Mordaunt Crook, *The Dilemma of Style* (London: John Murray, 1987)

J.D. Prown, *John Singleton Copley* (2 vols., Cambridge, Mass.: Harvard U.P., 1966)

Anita Brookner, *Jacques-Louis David* (London: Chatto & Windus, 1980*)

Paul Gassier and Juliet Wilson, *The Life and Complete Work of Francisco Goya* (New York: Reynal, 1971; revised edition, 1981)

Janis Tomlinson, *Goya* (London: Phaidon, 1994)

David Bindman, *Blake as an Artist* (Oxford: Phaidon, 1977)

Martin Butlin, *The Paintings and Drawings of William Blake* (2 vols., New Haven and London: Yale U.P., 1981)

— and Evelyn Joll, *The Paintings of J.M.W. Turner, a Catalogue* (2 vols., New Haven and London: Yale U.P., 1977; revised edition, 1984*)

Andrew Wilton, *The Life and Work of J.M.W. Turner* (London: Academy, 1979)

Graham Reynolds, *The Late Paintings and Drawings of John Constable* (2 vols., New Haven and London: Yale U.P., 1984)

Malcolm Cormack, *Constable* (Oxford: Phaidon, 1986)

Walter Friedländer, *From David to Delacroix* (Cambridge, Mass.: Harvard U.P., 1952*)

William Vaughan, *German Romantic Painting* (New Haven and London: Yale U.P., 1980*)

Helmut Börsch-Supan, *Caspar David Friedrich* (London: Thames & Hudson, 1974; 4th edition, Munich: Prestel, 1990)

Hugh Honour, *Neo-classicism* (Harmondsworth: Penguin, 1968*)

—, *Romanticism* (Harmondsworth: Penguin, 1981*)

Kenneth Clark, *The Romantic Rebellion* (London: Sotheby's, 1986*)

25

Permanent Revolution
The nineteenth century

Robert Rosenblum, *Ingres* (London: Thames & Hudson, 1967)
— and H.W. Janson, *The Art of the Nineteenth Century*
     (London: Thames & Hudson, 1984)
Lee Johnson, *The Paintings of Eugène Delacroix* (6 vols., Oxford U.P., 1981-9)
Michael Clarke, *Corot and the Art of Landscape* (London: British Museum, 1991)
Peter Galassi, *Corot in Italy: Open-Air Painting and the Classical Landscape*
     Tradition (New Haven and London: Yale U.P., 1991)
Robert Herbert, *Millet*
     (Paris: Grand Palais; and London: Hayward Gallery, 1975*)
Courbet (Paris: Grand Palais; and London: Royal Academy, 1977*)
Linda Nochlin, *Realism* (Harmondsworth: Penguin, 1971*)
Virginia Surtees, *The Paintings and Drawings of Dante Gabriel Rossetti*
     (Oxford U.P., 1971)
Albert Boime, *The Academy and French Painting in the Nineteenth Century* (London:
     Phaidon, 1971; reprinted New Haven and London: Yale U.P., 1986*)
Manet (Paris: Grand Palais; and New York: Metropolitan Museum of Art,
     1983)
John House, *Monet* (Oxford: Phaidon, 1977; 3rd edition, London, 1991*)
Paul Hayes Tucker, *Monet in the '90s: The Series Paintings*
     (New Haven and London: Yale U.P., 1989*)
Renoir (Paris: Grand Palais; London: Hayward Gallery; and Boston:
     Museum of Fine Arts, 1985*)
Pissarro (London: Hayward Gallery; Paris: Grand Palais; and Boston:
     Museum of Fine Arts, 1981*)
J. Hillier, *The Japanese Print: A New Approach* (London: Bell, 1960)
Richard Lane, *Hokusai: Life and Work* (London: Barrie & Jenkins, 1989)
Jean Sutherland Boggs et al., *Degas*
     (Paris: Grand Palais; Ottawa: National Gallery of Canada; and
     New York: Metropolitan Museum of Art, 1988*)
John Rewald, *The History of Impressionism* (New York: Museum of Modern
     Art, 1946; 4th edition, London: Secker & Warburg, 1973*)
Robert L. Herbert, *Impressionism: Art, Leisure and Parisian Society*
     (New Haven and London: Yale U.P., 1988*)
Albert Elsen, *Rodin* (New York: Metropolitan Museum of Art, 1963)
Catherine Lampert, *Rodin: Sculptures and Drawings*
     (London: Hayward Gallery, 1986*)

Andrew Maclaren Young, ed., *The Paintings of James McNeill Whistler*
(New Haven and London: Yale U.P., 1980)

K.E. Maison, *Honoré Daumier: Catalogue of the Paintings, Watercolours and Drawings* (2 vols., London: Thames & Hudson, 1968)

Quentin Bell, *Victorian Artists* (London: Routledge & Kegan Paul, 1967)

Graham Reynolds, *Victorian Painting* (London: Studio Vista, 1966)

26
In Search of New Standards
The late nineteenth century

Robert Schmutzler, *Art Nouveau*, translated by E. Roditi
(London: Thames & Hudson, 1964; abridged edition, 1978)

Roger Fry, *Cézanne: A Study of his Development* (London: Hogarth Press, 1927; new edition, Chicago U.P., 1989*)

William Rubin, ed., *Cézanne: The Late Work* (London: Thames & Hudson, 1978)

John Rewald, *Cézanne: The Watercolours* (London: Thames & Hudson, 1983)

John Russell, *Seurat* (London: Thames & Hudson, 1965*)

Richard Thomson, *Seurat* (Oxford: Phaidon, 1985; reprinted 1990*)

Ronald Pickvance, *Van Gogh in Arles*
(New York: Metropolitan Museum of Art, 1984*)

—, *Van Gogh in Saint Rémy and Auvers*
(New York: Metropolitan Museum of Art, 1986*)

Michel Hoog, *Gauguin* (London: Thames & Hudson, 1987)

Gauguin (Paris: Grand Palais; Chicago: Art Insitute; and Washington: National Gallery of Art, 1988*)

Nicholas Watkins, *Bonnard* (London: Phaidon, 1994)

Götz Adriani, *Toulouse-Lautrec* (London: Thames & Hudson, 1987)

—, *Post-Impressionism: From Van Gogh to Gauguin* (New York: Museum of Modern Art, 1956; 3rd edition, London: Secker & Warburg, 1978*)

27
Experimental Art
The first half of the twentieth century

Robert Rosenblum, *Cubism and Twentieth-Century Art* (London: Thames & Hudson, 1960; revised edition, New York: Abrams, 1992)

John Golding, *Cubism: A History and an Analysis, 1907-1914*
(London: Faber, 1959; 3rd edition, 1988*)

Bernard S. Myers, *Expressionism* (London: Thames & Hudson, 1963)

Walter Grosskamp, ed., *German Art in the Twentieth Century: Painting and Sculpture 1905-1985* (London: Royal Academy, 1985)

Hans Maria Wingler, *The Bauhaus* (Cambridge, Mass.: MIT Press, 1969)

H. Bayer, W. Gropius and I. Gropius, eds., *Bauhaus 1919-1928* (London: Secker & Warburg, 1)

William J.R. Curtis, *Modern Architecture since 1900* (Oxford: Phaidon, 1982; 2nd edition, 1987, reprinted London, 1994*)

Norbert Lynton, *The Story of Modern Art* (Oxford: Phaidon, 1980; 2nd edition, 1989; reprinted London, 1994*)

Robert Hughes, *The Shock of the New: Art and the Century of Change* (London: BBC, 1980; revised and enlarged edition, 1991)

William Rubin, ed., *'Primitivism' in 20th Century Art: Affinity of the Tribal and the Modern* (2 vols., New York: Museum of Modern Art, 1984)

Reinhold Heller, *Munch: His Life and Work* (London: John Murray, 1984)

C.D. Zigrosser, *Prints and Drawings of Käthe Kollwitz* (London: Constable; and New York: Dover, 1969)

Werner Haftmann, *Emil Nolde*, translated by N. Guterman (London: Thames & Hudson, 1960)

Richard Calvocoressi, ed., *Oskar Kokoschka 1886-1980* (London: Tate Gallery, 1987*)

Peter Vergo, *Art in Vienna 1898-1918: Klimt, Kokoschka, Schiele and their Contemporaries* (London: Phaidon, 1975; 3rd edition, 1993, reprinted 1994)

Paul Overy, *Kandinsky: The Language of the Eye* (London: Elek, 1969)

Hans K. Roethel and Joan K. Benjamin, *Kandinsky: Catalogue Raisonné of the Oil Paintings* (2 vols., London: Sotheby's, 1982-4)

Will Grohmann, *Wassily Kandinsky: Life and Work* (New York: Abrams, 1958)

Sixten Ringbom, *The Sounding Cosmos* (Åbo: Academia, 1970)

Jack Flam, *Matisse: The Man and his Art, 1869-1918* (London: Thames & Hudson, 1986)

John Elderfield, ed., *Henri Matisse* (New York: Museum of Modern Art, 1992*)

Pablo Picasso: A Retrospective (New York: Museum of Modern Art, 1980*)

Timothy Hilton, *Picasso* (London: Thames & Hudson, 1975*)

Richard Verdi, *Klee and Nature* (London: Zwemmer, 1984*)

Margaret Plant, *Paul Klee: Figures and Faces* (London: Thames & Hudson, 1978)

Ulrich Luckhardt, *Lyonel Feininger* (Munich: Prestel, 1989)

Pontus Hultén, Natalia Dumitresco, Alexandre Istrati, *Brancusi* (London: Faber, 1988)

John Milner, *Mondrian* (London: Phaidon, 1992)

Norbert Lynton, *Ben Nicholson* (London: Phaidon, 1993)

Susan Compton, ed., *British Art in the Twentieth Century: The Modern Movement*
      (London: Royal Academy, 1987*)
Joan M. Marter, *Alexander Calder, 1898-1976* (Cambridge U.P., 1991)
Alan Bowness, ed., *Henry Moore: Sculptures and Drawings*
      (6 vols., London: Lund Humphries, 1965-7)
Susan Compton, ed., *Henry Moore* (London: Royal Academy, 1988)
Le Douanier Rousseau (New York: Museum of Modern Art, 1985)
Susan Compton, ed., *Chagall* (London: Royal Academy, 1985)
David Sylvester, ed., *René Magritte, Catalogue Raisonné* (2 vols., Houston:
      The Menil Foundation and; London: Philip Wilson, 1992-3)
Yves Bonnefoy, *Giacometti* (New York: Abbeville, 1991)
Robert Descharnes, *Dali: The Work, the Man*, translated by E.R. Morse
      (New York: Abrams, 1984)
Dawn Ades, *Salvador Dali* (London: Thames & Hudson, 1982*)

28
A Story without End
The triumph of Modernism; Another turning of the tide; The changing past

John Elderfield, *Kurt Schwitters* (London: Thames & Hudson, 1985*)
Irving Sandler, *Abstract Expressionism: The Triumph of American Painting*
      (London: Pall Mall, 1970)
Ellen G. Landau, *Jackson Pollock* (London: Thames & Hudson, 1989)
James Johnson Sweeney, *Pierre Soulages* (Neuchâtel: Ides et Calendes, 1972)
Douglas Cooper, *Nicolas de Staël* (London: Weidenfeld & Nicolson, 1962)
Patrick Waldburg, Herbert Read and Giovanni de San Luzzaro, eds.,
      Complete Works of Marino Marini (New York: Tudor Publishing, 1971)
Marilena Pasquali, ed., *Giorgio Morandi 1890-1964* (London: Electa, 1989)
Hugh Adams, *Art of the Sixties* (Oxford: Phaidon, 1978)
Charles Jencks and Maggie Keswick, *Architecture Today*
      (London: Academy, 1988)
Lawrence Gowing, *Lucian Freud* (London: Thames & Hudson, 1982)
Naomi Rosenblum, *A World History of Photography*
      (New York: Abbeville, 1989*)
Henri Cartier-Bresson, *Cartier-Bresson Photographer*
      (London: Thames & Hudson, 1980*)
Hockney on Photography: Conversations with Paul Joyce
      (London: Jonathan Cape, 1988)
Maurice Tuchman and Stephanie Barron, eds., *David Hockney: A Retrospective*
      (Los Angeles: Los Angeles County Museum of Art; and London:
      Thames & Hudson, 1988)

List of illustrations
by location

Numbers refer to figures

Austria

Melk
Monastery 296-7

Vienna
Albertina: Bruegel, *The painter and the buyer* 245; Dürer, *Great piece of turf* 221; Dürer, *Hare* 9; Raphael, *Four studies for the 'Virgin in the meadow'* 18; Rembrandt, *Elephant* 10; Rubens, *Portrait of his son Nicholas* 1

Kunsthistorisches Museum: Bruegel, *Peasant wedding* 246-7; Cellini, *salt-cellar* 233; *Portrait head* 32; Raphael, *Virgin in the meadow* 17; Rembrandt, *Self-portrait* 273; Rubens, *Self-portrait* 258; *St Matthew* 105; Velázquez, *Prince Philip Prosper of Spain* 267

Upper Belvedere 293-4

Belgium

Antwerp
Koninklijk Museum voor Schone Kunsten: Memling, *Angel* 6

Bruges
Groeningemuseum: van der Goes, *The Death of the Virgin* 180-1
The Old Chancellery ('Le Greffe') 219

Brussels
Bibliothèque Royale: Le Tavernier, dedication page to *The Conquests of Charlemagne* 177

Hôtel Tassel 349
Musées Royaux des Beaux-Arts de Belgique: David, *Marat assassinated* 316

Ghent
Cathedral of St Bavo: van Eyck, *Ghent altarpiece* 155-7

Liège
St-Barthélemy: Reiner van Huy, font 118

Tournai
Cathedral 112

China

Hsian
'Terracotta army' 411-12

Nanjing
Tomb of Xiao Jing 94

Shantung provinc
Tomb of Wu Liang-tse 93

Czech Republic

Prague
Cathedral: Parler, *Self-portrait* 142
Národní Galerie: Mabuse, *St Luke painting the Virgin* 228

Denmark

Copenhagen
Statens Museum for Kunst: Pannini, *Interior of the Pantheon* 75

Greece

India

Detailed list of illustrations

1
Peter Paul Rubens, *Portrait of his son Nicholas*, c. 1620. Black and red chalks on paper, 25.2 × 20.3 cm, 10 × 8 in; Albertina, Vienna

2
Albrecht Dürer, *Portrait of his mother*, 1514. Black chalk on paper, 42.1 × 30.3 cm, 16½ × 12 in; Kupferstichkabinett, Staatliche Museen, Berlin

3
Bartolomé Esteban Murillo, *Street arabs*, c. 1670-5. Oil on canvas, 146 × 108 cm, 57½ × 42½ in; Alte Pinakothek, Munich

4
Pieter de Hooch, *Interior with a woman peeling apples*, 1663. Oil on canvas, 70.5 × 54.3 cm, 27¾ × 21⅜ in; Wallace Collection, London

5
Melozzo da Forlì, *Angel*, c. 1480. Detail of a fresco; Pinacoteca, Vatican

6
Hans Memling, *Angel*, c. 1490. Detail of a panel from an altarpiece; oil on wood; Koninklijk Museum voor Schone Kunsten, Antwerp

7
Guido Reni, *Christ crowned with thorns*, c. 1639-40. Oil on canvas, 62 × 48 cm, 24½ × 19 in; Louvre, Paris

8
Tuscan master, *Head of Christ*, c. 1175-1225. Detail of a crucifix; tempera on wood; Uffizi, Florence

9
Albrecht Dürer, *Hare*, 1502. Watercolour and gouache on paper, 25 × 22.5 cm, 9⅞ × 8⅞ in; Albertina, Vienna

10
Rembrandt van Rijn, *Elephant*, 1637. Black chalk on paper, 23 × 34 cm, 9 × 13⅜ in; Albertina, Vienna

11
Pablo Picasso, *Hen with chicks*, 1941-2. Etching, 36 × 28 cm, 14¼ × 11 in; illustration to Buffon's *Natural History*

12
Pablo Picasso, *Cockerel*, 1938. Charcoal on paper, 76 × 55 cm, 30 × 21½ in; private collection

13
Théodore Géricault, *Horse-racing at Epsom*, 1821. Oil on canvas, 92 × 122.5 cm, 36¼ × 48¼ in; Louvre, Paris

14
Eadweard Muybridge, *Galloping horse in motion*, 1872. Photograph sequence; Kingston-upon-Thames Museum

15
Caravaggio, *Saint Matthew*, 1602. Altar-painting; oil on canvas, 223 × 183 cm, 87⅞ × 72⅛ in; destroyed; formerly Kaiser-Friedrich Museum, Berlin

16
Caravaggio, *Saint Matthew*, 1602. Altar-painting; oil on canvas, 296.5 × 195 cm, 116⅞ × 76⅞ in; church of S. Luigi dei Francesi, Rome

17
Raphael, *Virgin in the meadow*, 1505-6. Oil on wood, 113 × 88 cm, 44½ × 34⅛ in; Kunsthistorisches Museum, Vienna

18
Raphael, *Four studies for the 'Virgin in the meadow'*, 1505-6. Leaf from a sketchbook; pen and ink on paper, 36.2 × 24.5 cm, 14¼ × 9⅝ in; Albertina, Vienna

19
Bison, c. 15,000-10,000 BC.
Cave paintings; Altamira, Spain

20
Horse, c. 15,000-10,000 BC.
Cave painting; Lascaux, France

21
Cave at Lascaux, France, c. 15,000-10,000 BC

22
Lintel from a Maori chieftain's house, early
19th century. Carved wood, 32 × 82 cm,
12⅝ × 32¼ in; British Museum, London

23
Head of a Negro, probably representing a ruler
(Oni), from Ife, Nigeria, 12th-14th century.
Bronze, height 36 cm, 14⅛ in; British
Museum, London

24
Oro, God of War, from Tahiti, 18th century.
Wood, covered with sinnet, length
66 cm, 26 in; British Museum, London

25
Ritual mask from the Papuan Gulf region,
New Guinea, c. 1880. Wood, bark cloth
and vegetable fibre, height 152.4 cm,
60 in; British Museum, London

26
Model of a nineteenth-century Haida chieftain's
house, north-west coast Indians. American
Museum of Natural History, New York

27
Head of the death-god, from a stone Mayan
altar found at Copan, Honduras, c. 500-600
AD. 37 × 104 cm, 14½ × 50 in; British
Museum, London

28
Inuit dance mask from Alaska, c. 1880.
Painted wood, 37 × 25.5 cm, 14½ × 10
in; Museum für Völkerkunde, Staatliche
Museen, Berlin

29
Vessel in the form of a one-eyed man, found
in the Chicanná Valley, Peru, c. 250-550 AD.
Clay, height 29 cm, 11½ in; The Art
Institute of Chicago

30
Tlaloc, the Aztec rain-god, 14th-15th
century. Stone, height 40 cm, 15¾ in;
Museum für Völkerkunde, Staatliche
Museen, Berlin

31
The Pyramids of Giza, c. 2613-2563 BC

32
Portrait head, c. 2551-2528 BC. Found
in a tomb at Giza; limestone, height
27.8 cm, 11 in; Kunsthistorisches
Museum, Vienna

33
The garden of Nebamun, c. 1400 BC.
Wall-painting from a tomb in Thebes,
64 × 74.2 cm, 25¼ × 29¼ in; British
Museum, London

34
Portrait of Hesire, from a wooden door in his
tomb, c. 2778-2723 BC. Wood, height 115
cm, 45¼ in; Egyptian Museum, Cairo

35
Wall-painting from the tomb of Khnumhotep,
c. 1900 BC. Found at Beni Hassan; from
a drawing after the original, published
by Karl Lepsius, Denkmäler, 1842

36
Detail of figure 35

37
Birds in an acacia bush. Detail of figure 35;
from a painting after the original by
Nina Macpherson Davies

38
The jackal-faced god Anubis supervising
the weighing of a dead man's heart, while the

ibis-headed messenger-god Thoth on the right
records the result, c.1285 BC. Scene from
an Egyptian 'Book of the Dead',
a painted papyrus scroll placed in the
deceased's tomb; height 39.8 cm,
15¼ in; British Museum, London

39
Amenophis IV (Akhnaten), c.1360 BC.
Limestone relief, height 14 cm, 5½ in;
Ägyptisches Museum, Staatliche
Museen, Berlin

40
Akhnaten and Nefertiti with their children,
c.1345 BC. Limestone altar relief,
32.5 × 39 cm, 12¾ × 15½ in;
Ägyptisches Museum, Staatliche
Museen, Berlin

41
Dagger, c.1600 BC. Found at Mycenae;
bronze inlaid with gold, silver and
niello, length 23.8 cm, 9½ in; National
Archaeological Museum, Athens

42
Tutankhamun and his wife, c.1330 BC.
Detail of gilt and painted woodwork
from the throne found in his tomb;
Egyptian Museum, Cairo

43
Fragment of a harp, c.2600 BC. Found
in Ur; gilt and inlaid wood; British
Museum, London

44
Monument of King Naramsin, c.2270 BC.
Found in Susa; stone, height 200 cm,
79 in; Louvre, Paris

45
Assyrian army besieging a fortress, c.883-
859 BC. Detail of alabaster relief from
the palace of King Asurnasirpal at
Nimrud; British Museum, London

46
The mourning of the dead, c.700 BC.
Greek vase in the Geometric style;
height 155 cm, 61 in; National
Archaeological Museum, Athens

47
Polymedes of Argos, *The brothers Cleobis
and Biton*, c.615-590 BC. Marble,
height 218 and 216 cm, 86 and 85 in;
Archaeological Museum, Delphi

48
Achilles and Ajax playing draughts, c.540 BC.
Vase in the 'black-figured' style, signed
by Exekias; height 61 cm, 24 in; Museo
Etrusco, Vatican

49
The warrior's leave-taking, c.510-500 BC.
Vase in the 'red-figured' style, signed
by Euthymedes; height 60 cm, 23½ in;
Staatliche Antikensammlungen und
Glyptothek, Munich

50
Iktinos, *The Parthenon, Acropolis, Athens*,
447-432 BC. A Doric temple

51
Athena Parthenos, c.447-432 BC. Roman
marble copy after the wood, gold
and ivory original by Pheidias, height
104 cm, 41 in; National Archaeological
Museum, Athens

52
Hercules carrying the heavens, c.470-460 BC.
Marble fragment from the Temple of
Zeus at Olympia, height 156 cm, 61½
in; Archaeological Museum, Olympia

53
Charioteer, c.475 BC. Found at Delphi;
bronze, height 180 cm, 71 in;
Archaeological Museum, Delphi

227
Albrecht Altdorfer, *Landscape*, c. 1526-8.
Oil on parchment, mounted on wood,
30 × 22 cm, 12 × 8⅝ in; Alte Pinakothek,
Munich

228
Mabuse, *St Luke painting the Virgin*, c. 1515.
Oil on wood, 230 × 205 cm,
90½ × 80¾ in; Národní Galerie, Prague

229, 230
Hieronymus Bosch, *Paradise and Hell*,
c. 1510. Left and right panels of
a triptych; oil on wood, each panel
135 × 45 cm, 53¼ × 17¾ in; Prado,
Madrid

231
Federico Zuccaro, *Window of the Palazzo
Zuccari, Rome*, 1592

232
Andrea Palladio, *Villa Rotonda, near Vicenza*,
1550. An Italian sixteenth-century villa

233
Benvenuto Cellini, *Salt-cellar*, 1543.
Chased gold and enamel on ebony
base, length 33.5 cm, 13¼ in;
Kunsthistorisches Museum, Vienna

234
Parmigianino, *Madonna with the long neck*,
1534-40. Left unfinished at the artist's
death; oil on wood, 216 × 132 cm,
85 × 52 in; Uffizi, Florence

235
Giambologna, *Mercury*, 1580. Bronze,
height 187 cm, 67 in; Museo Nazionale
del Bargello, Florence

236
Tintoretto, *The finding of St Mark's remains*,
c. 1562. Oil on canvas, 405 × 405 cm,
159⅝ × 159⅝ in; Pinacoteca
di Brera, Milan

237
Tintoretto, *St George and the dragon*,
c. 1555-8. Oil on canvas,
157.5 × 100.3 cm, 62 × 39½ in;
National Gallery, London

238
El Greco, *The opening of the Fifth Seal of
the Apocalypse*, c. 1608-14. Oil on canvas,
224.5 × 192.8 cm, 88½ × 76 in;
Metropolitan Museum of Art, New York

239
El Greco, *Brother Hortensio Felix Paravicino*,
1609. Oil on canvas, 113 × 86 cm, 44½ ×
33⅞ in; Museum of Fine Arts, Boston

240
Hans Holbein the Younger, *The Virgin
and Child with the family of Burgomaster
Meyer*, 1528. Altar-painting; oil on
wood, 146.5 × 102 cm, 57⅝ × 40⅛ in;
Schlossmuseum, Darmstadt

241
Hans Holbein the Younger, *Anne Cresacre,
Sir Thomas More's daughter-in-law*, 1528.
Black and coloured chalks on paper,
37.9 × 26.9 cm, 14⅞ × 10½ in; Royal
Library, Windsor Castle

242
Hans Holbein the Younger, *Sir Richard
Southwell*, 1536. Oil on wood, 47.5 ×
38 cm, 18 × 15 in; Uffizi, Florence

243
Hans Holbein the Younger, *Georg Gisze,
a German merchant in London*, 1532. Oil
on wood, 96.3 × 85.7 cm, 38 × 33¾ in;
Gemäldegalerie, Staatliche Museen,
Berlin

244
Nicholas Hilliard, *Young man among roses*,
c. 1587. Watercolour and gouache on
vellum, 13.6 × 7.3 cm, 5⅜ × 2⅞ in;
Victoria and Albert Museum, London

245
Pieter Bruegel the Elder, *The painter and the buyer*, c. 1565. Pen and black ink on brown paper, 25 × 21.6 cm, 9⅞ × 8½ in; Albertina, Vienna

246
Pieter Bruegel the Elder, *Peasant wedding*, c. 1568. Oil on wood, 114 × 164 cm, 45 × 64½ in; Kunsthistorisches Museum, Vienna

247
Detail of figure 246

248
Jean Goujon, *Nymphs from the Fontaine des Innocents*, 1547-9. Marble; each panel 240 × 63 cm, 94½ × 24¾ in; Musée National des Monuments Français, Paris

249
Jacques Callot, *Two Italian clowns*, c. 1622. Detail of etching from the series 'Balli di Sfessania'

250
Giacomo della Porta, *Church of Il Gesù*, *Rome*, c. 1575-7. An early Baroque church

251
Annibale Carracci, *The Virgin mourning Christ*, 1599-1600. Altar-painting; oil on canvas, 156 × 149 cm, 61⅜ × 58⅝ in; Museo di Capodimonte, Naples

252
Caravaggio, *Doubting Thomas*, c. 1602-3. Oil on canvas, 107 × 146 cm, 42⅛ × 57½ in; Stiftung Schlösser und Gärten, Sanssouci, Potsdam

253
Guido Reni, *Aurora*, 1614. Fresco, c. 280 × 700 cm, 110 × 276 in; Palazzo Pallavicini-Rospigliosi, Rome

254
Nicolas Poussin, 'Et in Arcadia ego', 1638-9. Oil on canvas, 85 × 121 cm, 33½ × 47⅝ in; Louvre, Paris

255
Claude Lorrain, *Landscape with sacrifice to Apollo*, 1662-3. Oil on canvas, 174 × 220 cm, 68½ × 86½ in; Anglesey Abbey, Cambridgeshire

256
Peter Paul Rubens, *Virgin and Child enthroned with saints*, c. 1627-8. Sketch for a large altar-painting; oil on wood, 80.2 × 55.5 cm, 31½ × 21¾ in; Gemäldegalerie, Staatliche Museen, Berlin

257
Peter Paul Rubens, *Head of a child, probably the artist's daughter Clara Serena*, c. 1616. Oil on canvas, mounted on wood, 33 × 26.3 cm, 13 × 10⅜ in; Sammlungen des Fürsten von Liechtenstein, Vaduz

258
Peter Paul Rubens, *Self-portrait*, c. 1639. Oil on canvas, 109.5 × 85 cm, 43⅛ × 33½ in; Kunsthistorisches Museum, Vienna

259
Peter Paul Rubens, *Allegory on the blessings of peace*, 1629-30. Oil on canvas, 203.5 × 298 cm, 80⅛ × 117¼ in; National Gallery, London

260
Detail of figure 259

261
Anthony van Dyck, *Charles I of England*, c. 1635. Oil on canvas, 266 × 207 cm, 104¾ × 81½ in; Louvre, Paris

262
Anthony van Dyck, *Lord John and Lord Bernard Stuart*, c.1638. Oil on canvas, 237.5 × 146.1 cm, 93½ × 57½ in; National Gallery, London

263
Diego Velázquez, *The water-seller of Seville*, c.1619-20. Oil on canvas, 106.7 × 81 cm, 42 × 31⅞ in; Wellington Museum, Apsley House, London

264
Diego Velázquez, *Pope Innocent X*, 1649-50. Oil on canvas, 140 × 120 cm, 55⅛ × 47¼ in; Galleria Doria Pamphilj, Rome

265
Detail of figure 266

266
Diego Velázquez, *Las Meninas*, 1656. Oil on canvas, 318 × 276 cm, 125½ × 108¾ in; Prado, Madrid

267
Diego Velázquez, *Prince Philip Prosper of Spain*, 1659. Oil on canvas, 128.5 × 99.5 cm, 50 × 39 in; Kunsthistorisches Museum, Vienna

268
Jakob van Campen, *The Royal Palace (former Town Hall), Amsterdam*, 1648. A Dutch seventeenth-century town hall

269
Frans Hals, *Banquet of the officers of the St George Militia Company*, 1616. Oil on canvas, 175 × 324 cm, 69 × 127½ in; Frans Halsmuseum, Haarlem

270
Frans Hals, *Pieter van den Broecke*, c.1633. Oil on canvas, 71.2 × 61 cm, 28 × 24 in; Iveagh Bequest, Kenwood, London

271
Simon de Vlieger, *Dutch man of war and various vessels in a breeze*, c.1640-5. Oil on wood, 41.2 × 54.8 cm, 16¼ × 21⅝ in; National Gallery, London

272
Jan van Goyen, *Windmill by a river*, 1642. Oil on wood, 25.2 × 34 cm, 10 × 13⅜ in; National Gallery, London

273
Rembrandt van Rijn, *Self-portrait*, c.1655-8. Oil on wood, 49.2 × 41 cm, 19⅜ × 16⅛ in; Kunsthistorisches Museum, Vienna

274
Rembrandt van Rijn, *Jan Six*, 1654. Oil on canvas, 112 × 102 cm, 44⅛ × 40⅛ in; Collectie Six, Amsterdam

275
Rembrandt van Rijn, *Parable of the Merciless Servant*, c.1655. Reed pen and brown ink on paper, 17.3 × 21.8 cm, 6¾ × 8½ in; Louvre, Paris

276
Rembrandt van Rijn, *The reconciliation of David and Absalom*, 1642. Oil on wood, 73 × 61.5 cm, 28¾ × 24¼ in; Hermitage, St Petersburg

277
Rembrandt van Rijn, *Christ preaching*, c.1652. Etching, 15.5 × 20.7 cm, 6⅛ × 8⅛ in

278
Jan Steen, *The christening feast*, 1664. Oil on canvas, 88.9 × 108.6 cm, 35 × 42 in; Wallace Collection, London

279
Jacob van Ruisdael, *A pool surrounded by trees*, c.1665-70. Oil on canvas, 107.5 × 143 cm, 42¼ × 56¼ in; National Gallery, London

318
Francisco Goya, *King Ferdinand VII of Spain*, c.1814. Oil on canvas, 207 × 140 cm, 81½ × 55⅛ in; Prado, Madrid

319
Detail of figure 318

320
Francisco Goya, *The giant*, c.1818. Aquatint, 28.5 × 21 cm, 11¼ × 8¼ in

321
William Blake, *The Ancient of Days*, 1794. Relief etching with watercolour, 23.3 × 16.8 cm, 9⅛ × 6⅞ in; British Museum, London

322
Joseph Mallord William Turner, *Dido building Carthage*, 1815. Oil on canvas, 155.6 × 231.8 cm, 61¼ × 91¼ in; National Gallery, London

323
Joseph Mallord William Turner, *Steamer in a snowstorm*, 1842. Oil on canvas, 91.5 × 122 cm, 36 × 48 in; Tate Gallery, London

324
John Constable, *Study of tree trunks*, c.1821. Oil on paper, 24.8 × 29.2 cm, 9¾ × 11½ in; Victoria and Albert Museum, London

325
John Constable, *The haywain*, 1821. Oil on canvas, 130.2 × 185.4 cm, 51¼ × 73 in; National Gallery, London

326
Caspar David Friedrich, *Landscape in the Silesian Mountains*, c.1815-20. Oil on canvas, 54.9 × 70.3 cm, 21⅝ × 27⅝ in; Neue Pinakothek, Munich

327
Charles Barry & Augustus Welby Northmore Pugin, *Houses of Parliament, London*, 1835

328
Jean-Auguste-Dominique Ingres, *The Valpinçon bather*, 1808. Oil on canvas, 146 × 97.5 cm, 57½ × 41⅛ in; Louvre, Paris

329
Eugène Delacroix, *Arab cavalry practising a charge*, 1832. Oil on canvas, 60 × 73.2 cm, 23⅝ × 28⅝ in; Musée Fabre, Montpellier

330
Jean-Baptiste Camille Corot, *Tivoli, the gardens of the Villa d'Este*, 1843. Oil on canvas, 43.5 × 60.5 cm, 17⅛ × 23¾ in, Louvre, Paris

331
Jean-François Millet, *The gleaners*, 1857. Oil on canvas, 83.8 × 111 cm, 33 × 43¾ in; Musée d'Orsay, Paris

332
Gustave Courbet, *The meeting, or 'Bonjour Monsieur Courbet'*, 1854. Oil on canvas, 129 × 149 cm, 50⅞ × 58¾ in; Musée Fabre, Montpellier

333
Dante Gabriel Rossetti, *'Ecce Ancilla Domini'*, 1849-50. Oil on canvas, mounted on wood, 72.6 × 41.9 cm, 28⅞ × 16½ in; Tate Gallery, London

334
Édouard Manet, *The balcony*, 1868-9. Oil on canvas, 169 × 125 cm, 66½ × 49¼ in; Musée d'Orsay, Paris

335
Édouard Manet, *The races at Longchamp*, 1865. Lithograph, 36.5 × 51 cm, 14⅜ × 20¼ in

336
William Powell Frith, Derby Day, 1856-8.
Oil on canvas, 101.6 × 223.5 cm,
40 × 88 in; Tate Gallery, London

337
Édouard Manet, Monet working in his boat,
1874. Oil on canvas, 82.7 × 105 cm,
32½ × 41½ in; Neue Pinakothek,
Munich

338
Claude Monet, Gare St-Lazare, 1877. Oil
on canvas, 75.5 × 104 cm, 29¾ × 41 in;
Musée d'Orsay, Paris

339
Pierre Auguste Renoir, Dance at the
Moulin de la Galette, 1876. Oil on canvas,
131 × 175 cm, 30¾ × 44½ in; Musée
d'Orsay, Paris

340
Camille Pissarro, The boulevard des Italiens,
morning, sunlight, 1897. Oil on canvas,
73.2 × 92.1 cm, 28⅞ × 36¼ in;
National Gallery of Art, Washington,
DC, Chester Dale Collection

341
Katsushika Hokusai, Mount Fuji seen
behind a cistern, 1835. Woodblock print
from 'One hundred views of Mount
Fuji', 22.6 × 15.5 cm, 9 × 6 in

342
Kitagawa Utamaro, Rolling up a blind for
the plum-blossom view, late 1790s. Wood-
block print, 19.7 × 50.8 cm, 7¾ × 20 in

343
Edgar Degas, Henri Degas and his niece
Lucie, 1876. Oil on canvas, 99.8 × 119.9
cm, 39⅜ × 47¼ in; The Art Institute of
Chicago

344
Edgar Degas, Awaiting the cue, 1879. Pastel
on paper, 99.8 × 119.9 cm, 39¼ × 47¼
in; private collection

345
Auguste Rodin, The sculptor Jules Dalou,
1883. Bronze, height 52.6 cm, 20¾ in;
Musée Rodin, Paris

346
Auguste Rodin, The hand of God, c.1898.
Marble, height 92.9 cm, 36⅝ in; Musée
Rodin, Paris

347
James Abbott McNeill Whistler,
Arrangement in grey and black: portrait of the
artist's mother, 1871. Oil on canvas, 144 ×
162 cm, 56⅝ × 63¾ in; Musée d'Orsay,
Paris

348
James Abbott McNeill Whistler, Nocturne
in blue and silver: old Battersea Bridge,
c.1872-5. Oil on canvas, 67.9 × 50.8 cm,
26¾ × 20 in; Tate Gallery, London

349
Victor Horta, Staircase, Hôtel Tassel, rue
Paul-Émile Janson, Brussels, 1893. An Art
Nouveau house

350
Paul Cézanne, Mont Sainte-Victoire
seen from Bellevue, c.1885. Oil on canvas,
73 × 92 cm, 37½ × 51¼ in; Barnes
Foundation, Merion, Pennsylvania

351
Paul Cézanne, Mountains in Provence,
1886-90. Oil on canvas, 63.5 × 79.4 cm,
25 × 31¼ in; National Gallery, London

352
Paul Cézanne, Mme Cézanne, 1883-7. Oil
on canvas, 62 × 51 cm, 24⅜ × 20 in;
Philadelphia Museum of Art

353
Paul Cézanne, Still life, c. 1879-82. Oil
on canvas, 46 × 55 cm, 18⅛ × 21⅝ in;
private collection

354
Georges Seurat, The bridge at Courbevoie,
1886-7. Oil on canvas, 46.4 × 55.3 cm,
18¼ × 21¾ in; Courtauld Institute
Galleries, London

355
Vincent van Gogh, Cornfield with cypresses,
1889. Oil on canvas, 72.1 × 90.9 cm,
28⅜ × 35¾ in; National Gallery,
London

356
Vincent van Gogh, View of Les Saintes-
Maries-de-la-Mer, 1888. Quill pen and
indian ink on paper, 43.5 × 60 cm,
17¼ × 23¾ in; Sammlung Oskar
Reinhart, Winterthur

357
Vincent van Gogh, The artist's room in
Arles, 1889. Oil on canvas, 57.5 × 74 cm,
22⅝ × 29⅛ in; Musée d'Orsay, Paris

358
Paul Gauguin, Te Rerioa (Day-dreaming),
1897. Oil on canvas, 95.1 × 130.2 cm,
37½ × 51¼ in; Courtauld Institute
Galleries, London

359
Pierre Bonnard, At the table, 1899. Oil
on board, 55 × 70 cm, 21¾ × 27⅝ in;
Stiftung Sammlung E.G. Bührle, Zurich

360
Ferdinand Hodler, Lake Thun, 1905. Oil
on canvas, 80.2 × 100 cm, 31⅝ × 39⅜ in;
Musée d'Art et d'Histoire, Geneva

361
Henri de Toulouse-Lautrec,
Les Ambassadeurs: Aristide Bruant, 1892.
Lithograph poster; 141.2 × 98.4 cm,
59¼ × 38¾ in

362
Aubrey Beardsley, Illustration to Oscar
Wilde's 'Salome', 1894. Line-block and
halftone on Japanese vellum;
34.3 × 27.3 cm, 13½ × 10¾ in

363
Frank Lloyd Wright, 540 Fairoaks Avenue,
Oak Park, Illinois, 1902. A house without
a 'style'

364
Andrew Reinhard, Henry Hofmeister
and others, The Rockefeller Center, New York,
1931-9. The style of modern engineering

365
Walter Gropius, The Bauhaus, Dessau, 1926

366
Mask of the Dan tribe, West Africa,
c. 1910-20. Wood, with kaolin around
the eyelids, height 17.5 cm, 7 in;
Von der Heydt Collection, Museum
Rietberg, Zurich

367
Edvard Munch, The scream, 1895.
Lithograph, 35.5 × 25.4 cm, 14 × 10 in

368
Käthe Kollwitz, Need, 1893-1901.
Lithograph, 15.5 × 15.2 cm, 6⅛ × 6 in

369
Emil Nolde, The prophet, 1912. Woodcut,
32.1 × 22.2 cm, 12⅝ × 8¾ in

370
Ernst Barlach, 'Have pity!', 1919. Wood,
height 38 cm, 15 in; private collection

371
Oskar Kokoschka, Children playing,
1909. Oil on canvas, 73 × 108 cm,
28¾ × 42½ in; Wilhelm Lehmbruck
Museum, Duisburg

372
Wassily Kandinsky, Cossacks, 1910-11. Oil
on canvas, 95 × 130 cm, 37½ × 51¼ in;
Tate Gallery, London

373
Henri Matisse, La Desserte (The dinner
table), 1908. Oil on canvas, 180 × 220
cm, 71 × 86¾ in; Hermitage, St
Petersburg

374
Pablo Picasso, Violin and grapes, 1912.
Oil on canvas, 50.6 × 61cm, 20 × 24 in;
The Museum of Modern Art, New York,
Mrs David M. Levy Bequest

375
Pablo Picasso, Head of a young boy, 1945.
Lithograph, 29 × 23 cm, 11½ × 9 in

376
Pablo Picasso, Head, 1928. Collage and
oil on canvas, 55 × 33 cm, 21¾ × 13 in;
private collection

377
Pablo Picasso, Bird, 1948. Ceramic
plate, 32 × 38 cm; 12½ × 15 in; private
collection

378
Paul Klee, A tiny tale of a tiny dwarf, 1925.
Watercolour on board, varnished, 43 ×
35 cm, 17 × 13¾ in; private collection

379
Lyonel Feininger, Sailing boats, 1929. Oil
on canvas, 43 × 72 cm, 17 × 28⅜ in;
Detroit Institute of Arts, gift of Robert
H. Tannahill

380
Constantin Brancusi, The kiss, 1907.
Stone, height 28 cm, 11 in; Muzeul de
Artă, Craiova, Romania

381
Piet Mondrian, Composition with red, black,
blue, yellow and grey, 1920. Oil on canvas,
52.5 × 60 cm, 20¾ × 23¾ in; Stedelijk
Museum, Amsterdam

382
Ben Nicholson, 1934 (relief), 1934.
Oil on carved board, 71.8 × 96.5 cm,
28¼ × 38 in; Tate Gallery, London

383
Alexander Calder, A universe, 1934
Motor-driven mobile; painted iron
pipe, wire and wood with string,
height 102.9 cm, 40½ in; The Museum
of Modern Art, New York, gift of Abby
Aldrich Rockefeller (by exchange)

384
Henry Moore, Recumbent figure, 1938.
Stone, length 132.7 cm, 52¼ in;
Tate Gallery, London

385
Henri Rousseau, Portrait of Joseph
Brummer, 1909. Oil on canvas, 116 × 88.5
cm, 45⅝ × 34¾ in; private collection

386
Marc Chagall, The cellist, 1939. Oil on
canvas, 100 × 73 cm, 39⅜ × 28¾ in;
private collection

387
Grant Wood, Spring turning, 1936. Oil on
board, 46.3 × 102.1 cm, 18¼ × 40¼ in;
Reynolda House Museum of American
Art, Winston-Salem, North Carolina

Index and glossary

Acknowledgements

The publishers wish to thank all private owners, museums, galleries, libraries and other institutions for permission to reproduce works in their collections. Further acknowledgement is made to the following (numbers in **bold** refer to figures):

Albright-Knox Art Gallery, Buffalo, New York, Gift of Mr and Mrs Samuel M. Kootz, 1958 **395**
Courtesy of the Department of Library Services, American Museum of Natural History, New York **26**
Archaeological Receipts Fund, Athens **41, 52, 59, 62, 406**
Archiv für Kunst und Geschichte, London **66, 115**
Archivi Alinari, Florence **72**
Artephot, Paris **111** (photo Brumaire), **297** (Nimatallah), **386** (A. Held)
Arti Galleria Doria Pamphilj, srl **264**
The Art Institute of Chicago **29** (Buckingham Fund, 1955.2339), **343** (Mr and Mrs Lewis Larned Coburn Memorial Collection 1933.429)
Artothek, Peissenberg **3, 202, 227, 326, 337**
Photograph © 1995 by The Barnes Foundation, All Rights Reserved **350**
Bastin & Evrard, Brussels **349**
Bavaria Bildagentur, Munich **104** (© Jeither), **295**
Bayerische Staatsbibliothek, Munich **107**
With the special authorization of the town of Bayeux, photos by Michael Holford **109, 110**

Bibliothèques Municipales, Besançon **131**
Bibliothèque Municipale, Épernay **106**
Bibliothèque Royale, Brussels **177**
Bildarchiv Preussischer Kulturbesitz, Berlin **28, 30, 39, 40, 68, 226, 256**
Bildarchiv Preussischer Kulturbesitz, Berlin, photo Jorg P. Anders **2, 178, 243**
Osvaldo Böhm, Venice **208**
The Trustees of the Boston Public Library, Massachusetts **315**
Bridgeman Art Library, London **5, 144, 159, 244, 263, 361**
By permission of the British Library, London: **103, 140**
Copyright British Museum, London **22, 23, 24, 25, 27, 33, 38, 43, 79, 95, 186, 216, 321, 368**
Foundation E.G. Bührle Collection, Zurich, photo W. Drayer **359**
Collectie Six, Amsterdam **274**
The Master and Fellows of Corpus Christi College, Cambridge **132**
Courtauld Institute Galleries, London **354, 358**
William Curtis **363**
The Detroit Institute of Arts, Gift of Robert H. Tannahill **379**
Ekdotike Athenon, S.A., Athens **51, 54, 61, 410**
English Heritage, London **270**
Ezra Stoller © Esto Photographics, Mamaroneck, NY **364**
Fabbrica di San Pietro in Vaticano **83**
Werner Forman Archive, London **34**
Foto Marburg **116, 128, 154, 268**
Frans Halsmuseum, Haarlem **269**
Giraudon, Paris **42, 124, 155, 156, 157, 174, 248, 253, 373, 389**